Mid-Atlantic

Delaware, Maryland, Virginia, and Washington, D.C.

Gardener's Guide

Mid-Atlantic

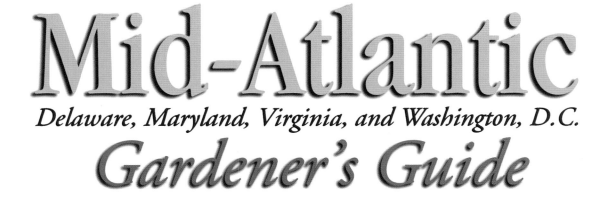

Delaware, Maryland, Virginia, and Washington, D.C.

Gardener's Guide

André and Mark Viette
with Jacqueline Hériteau

COOL
SPRINGS
PRESS
Home and Garden Experts™

MINNEAPOLIS, MINNESOTA

First published in 2004 by Cool Springs Press, an imprint of the Quarto Publishing Group USA Inc., 400 First Avenue North, Suite 400, Minneapolis, MN 55401 USA

Cool Springs Press titles are also available at discounts in bulk quantity for industrial or sales-promotional use. For details write to Special Sales Manager at Quarto Publishing Group USA Inc., 400 First Avenue North, Suite 400, Minneapolis, MN 55401 USA.

To find out more about our books, visit us online at www.coolspringspress.com.

ISBN-13: 978-1-93060-499-5

Library of Congress Cataloging-in-Publication Data

Viette, André.
    Mid-Atlantic gardener's guide : Delaware, Maryland, Virginia, Washington, D.C. / André and Mark Viette with Jacqueline Hériteau.
        p. cm.
    Includes bibliographical references and index.
    ISBN 1-930604-99-8 (pbk. : alk. paper)
    1. Landscape plants—Middle Atlantic States. 2. Landscape gardening—Middle Atlantic States. 3. Landscape plants—Washington, D.C. 4. Landscape gardening—Washington, D.C. I. Viette, Mark. II. Hériteau, Jacqueline. III. Title.
  SB407 .V54 2003
  635.9'0974--dc21
                          2002151413

Managing Editor: Jenny Andrews
Horticulture Editor: Michael Wenzel
Copyeditor: Julie Pinkerton
Production Artist: S.E. Anderson
Cover Designer: Sheri Ferguson

On the cover: 'Dad's Best Purple' Daylily, photographed by André Viette

Printed in China

Dedication

I dedicate this book to my mother and father, Jessie and Martin Viette, who instilled in me strong family values, a good work ethic, and a deep love of plants.

—André Viette

Acknowledgments

I want to thank the many people who have touched my life and made me a better person, especially my wife, Claire, who has been by my side throughout my career and has given me such wonderful children— Mark, Scott, Holly, and Heather. My son Mark works with me daily in the nursery, shares teaching duties with me at Blue Ridge Community College, and has been such an important part of the "In the Garden" radio programs. It has been a wonderful partnership. My father, a great plantsman, passed on to me his keen knowledge of plants and their culture. There is no substitute for the hands-on experience a parent gives to a child: digging and planting, weeding and hoeing, grafting and landscaping, that I learned at his side.

I also wish to thank the many fine professors at Cornell University who helped mold my scientific mind. Among the many who have shaped me as a nurseryman and gardener are my good friend and fellow Cornellian, Dr. Marc Cathey, President Emeritus of the American Horticultural Society, who has contributed so much to the world of floriculture; Rachel Carson who changed my approach to the way we use our planet, whom I met when I was just 24 years old; the late Harvey Barke, New York State University at Farmingdale, a great teacher from whom I learned so much about the field of biological science; my friend, Robert Hebb, first director of Virginia's Lewis Ginter Botanical Garden and world-class plantsman; and my thanks to the fine plantsman Kurt Bluemel, who is responsible for the many wonderful ornamental grasses in American gardens.

And I wish to recognize all my fellow members, past and present, of the New York Hortus Club, who through the years have represented the finest in horticulture from New York City, New York, Connecticut, and New Jersey. Some members have passed on but they leave their mark on many: Tom Everett, of the New York Botanic Garden; Harold Epstein, a keen plantsman and plant collector; Dr. Alfred Graf who wrote the impressive works *Tropica* and *Exotica*; Don Richardson, horticulturist and world-renowned orchid specialist who was in charge of the Whitney Collection.

And finally, my very good friend and fellow author, Jacqueline Hériteau. Jacqui is a knowledgeable gardener and author of many distinguished books in the field of gardening. She is fabulous to work with and has the organization and work ethic to get things done. It's been fun.

—André Viette, Fishersville, Virginia

Featured Plants *for the Mid-Atlantic*

Annuals

Ageratum, 26
Bedding Begonia, 27
Celosia, 28
Coleus, 29
Common Garden Verbena, 30
Cosmos, 31
Edging Lobelia, 32
Geranium, 33
Impatiens, 34
Lantana, 35
Marigold, 36
Pansy, 37
Petunia, 38
Pink Vinca, 39
Salvia, 40
Snapdragon, 41
Spider Flower, 42
Sunflower, 43
Sweet Alyssum, 44
Zinnia, 45

Bulbs, Corms, and Tubers

Crocosmia, 50
Crocus, 51
Daffodil, 52
Dahlia, 53
Fancy-Leaved Caladium, 54
Flowering Onion, 55
Grape Hyacinth, 56
Hyacinth, 57
Lily, 58
Tulip, 59

Conifers

Arborvitae, 62
Blue Atlas Cedar, 63
Canadian Hemlock, 64
Colorado Blue Spruce, 65
Douglas Fir, 66
Dwarf Hinoki Cypress, 67
Juniper, 68
Lacebark Pine, 69
Leyland Cypress, 70
Umbrella Pine, 71
White Fir, 72
Yew, 73

Ground Covers

Barrenwort, 78
Bearberry, 79
Bugleweed, 80
Christmas Fern, 81
Creeping Juniper, 82
Dead Nettle, 83
English Ivy, 84
Foamflower, 85
Golden Moneywort, 86
Japanese Painted Fern, 87
Japanese Spurge, 88
Leadwort, 89
Lenten Rose, 90
Lily-of-the-Valley, 91
Lily-Turf, 92
Periwinkle, 93

Herbs

Basil, 96
Chives, 97
Dill, 98
Lavender, 99
Mint, 100
Parsley, 101
Rosemary, 102
Sage, 103
Tarragon, 104
Thyme, 105

Ornamental Grasses

Blue Fescue, 108
Blue Oat Grass, 109
Chinese Silver Grass, 110
Feather Reed Grass, 111
Fountain Grass, 112
Japanese Blood Grass, 113
Northern Sea Oats, 114
Switch Grass, 115

Perennials

Astilbe, 120
Balloon Flower, 121
Bleeding Heart, 122
Blue False Indigo, 123
Chrysanthemum, 124
Columbine, 125
Coneflower, 126
Coral Bells, 127
Daylily, 128
Globe Thistle, 129
Hosta, 130
Japanese Anemone, 131
Lamb's Ears, 132
Marsh Rose Mallow, 133
Monarda, 134
Oriental Poppy, 135
Peony, 136
Phlox, 137
Pinks, 138
Purple Coneflower, 139
Red Hot Poker Plant, 140
Russian Sage, 141
Salvia 'May Night', 142
Scabiosa, 143
Sedum, 144
Siberian Iris, 145
Solomon's Seal, 146
Yarrow, 147

Roses

Climbing Rose, 150
Garden Rose, 151
Ground Cover Rose, 152
Hedge Rose, 153
Hybrid Tea Rose, 154
Miniature Rose, 155

Shrubs

Blue Spirea, 160
Boxwood, 161
Butterfly Bush, 162
Camellia, 163
Cotoneaster, 164
Daphne 'Carol Mackie', 165
Deciduous Azalea, 166
Dwarf Burning Bush, 167
Dwarf Fothergilla, 168
Evergreen Azalea, 169
Firethorn, 170
Flowering Quince, 171
Forsythia, 172
Glossy Abelia, 173
Hydrangea, 174
Japanese Andromeda, 175
Japanese Aucuba, 176
Japanese Kerria, 177
Lilac, 178
Mock Orange, 179
Mountain Laurel, 180
Nandina, 181

Oregon Grape Holly, 182
Purple Beautyberry, 183
Purple Japanese Barberry, 184
Rhododendron, 185
Rose-of-Sharon, 186
Spirea, 187
Sweet Pepper Bush, 188
Viburnum, 189
Weigela, 190
Witch-Hazel, 191

Trees

American Beech, 196
Birch, 197
Callery Pear, 198
Crape Myrtle, 199
Common Smoke Tree, 200
Dogwood, 201
Eastern Redbud, 202
Flowering Cherry, 203
Flowering Crabapple, 204
Franklin Tree, 205
Ginkgo, 206
Golden Rain Tree, 207
Holly, 208
Japanese Maple, 209
Japanese Pagoda Tree, 210
Japanese Snowbell, 211
Japanese Stewartia, 212
Katsura Tree, 213
Maple, 214

Oak, 215
Red Horse Chestnut, 216
Sour Gum, 217
Sourwood, 218
Southern Magnolia, 219
Sweet Gum, 220
Tuliptree, 221
White Fringe Tree, 222
Zelkova, 223

Vines

Carolina Jessamine, 226
Clematis, 227
Climbing Hydrangea, 228
Goldflame Honeysuckle, 229
Japanese Wisteria, 230
Trumpet Vine, 231

Water Plants

Anacharis, 234
Black Princess Taro, 235
Lotus, 236
Parrot's Feather, 237
Water Lily, 238
Yellow Flag, 239

(See individual entries for the corresponding botanical name of the above listed common plant names.)

Table of Contents

Welcome to Gardening in the Mid-Atlantic 10

How to Use the *Mid-Atlantic Gardener's Guide* 20

Cold Hardiness Zone Map 21

Annuals 22

Bulbs, Corms, and Tubers 46

Conifers 60

Ground Covers 74

Herbs 94

Ornamental Grasses 106

Perennials 116

Roses 148

Shrubs 156

Trees 192

Vines 224

Water Plants 232

More About Fertilizers and Plant Nutrition 240

More About Pruning Trees and Shrubs 242

Gardening with Wildlife, Welcome or Otherwise 244

Mid-Atlantic Public Gardens 248

Sources 250

Glossary 255

Photography Credits 259

Trademarked Product Credits 259

Bibliography 260

Plant Index 263

Meet the Authors 271

Welcome to Gardening
in the Mid-Atlantic

Wonderful gardens have flourished for 400 years in the Mid-Atlantic. We are blessed with a climate not too hot and not too cold for almost all of the garden plants we love. Winter is mild enough to let pansies bloom, and the hellebores flower early. From February on we are graced with lavish displays of flowering bulbs, shrubs, and trees. Summer is hot and stormy, but after mid-September many of the annual flowers revive and the flaming foliage of our maples, oaks, and burning bush light up the season of the falling leaves. A few bulbs bloom in early fall, and hollies, cotoneasters, winterberries, and barberries ripen fruits the birds love.

The plants we recommend are the best of the best for the Mid-Atlantic. We chose them for their lasting beauty, ease of maintenance, and immunity or strong resistance to pests and diseases. We're not recommending specific pesticides and other deterrents: they come and go too frequently. But more important to us is that we have learned from decades of experience that the best protection you can give your garden is (1) to choose pest and disease resistant plants that thrive in the Mid-Atlantic, and (2) to give them the light, nutrients, and moisture they need.

A very pleasant way to see how gardens grow in the Mid-Atlantic is to visit our magnificent public gardens. The Appendix includes the locations of many of our favorites. Strolling the grounds at Winterthur Museum and Gardens in Winterthur, Delaware, and Brookside Gardens in Maryland, you absorb so much about garden design. Buckeystown, Maryland, is home to Lilypons Water Gardens, which has wonderful annual programs for the public. And the Ladew Topiary Gardens are in Maryland. They're the finest example of topiary training in North America. In Tidewater, Virginia, you'll find beauty and wisdom in the sweet home gardens at the Colonial Williamsburg Restoration. In Richmond, Virginia, be sure to visit The Lewis Ginter Botanical Garden.

Central Virginia is home to a personal favorite, Jefferson's Monticello, where a sumptuous vegetable and herb terrace overlooks vineyards, orchards, and the valley below. In the District of Columbia there's so much to learn from the garden rooms at Dumbarton Oaks, the U.S. Botanic Garden on the Mall, and the many-storied collections at the U.S. National Arboretum. The American Horticultural Society, which is headquartered on a beautiful historic farm in Alexandria, offers membership to interested gardeners, and can also put you in touch with local garden groups, which are matchless sources of information

Patio garden with shrubs, perennials, and potted Mandevillas.

about plants and gardening where you live. They're able to explain, for example, which of the Mid-Atlantic's climate zones apply to you.

Our Climate

Planting the right plant in the right place is the key to a garden that gives joy for years. Climate dictates your choices. The USDA climate zone map numbers regions according to their average lowest winter temperature. Much of Delaware, Maryland, Washington, D.C., and Virginia are in Zone 6 and 7. The exceptions are a few cold spots in the mountains, which are Zone 5, and hot spots in the Tidewater and Piedmont (French for "foot of the mountain") areas of southern Virginia, which are Zone 8. Nursery plant tags usually state the plant's hardiness zones. About 99 percent of the plants we recommend thrive in Zones 6, 7, and 8. Where a plant has a problem with Zone 6 cold, or Zone 8 heat, we say so.

Light

On each plant page we tell you the light in which that plant thrives. When a flowering species fails to flower, check the hours of direct sun it receives: unless we say a plant flowers in part or full shade, or part sun, it requires at least six hours of intense direct sun, which occurs from 10:00 A.M. to 6:00 P.M., to bloom well. Plants that flop forward are telling you they need more light. In warm Zone 8 some noon and late afternoon shade can help certain plants—you can supply that by placing the plant under a trellis or in dappled shade under tall trees. Plants receiving full sunlight are often the most cold hardy.

Outwitting Your Climate

Your garden is not governed entirely by the zone in which you live. There are variables that explain unexpected failures, and successes. Cold sinks, so valleys on your property are cooler than high ground. High hills are colder than their respective zones. Cities are 5 to 10 degrees warmer than the suburbs and the countryside. Bodies of water modify temperatures, as do the miles of asphalt and concrete of a town or city. In spring the shore and 10 to 20 miles inland is colder by 10 degrees or more than it is farther inland because the ocean holds winter cold. In summer the shore is cooler because the ocean is cooler than the air.

Within every garden there are microclimates hospitable to plants normally beyond your zone. A south-facing wall can warm a corner, and shade can cool it. You can even create microclimates—a wall painted white or a reflective surface increases light and heat. The shade of a vine-covered pergola, a trellis, a tree, or a high hedge is cooling. Walls and windbreaks protect plants from sweeping winds that intensify cold. Mulch protects roots from extremes of heat and cold.

If you live in a borderline area—almost in cooler Zone 6, but not quite, for example—the safest choices are species that are well within their cold hardiness range in your garden. Borderline plants may live but not always bloom in a satisfying way. Late frosts can devastate the flower buds on a camellia though the plant itself may do well. Many plants are offered in varieties described as blooming early, midseason, or late. Where the growing season is short, plant varieties that will bloom early. If you wish to enjoy a very long season of bloom of any particular plant, plant varieties of all three types: early, midseason, and late.

Starting Seeds Indoors

You can extend the growing season by starting seeds early indoors—in winter for spring planting, in summer for early fall planting. (Starting seeds in a cold frame, or a hot bed, are projects beyond the scope of this book.) You can protect early starters from late and early cold by covering them with "hot caps," or plastic tenting. Two weeks after the date of the last annual frost, is usually safe to transplant seedlings into the open garden.

For slow-growing plants, seed packets will suggest starting seeds indoors ten to twelve weeks before the planting season. For fast growers the time is four to six weeks. We recommend flats that have individual planting pockets and plastic covers. Plant in moistened commercial seed starter mix and follow the packet instructions: some germinate best covered with soil, others need light. Label the seeds—don't forget!—and cover the flat for the germination period. Set it on a heat mat (or an old heating pad set on low and covered with plastic) to speed germination.

Seeds for most perennials are generally slow to germinate (some require cold temperature stratification), and more difficult than those for the pop-up annuals. Most annuals germinate at air temperatures of 65 to 70 degrees Fahrenheit. When they sprout, remove the cover and move the flat to good light. Water from the bottom, or mist the seedlings; pouring water over hair-thin stems flattens them. When they become crowded and have their first true leaves, transplant the seedlings to individual pots. Before moving seedlings to the open garden, wait for the daytime temperature to reach 55 degrees Fahrenheit. Seedlings sulk in cold soil. Before moving seedlings to the garden, harden them off for a week in bright shade out of the wind.

A fluorescent light "garden" is a worthwhile investment if you plan to start seeds indoors every year.

Soil Preparation and Improvement

Soil is your plant's support system, its drinking fountain, and its larder. In the Mid-Atlantic two types of soil prevail. Soil is sandy in the Tidewater, along the coasts of Maryland and Delaware, all along the Atlantic. There's a layer of hardpan under some sandy soils. Sandy soils are easy to dig and drain well, which is essential for many, many plants. But sandy soil doesn't retain water, or the nutrients dissolved in it. As the land rises on the Coastal Plain the soil still tends to sand, but moving inland and westward, clay appears and eventually dominates. Clay soils are rich in nutrients, but the very fine particles flock together, creating a condition of poor drainage and aeration, and making it difficult for roots to develop. Whichever your soil type, the way to make it right is to mix it with the humusy organic materials—such as compost, leaf mold (rotted leaves), or peat—and slow-release fertilizers.

The ideal garden soil has good drainage, lots of water-holding humus, and is loose enough so you can dig in it with your fingers. We evaluate garden soil in terms of its structure or composition, its pH, and its fertility. Structure governs the soil's ability to absorb and maintain moisture. Gritty particles create air spaces, allowing tender rootlets to seek oxygen, moisture, and the nutrients dissolved in it. They also allow water to drain. Soil containing humus retains enough moisture to keep the rootlets from drying out. Roots absorb the nutrients dissolved in water. We add to new planting beds lots of humusy organic amendments that improve soil structure.

A plant's access to nutrients also depends on the soil's "potential of hydrogen," its relative acidity or alkalinity. A soil pH of 7.0 is neutral; pH 4.0 is very, very acid; pH 8.0 is very alkaline. Most garden ornamentals do best in soil whose pH is between 5.5 and 6.5. Trees and shrubs are more apt to be finicky about pH than are herbaceous plants. You can use a relatively inexpensive testing kit to determine the pH of your soil. If it's above pH 6.5-7.0, apply water-soluble sulfur or iron sulfate. If the soil is below pH 5.5, spread finely ground limestone or hydrated lime. Ask your garden center or nursery for recommendations.

If you want plants to be all they can be, you must fertilize a new bed before planting, and all beds every year. The fertilizers we use are natural, organic, and release their nutrients slowly during the season, so we get solid stocky plants with loads of gorgeous foliage and flowers.

We plant in raised beds of improved soil. When we're digging a planting hole we add the same soil amendments and fertilizers in the same proportions. The best times to prepare a new bed are fall, and spring as soon as cold and moisture are out of the ground.

Preparing a New Bed

(1) Use a garden hose to outline the bed. A bed beside a fence, a wall, or a path can be formal or informal. For an informal look, lay out long, slow, gentle curves rather than scallops or straight

lines. For a formal look, make the bed symmetrical—a half circle, oval, square, or rectangle. Formal gardens many times are mirror images left and right of the central axis line. An island bed can be a large oval, an elongated S, or kidney shaped. Island beds are the easiest to work since you can get at the middle from any side.

(2) Thoroughly water the turf covering the area to get the roots activated.

(3) Spray the entire area with Roundup® weed and grass killer following the instructions on the label. It takes about two weeks to completely die. Alternately, you can remove the turf—the top layer of growth and its roots—but that's pretty hard work.

(4) Cover the area with enough of the most weed-free garden soil you can find to raise the soil level about 12 to 16 inches above ground level.

(5) Cover the bed with 3 to 4 inches of humus, enough so that one quarter of the content of the soil is organic matter. The humus can be decomposed bark, compost, partially decomposed leaves or seaweed, sphagnum peat moss, black peat humus, decomposed animal manures, or other decomposed organic material.

Blue-Eyed Grass and Golden Barberry

(6) Next, with a rear-tine rototiller, which you can rent from a garden center, mix all this deeply and thoroughly. The bed should now be, in André's words, "as soft as chocolate pudding."

(7) The next step is to determine the pH reaction of the soil, and amend it as needed to reach a pH between 5.5 and 6.5, following the steps described under Soil Preparation and Improvement.

(8) Next, for each 10 by 10 foot area (100 square feet), mix in the following and rototill or fork into the improved soil:

For a new garden in full sun:
Slow-release, organic fertilizer 5-3-3:
      5 to 10 pounds
Rock phosphate: 5 to 10 pounds
Greensand: 5 to 10 pounds
Clay soils only: gypsum 5 to 10 pounds
Slow-release fertilizer 8-month: 2 pounds

For a new garden in shade:
Slow-release, organic, acid fertilizer 4-6-4:
      4 to 7 pounds
Superphosphate: 3 to 5 pounds
Greensand: 5 to 10 pounds
Clay soils only: gypsum 5 to 10 pounds
Slow-release fertilizer 8-month: 2 pounds

For a new bed for bulbs:
Organic bulb fertilizer: 5 to 10 pounds

(9) When you are ready to plant, rake the bed smooth and discard rocks, lumps, and bumps.

(10) Finally, tamp the edge of the bed into a long, gradual slope and cover it with mulch to keep the soil from eroding. Or, frame the bed with low retaining walls of stone or painted cement blocks, 2 × 2 red cedar or pressure-treated wood, or railroad ties.

Planting

When you are planting in a new raised bed with improved, fluffed up soil, digging a generous planting hole is easy. Digging a big hole in a new spot, and even in an established garden, is tough. But the plant still needs a big planting hole, and soil mixed with 3 to 4 inches of humus (Step 5, above), enough so that one quarter of the content of the soil is organic matter mixed with slow-release organic fertilizers. Each chapter has directions for planting the plants in that chapter. Whether the plants are large or small, our basic approach is this:

Daylilies and Purple Coneflowers

(1) Make the planting hole big. For trees and shrubs make it three times as wide and two times as deep as the rootball; for perennials and annuals, dig a hole two times as wide and two times as deep as the rootball.

(2) For perennials, annuals, and bulbs provide a base of improved soil for the rootball to rest on by half filling the planting hole with improved soil before setting the plant in it. For shrubs and trees half fill the hole with improved soil, and tamp it down very firmly before setting the plant into the hole.

(3) With container plants, free the plant from matted roots. When possible, unwind roots that might be circling the rootball. If you can't untangle them, make four shallow vertical slashes in the mass. Cut off the matted roots on the bottom. Soak the rootball in a bucket containing starter solution.

(4) Set the plant in the hole. Half fill the hole with soil and tamp it down firmly; fill the hole all the way to the top with soil, then tamp it firmly. Shape the soil around the stem, crown, or trunk into a wide saucer. (The saucer is really important in collecting water for shrubs and trees, less so for perennials and annuals.)

Watering

Deep, slow, gentle watering is what keeps plants growing well. After planting, water the bed deeply, gently, and slowly. Ideal for a new bed is to put down $1^1/2$ inches of water after planting. Set an empty coffee tin, regular size, to catch the water, and record how long it takes your sprinkler to deliver $1^1/2$ inches. Water a newly planted shrub or tree by slowly pouring 10 to 15 gallons of water into the saucer around the plant. For a tree or a shrub's first season, unless there's a soaking rain, in spring and fall slowly and gently pour two to three bucketsful of water around the roots every two weeks; in summer every week or ten days. Remember, the larger the tree or shrub, the bigger the hole and the more water needed. Flower beds thrive with 1 to $1^1/2$ inches of gentle rain every ten days to two weeks; if the sky fails you, water long enough to lay down $1^1/2$ inches of water gently over a long period of time, at least six to eight hours, every ten days to two weeks. And, of course, water any time the plants show signs of wilting.

Overhead watering is fine as long as you water deeply. There's less waste if you water before the sun reaches the garden in the early morning, or late afternoon or evening. In hot, dry periods you need to water during the day. Daytime watering lowers leaf temperatures and reduces stress in very hot, dry periods. Evening watering is fine—dew does it and plants like it. We do not recommend electrically timed mechanical watering systems that ignore the weather and water too often and shallowly. However, they can do a good job if they are set up with the correct nozzles, and timed to run long enough to water deeply every week or ten days. Windy, hot times, such as occur in summer, require more water and the cool spring and fall days less.

Wisteria arbor in full flower.

Staking and Stem Protection

Only a few of the tallest flowers should need staking when grown in improved soil and fertilized with slow-release organic fertilizers. Tall, weak growth can be caused by force-feeding with non-organic fertilizers. Wide spacing improves air circulation, and reduces the risk of disease and mildew. Staking is easy: set a wood, bamboo, or metal stake close to the plant stem while it is still young. As it leafs out, it will hide the stake. Use soft green wool, raffia, or cotton string and tie the main stem loosely to the stake. Staking a tree isn't necessary unless the stem or trunk shows a tendency to lean over or to grow at an angle—and it should not need the stake for more than a year. In cold regions for their first winter a burlap windbreak is helpful to young shrubs and trees. You may need to protect a young tree trunk from rubbing or nibbling by deer: you can surround it with stakes wrapped with mesh, or attach a rubber or plastic stem guard. Remove the wrap in spring when growth starts. To protect the tender bark of a young tree from sun scald, paint it with a wash of calcium carbonate.

Mulches

If you love your plants, maintain a 2- to 3-inch organic mulch over the roots from early spring through fall and winter. Start the mulch about 3 inches from the main stem or stems. We mulch in part to buffer soil temperatures and maintain soil moisture, to prevent erosion and control weeds. An organic mulch does more: as it decomposes on the underside it replenishes the soil's supply of humus, which is dissipated during the growing season. The mulches we use suit all plants equally well. Tests have shown that an acid mulch, such as pine needles, has no lasting impact on the pH of the soil beneath. You can mulch with almost any healthy organic material available—seaweed or chopped leaves for example—as long as it is at least partially decomposed. The commercial mulches we recommend include: cypress mulch, pine needles, fir, pine and hardwood bark, and cocoa mulch.

Maintaining Fertility

We fertilize planting beds, not individual plants. The rule of thumb is to apply a slow-release organic fertilizer to the bed before growth begins in late winter (best) or in early spring; for some plants you'll see we recommend fertilizing again in the fall. In this region some soils have a rather high pH, that is, they are somewhat alkaline. In those situations we apply an organic, slow-release, complete fertilizer for acid-loving plants, because that tends to balance out the pH. Where soils test acid, we apply a slow-release organic fertilizer to balance out the acidity. For bulbs we use the same fertilizer or an organic fertilizer for bulbs. If plants need a boost in midseason we apply a water-soluble organic fertilizer such as fish emulsion. In high heat we don't try to force plant growth by feeding, and we avoid pruning at that time, which stimulates growth. It's natural for plants to slow their growth in extremes of weather. For more information on fertilizers, see the Appendix.

Grooming and Weeding

To realize their potential, plants need grooming. In early spring, gardens must be cleared of the previous year's dead foliage. In summer we deadhead and shear spent blooms to encourage flowering that year or the next. We prune woody plants to keep them shapely and healthy. We weed, eliminating the competition. Weeds can even be volunteers from last year's cosmos or phlox. They start up in spring and come into their own in midsummer, along with drought and high heat. A permanent mulch discourages weeds. But you can easily rake up the little green weeds if you do it before they're 1 inch high. When they're 6 inches high, you'll need a hoe. (After that you'll just be sorry you didn't get to it earlier!) Start clean and stay clean. Let weeds flourish in or near a newly established garden and go to seed, and they'll haunt you for years. If some get away from you, they are more difficult to dig out, especially in hard, dry soil. Water the garden first, then gently free the weeds and their roots.

Looking back on years of gardening, the moments that stand out in memory are those spent tending to the landscape. Grooming is a quiet time in the garden. Pruning boxwoods in the cool early morning, birds a-twitter; strolling the flower beds at sunset checking for spent blooms that need deadheading, weeding in summer, raking leaves in autumn—these homely chores lift us out of our everyday lives and into the life of the garden and a potential for beauty that nourishes the soul.

How to Use the Mid-Atlantic Gardener's Guide

Each entry in this guide provides information about a plant's characteristics, habits, and requirements for growth, as well as our personal experience and knowledge of the plant. Use this information to realize each plant's potential. You will find such pertinent information as mature height and spread, bloom period and seasonal colors, sun and soil preferences, water requirements, fertilizing needs, pruning and care tips, and pest information. Each section is clearly marked for easy reference.

Sun Preferences

Symbols represent the range of sunlight suitable for each plant. The symbol representing "Full Sun" means the plant needs 6 or more hours of sun daily. A ranking of "Part Sun" means the plant can thrive in 4 to 6 hours of sun a day. "Part Shade" designates plants for sites with fewer than 4 hours of sun a day, including dappled or high shade. "Full Shade" means the plant needs protection from direct sunlight. Some plants can be grown successfully in more than one exposure, so you will sometimes see more than one light symbol with an entry.

Full Sun   **Part Sun**   **Part Shade**   **Full Shade**

Additional Benefits

Many plants offer benefits that further enhance their appeal. These symbols indicate some of these benefits:

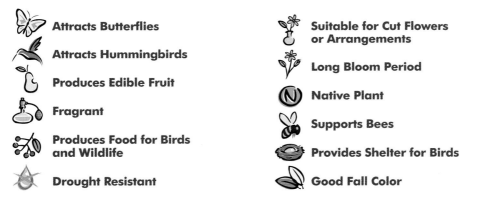

Attracts Butterflies

Attracts Hummingbirds

Produces Edible Fruit

Fragrant

Produces Food for Birds and Wildlife

Drought Resistant

Suitable for Cut Flowers or Arrangements

Long Bloom Period

Native Plant

Supports Bees

Provides Shelter for Birds

Good Fall Color

Companion Planting and Design

For most of the entries, we provide landscape design ideas as well as suggestions for companion plants to help you achieve striking and personal results from your garden.

Our Personal Recommendations

This section describes cultivars or varieties we have found particularly noteworthy, as well as interesting related plants and other relevant information.

USDA Cold Hardiness Zones

Delaware, Maryland, Virginia, and Washington, D.C.

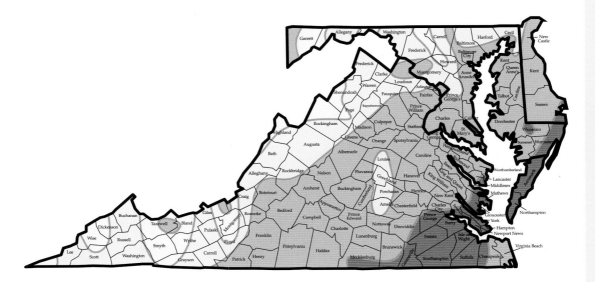

ZONE	Average Annual Minimum Temperature (°F)
5b	-10 to -15
6a	-5 to -10
6b	0 to -5
7a	5 to 0
7b	10 to 5
8a	15 to 10

Hardiness Zones

Cold-hardiness zone designations were developed by the United States Department of Agriculture (USDA) to indicate the minimum average temperature for an area. A zone assigned to an individual plant indicates the lowest temperature at which the plant can be expected to survive over the winter. The Mid-Atlantic region has zones ranging from 5b to 8a. Though a plant may grow (and grow well) in zones other than its recommended cold-hardiness zone, it is a good indication of which plants to consider for your landscape. If you don't know the zone in which you live, take a look at this map. Unless otherwise noted, each plant in this book is appropriate for all Mid-Atlantic zones.

Annuals *for the Mid-Atlantic*

Annuals and tender perennials last just one season but they're a delight to grow and dear to every gardener's heart. Just weeks after planting, annuals carpet empty spaces with lasting color and soon grow big enough to screen out the ripening of spring bulb foliage. The vivid zinnias and marigolds are so easy and so satisfying they're ideal for a child's garden. In dappled light impatiens, New Guinea impatiens, and coleus color well and grow more beautiful as summer advances; planted in complementary colors, they're stunning. Petunias, geraniums, and other tender (not winter hardy) perennials keep window boxes and patio planters blooming all summer long. Some annuals self-sow and may spare you the trouble of replanting the next year. Rogue out those you don't want and transplant the others for a late show.

Planter brimming with annuals and tropical Fuchsias.

Many annuals have a rewarding cut-and-come-again habit: the more flowers you harvest, the more the plant produces. Many of the best cutting flowers are annuals. Knowing how to harvest—where to cut the stems—is the key to keeping them blooming. We've described the process below, and, where relevant, with each plant in this chapter. For a continuous supply of vivid zinnias, giant golden marigolds, and late summer bouquets of pastel cosmos scented with basil, establish a cutting garden where your pleasure in harvesting won't spoil the view. Or, plant cutting flowers in a little kitchen garden with vegetables, herbs, and dwarf fruit trees.

Planting and Fertilizing

Annuals have modest root systems. To be all they can be, like vegetables they require sustained moisture and plenty of nutrients. Our Introduction explains how to prepare beds for annuals to bring the soil to pH 5.5 to 6.5, the ideal range for most. Organic fertilizers release their nutrients slowly so the plants should do well

Coleus 'Rusty'

the first season without further fertilization. Then every year, in late winter or early spring, fertilize beds for annuals with applications of slow-release, long-feeding organic fertilizers. If your annuals seem to slow after blooming, they may benefit from fertilization with one of the water-soluble organic fertilizers, such as seaweed or fish emulsion.

Nursery-grown seedlings of annuals are very tempting in mid-spring when you're looking for instant flowers. Those available at garden centers from early spring until late June are beautiful, already in bloom, healthy—and in everybody else's garden. Eventually you will want to try the alluring other varieties you see in garden magazines and catalogs. Then you will have to sow seeds—in the garden or, for a head start, indoors. (See Starting Seeds Indoors in the Introduction.) The time to sow seeds outdoors for the annuals that bloom in late spring and summer is about two weeks after the last frost for your area. Please don't rush the season! Most annuals just won't take off until the ground and the air warm up in mid-spring—seeds and seedlings set out too early sulk. Flowers whose seed packets say they are "cold hardy" you can sow outdoors a few weeks earlier than the others. Most annuals will come into bloom soonest when they are sown where they are to flower. Seeds for annuals whose show time is late summer and fall can be sown outdoors as late as June—cosmos, for example.

Sow smaller seeds by "broadcasting," that is, sprinkle them thinly over the area. Larger seeds you can sow in "hills," groups of four to six, or three to five, equidistant from each other. Flowers for edging beds can be sown in "drills," that is, dribbled at spaced intervals along a shallow furrow in the soil created by dragging the edge of a rake or hoe handle along the planting line. For planting depth, follow the instructions on the seed packet, or sow seeds at a depth that is about three times the seed's diameter, not its length. Seed packets usually suggest how much to thin seedlings to give the mature plants space to develop.

Cosmos

After sowing your seeds, give the planting bed a slow, thorough overhead soaking. See Watering in the Introduction. Water often enough during the next two or three weeks to maintain soil moisture. Thin the seedlings to 3 to 5 inches apart and apply a 2-inch layer of mulch. In periods of drought, water deeply every week or ten days, or when you see signs of wilting. For window box, basket, and container plantings we recommend using a commercial potting mix. If you mix into the soil a polymer such as Soil Moist™ you'll find maintaining moisture much easier. It holds twenty times its weight in water, and releases the water (and dissolved soil nutrients) slowly.

Annuals Can Take a Lot of Pinching

To be all they can be, some annuals need pinching at several points in the season. The pinching begins right at planting time. It's a fact that once an annual gets into flower production, the plant puts less strength into growing its root system. But the plant needs a big, healthy root system to get through hot summer days. The way to encourage the plant to grow its root system is to pinch out the flowering tips at planting time. If you are using the color of budded or opening flowers to decide where the plant goes, wait until it is in the ground to pinch out the flowers and buds. Then, at planting time, or very early in their careers, the branching tips of many, even most, annuals should be pinched out to encourage the production of side branches where flowers will develop.

Again, at midseason, when the plants are fully matured, you can encourage new branching and more flowering in some long-branching annuals, such as petunias, by shearing all the stems back by a third or half. And some annuals bloom more fully and over a longer period if you deadhead them consistently and persistently. Pinch them out between your thumb and forefinger—it's fast and easy. Frequent harvesting of most annuals has the same beneficial effect. Cut the stems for bouquets just above the next set of leaves: that's where the new flowering stems will rise. Some of the new petunias, impatiens, begonias, and vincas only need that first pinching when planting.

To Encourage Self-Sowers

Annual flowers that sow their own seeds will naturalize (come back year after year) under favorable conditions. Self-sown volunteers of petunias, snapdragons, cosmos, and little French marigolds pop up every year in our gardens. They're slow to flower, and can't be counted on for late summer and fall bloom. But we often transplant them for the fun of seeing what will happen. Other self-sowers are so productive they become weeds—morning glory comes to mind.

You can encourage self-sowing by spreading a 1- or 2-inch layer of humusy soil around the crowns of the parent plants and allowing flowers to set seed toward the end of the growing season. Keep the soil damp, and gather the seeds as they ripen and scatter them over the soil. Or, wait until the seeds are dry and loose in their casings, then shake the flower heads vigorously over the soil.

Other Good Options

The annuals on the following pages are on our best-of-the-best list. Others that are "good doers" in the Mid-Atlantic are:

Charming planting of annuals, with *Nicotiana sylvestris* and hanging baskets of Begonias.

Bachelor's-Button, Cornflower, *Centaurea cyanus*

Browallia, Bush Violet, *Browallia speciosa*

Butter Daisy, *Melampodium paludosum*

Corn Poppy, *Papaver rhoeas*

Flowering Tobacco, *Nicotiana alata* and *N. sylvestris*

Four O'Clock, *Mirabilis jalapa*

Garden Heliotrope, *Heliotropium arborescens*

Globe Amaranth, *Gomphrena globosa*

Gerbera, *Gerbera jamesonii*

Larkspur, *Consolida ambigua* (*Delphinium ajacis*)

Moss Rose, *Portulaca grandiflora*

Nasturtium, *Tropaeolum majus*

Ornamental Kale and Cabbage, *Brassica oleracea* (Acephala Group)

Wishbone Plant, Bluewings, *Torenia fournieri*

Ageratum

Ageratum houstonianum

Ageratum is the annual flower we rely on for mid-height, summer-long drifts of blue in flower borders. The blossoms are rounded clusters of tiny powder puffs, held in nosegays of pointed fresh green foliage. The varieties offered as seedlings by most garden centers now are dwarfish, 6 to 12 in. high. Seeds of old-fashioned varieties 18 in. high are out there but hard to find. The taller sorts are suitable for planting farther back in the garden and they make fairly lasting cut flowers. Deadheading keeps ageratum blooming, and while it may brown in the high heat of midsummer, ageratum comes back in our garden with the September rains. The plant known as the hardy ageratum, Eupatorium coelestinum, *is perennial here.*

Other Name
Flossflower

Bloom Period and Seasonal Color
Late spring to mid-autumn; blue, lavender-blue, pink, white.

Mature Height × Spread
$^1/_2$ to 1 ft × $^1/_2$ to 1 ft.

When, Where, and How to Plant
You can start ageratum seeds indoors in flats six to eight weeks before planting time. Ageratum seeds need light to germinate, so do not cover the seeds with soil. In mid-spring after the weather has become reliably warm, you can sow seeds or plant seedlings in the garden. Sow ageratum seeds where the plants are to bloom. For a quick show, plant seedlings already blooming in sets of three. Where summers are very hot ageratum benefits from dappled light; in cool, hilly regions, it can take direct sun. Ageratum does best in well-drained, humusy soil whose pH is 5.5 to 7.0. See Soil Preparation and Planting in the Introduction. Provide planting holes 8 to 12 in. deep. For smaller varieties, allow 6 in. between plants; for larger varieties, allow 12 in.

Growing Tips
For fuller plants, pinch out the first sets of flowering tips. For the first several weeks keep the soil around the plants well watered.

Care
During the flowering season, shear spent blooms often to keep the plants producing. If the tips brown out in heat, cut off the darkened portions and water the plants often enough to make sure they don't go dry. They will freshen in fall with cooler weather and rain, and go on blooming until the real cold comes.

Companion Planting and Design
Ageratum is lovely interplanted with pink-and-white snapdragons and silver artemisia. It makes a pretty border edging interplanted with white sweet alyssum and large-flowered pink wax begonias.

Our Personal Recommendations
Our favorites are compact, lavishly blooming, lavender-blue 'Blue Danube' ('Blue Puff'); extra-early, bright blue 'Adriatic'; and 'Blue Surf', which grows to 9 in. tall.

Bedding Begonia
Begonia Semperflorens-Cultorum Hybrids

When, Where, and How to Plant
You can start wax begonias indoors from seed in early January—but you will find lots of seedlings at the market gardens in April. They grow strong root systems and flower fully when planted right after the last frost date—April in Zone 8, early May in Zones 6 and 7. Wax begonias growing in bright dappled light bloom all season long. In cool regions, they'll do better with four to six hours of direct sun. In deep shade begonias keep their leaves but do not fill out. Wax begonias do best in soil with a pH of 5.5 to 7.0. See Soil Preparation and Planting in the Introduction. Work the soil 8 to 12 in. deep. Set the seedlings high, and 6 to 8 in. apart. Apply a 2-in. layer of mulch.

Growing Tips
To promote rapid, unchecked growth, for two or three weeks after planting water often enough to maintain soil moisture.

Care
After the first few weeks, water deeply when other flowers show signs of wilting. Wax begonias are able to remain crisp even in the first stages of water deprivation.

Companion Planting and Design
Wax begonias are perfect edgers for semi-shaded flower borders, and look just great planted in groups of three behind a ribbon of sweet alyssum.

Our Personal Recommendations
The prettiest wax begonias are the green-leaved Wing F1 hybrids, which are 10 to 12 in. tall and have 3-in. flowers. 'Picotee Wings' is a treasure, with soft white flowers rimmed in rose. For edging, choose dwarf Semperflorens-Cultorum hybrids; for hanging baskets, choose hybrids with cascading branches. The attractive 24-in. perennial begonia is *Begonia grandis*; it is also known as Evans begonia (formerly *B. evansiana*). It survives winters in Zone 7, though all runners from mother plants may overwinter in Zone 6 under mulch. It thrives under tall shrubs like laurel and rhododendrons. There are white and pink flowered varieties.

In dappled light the carefree Semperflorens-Cultorum hybrids produce small colorful flowers nestled in neat mounds of crisp, waxy, rounded leaves that stay handsome all season. Some strains have maroon-bronze leaves, others are bright green, and there are white-variegated forms. Bedding begonias are a maintenance-free delight, ideal edgers for partly shaded flower borders. We love them because they stay fresh in high heat, and with September rains grow even fuller and prettier. These wonderfully carefree little plants need no deadheading to keep blooming. They are tender perennials that can take a lot of cold at the end of the season, but no frost. Brought indoors in October, they bloom all winter. The wax begonia's gorgeous cousin, the tuberous begonia, is a superb but challenging bedding and basket plant that does best in cool areas of the Mid-Atlantic.

Other Names
Wax Begonia, Fibrous-Rooted Begonia

Bloom Period and Seasonal Color
Mid-spring to mid-fall; white, pale pink, rose, coral, deep pink, red, bi-colors.

Mature Height × Spread
6 to 9 in. × 12 to 18 in.

Celosia

Celosia argentea var. *cristata*

Celosia is one of the most colorful and enduring of the annuals. The "blooms" are either fanciful velvety crests (much like a cockscomb) or feathered plumes (feathered amaranth) that bloom from summer until frost touches them. The foliage is an asset and may be green or bronze, depending on the color of the blossom. There are dwarfs, and also taller types whose plumes may need staking. The feathery celosias provide strong color and graceful accents for bouquets of cut flowers. Celosia blooms are dryish to start with, so they are ideal subjects for drying: to make them into keepers, remove the lower foliage from stems 8 to 12 in. long, bundle the stems loosely, and hang them up to dry in an airy place out of bright sun. They will dry with little loss of color.

Other Names
Cockscomb, Feathered Amaranth

Bloom Period and Seasonal Color
Summer; red, pink, yellow, apricot, burgundy-red, gold, or cream.

Mature Height × Spread
6 to 24 in. × 8 to 12 in.

When, Where, and How to Plant
Start seeds indoors in late winter. Or, as soon as the soil has warmed, sow the seeds directly in full sun in fertile, well-drained soil worked to a depth of 8 to 12 in. The celosias do well in almost any soil. See Soil Preparation and Planting in the Introduction. Transplant seedlings, or thin garden-grown seedlings, to stand 12 in. apart. The plants start well but sulk if the roots are disturbed. Provide a 2-in. mulch starting 3 in. from the plant.

Growing Tips
Water the bed well after planting and maintain the moisture the first few weeks.

Care
During the summer growing season provide enough water so the plants do not dry out. But don't overwater, as celosias are susceptible to fungus. Once established, the plants withstand some drought.

Companion Planting and Design
Groups of celosias create solid splashes of vibrant color anywhere you plant them. A row of the cockscomb varieties makes a big color statement in the kitchen garden, and the feathery varieties are graceful wherever situated.

Our Personal Recommendations
The dwarf Fairy Fountains group has 4- to 6-in. plumes on 12-in. plants, and are charming edgers. The larger Century celosias are most effective massed in beds. The scarlet-plumed 'New Look' celosia endures hot climates.

Coleus
Solenostemon scutellarioides

When, Where, and How to Plant

Coleus grows quickly from seed sown in flats indoors any time. Garden centers offer flats of seedlings of mixed foliage color combinations when the weather warms in mid-May, just in time to plant. The leaf colors are more intense when grown in part shade. In warm parts of Zones 7 and 8, grow coleus on a shaded terrace, or in the bright shade of tall shrubs or trees, or in dappled light. In cool, hilly regions, coleus can take four to six hours of morning sun: the more red there is in the foliage, the more direct sun the plant can take. Plant coleus in moderately rich, humusy soil. See Soil Preparation and Planting in the Introduction. Make the planting holes 6 to 8 in. deep. Allow 12 to 14 in. between plants. Apply a 2-in. layer of mulch.

Growing Tips

To promote rapid, unchecked growth, for the first two or three weeks water to maintain soil moisture. When the plants show signs of new growth, encourage branching by pinching out the top 3 to 4 in. of the lead stem.

Care

Maintain moderate soil moisture. Encourage fuller growth by removing flower spikes as they start up, and pinch out the tips of branches that may become leggy.

Companion Planting and Design

A container planted in coleus in mixed colors is breathtaking. In flower boxes we like coleus combined with impatiens in matching or contrasting colors—scarlet-variegated coleus with scarlet impatiens, for example, and lime-green coleus with white impatiens. Sunny green and gold varieties planted with hosta lighten shaded shrub beds. Trailing varieties, like red and gold 'Scarlet Poncho', are great in hanging baskets.

Our Personal Recommendations

André still loves coleus! A pretty variety is 'Salmon Lace' which is salmon-edged, green, and cream-white. Yellow and green 'Highland Fling' pairs well with 'Molten Lava', whose red leaves have black-purple margins. The Stained Glassworks™ varieties have lacy leaves, and speckled and whorled foliage in sophisticated color variegations. Sun coleus cultivars include 'Gay's Delight', 'Kiwi Fern', and 'Alabama Sunset'.

Coleus was one of André's favorite plants as a child: he was amazed God could make a leaf to be so beautiful! Its gift is brightly patterned, mid-height foliage that brings eye-catching color to shaded areas. The large heart-shaped leaves emerge from lush, pale green stems that are squarish, a characteristic of the mint family. And coleus is as wonderfully (or terribly) generous as mint. If you keep the leaf tips and the untidy flower spikes pinched out, the plants grow bigger and more beautiful until killed by early frosts. This is a great container plant. The color combinations get wilder every year. Coleus cuttings root quickly in water and thrive indoors in a semi-sunny window. A whole new group of sun- and drought-tolerant coleus, called sun or solar coleus, has revolutionized the use of coleus in the landscape.

Other Name
Painted Nettle

Bloom Period and Seasonal Color
Colorful foliage all season; combinations of red, mahogany, chartreuse, yellow, white, rose, and near-black.

Mature Height × Spread
14 to 24 in. × 12 to 18 in.

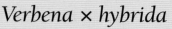

Common Garden Verbena
Verbena × hybrida

Common garden verbena is a spectacular basket plant and a fabulous shore-side performer. Fast growing and tolerant of drought, wind, and searing sun, it is a vigorous, free-blooming plant. It grows either as a fragrant mound or a trailer that covers itself with rounded heads of small, pale-eyed, primrose-like florets. The leaves are pretty, oval or lance-shaped, serrated, and dark-green. Verbena is a great bedding plant. In Washington, D.C., it is planted as a follow-on ground cover for bulbs and remains effective through the city's hot, muggy weather. Many varieties are very fragrant. Common garden verbena is the verbena for show. To see butterflies in action, plant its taller cousin, spring-flowering South American vervain, V. bonariensis, which, along with the cultivar V. canadensis 'Homestead Purple', is perennial in Zone 7 and warmer.

Other Names
Florist's Verbena, Vervain

Bloom Period and Seasonal Color
Summer till frost; colors are white, red, pink, yellow, blue, purple, and bi-colors.

Mature Height × Spread
6 to 12 in. × 8 to 18 in.

When, Where, and How to Plant
Common garden verbena is a tender perennial grown here as an annual. If you want to start your own plants, sow the seeds in January, just covering them with a little seed starting mix, and grow the seedlings in a cool room, between 64 and 70 degrees Fahrenheit. Because the seed germinates slowly, we buy seedlings and plant them outdoors, after all danger of frost is past, where they will get full sun, or sun until the afternoon. The verbenas need light, well-drained soil and they tolerate poor, dry soil. See Soil Preparation and Planting in the Introduction. Work the soil 8 to 12 in. deep and prepare planting holes 10 to 15 in. apart. Plant the seedlings high. Apply a 2-in. mulch starting 3 in. from the stems.

Growing Tips
To promote rapid, unchecked growth, for the first two or three weeks water the verbenas often enough to sustain the soil moisture. Encourage branching by pinching out the tips of each stem.

Care
During the growing season, water verbenas when you water the flower beds. After each flush of bloom, shear the spent flower heads.

Companion Planting and Design
We most often plant baskets of common garden verbena in a single color. For bedding we like red verbena with dianthus from the Charm series in mixed colors, dusty miller, and white sweet alyssum. A nice combination for window boxes is verbena with petunias in a contrasting shade, variegated vinca, and indoor foliage plants—on vacation out of doors.

Our Personal Recommendations
Many varieties of the mounded verbenas are very fragrant, especially the blue. One of the most popular series is the Showtime hybrids, which come in many brilliant colors, some with a bold contrasting eye. 'Sissinghurst' has bright rose-pink flowers. *V. tenuisecta* 'Imagination' has delicate leaves and produces flowers in a deep violet blue. 'Tappan Blue' has light blue flowers.

Cosmos
Cosmos bipinnatus

When, Where, and How to Plant

Sow seeds or transplant seedlings outdoors after the ground has warmed. Early-flowering strains bloom from seed in eight to ten weeks. Or, sow seeds indoors in late April and plan to transplant four to six weeks later. If you are starting seeds in the garden, sow them where the plants are to bloom. Cosmos does best in full sun but makes do with four to six hours a day. It withstands drying winds but may need staking in an exposed location. Cosmos is happy in well-drained soil of only average fertility. Overfeeding and rich soil create a need for staking. See Soil Preparation and Planting in the Introduction. Dig the bed 6 to 8 in. deep. Space seedlings of the tall varieties at least 12 in. apart. Apply a 2-in. layer of mulch.

Growing Tips

Water for two or three weeks often enough to sustain soil moisture, but grow the plants "hard." If the seedlings tilt, stake the central stem. When they reach 24 in., encourage branching by pinching out the top 3 to 4 in. of the lead stem. Repeat as the next set of branches develops.

Care

Once established, water cosmos only if it shows signs of wilting. Cosmos blooms lavishly even without deadheading, but it self-sows generously so remove spent blooms to avoid too many volunteers next season. When harvesting the flowers, cut the stems to just above a branching node.

Companion Planting and Design

Cosmos is essential in a cottage garden, great in a meadow garden, and makes a good follow-on plant for spring bulbs. Use varieties as fillers for the back of the flower border. For spectacular color, plant orange-juice colored *C. sulphureus* with wildly colorful Joseph's-coat, *Amaranthus tricolor* 'Molten Fire'. Cosmos combines especially well with snapdragons, blue salvia, and shasta daisies.

Our Personal Recommendations

For cutting, plant 'Sea Shells', which bears flowers that have creamy-white, shell-pink, or crimson and pink interiors; 'Psyche Mixed', for its semi-double and single flowers; and the bi-colored white and pink 'Candy Stripe'.

Willowy, drought-tolerant, no-problems cosmos brings to the late summer garden airy, fresh green foliage and bright, open-faced pastel flowers that bloom until early frosts. As the plant grows, lacy foliage fills in around the other flowers in the border so it makes a great filler. As they mature, the graceful 3- to 4-ft. branches are spangled with 2- to 4-in. flowers that have crested or tufted centers. Harvest the flowers, and the plants keep on producing. The flowers last well in arrangements and add lovely pastels to late summer bouquets of dahlias, blue salvia, and aromatic mint and basil. Cosmos is delicate, but tough. It self-sows exuberantly. We transplant volunteers to places left empty by the passing of spring flowers.

Bloom Period and Seasonal Color
Late summer to frost; crimson, orange, rose, yellow, white, pink, burgundy red, and bi-colors.

Mature Height × Spread
2 to 6 ft. × 2 ft.

Edging Lobelia
Lobelia erinus

In semi-shade these dainty little plants produce clouds of thin, fragile stems spangled with tiny florets in luminous, intense shades, often with a white eye. In the garden the stems spread to carpet nearby plantings; growing in a basket or an urn, they cascade. Some varieties have fresh green foliage, and some have decorative bronze foliage. In the cooler reaches of the Mid-Atlantic, in Zone 6, edging lobelia grows well throughout spring; with protection from direct sun it may continue into fall. In hot Washington, D.C., gardens, it disappears with the coming of high heat in June. If you love lobelia's intense colors, investigate the large, upright perennial blue and red lobelias (L. siphilitica *and* L. cardinalis).

Bloom Period and Seasonal Color
Spring into summer; light blue or intense deep blue, or wine-red spotted white.

Mature Height × Spread
4 to 6 in. × 8 to 12 in.

When, Where, and How to Plant
Plant seedlings two weeks after the last frost date in part sun or semi-shade. In cool regions, lobelia adapts to four hours of direct sun, if the soil is moist and the plants are mulched. See Soil Preparation and Planting in the Introduction. Prepare a well-drained humusy bed worked to a depth of 6 or 8 in. Set the seedlings 10 to 12 in. apart, water well, and apply a 2-in. mulch between plants.

Growing Tips
To promote rapid, unchecked growth, for the first two or three weeks water often enough to sustain the moisture in the soil.

Care
Maintain soil moisture throughout the growing season, especially when the weather heats up. After every flush of bloom, shear played-out stems.

Companion Planting and Design
We use edging lobelia to carpet empty spaces between fading early spring flowers. It is most beautiful dropping from a basket or an urn. For hanging baskets, choose the trailing Cascade or Fountain series, which bloom profusely.

Our Personal Recommendations
A favorite edging lobelia is deep blue 'Crystal Palace'. The Moon series is especially heat-resistant; 'Paper Moon' is an exquisite white, which covers itself with moon-shaped flowers. The blue cardinal flower, upright *L. siphilitica*, is a perennial that naturalizes and is a long-lasting cutting flower

Geranium
Pelargonium spp. and hybrids

When, Where, and How to Plant

Geraniums are safe planted after the last frost date. Although full sun plants, they may benefit from protection during the hottest part of the day; ideal is good morning light or a western exposure. Geraniums maintain themselves in hot, dry, windy exposures but do best where nights are cool. Plant zonal geraniums in well-drained potting or garden soil. Balcon and scented geraniums do best in a fertile humusy soil. All prefer soil with a pH of 5.5 to 6.5. See Soil Preparation and Planting in the Introduction. Plant the small bedding geraniums 8 in. apart. Do not mulch.

Growing Tips

When the plants show signs of new growth, encourage branching by pinching out the end 3 to 4 in. of the lead stem and the side branches. Repeat once more during the growing season.

Care

Allow the soil surface to dry between deep waterings. Deadhead consistently to encourage flowering. When fall comes, pot up your geraniums and bring them indoors for the winter; in a sunny window they will bloom for weeks to come. Softwood cuttings taken in January root easily in water or in a good rooting material. Geraniums like cool nights and can take quite a lot of cold at the end of the growing season.

Companion Planting and Design

Geraniums are great container plants. Bright red zonal geraniums combine well in a window box with silvery dusty miller, petunias, and variegated vinca. A handsome combination for a big container is pink zonal geraniums, blue ageratum, white sweet alyssum, and the cascading branches of ivy-leaved geranium. For bedding, use compact varieties like the Tango series; for landscaping, use the larger Rocky Mountain group. Scented geraniums grow tall in a flower bed, and must be brought indoors for the winter.

Our Personal Recommendations

Variegated zonal geranium 'Ben Franklin' has semi-double, rosy pink flowers and leaves splashed with beautiful, crisp white markings. The Orbit series is known for its ease of growth, compact form, and large flowers in a range of colors, including 'Apple Blossom', a favorite.

The showy geranium's special appeal is that it blooms all summer and has handsome foliage. There are many forms. The old-fashioned geranium with big, rounded flower heads and green horseshoe-shaped leaves banded maroon or bronze is called a zonal geranium, Pelargonium × hortorum. White-splashed variegated forms are perfect to feature in a container. The airy Balcon, or Alpine ivy geranium, P. peltatum, covers itself and its deeply cut foliage with florets that stand out on slender stems and is perfect for urns and lofty planters. Other ivy-leaved geraniums have fewer flowers but produce cascades of thick waxy foliage on drooping stems, and make beautiful basket plants; there are variegated forms. Martha Washington geraniums, P. × domesticum, have exceptionally showy flowers and are used as pot plants. The several species of scent-leaved geraniums have crinkly leaves that give off a strong aroma when brushed; they are grown for their foliage and scent. The geranium is a tender perennial. We bring our favorites indoors for the winter.

Bloom Period and Seasonal Color
Spring, summer, fall, some blooms in winter; colors are shades of red, salmon, fuchsia, pink, white, and bi-colors.

Mature Height × Spread
Zonal geranium can be trained to tree form; mature branches of the scent-leaved types reach 1 to 3 ft.

Impatiens
Impatiens walleriana

Impatiens has the rare ability to flower generously in partial or full shade, a quality that has made it a favorite in gardens and woodlands from coast to coast. It's a care-free plant that blooms early and more and more lavishly until the first frosts. By early September a mass planting looks like a low hedge. The foliage may be either dark green or bronzed, and there are white variegated forms. The blossoms of double-flowered impatiens are as pretty as miniature roses, but don't flower as fully as ordinary impatiens. The beautiful hybrid called New Guinea impatiens is a superb bedding plant and tolerates more sun; it is showier, more substantial, grows upright, and has large blossoms and colorful foliage, especially in the Painted Paradise series.

Other Names
Busy Lizzie, Sultana

Bloom Period and Seasonal Color
Late spring till frost; white, red, orange, salmon, melon, pink, lavender, orchid, spotted forms, and bi-colors.

Mature Height × Spread
6 to 36 in. × 8 to 24 in.

When, Where, and How to Plant
We recommend starting with seedlings, but wait to set them out until night temperatures are consistently in the high 50s to low 60s. Blooming starts when night temperatures are 60 to 65 degrees Fahrenheit. High and filtered shade are best, though modern cultivars tolerate four or five hours of direct sun, especially morning sun, when mulched and growing in humusy, moist soil. Impatiens needs well-drained soil rich in humus. In sandy areas, plant impatiens in containers or well-prepared topsoil that contains humus, peat moss, and other moisture-holding organic materials. Work the soil for impatiens 8 to 10 in. deep. See Soil Preparation and Planting in the Introduction. Set the seedlings 8 to 10 in. apart. After planting, apply a fine mulch 2 in. deep.

Growing Tips
Keep impatiens seedlings watered the first few weeks after planting. In high heat flowering may slow; a light shower to cool them off can be helpful.

Care
For compact plants, water impatiens only enough to keep it from wilting. Water early in the day or after the sun has gone by. Once flower buds have formed, fertilize rarely, if at all, and only lightly with an organic water-soluble fertilizer such as seaweed or fish emulsion.

Companion Planting and Design
Impatiens and coleus or caladiums in similar colors are beautiful together. Combinations we like are gray-white artemisia with light and dark pink and white impatiens, and a carpet of white impatiens with miniature white cushion mums. Impatiens is lovely with variegated hostas. New Guinea impatiens is a great follow-on plant for bulbs growing under deciduous trees. Plants of the compact Sonic series are suited to small containers. The larger Super Sonics are meant for landscaping.

Our Personal Recommendations
For containers and hanging baskets we like the Super Elfin® series. Under 10 in., they branch freely, and spread to 12 in. or more. For the front of the border, choose medium heights, 10 to 12 in. tall. For bedding, choose the tall Blitz series, 14 to 16 in. high, and New Guinea impatiens, hybrids of *I. hawkeri*.

Lantana
Lantana camara

When, Where, and How to Plant
You'll find good-sized container-grown plants and seedlings in 4-in. pots at garden centers toward mid-spring. The time to plant lantana is as soon as all danger of frost is past. It needs full sun to bloom well, but it is not very difficult as to soil. If you are planting in containers, consider using an enriched potting soil mix, and add Soil Moist™— grainy stuff that absorbs and holds twenty times its weight in water. If you are planting in the garden, provide generous planting holes worked 12 in. deep, and soil that is well drained and humusy. See Soil Preparation and Planting in the Introduction. Set the plants 2 to 3 ft. apart. Water well. Surround the plants with a mulch 2 in. deep.

Growing Tips
Pinch off the branch tips of new plants to encourage lots of bushy growth. Keep the plants well watered until you see fresh new growth at all the branch tips.

Care
Mature plants tolerate drought but should be watered deeply if they show signs of wilting. Shear after every flush of bloom.

Companion Planting and Design
We love butterflies, so we place lantana near other plants that attract these lovely insects. *Buddleja*, butterfly bush, is one. Blue passion flower, *Passiflora caerulea*, a vigorous exotic vine that bears fragrant flowers, is another. Others are *Asclepias tuberosa* (butterfly weed), *Cosmos sulphureus* 'Bright Lights', purple coneflower, pentas, and parsley in its second year (when it flowers).

Our Personal Recommendations
There are reports from the Tidewater area that *Lantana camara* 'Miss Huff' sometimes winters over. If you'd like to try your hand at training lantana as a standard, work with a good-sized container-grown specimen of weeping lantana, *L. montevidensis*. Trained as a standard, it is lovely in bloom.

In color, shape, and nectar production, lantana is second only to the butterfly bush, Buddleja, as a butterfly magnet. A tender perennial sub-shrub, it develops quickly so we can grow it here as an annual. The cascading limbs are tipped eventually with dense, rounded or flat-topped clusters of tiny tubular florets. It's an attractive basket and container plant that provides non-stop colorful blooms summer till frost. In the species the flowers are cream to yellow and in some plants the color changes to orange, lavender, and red. There are all-white and all-red hybrids. Trained as a standard, lantana makes a handsome garden centerpiece. It thrives by the seashore. The drooping stems of the lavender species L. montevidensis, weeping or trailing lantana, can reach 36 in.

Other Name
Yellow Sage

Bloom Period and Seasonal Color
Summer till frost; white, cream to yellow changing to orange, lavender, yellow, and red.

Mature Height × Spread
2 to 6 ft. × 3 to 5 ft.

Marigold
Tagetes spp. and hybrids

Marigolds fill the garden with bursts of sunny colors, from yellow-white to gold to burnt orange. They bloom non-stop until frosts and have lacy foliage and a sharp, if not universally popular, aroma. They grow quickly from seed and tolerate drought, heat, and neglect. There are two major groups. The small French marigolds are varieties of Tagetes patula. *The big, round, fluffy African or Aztec marigolds are varieties of T. erecta; near-white and "odorless" marigolds belong to this group. The big-flowered varieties come in sizes from semi-dwarf, to 4-ft. hedge forms. "Triploid" marigolds are crosses between these species; they bloom early, are as durable as the French marigolds, and they are also as full as the African marigolds—and almost indestructible.*

Bloom Period and Seasonal Color
Summer until frost; off-white, shades of gold, orange, yellow, mahogany, and bi-colors.

Mature Height × Spread
8 in. to 3 ft. × 10 in. to 3 ft.

When, Where, and How to Plant
Indoors or in the garden, marigolds are easy to grow from seed. Sow seeds in the garden after the soil warms, or get a head start by sowing seeds indoors four to six weeks earlier. Small early marigolds bloom in as little as six to seven weeks from seed sown where they are to grow. The larger types need twelve or thirteen weeks to bloom. Marigolds need full sun to develop fully, except for the white varieties, which prefer a little shade. They all do best in well-drained, moderately fertile soil enriched with humus. See Soil Preparation and Planting in the Introduction. Space small marigolds 6 to 8 in. apart; allow 15 to 24 in. between tall marigolds. Apply a 2-in. layer of mulch.

Growing Tips
To encourage branching in big marigolds, as the plant develops pinch out the lead stem and branch tips.

Care
Deadhead, or shear, marigolds to keep blooms coming. The big-flowered marigolds are handsome in a vase, and last well if you strip the leaves from the part of the stem that will be immersed. The little French marigolds often self-sow, even in window boxes. Gather seed for next year's garden.

Companion Planting and Design
You can use marigolds large and small to ornament dry, neglected corners. They're also great follow-on flowers for spring bulbs. When marigolds are touched by frost, replace them with ornamental cabbages, kales, or potted mums in bloom. The little French marigolds are believed to discourage soil nematodes, mosquitoes, and some insects that attack vegetables. Rototilling the big orange African marigolds into the soil seems to protect flowers planted later in the same ground from nematodes. Rows of them planted between rows of nematode-susceptible vegetables and flowers reduces nematode infestations.

Our Personal Recommendations
Our favorites are the big Climax series whose dramatic blooms are over 4 in. across on plants that grow to 3 and 4 ft. tall. You can use them to create a fast-growing, bushy, eye-catching annual hedge.

Pansy
Viola × wittrockiana

When, Where, and How to Plant
Pansies here are planted in early spring and again in early fall. We set seedlings out when the weather cools and replenish the plantings with new seedlings in early spring. They live longest where the light will become dappled when the trees leaf out. In cool, hilly regions, pansies can take a little more sun and often live through the summer. The ideal soil for pansies is well drained and humusy. See Soil Preparation and Planting in the Introduction. Make the planting holes 8 to 10 in. deep. Plant seedlings with about 3 in. between plants. Apply a 2-in. layer of mulch.

Growing Tips
As spring advances pansies become leggy. Keep the soil well moistened and deadhead consistently—a killer job when done correctly since some bloom into summer. In the Washington, D.C., climate about half are gone by June, replaced by long-lasting annuals for summer and early fall.

Care
To encourage fall-planted pansies to keep going, deadhead after the first flush of fall bloom. When the weather begins to warm in late winter, fertilize the bed with an organic liquid fertilizer. When the plants show vigorous growth in mid-spring, resume deadheading.

Companion Planting and Design
For a showy fall and spring display, plant a color mix of large-flowered pansies, including lots of yellows, and interplant with early tulips. For loads of blooms, plant mixed varieties of the solid-color hybrids. For a lovely spring show, carpet under daffodils with 'Sorbet Blueberry Cream' Johnny-jump-ups. Pansies make handsome window box and container plants, and are delightful as accent plants and edgers for moist places in rock gardens, wild gardens, and woodsy places. Replace fading pansies with shade-loving edging lobelia, forget-me-not 'Victoria Blue', wax begonias, or impatiens.

Our Personal Recommendations
'Maxim Marina', an All-America Selections winner, bears 2-in., pansy-faced, lavender-blue blossoms on 4-in. stems. André loves the clear colors of the slightly smaller pansies called 'Clear Crystal' or the "crystal clears." They stay in bloom longer than the other pansies.

The pansy is a strange breed of annual: sown and planted in fall, it can survive 15 to 20 degrees Fahrenheit, one of very few winter-flowering plants. A hybrid violet beloved at least since the Elizabethan era, over the centuries this lovely little flower has acquired a string of delightful common names—heartsease, ladies-delight, and stepmother's flower. Old-fashioned pansies with painted faces in combinations of white, yellow, pink, blue, purple, near-black, and mahogany red have the biggest blooms and are the showiest. Modern pansy strains are smaller-flowered and come in solid colors and tender shades. They have a faint, sweet perfume. The small-flowered Johnny-jump-ups are true violas: their little painted faces do jump everywhere, even into next year.

Other Name
Heartsease

Bloom Period and Seasonal Color
Fall through early summer in shades and combinations of yellow, blue, white, orange, pink, rose, purple, and black.

Mature Height × Spread
8 to 10 in. × 8 to 18 in.

Petunia

Petunia × hybrida

The old-fashioned petunia with its single or double trum-pet-shaped blooms comes in colors to match every dream. *Cascade varieties tumble from window boxes and hang-ing baskets, growing fuller as summer advances. Upright forms make superb full-flowered bedding plants. Some purple and white varieties spread a sweet cinnamon scent over the evening air; those include in their genetic makeup the night-scented* Petunia axillaris, *the large white petunia. Newer varieties don't set seed, so they last longer. The* F1 Hybrid Single Multifloras *seem better able to stand high heat. Wave*™ *petunias are low, dense, wide spreading, and hold their flowers up. Supertunias*™ *are stronger, fuller plants. Common petunias are perennials that can't stand our winters, but the scented, full-flowering, hot magenta P. integrifolia is quite hardy.*

Bloom Period and Seasonal Color
Summer; in white, yellow, orange, pink, red, blue, lavender, magenta, purple, and showy bi-colors.

Mature Height × Spread
$^{1}/_{2}$ to 2 ft. x 3 to 4 ft.

When, Where, and How to Plant
You can start petunias indoors from seed ten to twelve weeks before the weather warms. See Starting Seeds Indoors in the Introduction. We prefer to choose from the many varieties of seedlings available at garden markets. Plant petu-nias when temperatures reach 60 to 65 degrees Fahrenheit. In midsummer we add fresh seedlings to containers to keep the displays going longer. For the fullest bloom, grow petunias where they will receive at least six hours of direct sun daily. Provide well-drained, humusy soil, with a pH of 6.0 to 7.0, worked to a depth of 8 to 10 in. See Soil Preparation and Planting in the Introduction. Allow 4 to 6 in. between plants. Spread a 2-in. layer of mulch around bedding petunias.

Growing Tips
Pinch out the tips of young petunias to encourage branching. Keep the soil evenly moist.

Care
Deadhead most petunias to keep them blooming. Midsummer, trim the stems back by a third to encourage late blooming, and repeat as blooms become sparse. Surprisingly, petunias last well as cut flowers; individual blossoms fade but others on the stem open. Wave™ petunias need no deadheading, pinching, or pruning, but are heavy feeders; add slow-release organic fertilizer at planting time.

Companion Planting and Design
Bedding petunias make good follow-on plants for spring flowers. The sparkling whites of the Cascade varieties harmonize mixed colors in bas-kets and planters. The grandiflora (big-flowered) forms and doubles produce fewer flowers, but they are magnificent, worth featuring on their own. The multiflora (many-flowered) forms cover themselves with smaller, single blossoms that froth into summer's prettiest multicolor display.

Our Personal Recommendations
Charming Fantasy miniatures will bloom all winter indoors. For a cascade of flowers we plant the Surfinia® and the Supertunia™ hybrids; for mixed baskets and planters, we like the tiny Million Bells® petunias; for bedding we use Wave™ and Tidal Wave™ hybrids. We love the new 'Blue Wave'™ for its velvety 2-in. blooms.

Pink Vinca
Catharanthus roseus

When, Where, and How to Plant

Seeds can be started indoors ten to twelve weeks before the average last frost. But, the plants are very sensitive to cold and over-watering, so we recommend buying nursery seedlings when they come on the market in late spring. In warm Zone 8, you'll find protection from mid-afternoon sun beneficial; in cool regions pink vinca does well in full sun. The ideal pH for pink vinca is 6.0 to 6.5. Any well-drained improved garden soil suits pink vinca. See Soil Preparation and Planting in the Introduction. Prepare planting holes 6 in. deep. Set standard vincas 8 to 12 in. apart; allow 12 to 14 in. between plants of the Mediterranean series and 'Cascade Appleblossom'. Apply a 3-in. mulch starting 3 in. from the stems.

Growing Tips

For the first two or three weeks water lightly at ground level without wetting the foliage, just often enough to keep the seedlings from drying out. Once the plants show signs of new growth, to encourage branching, pinch out the top 3 to 4 in. of the lead stem. Pinch out the next two sets of branches as they develop.

Care

If the leaves curl in periods of drought and heat, don't be concerned since they'll uncurl when dew falls in the evening.

Companion Planting and Design

Pink vinca's clear colors, bright contrasting eyes, and crisp green foliage have a cooling effect that enhances flowers with hot colors. It's attractive with blue or scarlet salvia, and makes a pretty low hedge for the front of the garden.

Our Personal Recommendations

For very hot situations we recommend the 'Magic Carpet' strain, whose flowers are white and shades of pink and rose, for they tolerate a lot of heat. 'Bright Eye' is a white dwarf with a carmine eye. 'Pink Panther' is under 12 in. and has clear, rose-red flowers with a darker eye. A wide-spreading, trailing habit makes the Mediterranean series good for baskets. The dwarfish 'Jaio Scarlet Eye' and 'Stardust Orchid' have won All-America Selections awards.

You can count on pink vinca to fill the front of your garden with pretty flowers nestled in crisp, fresh foliage from late spring until frost. It tolerates heat, drought, and pollution. The flower color never fades and the blossoms never need deadheading. The shiny leaves are dark green, and the single flowers have overlapping petals and, usually, an eye in a contrasting color. Cut, the flowers continue to open buds for several days, and the leaves stay fresh. Both the leaves and the flowers resemble pink vinca's trailing cousins, the evergreen periwinkles or myrtles, Vinca minor and V. major. Pink vinca's standard height is 1 to 1 1/2 ft. but new strains provide plants of varying heights, some with wide-spreading, trailing branches suited to containers.

Other Names

Madagascar Periwinkle, Rose Periwinkle, Rose Vinca

Bloom Period and Seasonal Color

Late spring until frosts; pink, deep rose, red, scarlet, white with a red eye, lavender blue with a white eye, peach, apricot, orchid, raspberry, burgundy.

Mature Height × Spread

12 to 18 in. × 18 to 20 in.
6 to 9 in. × 10 to 12 in.

Salvia
Salvia splendens

Scarlet sage is the reddest of the summer flowers, and the parent of today's short, spiky cultivars in designer shades—aubergine to purple, gold to salmon, and, of course, red. The plant, a perennial sub-shrub we grow here as an annual, has glossy green foliage and small tubular red flowers clustered at the tops of leafy stems in thick, showy spikes. Massed in the sun, the scarlet sages make a striking display! Scarlet sage is a cousin of the lovely blue sage, S. farinacea and its varieties, which are less showy but wonderful filler plants for borders and bouquets. The blue sages bush out and produce masses of lovely, slender, lavender-blue flower spikes that are beautiful in the garden, in late summer bouquets, and in dried arrangements.

Other Names
Sage, Scarlet Sage

Bloom Period and Seasonal Color
Midsummer till frosts; many colors including lavender blue.

Mature Height × Spread
1 to 3 ft. × 1 to 1^1/$_2$ ft.

When, Where, and How to Plant
You can start salvia seeds indoors ten to twelve weeks before mid-spring; grow the seedlings at about 55 degrees Fahrenheit. Or, sow seeds in the garden in late fall or in mid-spring. Full sun is best but blue sages flower moderately well with morning sun, particularly in Zone 8. Any well-drained humusy soil is suitable. See Soil Preparation and Planting in the Introduction. Work the planting holes to a depth of 8 to 10 in. Space the seedlings 6 to 8 in. apart. Apply a 2-in. layer of mulch.

Growing Tips
To promote rapid, unchecked growth, for the next two or three weeks water often enough to maintain the soil moisture. To encourage branching, pinch out the top 3 to 4 in. of the lead stem.

Care
After every flush of bloom, remove spent stalks to promote further flowering. The sages are drought-tolerant but need watering during prolonged dry spells.

Companion Planting and Design
Aubergine scarlet sage planted with coral New Guinea impatiens makes a striking show. The blue salvias are beautiful filler plants for shrub roses and lovely with snapdragons and cosmos in complementary colors.

Our Personal Recommendations
Heat- and drought-tolerant *S. farinacea* 'Victoria', which is 18 to 20 in. tall, and the slightly taller Wedgewood blue 'Blue Bedder', are among the best blue salvias. 'Rhea' is a 14-in. blue salvia recommended for planters and small gardens. *S. coccinea* 'Lady in Red' is one of the best salvias to attract hummingbirds.

Snapdragon
Antirrhinum majus

When, Where, and How to Plant

Planting time for snapdragon seeds and seedlings is mid-spring, two weeks after the last frost date. For early bloom, start snapdragon seeds indoors ten to twelve weeks earlier, or buy seedlings. In Zones 7 and 8, snapdragons do best in bright, dappled light but make do with four to six hours of morning sun. In cool, hilly regions, plant snapdragons in full sun. The ideal soil pH for snapdragons is 5.5 to 7.0. See Soil Preparation and Planting in the Introduction. For seedlings make the planting holes 8 to 12 in. deep, and space them 6 to 10 in. apart. Apply a 3-in. mulch layer starting 3 in. from the stems.

Growing Tips

For the first several weeks after planting, water often enough to keep the soil damp. When the seedlings are 4 in. high, pinch out the tips of the lead stems, and repeat for the next two sets of branches. When the tall varieties are 18 in. high, stake the lead stem. Where rust is a problem, plant only rust-resistant strains.

Care

In midsummer, water deeply every week to ten days unless you have a soaking rain. When harvesting or deadheading snapdragons, cut the stem just above the next branching node to encourage continued blooming. When snapdragons that survive winter become woody, plant new seedlings beside them in the spring and discard the older plants after their first flush of bloom. Shear dwarf snapdragons after every flush of bloom.

Companion Planting and Design

The tall pastel snaps in rosy colors are beautiful with tall ageratum and silver artemisia. For windy places, choose large-flowered tetraploids like 'Ruffled Super Tetra' for their strong stems.

Our Personal Recommendation

For big bouquets and a back of the border show, plant Double Supreme hybrids which reach to 36 in. tall and bloom in clear, solid shades of red, pink, rose, and yellow.

Spring through fall snapdragons fill cutting gardens and borders with spires of colorful flowers in many colors and bi-colors. There's a size and a variety for every garden purpose. Very tall snapdragons are perfect for cutting and for color at the back of a flower bed. The Princess strain's luscious bi-colors are mid-height and also good cutting flowers. Mid-height, open-faced Monarch and "butterfly" hybrids are excellent border flowers. Dwarfs like 'Tahiti' make full, fluffy edgers. In the Mid-Atlantic we class snapdragons with the annuals, but in Washington, D.C., and Zone 8 they usually come back a year or two to provide one of spring's loveliest early displays.

Other Name
Snaps

Bloom Period and Seasonal Color
Spring through early fall; clear solid shades of red, pink, rose, yellow, and bi-colors.

Mature Height × Spread
7 to 30 in. × 8 to 15 in.

Spider Flower
Cleome hassleriana

Spider flower is an airy, wonderfully useful back-of-the-border filler flower that develops a big, rangy, multi-branched, and interesting structure. It produces masses of big, open, globe-shaped flower heads in white, pink, or purple, and elegant divided leaves. The flowers are somewhat scented and are followed by attractive seedpods. Spider flower seedlings, and even seeds planted in the open garden, fairly leap to full maturity by midsummer and they stay beautiful well into the fall. The plant handles high heat and drought and is absolutely trouble free, but often gets to be so big it needs staking. It self-sows prolifically (unless you deadhead) and will save you the trouble of replanting next year.

Bloom Period and Seasonal Color
Midsummer till frosts in white and shades of pink, rose, lilac, purple.

Mature Height × Spread
3 to 5 ft. × 1 1/2 to 2 ft.

When, Where, and How to Plant
You can start seeds for spider flower indoors eight to ten weeks before the last local frost date; they grow well where temperatures are about 64 degrees Fahrenheit. Cleome also flowers readily from seed sown in mid-spring in the open garden in full sun. Not all garden markets offer spider flower seedlings, but the plants self-sow so generously, once you have planted cleome it probably will maintain itself in your garden. Almost any well-worked, well-drained, light soil suits the spider flower, and it does well even in sandy soil. See Soil Preparation and Planting in the Introduction. Space seedlings 15 to 20 in. apart and mulch 2 in. deep.

Growing Tips
Maintain soil moisture until the seedlings are growing well. If you have sown seeds outdoors in the open garden, once the seedlings are up, water them weekly.

Care
Water deeply if the plants show signs of wilting in a drought. If the plants take off and begin to look like they're headed for shrub size, tie the lead stem to a sturdy stake. Since cleome self-sows abundantly, deadhead now and then to minimize the thinning you will have to do next year.

Companion Planting and Design
A mass planting of spider flowers is handsome growing against a stone wall, and it is an excellent background plant for the flower border, and a lovely addition to a meadow garden.

Our Personal Recommendations
'Rose Queen', with its deep pink buds and pale pink flowers is a favorite, along with 'Purple Queen' and 'Helen Campbell', a beautiful white spider flower. New dwarf varieties such as 'Linde Armstrong' and 'Sparkler Blush' are excellent fillers for the middle of the flowering border.

Sunflower
Helianthus annuus

When, Where, and How to Plant

Sunflowers pop up and grow so quickly, you can sow the seeds directly in the garden once the soil is warm. Thin the seedlings to stand about 18 in. apart. Sow seeds where the plants are to grow. We have started sunflowers successfully indoors about four weeks before planting season, which is mid-spring; however, they quickly become leggy, so don't start them too early. See Starting Seeds Indoors in the Introduction. Sunflowers bloom most fully in full sun, thrive in ordinary even poor soil, and tolerate drought. See Soil Preparation in the Introduction, and Planting in the beginning of this chapter. Thin, or plant, the seedlings to stand about 18 in. apart. The very tall varieties may need staking as the seedheads become very heavy. Mulch 2 in. deep between plants. When deer have chomped the tops off a row of tall sunflowers, we have learned that the plants will branch if topped, so now we shorten the sunflowers at the front of the row to about 2 to 3 ft. and that makes a prettier picture.

Growing Tip

Keep the soil moist until the sunflowers are growing lustily.

Care

To save the seedheads from the birds, wrap the heads in gauze before the seeds ripen—then you can harvest the seeds for winter use.

Companion Planting and Design

The tall sunflowers belong in a row of their own in the kitchen garden, or lining a fence or a blank wall. The new dwarfish forms look well in a flowering border: we plant them with the vegetables and herbs in our kitchen gardens.

Our Personal Recommendations

A favorite sunflower is 'Golden Pheasant': instead of ray petals around a disc of seeds, the whole flower head is a mass of glorious golden yellow petals. Another favorite for cutting is 'Sunburst Mixed', which bears 4-in. flowers in deep crimson, lemon, bronze, and gold on strong branching stems to 4 ft. high.

The sunflower isn't the most beautiful, nor the most exotic, nor the most colorful flower we have, but it's a real charmer where children are concerned, and newer branching varieties provide masses of glorious, huge, cutting flowers. The annual species, planted in spring, sends thick stalks soaring as high as 12 ft. and the flower heads often are 12 in. across, with a central disk surrounded by yellow ray petals. The flowers are best picked in evening or early morning. Remove the leaves and plunge the stems into boiling water for one and a half to two minutes then condition the stems in water in a tall container overnight. Once hardened, the stems can usually be re-cut and used without further treatment. Birds love the seeds and deer relish both leaves and flowers, alas!

Bloom Period and Seasonal Color
Summer to fall; yellow, orange, maroon, creamy white, bi-colors; some with green centers, some with maroon or black centers.

Mature Height × Spread
2 to 12 ft. × 2 to 2^1/$_2$ ft.

Sweet Alyssum

Lobularia maritima

Sweet alyssum is a fragrant, frothy little edging plant that from summer through late fall just covers itself with tiny, scented florets in sparkling white, rosy violet, or purple. The plant has a dainty appearance and spreads outward, becoming a low sprawling mound by the end of the season. In extreme heat in midsummer, a slump in flower production can occur, but the blossoms return when cooler weather arrives. However you use alyssum, be sure to set at least a few plants by the porch or patio where you can enjoy its sweet scent in late summer. Alyssum is one of the plants that does exceptionally well near the sea and it can be set out around taller plants as a living mulch to keep the ground cool.

Bloom Period and Seasonal Color
June until frosts in white, purple, and pastel colors.

Mature Height × Spread
4 to 8 in. × 12 to 18 in.

When, Where, and How to Plant

If you want to grow your own alyssum, start the seeds indoors between February 1 and 15, but be aware that alyssum is slow to germinate. Plant the seedlings outside when the soil has warmed. Sweet alyssum can do with a little less than direct sun all day, but it needs at least four to six hours of direct sun to flower at all well. The ideal for sweet alyssum is well-drained humusy soil with a pH between 6.0 and 7.0. Dig the bed, or generous planting holes, 6 in. deep. See Soil Preparation and Planting in the Introduction. Set the seedlings 6 to 8 in. apart. Apply a 2-in. mulch starting 3 in. from the stems.

Growing Tips

To promote rapid, unchecked growth, for the first two or three weeks water often enough to sustain the soil moisture.

Care

In midsummer, water deeply when you water the flower garden. Shear after each flush of bloom to discourage seed-setting and to encourage flowering. Sweet alyssum self-sows and can spread like wildfire to other parts of the garden. Discard volunteers, because chances are these will turn out to be plants that have reverted to the original, less-interesting species, not the beautiful cultivar you planted originally.

Companion Planting and Design

Sweet alyssum makes a neat, fragrant edger for flowering borders and walks. We add sweet alyssum in hanging baskets, planters, and tubs, set so the stems will spill over the container edges as the plant fills out. It thrives tucked into moist planting pockets in a dry stone wall and is very pretty with purplish ornamental peppers.

Our Personal Recommendations

Some of our favorite varieties are 'Little Dorrit', 'New Carpet of Snow', 'Noel Sutton', 'Elizabeth Taylor', 'Royal Wedding', 'Creme Beauty', and 'Geranium Pink'. 'Snowcloth' is a really small form.

Zinnia

Zinnia elegans and hybrids

When, Where, and How to Plant

You can sow seeds indoors about four weeks before planting time, which is when the soil has warmed. The smaller varieties bloom in four to five weeks from sowing. Zinnias do best with full sun, but bloom with four to six hours of sun. Dig the soil 8 to 12 in. deep. See Soil Preparation and Planting in the Introduction. Set seedlings of miniatures 6 in. apart, and the larger zinnias 18 in. apart. We can't do without zinnias, but they are subject to leaf spot and mildew so avoid mulch and crowding, which encourages mildew.

Growing Tips

When the seedlings are 6 in. high, pinch out the tips of the lead stems to encourage branching. Deadhead consistently, and harvest flowers at will. Cut the stem just above the next branching node and new flowering stems will develop, rising from between each pair of leaves and the main stem.

Care

In a drought, water every ten days to two weeks; overwatering encourages mildew. Where mildew is a problem, choose mildew-resistant cultivars. Cornell University research suggests that spraying with a solution of 1 tablespoon of ultrafine or horticultural oil plus 1 tablespoon of baking soda (sodium bicarbonate) per gallon of water protects against mildew.

Companion Planting and Design

Zinnias are ideal follow-on plants for spaces left empty by the passing of spring flowers. Dwarfs like 'Dasher' and 'Liliput' make colorful edgers. Ribbons of award-winning 'Peter Pan' zinnias, small plants with big flowers, brighten a garden path. Little *Z. angustifolia* is a spreading form to use in hanging baskets and as an edger. An annual that makes a delightful edger for zinnias is the pretty little "creeping zinnia," *Sanvitalia procumbens*.

Our Personal Recommendations

For cutting and show, we like tall zinnias with blooms 4 to 5 in. across on 30-in. stems, and showy 'Candy Cane', 17-in. plants with semi-double and double flowers striped pink, rose, and cerise. The 12- to 14-in. 'Small World Pink' hybrid zinnia is pretty and billed as disease-resistant.

We love the zinnia's sparkling colors, wild and wonderful flower forms, and cut-and-come-again attitude. One of the very best annuals for vibrant color and lasting vase life, it's a staple in our gardens. Zinnias are fun because there are so many varieties to experiment with. These are upright plants that branch when the tips are pinched, and they come in colors and sizes suited to every design purpose. The petals of some varieties are quilled like a cactus, others curl, and some are ruffled. There are flat-petaled forms, doubles, and singles. The large-flowered zinnias bloom less freely than the small-flowered forms, and need more time to come into bloom.

Bloom Period and Seasonal Color

When deadheaded, zinnias bloom from summer through early fall. Colors include shades of red, pink, orange, magenta, yellow, white, and bi-colors.

Mature Height × Spread

$^1/_2$ to 3 ft. × 1 to $3^1/_2$ ft.

Bulbs, Corms, and Tubers *for the Mid-Atlantic*

The earliest flowers come from bulbs, tubers, and corms planted September and October the fall before. The little bulbs open first, about February when the witch-hazels bloom at the National Arboretum. We plant these early risers under shrubs and trees tall enough to allow them dappled light. We edge flower beds with them, and woodland paths, and set them adrift in rock gardens. We keep a few near entrances so they can report on the progress spring is making. Each small bulb adds just a scrap of color to the winter landscape, so we plant them in drifts of twenty to a hundred. Small bulbs thrive and perennialize even in lawns. They may be grown in large containers outdoors in Zones 7 and 8 and some can be forced into flower indoors.

The next wave of color from fall-planted bulbs peaks in April and May. The earliest of the big bulbs are the perfumed hyacinths, which we plant near entrances. Then come the daffodils and the tulips. The large spring bulbs are most effective planted in groups of ten in flower borders and naturalized in drifts of twenty or more. We plant dozens in flower borders accompanied by perennials (and annuals) that will grow up and hide the fading bulb foliage, which must be allowed to ripen before it is removed. That's their major drawback: for the larger bulb flowers to bloom well the following year, the foliage must be allowed to ripen—yellow—before it is removed. It takes weeks and the process is unsightly.

Oriental Lilies

Summer-flowering bulbs provide great screening for the fading foliage of spring flowering bulbs. They come into bloom when the nights turn warm—mid- to late June, and some last until mid-September. Those that are winter hardy can be planted the fall before; tender bulbs should be set out in the spring. To be effective these big bulbs need to be in sets of five or ten. We like to add a few real tropicals, including canna and the ornamental banana, for their exotic foliage: they're available pot-grown in late spring. They often winter over successfully stored in their containers in a cool basement.

Bulbs that bloom when all other flowers have faded have a special place in the gardener's heart. The silky petals and tender colors look so fragile, but they endure fall rains and wind storms. Fall-

Cactus-Flowered Dahlias

flowering bulbs can be planted in spring and any time up until July—as soon as they're available. These small bulbs are most effective planted in groups of twenty, fifty, and 100.

When, Where, and How to Plant

Bulbs-in-waiting can be stored in the crisper, or a cool garage or cellar. (Do not store them with apples, which put out a gas that will cause the bulbs to rot.) If you can, plant them as soon as you get them. Planted late they have shorter stems and late blooms. Most bulbs bloom earliest growing in full sun; in part shade they open later. Their first year, spring flowering bulbs will bloom planted in shade. But to perennialize and bloom fully, they need at least bright or dappled light under deciduous trees, or bright shade under a tall evergreen. Ideal is a sunny, sheltered location where the soil is dryish in summer and in winter.

The ideal soil for bulbs is light, very well drained, and improved by additions of organic matter such as peat moss, compost, or aged pine bark, along with an organic, blended bulb fertilizer at the rate of 5 to 10 pounds per 100 square feet. The ideal pH range for most is 6.0 to 7.0. See Soil Improvement in the Introduction. Set bulbs so the pointed tips are upright; set corms and tubers with the roots facing down. For bulbs under 2 inches tall, provide holes at least 5 inches deep and 1 inch wide. Or, prepare a planting bed 5 to 6 inches deep. Set the small bulbs 2 inches apart. Plant bulbs that are 2 inches or larger in holes 8 inches deep and 3 inches wide. Or prepare a planting bed 8 to 10 inches deep. Set the bulbs 4 to 6 inches apart. To create naturalized drifts, dig an irregularly shaped planting bed, throw the bulbs out by the handful and plant where they fall.

But before planting bulbs, inventory the vole population. For voles your bulbs are the local gourmet counter. Squirrels shop there, too, and store their catch for later use. When they forget where they stored your bulbs, they come up in totally unexpected, sometimes delightful, places. To foil the sweet dears, plant your bulbs in pockets of VoleBloc™ or PermaTill®. Either one improves drainage, by the way. Daffodils don't need protection from voles: they're toxic to wildlife. Place 2 inches of VoleBloc™ or PermaTill® in the bottom of the hole. Set the bulb on top of it, and fill in all around with VoleBloc™ or PermaTill® leaving just the tip exposed. Fill the hole with a mix of 50 percent VoleBloc™ or PermaTill® and improved soil from the hole. Mulch with 2 inches of pine needles, oak leaves, composted wood chips, or shredded bark.

Care

Most of the bulbs we recommend come back, at least for a season or two. Allow the stems and foliage of the large bulbs to ripen six to seven weeks before removing them. Daffodils and some of the small bulbs are likely to rebloom and to multiply indefinitely without deadheading. Large bulbs benefit from dead-heading. Remove only the flower itself. Allowing the flower stem as well as the foliage to ripen nourishes the bulb and that enhances next year's flowering. Small bulbs do not need deadheading. Tulip foliage may be cut when it yellows halfway down. If well fertilized, some tulips perennialize, but the following year many just put up puny foliage and fail to bloom. We dig and discard those. Most bulbs require ample moisture during the season of active growth, from the moment the first pip breaks ground. Once the foliage disappears the bulbs are dormant, and excess watering can be detrimental. After flowering, but before the foliage disappears, spread an organic, slow-release fertilizer over the bulb plantings, 4 to 6 pounds per 100 square feet.

A Seasonal Approach

There are so many wonderful bulbs to choose from, it can be overwhelming. One way to simplify the selection is to categorize them by seasons.

Late Winter and Early Spring Bulbs

Dwarf Beardless Iris, *Iris reticulata*

Early Crocus, *Crocus vernus*

Glory-of-the-Snow, *Chionodoxa luciliae*

Grape Hyacinth, *Muscari* spp.

Miniature Cyclamen, *Cyclamen coum*

Miniature Daffodils, *Narcissus* 'Tete a Tete' and other early daffodils

Snowdrops, *Galanthus nivalis*

Species Tulips, *Tulipa saxatilis, T. tarda, T. turkistanica,* and others

Squill, *Scilla tubergeniana*

Striped Squill, *Pushkinia scilloides*

Windflower, *Anemone blanda*

Winter Aconite, *Eranthis hyemalis*

Early and Mid-Spring Bulbs

Bearded Iris, *Iris* hybrids

Daffodils, *Narcissus*

Fritillaria, *Fritillaria imperialis*
   'Rubra Maxima'

Hyacinth, *Hyacinthus* hybrids

Late Crocus, *Crocus*

Lily-of-the-Valley, *Convallaria majalis*

Silver Bells, *Ornithogalum nutans*

Starflower, *Ipheion uniflorum*
   'Wisley Blue'

Tulips, *Tulipa*

Wild Hyacinth, Wood Hyacinth,
   Hyacinthoides hispanica
   (syn. *Scilla campanulata*)

Wood Sorrel, *Oxalis adenophylla*

Summer Bulbs

Crocosmia, *Crocosmia* spp. and hybrids

Dahlias, *Dahlia* hybrids

Dwarf Canna, *Canna* hybrids

Flowering Onion, *Allium giganteum*

Gladiolus, *Gladiolus*

Lilies, *Lilium*

Peacock Orchid, *Acidanthera bicolor*

Peruvian Daffodil, *Hymenocallis narcissiflora*
   (syn. *Ismene calathina*)

Poppy Anemones, *Anemone coronaria*

Rain Lily, *Zephyranthes*

Spider Lily, *Lycoris* spp.

Summer Hyacinth, *Galtonia* hybrids

Tuberose, *Polianthes tuberosa* hybrids

Fall and Winter Bulbs

Colchicum, *Colchicum autumnale*

Fall Crocus, Saffron Crocus, *Crocus sativus,*
   C. kotschyanus (syn. *C. zonatus*), *C. speciosus*

Hardy Cyclamen, *Cyclamen hederifolium*

Lily-of-the-Field, *Sternbergia lutea*

Winter Daffodil, including Tenby Daffodils,
   Narcissus asturiensis and
   N. 'Grand Soleil d'Or'

Other Options

This chapter presents the best bulbs, corms, and tubers for the Mid-Atlantic, but there are others we like also:

Canna, *Canna* × *generalis* cultivars

Hardy Cyclamen, *Cyclamen hederifolium*

Ornamental Banana, *Musa velutina*

Peacock Orchid, *Acidanthera bicolor*

Peruvian Daffodil, *Hymenocallis narcissiflora*
   (syn. *Ismene calathina*)

Rain Lily, *Zephyranthes* spp.

Spider Lily, *Lycoris* spp.

Summer Hyacinth, *Galtonia* spp.

Tuberose, *Polianthes tuberosa*

Crocosmia

Crocosmia spp. and hybrids

Crocosmia is a tall, exceptionally beautiful and showy summer-flowering bulb that will remind you of a gladiola. Like the gladiola it grows from a corm and sends up fresh, handsome sword-shaped leaves followed by slender, branching spikes of deep orange-scarlet flowers. The blossoms must be loaded with nectar because they are dearly loved by butterflies and hummingbirds. The most famous of the cultivated varieties is 'Lucifer' whose large, silky flowers are a vivid flame red. Crocosmia is a long-lasting garden perennial that lives through winters without cover even in Zone 6. In Zone 7 and southward it perennializes, multiplies, and provides many weeks of vivid color for the garden in the dull summer months. Crocosmia is also an excellent cutting flower.

Bloom Period and Seasonal Color
July and August; orange-red, red, yellow.

Mature Height × Spread
2 ft. × 1 to 1 1/2 ft.

When, Where, and How to Plant
Crocosmia may suffer in cold winters in Zone 6, so plant it in a protected spot and provide a winter mulch. If your winters are colder than Zone 6, plant corms and plan to lift and store them for the winter. Garden centers offer container-grown crocosmia in spring, the planting season. In cool regions crocosmia needs full sun to be all it can be, but where summer gets very hot it needs some protection from noon sun. Crocosmia is tolerant as to pH, but needs a well-drained site and humusy, fertile soil. See Soil Preparation in the Introduction. Set corms 3 in. deep and 5 in. apart. Plant container-grown crocosmia according to the planting instructions at the beginning of the Perennials chapter. Water well. Mulch 2 in. deep starting 3 in. from the edge of the planting.

Growing Tips
Water deeply every week to ten days the first four to six weeks unless you have a soaking rain.

Care
Crocosmia is self-cleaning, so doesn't need dead-heading. The flowers are followed by attractive seed capsules that can be left until fall, then the foliage should be cut down to a few inches above the crown. For winter protection in Zone 6, mulch with evergreen boughs or hay; in cooler regions lift the corms and store them for the winter. Fertilize the bed between late winter and early spring with slow-release, organic, acid fertilizer. Crocosmia does best given sustained moisture, but the plant is adaptable.

Companion Planting and Design
Use crocosmia to screen the last of the foliage of the late spring bulbs: it will grow up and make a wonderful splash of color in the hot dry months. Plant crocosmia in a flowering border in groups of five or ten and toward the center of the bed. It needs lots of space all around.

Our Personal Recommendation
'Lucifer' is our favorite.

When, Where, and How to Plant

Plant the bulbs in September or October, and set them out in full sun; in part shade they open later. The ideal location is a sunny, sheltered place where the soil is dryish in summer and in winter. The ideal soil is light, well drained, and improved by additions of organic matter and an organic, blended fertilizer. The ideal pH range is 6.0 to 7.0. See Soil Preparation in the Introduction and the planting instructions at the beginning of this chapter, including instructions on discouraging voles and squirrels. Provide holes 5 in. deep and 1 in. wide, or a planting bed 5 to 6 in. deep. Set the bulbs 2 in. apart. Avoid leaving bits of bulb casing around the planting: squirrels notice. Mulch the area.

Growing Tips

Crocus naturalize easily, and will perennialize in lawns. If you plant crocus in the lawn, you must be prepared to allow the foliage a little time to ripen before the grass can be mowed.

Care

After flowering, and before the foliage disappears, spread an organic, blended fertilizer over the area where the bulbs have been planted, at the rate of 4 to 6 pounds for every 100 sq. ft.

Companion Planting and Design

To show, they need to be planted in drifts of twenty to 100. We like lots of spring blooming crocuses near house entrances, early reminders that spring is coming, and edging flower beds and borders, fronting shrub borders, along woodland paths. With fall blooming crocus André plants *Colchicum autumnale* under tall trees.

Our Personal Recommendations

André's choices are: hybrids of *Crocus vernus*, with 3-in. flowers, some striped or feathered, which has been in cultivation since 1765; and the Dutch hybrid cultivars. For fall flowering *C. speciosus*, which blooms early, is the showiest, the easiest, and can stay in bloom until hard frosts; *C. kotschyanus* (syn. *C. zonatus*), which bears 4- to 6-in. tall rose-lilac flowers; and the later blooming saffron crocus, *Crocus sativus*.

There are both fall blooming and spring blooming crocus. The late winter, early spring crocuses are planted the fall before, and begin to bloom about the same time as the snowdrops raise their tiny white bells. Often enough these early birds face up to and bloom through the last snowfall. The brightly colored, little, cup- or chalice-shaped flowers have vivid yellow anthers and come in many colors. Some have beautiful contrasting stripes or streaks. The grassy green leaves come up after the flowers and in some varieties have white or silver midribs. The fall crocuses produce their elegant cup-shaped blooms in early and mid-fall. They are planted in August or September. The following year the grassy leaves come up in the spring, then die down in summer.

Bloom Period and Seasonal Color

Late winter and early spring; white, pink, lavender, purple, yellow, orange; many are striped or streaked with contrasting colors.

Mature Height × Spread

2 to 6 in. × 2 to 6 in.

Daffodil

Narcissus spp. and hybrids

Daffodils are big bulb flowers that announce the coming of spring with a splashy show of gold, cream, or bi-colored "ta-da-ta-da" trumpets on straight 4- to 20-in. stems. In the hills of Virginia and Maryland, Zone 6, the early daffodils often bloom with the thawing of the snow. But in southern Virginia and along the shore, early daffodils and miniatures such as 'Tete-a-Tete' often flower in December and January, or even earlier. Daffodils perennialize readily and are safe from squirrels and other rodents because they are toxic to them. The names "daffodil," "Narcissus," and "jonquil" cause confusion: Narcissus is the botanical name, though "daffodil" may be used in its place. Jonquils are a specific type related to the species N. jonquilla, late bloomers that bear a cluster of flowers on each stem and are exquisitely scented. The paperwhites we force for winter bloom are jonquils too tender to survive our winters.

Other Name
Jonquil

Bloom Period and Seasonal Color
Spring; white, yellow, gold, orange, bi-colors, pink.

Mature Height × Spread
4 to 20 in. × 3 to 5 in.

When, Where, and How to Plant
Plant the bulbs in September or October in full or partial sun. The ideal soil is well drained and slightly acid. Provide well-worked fertile loam with excellent drainage. See the Soil Preparation section of the Introduction. Some of the bigger daffodil bulbs are really two or three bulbs attached—don't separate them. Set the bulbs 8 in. deep, about 3 to 6 in. apart. Mulch the area.

Growing Tips
To perennialize daffodils, after flowering and before the foliage disappears, spread an organic, blended fertilizer over the area, 4 to 6 pounds for every 100 sq. ft.

Care
Deadheading isn't essential. Allow the foliage to yellow about six weeks before cutting it back. Don't bind the leaves during that period—that cuts off light and oxygen. When daffodils get smaller and crowded, divide them just before the foliage has died. Replant them at once, or store them in well-ventilated trays at 50 to 80 degrees Fahrenheit. Cut daffodils last well. A note of caution: before combining just-cut daffodils (which contain toxic substances) with other flowers, soak the daffodils in water overnight and discard the water.

Companion Planting and Design
Plant daffodils in irregular drifts of ten, twenty, or more. Large daffodils are breathtaking in woods, fronting evergreens, edging meadows, and along the banks of ponds and streams. The miniatures are exquisite in rock gardens, containers, tucked into rocky nooks. By choosing bulbs that come up early, midseason, and late there can be daffodils from late winter until early summer. In warm climates a few will flower (whether you want them to or not) before Christmas.

Our Personal Recommendations
For over fifty years nurseryman Martin Viette, André's father, tested daffodils to find those that perennialize best. Here are a few culled from his lists: 'February Gold', 'Avalanche', 'Geranium', 'Hawera', 'Ice Wings', 'Quail', 'Sir Winston Churchill', and 'Tete-a-Tete'. A few are fragrant such as 'Cheerfulness' and 'Old Pheasant Eyes'.

Dahlia

Dahlia × hybrida

When, Where, and How to Plant

Plant tubers, or container-grown dahlias, when lilacs bloom. Provide an open sunny site and soil improved as described in the Introduction—light, fertile, well drained, humusy, pH 6.0 to 7.5. Set tubers, or container-grown plants, 18 to 24 in. apart. For 5-footers, provide sturdy, equally tall stakes. For tubers, dig planting holes 6 to 8 in. deep with the eye portion nearest the stake, if there is to be one. Cover the tuber with 2 to 3 in. of soil. Water when a shoot appears about four weeks later. Then add a few more inches of soil, water, and repeat at intervals as the plant grows until the hole is filled. When the stem is 12 in. tall, tie the stem to its stake. Tie on other branches as the plant matures.

Growing Tips

Dahlias require watering every week to ten days unless there's a good soaking rain. Harvest the blooms or deadhead.

Care

Place cut dahlia stems in water at 150 to 160 degrees Fahrenheit to harden overnight before re-cutting the stems and arranging them. Given a deep winter mulch, dahlias may perennialize. But growers recommend digging and storing the tubers when the yellowing tops die back after the first killing frost. Lift the crown with a spading fork, remove the foliage, and wash off the dirt. Dry them out of direct sunlight for a day or so. Label and store them in cedar chips, vermiculite, sand, or peat moss in a cool dry place at 40 to 45 degrees Fahrenheit. In spring when the eyes begin to sprout, divide the tubers, providing each with at least one eye, and replant.

Companion Planting and Design

We plant dahlias in the cutting and vegetable gardens—5-footers get a row of their own. We use bedding dahlias to edge perennials and with blue salvia, mint, asters, lavender, purple basil, and statice. In the flower beds, we front tall dahlias with baby's breath, and grassy liriope.

Our Personal Recommendation

For cutting, we favor the long-stemmed cactus-flowered dahlias.

The dahlia is one of the great flowers of late summer and early fall, an easy-to-grow bushy perennial with lush foliage and many-petaled flowers in extraordinary forms. The American Dahlia Society recognizes fourteen distinct types of this New World flower, discovered in the sixteenth century in the mountains of Mexico by members of the Cortez expedition. But for gardeners, there are two main groups: the seed-grown bedding plants sold in flats of mixed colors; and the big show dahlias grown as staked specimens in containers or at the middle or back of the border. The flowers range from 6- and 7-in. "dinner plates" to 1½- and 2-in. pom-pom charmers. Dahlias last well cut. The crisp, almost translucent petals catch the light and in paler shades can be luminous.

Bloom Period and Seasonal Color

Late summer, early fall; pastels and jewel tones of pink, salmon, white, cream, lemon, heliotrope mauve, red, bi-colors.

Mature Height × Spread

1½ to 5 ft. × 1 to 2½ ft.

Fancy-Leaved Caladium
Caladium bicolor

Caladiums, which grow from tubers, are not winter hardy in our area, but we can't imagine summer without these beautiful foliage plants brightening semi-shaded areas with their incredible colors. Unlike the time-bound show that flowers provide, the caladium's rich glow is with you all season long, growing more beautiful as the plants fill out. The leaves are large and shield-shaped, held on slender stems 12 to 24 in. tall. The old-fashioned name for them is "dancing ladies" because they flutter in the wind. The fanciful leaf patterns are pink, red, and/or white on green, and in some varieties almost translucent. The leaves are used in flower arrangements; the flowers are insignificant and should be removed so the strength of the plant can go to the leaves.

Other Name
Dancing Ladies

Bloom Period and Seasonal Color
All season foliage color; green overlaid with patterns in white, pink, rose, salmon, crimson.

Mature Height × Spread
20 to 30 in. × 12 to 18 in.

When, Where, and How to Plant
We start caladium tubers indoors in a warm room about eight weeks before the weather turns warm enough to put out tropicals—55 degrees Fahrenheit. We lay them on 2 to 3 in. of peat moss or sterile soilless mix on shallow trays. Place them about 8 in. apart with the knobble side up and the little straggle of dry roots facing the bottom: even if you plant them upside down, they'll grow but may have smaller leaves. They're rather slow to start up but then they grow quickly. They develop well on a grow-light stand and in a sunny glassed-in porch. Once the tubers sprout, transplant them to pots filled with soil fertilized with a slow-release fertilizer. You can also plant caladiums outdoors when nights are above 60 and day temperatures are at or above 70 degrees Fahrenheit. Set them out in groups of four to six, about 2 in. under well-drained, rich soil mixed with humus or peat moss. They do best in a semi-sunny or a lightly shaded location. Deer love caladiums.

Growing Tip
Keep the soil evenly moist.

Care
In autumn as the temperature drops, gradually dry out caladium tubers and store them in dry peat moss, vermiculite, or perlite at 70 to 75 degrees Fahrenheit.

Companion Planting and Design
Caladiums are superb bedding and pot plants, glorious growing with impatiens whose colors complement the leaves: red impatiens with red-centered caladiums, white impatiens with white-green caladiums. We also use caladiums to keep color in late spring, summer, and early fall borders.

Our Personal Recommendations
The *C. bicolor* cultivars of great beauty include 21-in. tall, cool, white and green 'White Christmas'; the lovely, light-as-air, 18- to 20-in. white and green-lined-red 'White Queen'; 18-in., dark green, white frosted rose and red 'Rose Bud'; solid red bordered green 'Frieda Hemple'; rosy 15-in. 'Florida Sweetheart'; luminous 16- to 18-in., shell pink touched with green 'Pink Symphony'; and 8-in. 'Miss Muffet'.

Flowering Onion
Allium spp. and cultivars

When, Where, and How to Plant
Plant the bulbs for flowering onions in late fall in full sun or light shade. The ideal soil is well-drained, humusy, and fertile, pH 6.0 to 7.5. You'll find instructions on improving soil for bulbs in the Soil Preparation section in the Introduction. Plant the bulbs, large or small, following the instructions at the beginning of this chapter. Set the bulbs, depending on their size, 3 to 5 or 8 in. deep, 3 to 6 or 8 in. apart. Mulch the area.

Growing Tips
Maintain moisture during the flowering onion's growth period: after that it can be according to the weather, average to dry. To encourage the plants to come back, after flowering, and before the foliage disappears, spread an organic, blended fertilizer, 4 to 6 pounds for every 100 sq. ft.

Care
In the cooler reaches of the flowering onion's hardiness range, plants come back at least two or three years if the flower is removed after flowering and the foliage is allowed to mature fully before it is removed. Deadheading helps.

Companion Planting and Design
Plant flowering onions where the foliage of other flowers serves as a filler and screens the onion foliage while it is fading. The giant onion is striking in arrangements of flowers fresh or dried.

Our Personal Recommendations
There are dozens of interesting ornamental onion species. *A. aflatunense* is a smaller version of the giant allium that blooms earlier. *A. christophii* (syn. *A. albopilosum*), star-of-Persia, has a much larger flower, 8 to 10 in. around. *A. sphaerocephalum*, called drumsticks or round-headed garlic, bears small, perfectly round, reddish-lavender flower heads on stalks 20 in. tall. *A. karataviense*, a superior bedding plant recommended for rock gardens, bears fragrant, round, lilac-pink flowers and has decorative gray-purple leaves spotted violet. *A. schubertii* is an early summer bloomer with large flower heads composed of forty or more little pink or purple florets on stems of very unequal length. The flower of the lily leek, or golden garlic, *A. moly,* is made up of clusters of bright yellow, star-shaped florets.

The strap-shaped leaves of flowering onions do smell like onions but several species have appealing flowers, and all are excellent pest proof plants. There are two types of flowers. The most interesting are perfect spheres composed of many blue-purple or white-pink florets, on leafless stalks above tufts of dark green, strap-shaped foliage. Think huge chives. The tallest is A. giganteum, giant onion, whose round 6-in. reddish-purple flower heads top stems 35 to 45 in. tall. The flowers of A. tuberosum, which is known as garlic chives or Oriental garlic, are spreading clusters of fragrant white florets, typical of the other type of ornamental onion. The ornamental onions create striking accents in a mixed border. They're also lasting, eye-catching cut flowers and excellent for drying.

Other Name
Ornamental Onion

Bloom Period and Seasonal Color
Late spring and late summer; blue, purple, pink, white, yellow.

Mature Height × Spread
10 to 45 in. × 10 to 15 in.

Grape Hyacinth

Muscari spp.

The most familiar grape hyacinths are blue as blue can be, a tribe of little bulb flowers that bloom toward mid-spring almost anywhere there is sun or dappled light. Muscari *perennializes and naturalizes readily, and growing in good soil in open sunny woodlands, will eventually carpet the earth with an extraordinary "river" of blue. The flowers of the grape hyacinth are thickly clustered on stems to 6 to 8 in. high. In some forms the flowers are open and fertile, so they look a little like miniature hyacinths. Other types are sterile and the unopened buds look like tiny grapes enveloping the stems. Some varieties combine both fertile and infertile flowers. The leaves are grassy. There are white varieties. Some have a faint spice-and-grape fragrance, especially* M. macrocarpum, *a rather rare yellow species.*

Bloom Period and Seasonal Color
Early to mid-spring; many shades of blue, white, yellow.

Mature Height × Spread
5 to 12 in. × 6 to 8 in. to indefinite spread

When, Where, and How to Plant
Plant grape hyacinths in September or October, in full or part sun. The ideal soil is light, well drained, and improved by additions of organic matter and an organic, slow-release 4-10-6 fertilizer. The ideal pH range is 6.0 to 7.0. See Soil Preparation in the Introduction and the planting instructions at the beginning of this chapter, including instructions on discouraging voles and squirrels. Provide holes 5 in. deep and 1 in. wide, or a planting bed 5 to 6 in. deep. Set the bulbs 2 in. apart. Mulch the area.

Growing Tips
To encourage grape hyacinth to multiply, after flowering, and before the foliage disappears, spread a blended, organic fertilizer over the area, 4 to 6 pounds for every 100 sq. ft.

Care
Plant blue grape hyacinths in large groups, drifts of twenty to 100. White grape hyacinths stand out more, so fewer are effective. There's no deadheading. Grape hyacinths will multiply if they are well fertilized after blooming every year.

Companion Planting and Design
Grape hyacinths add solid blue to the front of flower beds. We like them naturalized in drifts, along paths, and at the foot of stone walls and white picket fences. They're pretty at the edge of the lawn, as a carpet between larger bulbs, in bulb baskets or shallow pots, and as underplanting for large white daffodils. 'Blue Spike' is lovely with daffodils like white 'Thalia' and early, pale yellow 'Hawera'.

Our Personal Recommendations
André favors 6- to 8-in. *M. botryoides* 'Caeruleum'. *M. azureum* has both infertile (buds) flowers and fertile, open flowers and these have a darker stripe of blue on the lobes. He likes *M. armeniacum* 'Blue Spike', a popular cultivar whose flowers are light blue and double. It is the *Muscari* usually chosen for planting in "rivers." The feather hyacinth, *M. comosum* ('Plumosum' in the trade) has fluffy, double, mauve-lilac flowers that bloom on 6-in. stems a little later than the other species. It's a historic bulb flower used in restoration gardens at Monticello and Mount Vernon.

Hyacinth
Hyacinthus orientalis

When, Where, and How to Plant
Plant hyacinth bulbs in September or October in full sun or partial shade. Some shade can prolong the hyacinth's flowering but in our cooler regions full sun is recommended. Provide well-worked fertile loam with excellent drainage. Look up the information about soil for bulbs in the Soil Preparation section in the Introduction. Plant following the instructions at the beginning of this chapter. Set the bulbs 8 in. deep, about 3 to 4 in. apart. Mulch the area.

Growing Tips
To encourage hyacinths to come back, after flowering, and before the foliage disappears, spread a blended, organic fertilizer over the area, 4 to 6 pounds for every 100 sq. ft.

Care
In the cooler reaches of their hardiness range, hyacinths come back for at least two or three years if the flower is removed after flowering and the foliage is allowed to mature fully before it is removed. In the South the sudden onset of summer heat often prevents this. Maintain moisture in spring, but avoid it in summer and winter.

Companion Planting and Design
Plant early, mid-season, and late types in groups along paths, in pockets near patios and entrances. In flower beds, plant hyacinths in groups of five to fifteen; in containers, plant the bulbs in sets of three to five. For bedding, choose slightly smaller bulbs; they'll have outstanding blooms the first year and a looser cluster the second. For forcing indoors, choose the largest bulbs of white 'Carnegie', 'Pink Pearl', deep blue 'Ostara', and clear pink 'Anna Marie'.

Our Personal Recommendations
Generally, white hyacinths are the most fragrant, then the pastels, but some deeply colored hyacinths have a powerful scent. Light blue 'Cote d'Azure' is unsurpassed for perfume. Among notably scented large doubles are the white 'Mme Sophie' and 'Ben Nevis' and the luscious pink 'Chestnut Flower'. Some related species André recommends are: endymion, *Hyacinthoides*, a frost hardy European bluebell that naturalizes easily; the Spanish bluebell, *H. hispanica*; and the English bluebell, *H. non-scripta* (syn. *Scilla non-scripta*).

The Oriental hyacinths open with the daffodils and the early tulips and they bring us spring's most extraordinary perfume. The plant is composed of wide grass-like leaves and a thick, fleshy flower stem that rises right up out of the middle, completely covered with starry, outfacing bells. Hyacinths are rather rigid, which makes them somewhat difficult to fit into a casual garden design. But the perfume is worth the effort. Hyacinths grow from bulbs that are quite large, a fair handful. Some varieties bloom early, others at midseason, and some quite far along in spring, so you can, if you plan carefully, keep hyacinth perfume on your garden all spring. Hyacinths can be forced to bloom indoors long before they come into flower out in the garden.

Other Names
Oriental Hyacinth, Dutch Hyacinth

Bloom Period and Seasonal Color
Early to mid-spring; pure white, yellow, coral, pink, rose, shades of blue and purple, midnight purple.

Mature Height × Spread
8 to 12 in. × 3 to 6 in.

Lily
Lilium spp. and hybrids

The lilies are among the tallest of all garden flowers. They're also the most stately, probably the most beautiful, and, in the case of the Oriental lilies, the most exquisitely perfumed. A 6- or 7-ft. lily is a commanding plant, not at home everywhere. But there's a place in every garden for medium and small lilies which, planted in groups, provide welcome color just when you need it most in summer. They bloom in a wide range of colors for three to four weeks beginning in most areas in June. The three major groups—Asiatics, Trumpets, Orientals—bloom in that order. Their periods of bloom overlap since there are late Asiatics and early Trumpets and Orientals. By thoughtful selection you can have lilies flowering from late spring until frost.

Bloom Period and Seasonal Color
June to August; white, every color but the blue range, bi-colors, spotted, brush-marked.

Mature Height × Spread
$1^1/_2$ to 6 ft. × $1^1/_2$ to 2 ft.

When, Where, and How to Plant
A container-grown lily in bloom adapts to transplanting almost anytime during the growing season, but to plant a bulb with a shoot over 2 in. long is death—believe us! Growers ship big dormant bulbs in damp peat: keep them there until planted, or in a crisper. Six hours of full sun, plus partial sun the rest of the day, is the rule of thumb; where temperatures soar over 90 degrees Fahrenheit, lilies benefit from protection from noon and afternoon sun. Pastel shades are more successful in bright shade. A lily requires perfect drainage and very fertile soil, with enough humus to keep moisture around the roots. Most need rather acid soil and will fail where lime or wood ashes have been applied. The exceptions are the Martagons and the species *L. candidum,* which thrive in alkaline soils. See Soil Preparation in the Introduction. Provide planting holes worked to a depth of 24 in. to guarantee good drainage, and space the big lilies 12 to 18 in. apart. Stake taller varieties. Water well. Mulch 3 in. deep.

Growing Tip
Lilies tolerate a dry period after flowering.

Care
As they fade, pinch blooms off the stalk. For bouquets, cut the stalks less than a third of the overall height of the plant, or the lily will be smaller next year. When flowering is over, cut the stalks to just above the leaves; when the leaves yellow, cut the stalks to the ground—or leave them to mark the locations. In fall and late winter fertilize the bed with a slow-release, organic fertilizer for acid-loving plants. Mulch the area. Move or divide lilies every four years in the fall.

Companion Planting and Design
All lilies enjoy cool feet. A mulch of ground cover such as alyssum or petunias or short marigolds does that job beautifully. For tubs or flower beds, group mid-size lilies three to five. For big borders, mass taller lilies in sets of ten to fifteen.

Our Personal Recommendation
An extraordinarily fragrant, beautiful lily is pure white, 3-ft. 'Casa Blanca', which has wide petals, and colorful stamens (that stain!). It blooms mid-season.

Tulip

Tulipa spp. and hybrids

When, Where, and How to Plant

Plant tulips in September or October, well before the ground freezes. Results past mid-December are poor. Tulips need only six hours of sun daily to perform well, preferably six hours of morning or afternoon sun. Deer love tulips, so avoid planting tulips where deer nibble. Ideal soil for tulips is slightly acid, well drained, deeply dug, enriched with compost and humus. You will find information about soils for bulbs in the Soil Preparation section in the Introduction. Plant tulip bulbs following the instructions at the beginning of this chapter and do follow the instructions on discouraging voles and squirrels. Squirrels really love tulips! Set large tulips 4 to 6 in. apart, 8 in. deep; set small bulbs 3 to 4 in. apart, 4 to 5 in. deep. Deeper planting can be successful but is not recommend below 10 in. Mulch the area.

Growing Tips

To encourage tulips to perennialize, after flowering and before the foliage disappears, spread a slow-release organic bulb fertilizer over the area, 4 to 6 pounds for every 100 sq. ft.

Care

In ideal conditions, some tulips perennialize and multiply. Some come back under most conditions for at least four years. Deadheading helps: take just the bloom, leaving the stem intact. Allow the foliage to yellow about seven weeks before cutting it back. Don't bind the leaves during that period—that cuts off light and oxygen. If the following year all you get is foliage, dig and discard the little bulbs that produce it. They may never bloom well.

Companion Planting and Design

Plant the little early botanical tulips with small bulbs. Big annual flowers make fine screening for ripening tulip foliage: tall snapdragons and big marigolds and zinnias, for example. André likes pastel tulips growing with creeping phlox, (*Phlox subulata*), white candytuft (*Iberis*), big multicolored pansies, scilla, crocuses, and snow drops.

Our Personal Recommendations

Good tulips include 'Apricot Beauty', 'Ollioules', 'Beau Mond', 'Temple of Beauty', 'Marilyn', and 'Duke of Wellington'.

Tulips are with us from very early spring, or late winter, right through late spring. There's every size and shape, almost every color, including midnight purple, and almost every combination of colors you can imagine. You really can have tulips blooming in your garden for months on end. We group them for design purposes according to their season of bloom. The earliest ones are the low-growing little species (botanical) tulips—bright, perky, and informal. The big cup-shaped tulips on round jade-green stems are showstoppers from late March through May. Some bloom as singles, others are bunch-flowering. There are early, midseason, and late bloomers in a range of colors and forms that are a delight to explore; plant a series of all types for a long season of bloom. Put your nose right into a tulip cup, and you'll discover a faint, hauntingly sweet scent, more pronounced in a few hybrids. Many Single Early tulips are scented, and the vivid orange, lily-flowered 'Ballerina' has fragrance.

Bloom Period and Seasonal Color
Late winter to late spring; every color but true blue.

Mature Height × Spread
4 to 24 in. × 6 to 8 in.

Conifers *for the Mid-Atlantic*

Evergreens are key foundation plants. In this chapter we've grouped the needled and scale-leaved conifers, large and small. The shrub sizes of familiar tree species—pines, yews, cedars, junipers, spruce, and hemlock—are discussed on the same pages as the tree sizes.

We find the small, shrubby conifers extremely useful for anchoring color and as background in flower beds and shrubbery borders. The shrubby evergreens also make the best dense hedges and windbreaks,

Cedar of Lebanon

and sturdy edgers for paths and driveways. For tall privacy screening and windbreaks we use big, naturally columnar evergreens, such as American arborvitae. To furnish neglected corners, and for mid-height or low screening, we like the bold branching of the sprawling dwarf junipers, and upright little yews like 'Pygmaea', which stay under 2 feet. Elegant columnar junipers—like 'Gray Gleam' and 'Skyrocket'—are ideal where a stylish accent is wanted and they make great verticals for small spaces.

A big, needled evergreen that has a considerable presence is the Canadian hemlock, a pyramidal conifer with short needles. Hemlock grows into a handsome shade tree, and a hemlock hedge can be pruned for decades. A hemlock and a holly make a lovely background for white-barked birch, and for azaleas and ornamental grasses. For a hurry-up tree and for really tall screening nothing beats the Leyland cypress, which grows at least 3 feet a year. It can be pruned for many years without losing its beauty. Mature, it becomes a big stately tree with graceful, feathery, bluish green, scale-like foliage and red-brown bark. Weeping evergreens, like the blue Atlas cedar, *Cedrus libani* spp. *atlantica* 'Glauca Pendula', add grace notes to the landscape.

Other lovely conifers that do very well here are varieties of blue spruce, silver fir, lacebark pine, and the beautiful dwarf hinoki cypress. The tall, longleaf pine that is native to our sandy coastal plain is too tall and coarse to be considered a garden ornamental.

Delayed leaf drop is one of the advantages you gain by planting conifers: practically no leaves to gather and grind in the fall. It's reassuring to know that yellowing needles most often are a normal part of a needled evergreen's cycle and not symptomatic of a problem. The term "evergreen" is misleading. Every plant must renew its foliage. White pines shed aging needles every year. And most other conifers shed *some* aging needles every year, but they don't, like the deciduous trees, lose *all* their older needles at once.

Planting and Pruning Evergreens

Conifers need well-drained soil and are moderate drinkers. You will find general information on planting and care for shrubs in the Shrubs chapter, and for trees in the Trees chapter. Specific soil needs and planting information for each conifer appears with the plant.

A collection of conifers, including Dwarf Alberta Spruce and False Cypress

Most often we prune an evergreen only to shape the plant or to make it bushier. To encourage dense branching to the ground, begin pruning when the evergreen is three to five years old. Summer after its main spurt of growth is the time to prune an evergreen to slow, dwarf, or maintain its shape. The rule is to prune strong growth lightly, and weak growth hard. Never trim more than a third from a conifer. You should not remove more of the top growth (the leader) than the growth of the last year or two. You can cut the main stem back to the first side shoots. This doesn't apply for trimmed hedges.

Light pruning of the branch ends of many evergreens, including hemlocks, junipers, and yews, is acceptable throughout the growing season, but not when they are dormant. Yews and junipers can take heavy pruning and fill out again very quickly. Firs, pines, spruces, and other conifers whose growth is initiated by "candles" should be pruned in spring when the candles appear at the branch tips. Cutting back the new candles by one-half to two-thirds will make the tips branch. Heavy pruning in fall isn't a good idea, because the pruning may stimulate a new flush of growth which could be damaged by winter weather, and wounds heal more slowly in seasons of reduced activity. But you can save some pruning of your coniferous evergreens, and the hollies, too, to make swags and roping for the holiday season.

Other Good Conifers

Dawn Redwood, *Metasequoia glyptostroboides* (a deciduous conifer)

Lawson's False Cypress, *Chamaecyparis lawsoniana,* and its cultivars

Arborvitae
Thuja occidentalis

Arborvitae is perhaps the most beautiful of all the formal conifers. A tall shrub, it is used as a specimen, windbreak, hedge, and foundation plant. Densely clothed with scale-like, lacy leaves in flat sprays that are an attractive deep green, and aromatic when crushed, the plant is symmetrical, slow growing, long lived, and can be sheared repeatedly. It also is easy to grow. In cultivation, the height of American arborvitae is between 12 and 15 ft. The fruits are small, erect cones. Cultivars in many shapes and shades are available. There are narrow forms, round forms, and broadly pyramidal forms, and cultivars in shades of blue-green and yellow tones. 'Emerald' maintains its brilliant color in winter and has considerable heat tolerance. 'Holmstrup' is a slow-growing arborvitae that stays under 10 ft. Deer love them all.

Other Names
American Arborvitae, Eastern Arborvitae

Bloom Period and Seasonal Color
Insignificant blooms; small erect cones.

Mature Height × Spread
12 to 15 ft. × 3 to 5 ft.

When, Where, and How to Plant
Container-grown and balled-and-burlapped arborvitae transplant easily in early spring and fall. The plant adapts to light shade but unless it is growing in full sun it loses the furry texture that is one of its major assets. It flourishes in soil that is slightly acid, with a pH of 6.0 to 7.0, neither very wet nor very dry. It tolerates clay and limestone soils as long as the site is fertile, well drained, and sustains moisture. See Soil Preparation in the Introduction, and planting instructions in the Trees chapter, because it is a big plant. Provide a planting hole three times the width of the rootball and twice as deep. Set the shrub so the crown will be an inch or two above ground level. Shape the soil around the crown into a wide saucer. Water slowly and deeply. Apply mulch 3 in. deep starting 3 in. from the trunk.

Growing Tips
The first year, unless there's a soaking rain, in spring and fall slowly and gently pour two to three bucketsful of water around the roots every two weeks; in summer every week or ten days. Maintain the mulch throughout the summer.

Care
Using a slow-release organic fertilizer, fertilize lightly in fall and again in spring. Replenish the mulch. Water deeply in periods of drought. Arborvitae generally does not need pruning. A heavy snowfall can open up the tight branching at the top: the solution is to tie the top of the plant in the fall. Any pruning should be done before spring growth begins.

Companion Planting and Design
Arborvitae is excellent as a formal specimen in the lawn, as a backdrop for deciduous trees and flowering shrubs, and in windbreaks and hedges. Deer crop arborvitae to the core at grazing height; the radical solution is to surround the plants with 8-ft. wire fencing.

Our Personal Recommendations
For the warmest reaches of our area 18- to 25-ft. Oriental arborvitae, *T. orientalis*, might be a better choice. It's a small tree with grass-green foliage when young that changes to a darker green as it matures. A 30- to 50-ft. tree form that does well in wet places is fast growing, cinnamon-barked Western or giant arborvitae, *T. plicata*. It doesn't tolerate salt spray.

Blue Atlas Cedar
Cedrus libani ssp. *atlantica* 'Glauca'

When, Where, and How to Plant
The true cedars are difficult to transplant, so set out a *young* container-grown plant in early spring, and handle the rootball with great care. Cedars require lots of space all around as they develop, but they do not do well exposed to icy blasts of wind—so avoid the crest of a hill with a northern exposure, and areas where there is pollution. The Atlas cedar tolerates partial shade but the other species named need full sun. The cedars as a group do best in soil that is somewhat acid, pH 5.0 to 6.5, but the Atlas cedar withstands some alkalinity in the soil. It tolerates clay and sandy soils as long as they are well drained. See Soil Preparation in the Introduction, and planting instructions in the Trees chapter. Provide a planting hole three times the width of the rootball and twice as deep. Set the tree so the crown will be about 1 or 2 in. above ground level. Shape the soil around the crown into a wide saucer. Water slowly, deeply, thoroughly. Apply mulch 3 in. deep starting 3 in. from the main stem.

Growing Tips
The first year, unless there's a soaking rain, in spring and fall slowly and gently pour two to three bucketsful of water around the roots every two weeks; in summer every week or ten days. Maintain the mulch throughout the summer.

Care
Using a slow-release organic fertilizer for acid-loving plants, fertilize lightly in fall and again in spring. Replenish the mulch as needed.

Companion Planting and Design
Blue Atlas cedar is superb in a group with 'October Glory' red maple, and low-growing evergreen azaleas. Use blue trees with discretion: more than one in a small landscape can be too much.

Our Personal Recommendations
If you like picturesque plants, consider also the deodar cedar, *C. deodara*, which has needles that are light blue or grayish green. Zone 7 is the northern end of its hardiness range. The variety 'Kashmir' is hardy to -25 degrees Fahrenheit. *C. libani*, the legendary cedar of Lebanon celebrated since biblical times, is like the blue Atlas cedar in form, but has dark green needles; *C. libani* var. *stenocoma* can stand severe winters.

The cedar is a needled evergreen: when mature, it is perhaps the most beautiful of the large evergreens, especially when featured as a specimen in a large landscape and surrounded by green lawn. The blue Atlas cedar is narrowly pyramidal in youth, and with maturity becomes a picturesque, flat-topped tree, 40 to 60 ft. tall, with slightly drooping horizontal branches, steel blue needles, and handsome upright cones. It grows quickly when young. For a smaller landscape, consider the weeping form, 'Glauca Pendula', which has pendulous branches 15 to 20 in. wide that drip icy blue foliage. This cedar will be fine in warm Zones 7 and 8, but it is borderline hardy near the West Virginia border, in Zone 6.

Bloom Period and Seasonal Color
Insignificant blooms; 3-in. upright cones.

Mature Height × Spread
40 to 60 ft. × 25 to 30 ft.

Canadian Hemlock

Tsuga canadensis

Long-lived, tolerant of years of shearing, easy to transplant, the Canadian hemlock is a superb evergreen for screening, shade, and display as a specimen. The shape is pyramidal and the branches are graceful, feathery, slightly drooping, and covered with short, aromatic, deep green needles that have two white bands beneath. It's a favorite nesting place for birds. The fruits are pretty little coppery-brown cones $1/2$ to 1 in. long. The cinnamon-brown bark in time becomes attractively ridged and deeply furrowed. The Canadian hemlock grows to between 40 and 70 ft. in cultivation, but in its native lands—the Midwest, Northeast, and the Appalachian regions—it can reach 100 ft. and more. The boughs are harvested for Christmas decorations and roping.

Other Name
Eastern Hemlock

Bloom Period and Seasonal Color
Insignificant blooms; the cones are coppery-brown and $1/2$ to 1 in. long.

Mature Height × Spread
40 to 70 ft. × 25 to 36 ft.

When, Where, and How to Plant
Plant a young balled-and-burlapped, or container-grown, hemlock in fall before Indian summer, or in early spring, while the tree is still dormant. Canadian hemlock does well in full sun or in partial shade. It does best in cool, moist, acid soil, pH 5.0 to 6.5. It also succeeds on rocky bluffs providing there is shelter from icy winds, and in sandy soil, providing there's enough humus in it to keep moisture around the roots. See Soil Preparation in the Introduction, and planting instructions in the Trees chapter. Provide a planting hole three times the width of the rootball and twice as deep. Set the tree so the crown will be an inch or two above ground level. Shape the soil around the crown into a wide saucer. Water slowly and deeply. Apply mulch 3 in. deep starting 3 in. from the trunk.

Growing Tips
The first year, unless there's a soaking rain, in spring and fall slowly and gently pour two to three bucketsful of water around the roots every two weeks; in summer every week or ten days. Maintain the mulch throughout the summer.

Care
Using a slow-release, organic, acid fertilizer, fertilize lightly in early spring. Replenish the mulch as needed. Prune away dead wood any time of year. Light pruning or shearing of new growth on the branch ends is acceptable after the main spurt of growth and throughout the growing season, but not after the plant becomes dormant.

Companion Planting and Design
Canadian hemlock is an excellent tall foundation plant. Limbed up, it becomes a graceful evergreen shade tree. Trimmed, it makes a superb 6-ft. hedge that can be maintained for decades.

Our Personal Recommendations
We recommend the eye-catching variety 'Sargentii', a spreading, weeping tree. 'Pendula', weeping Canadian hemlock, is a dark green, prostrate form that takes decades to reach 5 ft. by 8 to 10 ft. and thrives in shade. The Carolina hemlock, *T. caroliniana*, is somewhat less graceful than the Canadian hemlock, but is the best hemlock for city conditions.

Colorado Blue Spruce

Picea pungens 'Glauca'

When, Where, and How to Plant
Plant balled-and-burlapped or container-grown spruces in early fall or early spring. They have spreading root systems (rather than deep ones), so large specimens can be transplanted successfully. The Colorado blue spruce needs full sun to color well and does best in well-drained, moderately moist soil in the acid range, pH 5.0 to 6.0. See Soil Preparation in the Introduction, and planting instructions in the Trees chapter. Provide a planting hole three times the width of the rootball and twice as deep. Set the tree so the crown will be about 1 or 2 in. above ground level. Shape the soil around the crown into a wide saucer. Water slowly and deeply. Apply mulch 3 in. deep starting 3 in. from the main stem.

Growing Tips
The first year, unless there's a soaking rain, in spring and fall slowly and gently pour two to three bucketsful of water around the roots every two weeks; in summer every week or ten days. Maintain the mulch throughout the summer.

Care
In early spring before growth begins, broadcast the recommended dose of a slow-release organic fertilizer for acid-loving plants. Water it in. Replenish the mulch. To encourage density, or to change the shape of the plant, periodically prune the tips.

Companion Planting and Design
The Colorado blue spruce is best featured as a specimen out in the open in a large landscape; parked in a small lawn it soon grows out of scale with the dwelling. Grouped with smaller evergreens and planted at a distance from a dwelling, it becomes the anchor for a beautiful screen.

Our Personal Recommendations
Our favorite compact varieties of *P. pungens* are bluish-white 3-ft. 'Glauca Globosa', and silver-blue 'Montgomery'. For screening we suggest fast-growing green Norway spruce, *P. abies* and *P. abies* forma *pendula*, and the compact 4- to 6-ft. bird's-nest spruce, 'Nidiformis'. For high style there's the narrow 100-ft. Serbian spruce, *P. omorika*, whose cascading branches droop, then curve upward. The graceful Oriental spruce, *P. orientalis*, is beautiful and has exfoliating bark.

The spruces are the aromatic, symmetrical, conical evergreens we buy for Christmas trees, both cut and live. The needles are thin, rigid, 1/2 to 1 1/4 in. long with four sides and sharp points. The 2- to 4-in. cones start out green and turn light brown. A hardy native of the high Rocky Mountains, it lives 600 to 800 years. Majestic 'Glauca' has soft, blue-gray foliage that turns silver-gray to blue-green as the tree grows slowly to from 30 to 50 ft. There's a gorgeous weeping form, 'Glauca Pendula', and several other cultivars with special characteristics: 'Hoopsii' has the bluest needles; 'Moerheim' is a narrow, conical, blue tree; 'Thompsonii' has whitish silver-blue foliage and is considered one of the best of the blue spruces.

Bloom Period and Seasonal Color
Insignificant blooms; cones are green and mature to light brown.

Mature Height × Spread
30 to 50 ft. × 10 to 20 ft.

Douglas Fir
Pseudotsuga menziesii

The Douglas fir is a stately pyramidal evergreen straight as a spear at maturity, and one of North America's most important timber trees. It's also used as a cut or live Christmas tree. A dramatic landscape ornamental 40 to 50 ft. tall, in the wild it towers to heights of 250 and 300 ft. and lives 800 to 1,000 years! When young, the upper branches of the Douglas fir are ascending while the lower branches are somewhat drooping, a characteristic that becomes accentuated as the tree matures. The needles are flattish and blue-green. The pendulous cones are 3 to 4 in. long and bear seeds; when they mature in late summer they become an important source of food for small mammals and birds.

Other Name
Green Douglas Fir

Bloom Period and Seasonal Color
Insignificant blooms; 3- to 4-in. seed-bearing cones.

Mature Height × Spread
40 to 50 ft. × 12 to 20 ft.

When, Where, and How to Plant
Balled and burlapped, or container grown, the Douglas fir transplants well in early spring. The ideal site is open, airy, and sunny with space all around and moist air. It does not succeed in dry, windy areas. Plant a Douglas fir where the soil is well drained, with enough humus to maintain moisture around the roots, and slightly acid, pH 6.0 to 7.0. See Soil Preparation in the Introduction, and planting instructions in the Trees chapter. Provide a planting hole three times the width of the rootball and twice as deep. Set the tree so the crown will be about 1 or 2 in. above ground level. Shape the soil around the crown into a wide saucer. Water slowly and deeply. Apply mulch 3 in. deep starting 3 in. from the main stem.

Growing Tips
The first year, unless there's a soaking rain, in spring and fall slowly and gently pour two to three bucketsful of water around the roots every two weeks; in summer every week or ten days. Maintain the mulch throughout the summer.

Care
Using a slow-release, organic, acid fertilizer, fertilize lightly in fall and again in early spring. Replenish the mulch as needed.

Companion Planting and Design
The Douglas fir is a dramatic ornamental tree for large landscapes, such as parks, golf courses, and estates.

Our Personal Recommendation
The beautiful Douglas fir variety *glauca*, or Rocky Mountain Douglas fir, grows more slowly and makes a long-lasting live Christmas tree. The needles are a beautiful soft blue. Unfortunately, after Christmas it often gets lovingly planted on a small front lawn where it soon grows out of scale in relation to the grounds and the dwelling.

Dwarf Hinoki Cypress
Chamaecyparis obtusa 'Nana Gracilis'

When, Where, and How to Plant
Plant a young container-grown false cypress in fall before Indian summer, or in early spring, while the tree is still dormant. The hinoki cypress requires full sun and does best with some protection from wind. It prefers soils that are well drained, with enough humus to maintain moisture around the roots, and neutral to slightly acid, pH 6.0 to 7.0. See Soil Preparation in the Introduction, and planting instructions in the Shrubs chapter. Provide a planting hole three times the width of the rootball and twice as deep. Set the shrub so the crown will be an inch or two above ground level. Shape the soil around the crown into a wide saucer. Water slowly and deeply. Apply mulch 3 in. deep starting 3 in. from the crown.

Growing Tips
The first year, unless there's a soaking rain, in spring and fall slowly and gently pour two to three bucketsful of water around the roots every two weeks; in summer every week or ten days. Maintain the mulch throughout the summer.

Care
Using a slow-release organic fertilizer for acid-loving plants, fertilize lightly in fall and again in early spring. Replenish the mulch as needed. Pruning is rarely needed.

Companion Planting and Design
This is a first-rate, shrub-size evergreen for use in hedges, as background to a shrub border of azaleas, and as a foundation plant. The golden foliage of 'Crippsii' is striking against darker evergreens.

Our Personal Recommendations
A fascinating relative is the blue- or gray-green weeping Nootka, or Alaska, false cypress, *C. nootkatensis* 'Pendula', a variety with pendulous branches that droop. It can live to be over 1,000 years old. In cultivation it reaches 30 to 45 ft. A yellow species that is hardier than 'Crippsii' and holds its striking yellow hue in summer, is the 8- to 12-ft. golden threadleaf sawara, or Japanese cypress, *C. pisifera* 'Filifera Aurea'.

Shrubby forms of the false cypress are first-rate landscape plants. The dwarf hinoki cypress, 'Nana Gracilis', is an exceptionally graceful shrub 4 to 6 ft. tall with deep green, lustrous foliage that is white on the underside, flat, and scale-like. The branch tips turn down in an interesting half-twist that gives the plant an appealing texture and the appearance of greater softness than is usual in a conifer. An excellent yellow form is the golden cypress, C. obtusa 'Crippsii', a dense, pyramidal evergreen, whose branchlets are tipped a rich yellow-gold. It's a slow-growing shrub that needs a decade or two to reach 8 to 10 ft. but may eventually reach 30 ft.

Other Name
Dwarf False Cypress

Bloom Period and Seasonal Color
Insignificant blooms; bluish cones changing to red-brown.

Mature Height × Spread
6 ft. × 3 to 4 ft.

Juniper

Juniperus spp., cultivars, and hybrids

The junipers are really tough conifers that come in amazingly variable shapes, from 60-ft. trees to 2-ft. ground-hugging plants like the creeping juniper, J. horizontalis, covered in the Ground Covers chapter. Juvenile growth has awl-shaped needles and the adult growth is scale-like; when that transition occurs depends on the variety. The male cones are yellow, and resemble catkins; the female fruits are berry-like cones. Many superb shrubs have been developed from the Chinese juniper, J. chinensis, whose foliage may be bright green or blue- or gray-green. 'Hetzii' is a beautiful gray-green shrub about 10 ft. by 10 ft. at maturity. 'Mint Julep' is a compact, bright green, fountaining shrub, 4 ft. by 6 ft. 'Pfitzeriana', the most hybridized, has drooping branches, bright green foliage, and averages 5 ft. by 7 ft.

Bloom Period and Seasonal Color
Insignificant blooms; berrylike cones.

Mature Height × Spread
Variable, according to species and variety.

When, Where, and How to Plant
The junipers have a spreading root system that transplants easily. Set out container-grown plants in spring or fall. Plant in full sun; they accept some shade when young, but will get open and ratty unless growing in full sun. The eastern red cedar, *J. virginiana*, does well in acid and in alkaline soils, but most junipers prefer soil in the pH 5.0 to 6.5 range that is light, even sandy, and moderately moist. But they are tolerant of dry, clay soils and pollution. See Soil Preparation in the Introduction, and planting instructions in the Shrubs chapter. Provide a planting hole three times the width of the rootball and twice as deep. Set the shrub so the crown will be an inch or two above ground level. Shape the soil around the crown into a wide saucer. Water slowly and deeply. Apply mulch 3 in. deep starting 3 in. from the trunk or main stem.

Growing Tips
The first year, unless there's a soaking rain, in spring and fall slowly and gently pour two to three bucketsful of water around the roots every two weeks; in summer every week or ten days. Maintain the mulch throughout the summer.

Care
Using a slow-release organic fertilizer for acid-loving plants, fertilize lightly in fall and again in late winter or early spring. Replenish the mulch as needed. Minimize shearing and pruning by choosing junipers whose growth habits fit your purpose. The best time to prune junipers to minimize growth or enhance their shape is just after new growth.

Companion Planting and Design
For ground cover we use 24-in., slow-spreading *J. sabina* 'Tamariscifolia' which spreads 8 to 10 ft. For edging, graceful 3- to 4-ft. creeping juniper, *J. horizontalis* 'Plumosa' and 'Compacta', whose foliage turns purplish in winter. For columnar accents we like *J. scopulorum* 'Skyrocket' and 'Pathfinder', elegant, narrow, 20-ft., blue or blue-gray trees.

Our Personal Recommendations
A 40- to 50-ft. tree we recommend for landscaping and seashore planting is eastern red cedar, *J. virginiana*, available in both pyamidal and columnar forms. Another we like is the rare temple juniper, *J. rigida* 'Pendula', a weeping shrub or small tree.

Lacebark Pine
Pinus bungeana

When, Where, and How to Plant
Pines have taproots and are best moved as *young*, container-grown or balled-and-burlapped plants in early spring. They require full sun and well-drained, somewhat acid soil, pH 5.0 to 6.0. The lacebark pine tolerates some alkalinity. See Soil Preparation in the Introduction, and the planting instructions in the Trees chapter. Provide a planting hole three times the width of the rootball and twice as deep. Set the shrub so the crown will be an inch or two above ground level. Shape the soil around the crown into a wide saucer. Water slowly and deeply. Apply mulch 3 in. deep starting 3 in. from the trunk.

Growing Tips
The first year, unless there's a soaking rain, in spring and fall slowly and gently pour two to three bucketsful of water around the roots every two weeks; in summer every week or ten days. Maintain the mulch throughout the summer.

Care
Using a slow-release organic fertilizer for acid-loving plants, fertilize lightly in fall and again in late winter or early spring. Replenish the mulch. To encourage density, or to change the shape of a pine, in June, when new candles are fully grown, cut them back by half.

Companion Planting and Design
Several species of pine are used in landscaping. For edging urban gardens and anchoring perennial beds we like dwarfs of the mugo pine, *P. mugo*, which have small, attractive, dark green bundles of needles. They also do well by the shore. Plant lacebark pine where you can appreciate the mottled bark.

Our Personal Recommendations
One of the hardiest and most attractive of the big trees is *P. strobus*, the eastern white pine, straight as a ship's mast with long, bluish-green needles, 6- to 8-in. cones, and rapid growth to 50 to 80 ft. The drooping branches of 'Pendula' sweep the ground; 'Nanus' is slow-growing and can take seventy-five years to reach 15 ft. Coastal gardeners love the Japanese black pine, *J. thunbergii*, a salt-tolerant tree sometimes used as a sand binder. It will grow to between 20 and 80 ft. depending on the environment.

You can tell a pine from similar conifers by its needles, which are soft, thin, 2 to 5 in. long, and grow in bundles of two to five. The pine group includes dwarf, compact forms that are useful in landscaping, as well as tall, pyramidal trees. Lacebark pine is one of the most appealing species—a multiple-stemmed tree that grows very slowly to 30 to 50 ft. Its major and unique asset is bark that exfoliates and becomes mottled. When the tree is young, the several stems are a mixture of green with white and brown. As the trunks mature, they show a great deal of chalky white. Where winters are severe, try the Korean pine, P. koraiensis, *a similar, faster-growing tree.*

Bloom Period and Seasonal Color
Insignificant blooms; cones have scale-like surface, and are 2 to 3 in. long.

Mature Height × Spread
30 to 50 ft. × 20 to 35 ft.

Leyland Cypress
× *Cupressocyparis leylandii*

The Leyland cypress is a stately columnar hybrid of the cypress family, a group of narrow shrubs and trees with flat, scale-like leaves. It has graceful branches and bluish green, feathery foliage. The red-brown bark is a nice warm color, interestingly scaly, and it bears small roundish cones that are dark brown. In addition to its grace, what makes the Leyland cypress unusual is that it grows up to be a big tree 60 or 70 ft. tall very quickly— 3 ft. a year. That makes it an exceptionally good evergreen for screening. It tolerates heavy shearing, and makes a fine tall hedge. It also tolerates salt, and is used along the coast as a screen to protect the garden from salt spray.

Bloom Period and Seasonal Color
Insignificant blooms; roundish, dark brown cones.

Mature Height × Spread
60 to 70 ft. × 25 to 30 ft.

When, Where, and How to Plant
Plant a container-grown or balled-and-burlapped tree in fall before Indian summer, or in early spring. In shade, the branching is more open and informal; in full sun the foliage grows more dense. Leyland cypress adapts to a variety of soils, acid or alkaline, but grows most rapidly in moist, fertile soil containing enough humus to maintain moisture around the roots. If you are planting a hedge, make the bed at least 5 ft. wide. See Soil Preparation in the Introduction, and planting instructions in the Trees chapter. Provide a planting hole at least three times the width of the rootball and twice as deep. Set the tree so the crown will be about 1 or 2 in. above ground level. Shape the soil around the crown into a wide saucer. Water slowly and deeply. Apply mulch 3 in. deep starting 3 in. from the main stem.

Growing Tips
The first year, unless there's a soaking rain, in spring and fall slowly and gently pour two to three bucketsful of water around the roots every two weeks; in summer every week or ten days. Maintain the mulch throughout the summer.

Care
Using a slow-release, organic, acid fertilizer, fertilize in fall and again in late winter or early spring. Replenish the mulch. Maintain soil moisture during droughts. Periodically prune or shear a Leyland cypress during July. For a formal hedge, allow the tops to grow 6 to 12 in. beyond the intended height, then cut the leaders off to just above a lateral branch 6 in. below the intended height.

Companion Planting and Design
Provide Leyland cypress plenty of room as it is too vigorous for narrow spaces that restrict growth. In a new landscape, Leyland cypress is sometimes planted with a slow-growing evergreen that is more desirable for the long term, then, when the star specimen attains a desired height, the Leyland cypress is cut down to allow space for the other.

Our Personal Recommendations
A very graceful Leyland is 30- to 40-ft. 'Naylor's Blue', whose bright, gray-blue foliage is intensely colored in winter. The new growth of narrow 20-ft. 'Castlewellan Gold' is tipped yellow-gold, bronze in winter.

When, Where, and How to Plant

The best time to plant an umbrella pine is in early spring. Buy a *young*, container-grown or balled-and-burlapped plant and handle the rootball with great care. The site can be in partial shade or in full sun as long as there is protection from the hot late afternoon sun and from sweeping winds. The umbrella pine does not tolerate pollution or drought. The ideal site is well drained and has rich, moist, and somewhat acid soil. See Soil Preparation in the Introduction, and planting instructions in the Trees chapter. Provide a planting hole three times the width of the rootball and twice as deep. Set the tree so the crown will be about 1 or 2 in. above ground level. Shape the soil around the crown into a wide saucer. Water slowly and deeply. Apply mulch 3 in. deep starting 3 in. from the main stem.

Growing Tips

The first year, unless there's a soaking rain, in spring and fall slowly and gently pour two to three bucketsful of water around the roots every two weeks; in summer every week or ten days. Maintain the mulch throughout the summer.

Care

Using a slow-release organic fertilizer for acid loving plants, fertilize lightly in fall and again in early spring. Replenish the mulch. The umbrella pine should not be sheared and should not need pruning.

Companion Planting and Design

The umbrella pine is best used as an accent tree in a group of trees and shrubs, or as a specimen out in the open.

Our Personal Recommendation

Plant the species.

Consider an umbrella pine if you'd like something different in an evergreen. It's a rather small tree with a strongly textured look that to some seems primitive, as though it belonged to an earlier time. Considered unique and artistic in appearance, it has two types of needles: one type is small and scale-like, arranged at the tips of the twigs; and the other is 2- to 5-in. long, dark green needles bunched at the ends of the branches. When the tree begins to mature, the bark turns orange to red-brown and begins to peel in plates and strips. A young umbrella pine has a compact pyramidal shape and the branches are stiff, twiggy, and spread in whorls. As it matures, the branches droop and loosen. It grows very slowly.

Other Name

Japanese Umbrella Pine

Bloom Period and Seasonal Color

Insignificant blooms; green 2- to 4-in. cones turning to brown.

Mature Height × Spread

20 to 30 ft. × 15 to 20 ft.

White Fir

Abies concolor

The firs are long-lived, stately trees native to the Rockies. Pyramidal conifers like the spruces, they also are used as live Christmas trees, and the boughs sold to make Christmas decorations. In silhouette, the white fir looks like a blue spruce, but it's more refined. The silvery, blue-green needles are flatter than those of the spruces, soft, 2 to 3 in. long, and have two pale, bluish bands underneath. The cones are 3 to 5 in. long and greenish when new, shading to purple. Most other fir species are big forest trees that live at high altitudes and do poorly in hot, dry cities. The white, or silver, fir has some tolerance for long, hot summers like those in Washington, D.C., and it endures city conditions, heat, cold, and drought. But it may not do well in the Tidewater area.

Other Names
Colorado Fir, Silver Fir, Concolor Fir

Bloom Period and Seasonal Color
Insignifican blooms; cones are 3 to 5 in., green shading to purple.

Mature Height × Spread
30 to 50 ft. × 15 by 30 ft.

When, Where, and How to Plant
Plant a *young*, container-grown or balled-and-burlapped tree in early spring. The white fir prefers full sun, but tolerates all-day, bright filtered light. Firs do best in acid soil, pH 5.0 to 6.0. The white fir can live on almost bare rock, but it does poorly in heavy clay soil. Ideal soil is rich, moist, sandy loam. Prepare the soil well! See Soil Preparation in the Introduction, and planting instructions in the Trees chapter. Provide a planting hole three times the width of the rootball and twice as deep. Handle the rootball with great care. Set the tree so the crown will be about 1 or 2 in. above ground level. Shape the soil around the crown into a wide saucer. Water slowly and deeply. Apply mulch 3 in. deep starting 3 in. from the main stem.

Growing Tips
The first year, unless there's a soaking rain, in spring and fall slowly and gently pour two to three bucketsful of water around the roots every two weeks; in summer every week or ten days. Maintain the mulch throughout the summer.

Care
Using a slow-release organic fertilizer for acid-loving plants, fertilize lightly in fall and again in early spring. Replenish the mulch.

Companion Planting and Design
The dark green needles make a handsome backdrop for ornamental plants and in fall and winter they lend life to the sleeping garden. It is generally used as a specimen in lawns and parks.

Our Personal Recommendations
In addition to the white fir, we recommend the graceful Caucasian, or Nordmann fir, *A. nordmanniana*, whose tired branches sweep downward and then curve up. It's a big tree, 40 to 60 ft., whose needles are a lustrous black green. The ideal pH for the Caucasian fir is soil in the 5.8 to 7.0 range; it needs full sun, a very well-drained site, and does best in a somewhat sheltered situation.

Yew

Taxus × media

When, Where, and How to Plant

Plant a balled-and-burlapped or container-grown yew in fall before Indian summer, or in early spring while the shrub still is dormant. A yew will do well growing in full sun or bright shade, but the needles will brown in winter if the plant is exposed to strong, cold winds. Yews generally prefer somewhat alkaline soil; they are not good companion plants for azaleas, rhododendrons, or other acid-loving evergreens. The ideal site has excellent drainage—yews do not tolerate wet feet. See Soil Preparation in the Introduction, and planting instructions in the Trees chapter. Provide a planting hole three times the width of the rootball and twice as deep. Set the tree so the crown will be about 1 or 2 in. above ground level. Shape the soil around the crown into a wide saucer. Water slowly and deeply. Apply mulch 3 in. deep starting 3 in. from the main stem.

Growing Tips

The first year, unless there's a soaking rain, in spring and fall slowly and gently pour two to three bucketsful of water around the roots every two weeks; in summer every week or ten days. Maintain the mulch throughout summer.

Care

Using a slow-release organic fertilizer, fertilize lightly in fall and again in spring. Prune away yew dead wood any time of year, but do not cut beyond the area where green needles are growing. Yews accept shearing of the branch ends throughout the growing season. To keep a yew compact, follow an early spring pruning by the removal of the soft new summer growth. To create a natural looking hedge, remove the longest growth every other year.

Companion Planting and Design

Yews are enduring foundation plants.

Our Personal Recommendations

The tree form we favor is 'Capitata', a pyramidal 40- to 50-ft. cultivar of the very hardy light green Japanese yew, *T. cuspidata*. A single plant that can make a hedge almost by itself is 'Repandens', a cultivar of the big English yew, *T. baccata*, which grows 2 to 4 ft. tall and 10 to 15 ft. wide. It has beautiful dark or black-green foliage.

The yews are the most adaptable, durable, and useful of evergreens. Dark-needled shrubs and trees with reddish brown, scaly bark, they bear pea-sized fleshy red berries. Native to the Northern Hemisphere, the yews are disease resistant. They grow slowly and are tolerant of extensive pruning, so they're often used for clipped hedges, green screens, and walls, archways, topiary, and foundation plants, small and tall. Yews come in almost all sizes, shapes, and colors. Among the very best for hedges, screening, and foundation plantings are cultivars of the medium- to deep-green intermediate yews, including pyramidal 10- to 12-ft. by 10-ft. 'Hatfieldii'; columnar 'Hicksii'; low, spreading, 4- to 5- ft. 'Densiformis'; and rounded, 6-ft. 'Brownii'. The seeds and foliage contain toxic compounds.

Other Name

Intermediate Yew

Bloom Period and Seasonal Color

Insignificant blooms; fleshy, red berries in winter.

Mature Height × Spread

Cultivars vary in size; many are as wide as they are tall, or wider.

Ground Covers *for the Mid-Atlantic*

Ground covers create a unified field that harmonizes and pulls together the various elements of the landscape—shrub borders, flower beds, and specimen trees. Ground covers can be any height. Even daylilies can be a ground cover. Those we recommend here are low-growing, need almost no maintenance once estab- lished, can do what lawn grasses do where mowers can't go, and can replace lawns you are weary of mowing. The most attractive and enduring ground covers for Mid-Atlantic gardens are the plants on the pages that fol- low, but not every one of these is perfect for every site. They are designated as ground covers because, like weeds, most of them spread rapidly: so think twice about planting any of these where they might later invade stands of native plants or woodlands we are trying to preserve.

Periwinkle

The toughest low evergreen ground covers are ajuga, periwinkle, ivy, and creeping juniper. Ajuga and periwinkle bear sweet little flowers in early spring and can be walked on—with discretion. Ivy can take months to expand, but once started spreads irrepressibly. Creeping juniper withstands sun, heat, drought, and salt, and it's a good bank holder.

A beautiful ground cover for shade is silvery lamium, which produces masses of small hooded flowers in spring. Leadwort has handsome glossy foliage and in late summer bears long-lasting, gentian-blue flowers. For cooler regions, dappled light, and a formal look, pachysandra is the perfect choice. The ferns we recommend also do well in dappled light and are lovely in transitional areas edging woodlands.

Combining several compatible ground covers adds texture to an area and it's a safeguard should one of the plants run into difficulties. For a richly varied lawn substitute we like drifts of small winter- flowering bulbs, overplanted with aromatic Greek oregano and thyme, ajuga in the sunny places, periwinkle in part sun, and lamium under the trees.

Planting Ground Covers

We recommend starting ground covers with flats or pots of rooted cuttings. If you will be replacing turf, in early spring or fall when the soil is dry, spray the area with Roundup® according to the directions on the label, or remove the top layer. Top the area with 2 or 3 inches of compost or decomposed leaves and broadcast over it slow-release fertilizers, along with greensand (with its thirty-two micro-nutrients) and rock phosphate. Follow the rates recommended on the packages. Rototill all this 8 inches deep three times over a two-week period. If you are installing an invasive ground cover such as ivy or ajuga, bury a 6-inch metal barrier around the perimeter to keep it from overrunning neighboring plantings.

At planting time, cover the area with 3 inches of mulch and plant through it. Working in even rows and starting at the widest end, dig a row of evenly spaced planting pockets 8 to 14 inches apart. Set the plants into the pockets and firm them into place. On a slope, set the plants so their backs are a little lower than their fronts. Position the second row plants zig-zag style between those of the row above. Row three repeats row one, and row four repeats row two. Maintain the mulch until the ground cover shades out weeds. Plan on at least two years for the plants to grow enough to cover well.

If weeding won't be possible, plant your ground cover through a porous landscape fabric. Push the edges of the fabric sheet into the ground and weight them with rocks, or heel them in. Make rows of x-shaped slits in the fabric, and insert the plants through the slits with a trowel. Landscape fabric slows the rooting of the aboveground branches, so plant densely. In fall clear your ground cover of fallen leaves with a blow-vac. Certain ground covers when fully mature benefit from shearing every year or two in early spring before growth begins.

Japanese Pachysandra

Companion Planting and Design

We use ground covers in one-of-a-kind plantings to carpet, protect, and enhance untended slopes and the areas at the feet of tall trees where shade is too intense for grass to flourish. We also combine ground covers with trees, shrubs, ornamental grasses tall and small, flowers, and bulbs to natualize rocky fields and transitional areas between gardens and woodlands, bodies of water, the road, or the next property. No-maintenance shrubs that work well in this type of planting include several roses, such as the rugosa rose, and the Virginia rose. *Rosa virginiana* and the ground-hugging memorial rose, *R. wichuraiana*, are good choices for erosion control of slopes. You can combine low-growing ground covers with *Forsythia* × *intermedia* 'Arnold Dwarf' in full sun almost anywhere. Summer-flowering shrubs and trees that go well with ground covers are crape myrtle, butterfly bush, and blue spirea, which all bloom on new wood so they can be cut back every spring. Some of the flowers we like to include in these naturalized areas are columbine, butterfly weed, coreopsis, purple coneflower, rudbeckia, and goldenrod.

The plants on the following pages are the best of the best, but we have other favorites:

Variegated Liriope

Golden Moneywort

Other Ground Covers Worthy of Consideration

Barren Strawberry, *Waldsteinia fragarioides*

Bloody Cranesbill, *Geranium sanguineum*

European Ginger, *Asarum europaeum*

Golden Star, *Chrysogonum virginianum*

Mountain Pink, *Phlox subulata*

Soapwort, *Saponaria officinalis* 'Rosea Plena'

Sedum, *Sedum spurium* 'John Creech' and
other cultivars

Snow-in-Summer, *Cerastium tomentosum*

Sweet Woodruff, *Galium odoratum*

Wintergreen, Checkerberry,
Gaultheria procumbens

Other Ferns Worthy of Consideration

Beech Fern, *Thelypteris hexagonoptera*

Cinnamon Fern, *Osmunda cinnamomea*

Deer Fern, *Blechnum spicant*

Japanese Shield Fern, *Dryopteris erythrosora*

Maidenhair Fern, *Adiantum pedatum*

Marsh Fern, *Thelypteris palustris* forma *pufferae*

Massachusetts Fern, *T. simulata*

New York Fern, *T. noveboracensis*

Ostrich Fern, *Matteuccia struthiopteris*

Rock Polypody, American Wall Fern,
Polypodium virginianum

Royal Fern, *Osmunda regalis*

Barrenwort
Epimedium spp. and hybrids

The barrenworts are spring-flowering plants that, given time, carpet the earth under trees, shrubs, and in woodlands with clumps of beautiful, long, heart-shaped semi- or evergreen (Zones 7 and 8) leaves. The foliage colors reddish or gold in cold weather, bringing new vitality to the fading fall scene. In spring exotic little flowers rather like columbines, some long-spurred, are borne in clusters on slim, gracefully arching stems. Among many wonderful barrenworts for our area are red alpine epimedium, E. × rubrum, whose graceful sprays of flowers are red with yellow or white; bi-color barrenwort, E. × versicolor 'Sulphureum', which bears delicate yellow flowers with long rosy spurs; and E. pinnatum (syn. E. colchicum), which has handsome brownish foliage and bears up to twenty-four short-spurred yellow flowers.

Other Name
Bishop's Hat

Bloom Period and Seasonal Color
Spring foliage and flowers; fall foliage. Flowers are yellow, pink, orange, rose, lavender, white, or bi-colors.

Mature Height × Spread
6 to 10 in. × 12 to 18 in.

When, Where, and How to Plant
You can set out container-grown epimediums at any time during the growing season. The plants do best in bright shade. But in the cooler regions of the Mid-Atlantic, especially in Zone 6, epimediums can tolerate full sun. Once established, they grow well in dry shade. They thrive in well-drained, rich soil with an acid pH of 4.5 to 5.5. It's an ideal ground cover for land that was forest and for wooded areas. Follow the planting instructions at the beginning of this chapter, and provide planting holes 8 to 12 in. deep. Space the plants, which are slow to establish, about 12 in. apart. Spread a permanent 1-in. mulch of pine needles, or rotted leaf mold.

Growing Tips
Keep the plants well watered the first two months, and weekly thereafter unless you have a good soaking rain. Established epimediums can handle some drought, but they need sustained moisture to get off to a good start.

Care
In late winter fertilize and replenish the mulch in new beds; once established, epimidiums make a dense mat so they will need no mulch in subsequent years. In early spring just before new foliage emerges, shear old foliage. You can multiply your holdings by dividing mature clumps of epimediums in very early spring or toward the end of summer.

Companion Planting and Design
The barrenworts make beautiful ground covers for the earth under trees, shrubs, and in woodlands. We love seeing them bordering a woodland path planted with fall flowering anemones, ferns, and hostas. They're handsome growing with hellebores in the shade of a tall shrub border.

Our Personal Recommendations
We especially like *E. × versicolor* because it is beautiful and grows vigorously. We use *E. grandiflorum* 'Rose Queen', a long-spurred epimedium, for planting nooks and crannies of stone walls.

Bearberry
Arctostaphylos uva-ursi

When, Where, and How to Plant
Set out container-grown plants in very early spring. If local people do not carry bearberry, you will find it in catalogs like Ray and Peg Prag's Forest Farm Nursery, in Williams, Oregon. Do not dig bearberry in the wild—it is protected in many states, and it will die anyway. An ideal ground cover for land that was forest and for wooded areas, it does best where it receives some direct sun and some shade. Though it succeeds in neutral and even in limestone soils, it prefers well-drained, infertile soil with an acid pH 4.5 to 5.5. Bearberry is difficult to transplant and the plants are fairly costly, so put the effort necessary into soil preparation. Follow the soil preparation and planting instructions at the beginning of this chapter, but omit the fertilizer. Dig generous planting holes, spacing the plants 12 to 24 in. apart. Water well. Apply a permanent mulch of pine needles, or rotted leaf mold.

Growing Tip
Water a new planting every week or two the first season.

Care
Replenish the mulch in late winter until the plants have spread widely enough to shade out weeds. Do not fertilize. Pruning is rarely needed. Once the plants are established, local rainfall should be enough to keep bearberry healthy and growing, except during our mid- and late-August droughts.

Companion Planting and Design
Bearberry is used as a soil stabilizer on sandy banks beside highways and at the shore as it survives without much water in poor, sandy or gravelly soil, and hot sun. It is especially attractive as ground cover for hillside terraces, and we love to see it rambling over stony slopes.

Our Personal Recommendations
At 18 in. *A. uva-ursi* 'Radiant' is taller than most and has beautiful red berries in fall. It is an excellent shore plant. Little 'Wood's Compact' is just 4 in. high. 'Bear' is large and tinged with red in winter. 'Wood's Red' is a dwarf with unusually large red fruits. 'Massachusetts' is very tolerant of wet conditions. 'Emerald Carpet' has pink flowers and tolerates shade.

Bearberry is one of the most beautiful of all low-growing trailing ground covers. A broad-leaved evergreen, it is not used nearly as often as it should be because it is hard to transplant and slow to spread. But it is rugged, and in time can spread to 15 ft. The leaves are shiny and dark green in summer, bronze-red in cold weather. In spring, clusters of tiny pink or white flowers bloom, followed by lasting red berries that birds love. Bearberry does well as far south as Richmond, and in our cool upland regions. We recommend it for full sun in Northern Virginia and for light shade farther south. It tolerates sandy soil, and makes an excellent ground cover for seashore gardens.

Other Name
Kinnikinick

Bloom Period and Seasonal Color
Tiny pink or white flowers in spring.

Mature Height × Spread
$^1/_2$ to 1 ft. × 2 to 4 ft.

Bugleweed
Ajuga reptans

Ajuga covers the earth with flat rosettes of colorful leaves 3 to 4 in. long, an excellent ground cover for small, partially shaded areas, and poor soil. It's a tough plant that can be walked on, in moderation. Fast-growing A. reptans is our choice for quick cover. Some forms are green-leaved; others are splashed with cream or pink or have a metallic sheen. In mid- to late spring ajuga is misted with blue florets on short, squarish flower spikes. Ajuga is evergreen here and the leaves take on an attractive bronze-plum tint when the weather turns cold. In severe winters the leaves flatten and some turn brown. Cold that persists without snow cover damages the leaf tips but in spring the plants soon fill out.

Other Names
Carpet Bugleweed, Ajuga

Bloom Period and Seasonal Color
Foliage may be green, or multicolored, rose, and burgundy; in early spring flowers are white, reddish blue, deep blue, pink, and rose.

Mature Height × Spread
4 to 8 in. × 12 to 14 in.

When, Where, and How to Plant
Plant clumps of rooted plantlets in early spring or early fall. Where summers are muggy, ajuga does best in high, bright shade; in dense shade the leaves will be smaller and it will spread toward the sunlight. In cool upland areas, ajuga can handle full sun. The colored varieties are showiest growing in some direct sun. Rooted plants are fairly expensive, but you can minimize the cost by choosing the rapidly spreading species *A. reptans* and setting the plants 6 to 12 in. apart. You can also divide the clumps into individual plantlets and make more. Ajuga does best in well-drained ordinary garden soil whose pH range is between 6.0 and 7.0. Follow the soil preparation and planting instructions at the beginning of this chapter, but omit the fertilizer. Prepare a planting bed 6 to 8 in. deep. Space slower-spreading ajuga species 3 in. apart and be prepared to divide the plants—or prune them back—the following summer. Mulch the area.

Growing Tip
Water a new bed every week to ten days the first season, unless rain is plentiful.

Care
Too well fed, ajuga will "melt out" with diseases. In early spring, scratch a little slow-release fertilizer in beside young plants. In the following years, when you fertilize your lawn, water in a long-lasting organic fertilizer. Ajuga growing in full sunlight in Zones 7 and 8 may need watering during droughts. Clear autumn leaves to avoid crown rot; if a fungal problem develops, ask your garden center to recommend a fungicide. Rooted plantlets of *A. reptans* can be cut from the parent and replanted during the growing season; divide other species in early spring.

Companion Planting and Design
We use ajuga to cover a small area with a low dense mat. Its growth is expansive, so avoid growing it close to flower beds and other areas easily invaded.

Our Personal Recommendations
For something different, plant *A. reptans* 'Alba', whose flowers are off-white. Or 'Burgundy Glow', whose leaves are cream, pink, rose, and green. 'Rosea' has green leaves and showy rose-pink flower spikes. Where crown rot is a problem, choose *A. genevensis*.

Christmas Fern
Polystichum acrostichoides

When, Where, and How to Plant
Set out container-grown plants of Christmas fern after the last frost. They do best in partial shade. Some direct morning sun is acceptable if the soil has been well prepared. Like most ferns, the Christmas fern thrives in moist, humusy soil in the pH range 5.0 to 6.0. Follow the planting and soil preparation instructions at the beginning of this chapter, and enhance the soil mix by mixing in 50 to 75 percent of humusy forest soil or decayed shredded leaves, and a natural or slow-release organic fertilizer for acid-loving plants. Since the fern lives long and multiplies all around, dig wide planting holes 18 to 20 in. apart. Set the rootball just a little higher than the level at which it was growing before. Mulch all around with pine needles, shredded leaves, or leaf compost.

Growing Tips
Maintain soil moisture for the first season. A little overhead watering in high heat and drought is helpful. Fern glades are often misted.

Care
In following seasons, in late winter scatter a light application of organic fertilizer for acid-loving plants under the foliage. Allow the duff (layer of decaying vegetation covering the soil) to remain undisturbed. Avoid cultivating next to the crown; pull weeds by hand.

Companion Planting and Design
This evergreen fern is a beautiful ground cover and it is especially lovely in a ferny glade planted with hostas and astilbes. Christmas fern fills its space throughout the year so it makes a charming background for garden plants such as wildflowers, begonias, columbines, lilies-of-the-valley, primroses, Solomon's seals, trilliums, and lady's-slippers. Shallow-rooted, Christmas fern competes successfully with tree roots and in rock gardens for moisture and space.

Our Personal Recommendations
Evergreen and long-lived, Christmas fern is André's favorite. But in alkaline soils, you will do better with the shield, or holly, fern, *P. braunii*. It is semi-evergreen with graceful, arching fronds to 36 in. tall, and has twice divided leaves covered with hair-like scales at the edges. It needs cool, deep shade and tolerates somewhat alkaline soil.

Ferns have a cool graceful presence that no other type of plant quite duplicates. The lush greens evoke woodlands and romantic glades and no cottage garden is complete without them. The Christmas fern is a forever plant, a lifetime fern with beautiful lance-shaped leathery fronds up to 24 in. long by 5 in. wide, growing in arching, circular clusters from the crown. And it is evergreen here! A woodland native, it offers practical solutions to the challenges presented by the north side of a house, the north slope of a wooded stretch, and sun-dappled stream edges with poor drainage. It can tolerate more sun than many ferns if given adequate moisture. Please insist on purchasing only plants propagated by nurseries, not gathered from the wild.

Other Names
Dagger Fern, Canker Brake

Bloom Period and Seasonal Color
Evergreen crown of dark green foliage.

Mature Height × Spread
1 to 1 1/2 ft. × 1 to 1 1/2 ft.

Creeping Juniper
Juniperus horizontalis

This is a creeping form of the familiar evergreen tree or shrub. It grows just 6 to 12 in. high, and the branches spread horizontally about a foot a year to 5 ft. and more. Tough, drought-resistant, creeping juniper performs beautifully in sun-baked situations, saves hot dry slopes from erosion, makes a great small lawn, and is a favorite for bordering paths and driveways. Along with the somewhat taller shore juniper, J. conferta, it thrives in sandy soils. The junipers are either male or female plants: the females bear pea-sized gray-blue or green berry-like cones. Some varieties are dark green; others are shaded soft gray-green or blue-green, and there are gold- and silver-tipped forms. In cold weather, many varieties color plum to purple.

Other Name
Ground Cover Juniper

Bloom Period and Seasonal Color
The foliage turns plum in winter, or deeper green or deeper blue, depending on the variety.

Mature Height × Spread
6 to 12 in. × 5 to 8 ft.

When, Where, and How to Plant
Container-grown junipers can be planted at any season. If the plants are root-bound, make shallow vertical cuts through the binding roots, and slice 1 in. off the bottom. Junipers need six hours or more of direct sun; in shade they get thin and ratty. The creeping junipers do best in soil with a pH of 5.0 to 6.0, but can handle slightly alkaline soils. The shore juniper, *J. conferta*, can be planted in areas reached by salt spray. Juniper colors most intensely in infertile sandy loam that is somewhat moist. Follow the soil preparation and planting instructions at the beginning of this chapter but omit the fertilizer. Set the plants about 3 ft. apart in generous planting holes and spread out the roots. Water thoroughly. Spread a 3-in. mulch of pine needles, bark chips, or rotted leaf mold.

Growing Tip
Water a new planting every week or two the first season.

Care
Local rainfall should be enough for established plants. They grow without extra watering among the rocks at Bar Harbor, Maine. Do not fertilize unless the soil is extremely poor. Replenish the mulch in late winter. If the branches are rusty, chances are spider mites are at work: spray with a miticide. Where branches are beginning to overlap, prune in midsummer. Where branches touch the soil they will eventually root; in early spring you can sever rooted branches and replant them.

Companion Planting and Design
We plant creeping juniper as a bank holder, and as a ground cover for neglected areas among rocks and edging masonry walls. These low-growing junipers can be interplanted with early daffodils and other medium-height spring flowering bulbs.

Our Personal Recommendations
Among the finest junipers are: 6-in.-high, silver-blue 'Blue Rug' creeping juniper; gray-green, 12-in.-high 'Bar Harbour'; 12- to 28-in.-high shore juniper, *J. conferta*, which thrives by the sea; little 6-in.-high, dense blue-green, mosslike *J. procumbens* 'Nana', dwarf Japanese garden juniper. For a taller ground cover we use Chinese juniper, including 18-in., blue-green *J. chinensis* var. *sargentii*, and 4- to 6-in-high, dark green 'Green Carpet'.

82

Dead Nettle

Lamium maculatum

When, Where, and How to Plant

Plant root divisions in early spring in partial shade. *Lamium* can take full shade and tolerates more sun in the cool upland areas. Nettles do well in almost any soil, but spread rapidly in light, well-drained loam. Follow the soil preparation and planting instructions at the beginning of this chapter. Prepare planting holes 6 to 8 in. deep and set the plants 12 to 18 in. apart. Water well. Mulch between the plants to keep weeds at bay until the plants completely shade the ground.

Growing Tips

For the first month or two, water weekly or bi-weekly, unless there is a good supply of rain. If the plants become straggly toward midsummer, cut them back to 6 to 8 in. to keep the growth full and within bounds.

Care

Water lamium when you water the flowers. If it dries repeatedly, it will die back to scattered plantlets that take months to re-establish vigorous growth. In spring, remove winter-damaged stems and scatter a little slow-release fertilizer and compost through the bed. Replenish the mulch if weeds begin to take hold. In late fall, remove dead stems and clear away fallen leaves. To multiply your holdings, dig rooted plantlets *that have not reverted to an unwanted color* and replant at once. Terminal cuttings taken from parent plants during the growing season will root easily in water and can be planted once the heat of summer has gone by.

Companion Planting and Design

Dead nettle lightens the shade under trees, is quite lovely edging shaded flower beds, and as a filler in a bed in a formal parterre.

Our Personal Recommendations

André recommends 'Album', which bears white flowers and has a silver stripe down the middle of the leaves. The most beautiful for foliage is 'Beacon Silver', whose silver leaves are edged with a narrow band of green; the leaves of 'White Nancy' are a lovely pale jade, and the blossoms are white.

Beautiful but tender-leaved, nettle (André hates the term "dead" nettle) produces a year-round froth of silvered leaves in the shade where even hostas and impatiens do poorly. A low, fast-growing creeper of the mint family, its dark-green, oval leaves are splashed or striped silver or white along the midrib. Between late spring and midsummer, it sends up small hooded flowers. In summer, it throws 1- to 2-ft. horizontal stems toward sunnier reaches of the garden. The stems root at the nodes and the plantlets can revert to other foliage and flower colors. Nettle is evergreen most years in Washington, D.C., but in sizzling heat and in very cold winters without snow cover, the new stems may die back; the rooted parent plants remain and re-grow in the spring.

Other Names

Spotted Dead Nettle, Lamium

Bloom Period and Seasonal Color

The foliage is green and silver; flowers appear in late spring and are pink, lavender-pink, or white.

Mature Height × Spread

8 to 12 in. × 12 to 16 in.

English Ivy
Hedera helix

Tough, reliable English ivy fills the bill where a vigorous ground cover is needed. It stands hot sun, heat, drought, or lack thereof, and cold or too much rain. Any vigorous non-native can become a pest, ivy especially, so don't plant it where it can escape your control, and especially never near woodlands. It succeeds in shade under trees, though the vines will run toward better light, and it competes well with tree roots. Thickly planted, it makes a dense "lawn" 6 to 8 in. high. English ivy is a running or climbing woody vine that has an adult form that is shrub-like and not viny. Allowed to run, it develops a shrubby form and, if supported, climbs, irrepressibly. Ivy cultivars make beautiful container plants.

Bloom Period and Seasonal Color
The flowers are insignificant. Evergreen foliage; some forms are variegated.

Mature Height × Spread
8 to 10 in. × 25 to 50 and even 90 ft.

When, Where, and How to Plant
Plant flats of rooted cuttings in early spring or early fall in part shade or sun. It grows most vigorously in fall and thrives in acid and non-acid soils with a pH range of 6.0 to 7.5. To encourage rapid growth, follow the soil preparation and planting instructions at the beginning of this chapter and provide a planting bed with soil that is rich, fairly humusy, and well drained. In sandy soil, mix in 40 percent humus. Set the plantlets 6 in. apart. Prune straggly stems back to 6 in., then soak the ground with water containing a liquid fertilizer such as seaweed or fish emulsion. Provide a permanent mulch of pine needles, rotted leaf mold, or bark. The vines can take two or three seasons to cover the area.

Growing Tips
The first season water the plants deeply every week in hot and dry weather. The second year keep the soil moderately damp until the plants are well established and the vines are running (growing).

Care
Do not fertilize established beds unless the foliage yellows. Water during droughts. Keep ivy trimmed, tidy, and well groomed, and shear it back every three or four years to maintain the density of the foliage. To encourage ivy to root, peg a stem to the soil; when it shows new growth in the spring, dig it, sever it from the parent, and transplant.

Companion Planting and Design
Ivy is beautiful dripping from hanging baskets, urns, and in tall flower arrangements. It's also a great edger between strips of pavement. But ivy-clad walls are bad news, especially for clapboard siding, and the vines can get under shutters and gutters. Stop ivy from climbing walls and tree trunks by pruning it yearly.

Our Personal Recommendations
'Baltica' and '238th Street' withstand our winters and do not scald in winter sun. 'Thorndale' is another very hardy ivy. 'White Helix' is a handsome variegated form to feature in a container; there's a superb collection at the Lewis Ginter Botanical Garden in Richmond, Virginia. Beautiful Algerian ivy, *H. canariensis*, which has large leaves and burgundy red twigs, succeeds in the warmer areas.

Foamflower
Tiarella cordifolia

When, Where, and How to Plant
Plant root divisions or runners of foamflower in early spring in partial or full shade. Good-sized plants of the new varieties are now being offered by growers, with many more anticipated in the years ahead. Foamflower thrives in soil with pH between 5.0 and 6.0 and is an excellent low ground cover for damp, shady places where the soil is rich in humus. Follow the soil preparation and planting instructions at the beginning of this chapter, and mix in 50 to 75 percent of humusy forest soil or decayed shredded leaves; fertilize with a slow-release organic fertilizer for acid-loving plants. Provide planting holes 6 to 8 in. deep, and 8 to 12 in. apart. Water well after planting and mulch 2 in. deep between the plants with shredded leaves, leaf compost, or peat moss.

Growing Tips
Maintain soil moisture for the first season. Mature plants tolerate brief periods of drought.

Care
In late winter scatter a light application of acid fertilizer under the foliage. Pull weeds by hand, selectively. *T. cordifolia* sends out runners that creep over or just under the soil surface, between fallen logs, and over or between rocks. You can control its growth by chopping off the runners; and you can multiply your holdings by clipping off rooted plantlets and transplanting those with good root systems.

Companion Planting and Design
With ferns, *Tiarella* makes a lovely living mulch for clematis. We use it as underplanting for drifts of bleeding heart along woodland paths and in sun-dappled glades. In shaded corners, it's pretty with hellebore, creeping phlox, and ferns. The new hybrids make attractive container plants.

Our Personal Recommendations
'Pink Brushes' is a new, very cold hardy *Tiarella* cultivar whose pink blooms gradually change to white. 'Pink Pearls' blooms over a long period. The foliage of both these cultivars acquires bronze-red tones in the fall. The leaves of 'Rambling Tapestry' are marked attractively with maroon veins; the leaves of 'Eco Running Tapestry' have wine-red centers. *T. wherryi*, is a clump-forming foamflower—no runners—grown for the flowers.

The foamflower is a charming wildflower native to the rich, moist woodlands of the Eastern U.S. and Canada. Evergreen in the warmer areas of the Mid-Atlantic, it forms small clumps of overlapping crinkled leaves that spread by runners. In mid-spring the foliage is covered with a foam of fluffy little white flowers on tall stems. The blooms fade in a couple of weeks revealing fresh new foliage. Foamflower is easy to grow and spreads so energetically that it makes an excellent woodland ground cover. Breeding by our friend Sinclair Adams has extended the beauty of the foliage color and markings so that now many interesting new hybrids are coming onto the market, some with flowers that are white, cream, pink, or deep rose.

Other Name
Allegheny Foamflower

Bloom Period and Seasonal Color
May; the species flowers are white; some cultivars and hybrids are pink.

Mature Height × Spread
6 in. (with 10-in. flower spikes) × 24 in.

Golden Moneywort
Lysimachia nummularia 'Aurea'

Great in shaded areas with moist soil, Lysimachia is a rapidly spreading perennial with round, dark green leaves that are evergreen in all but the coldest areas of the Mid-Atlantic. It bears masses of small, bright-yellow, cup-shaped flowers and is an excellent ground cover for stream borders, wet banks, and the edges of damp woodlands. A European plant that has naturalized here, it rambles along the ground, rooting as it goes and forming a ruffled carpet. This golden-leaved variety produces rounded, penny-shaped, 1-in. leaves that start out yellowish in spring then turn lime-green in summer. In the shade the foliage fairly glows. The flowers are yellow and faintly fragrant. It can grow in water up to 2 in. deep.

Other Name
Golden Creeping Jenny

Bloom Period and Seasonal Color
Early summer; blooms in yellow.

Mature Height × Spread
1 to 2 in. × indefinite spread

When, Where, and How to Plant
Set out container-grown plants any time after the last spring frost and before the first frost in autumn. In Zone 8, *Lysimachia* does best in bright shade and it can multiply even in deep shade. In Zone 6, it can stand sun. *Lysimachia* prefers somewhat neutral soil. If the planting bed is in or near woodlands, and somewhat acidic, apply lime to raise the pH to between 6.5 and 7.0. Follow the soil preparation and planting instructions at the beginning of this chapter. If the bed is not naturally moist, increase the humus content by digging in a 2-in. layer of peat moss or chopped leaves, along with a 1-in. layer of compost, or an application of a slow-release organic fertilizer. Set the plants 12 to 18 in. apart. Water thoroughly. Provide a permanent mulch of well-rotted leaf mold to keep weeds at bay until the plants cover the ground completely.

Growing Tips
Water a new planting every week to ten days unless the ground is naturally moist. Golden creeping Jenny spreads aggressively in moist conditions and can become invasive, so keep an eye on its development. You can multiply your holdings in early spring or in early fall by digging up and replanting rooted sections of the stems or small divisions of the crown.

Care
Fertilize a new planting early in the spring after you set out the plants by scratching a slow-release fertilizer into the soil beside young plants. Prune the plants back in late winter if they are becoming matted. Once established, these plants do well on their own without fertilization or spraying. Neither pests nor diseases seem to come their way—but they will suffer if the soil surface is dry for days at a time. Maintain mulch until the plants spread enough to shade out weeds.

Companion Planting and Design
'Aurea' is an excellent ground cover for wet, difficult places. It's lovely in rock gardens, between paving stones, and as an edger in patio containers. It's attractive planted with golden-leaved coleus.

Our Personal Recommendations
For golden cover, we plant 'Aurea'. For green cover, we plant the species.

Japanese Painted Fern
Athyrium nipponicum 'Pictum'

When, Where, and How to Plant

Root divisions of Japanese painted fern are available from nurseries and through garden catalogs. Set them out after the last frost in partial to deep shade. Some direct morning sun is acceptable if the soil has been well prepared. This fern thrives in moist, humusy soil in the pH range 5.0 to 6.5. It lives long and multiplies all around, so dig wide planting holes 25 to 30 in. apart. Follow the soil preparation and planting instructions at the beginning of this chapter and improve the soil by mixing in 50 to 75 percent of humusy forest soil or decayed shredded leaves fertilized with a slow-release organic fertilizer for acid-loving plants. Set the rootball a little higher than it was growing before and mulch with shredded leaves, leaf compost, or peat moss.

Growing Tips

Maintain soil moisture for the first season. A little overhead watering in high heat and drought is helpful.

Care

In following seasons, in late winter scatter a light application of acid fertilizer under the foliage. Allow the duff (a layer of decaying vegetation that covers the soil) to remain undisturbed; pull weeds by hand. Protect from frosts; in spring it is as sensitive to frost as impatiens. Japanese painted fern can be divided in early spring or fall by digging and separating the crown into smaller divisions.

Companion Planting and Design

We love Japanese painted fern paired with white impatiens and with wild ginger and creeping thyme. We have edged a water garden set in a rocky outcropping with Japanese painted fern, astilbes, white bleeding heart, and Japanese irises and they are pretty together.

Our Personal Recommendations

The silvery Japanese painted fern is our first choice, and we also recommend 'Pictum Red', which has a reddish tinge in the fronds. We love Japanese painted fern's green cousin, the lady fern, *A. filix-femina*, which forms thick clumps of graceful, lacy fronds 24 in. long that appear throughout the growing season. It spreads at a moderate rate in moist conditions but is tolerant of fairly dry soils.

Japanese painted fern is a strikingly beautiful specimen plant for the wild garden. An exotic looking variegated fern, it has gray-silver, lance-shaped fronds with wine red stems and a graceful weeping habit. It grows vigorously and easily in partial shade almost anywhere. Unlike the Christmas fern, which is evergreen here, the Japanese painted fern dies down in winter but it stands up to a lot of cold, greening wooded lots long after the trees have dropped their leaves. In a suitable habitat—partially shaded, moist soil—it grows more lush every year, doubling and tripling its size and competing successfully with tree roots. In the 1940s, Alex Summers, founder of the American Hosta Society, introduced the plant to André's father, nurseryman Martin Viette, who introduced it to the trade.

Other Name
Painted Fern

Bloom Period and Seasonal Color
Blended silver-green and maroon fronds.

Mature Height × Spread
14 to 24 in. × 18 to 30 in.

Japanese Spurge
Pachysandra terminalis

Pachysandra is a beautiful, rather formal, low-growing evergreen ground cover that does best in light shade and in the cooler areas of the Mid-Atlantic. It makes a handsome "lawn" though it cannot be walked on, and succeeds under tall shrubs and even under maples, beeches, and sycamores where roots are shallow and competitive. The plant consists of upright rosettes of rich-green, scalloped, or saw-toothed leaves on fleshy stems 8 to 10 in. tall. In early spring, there is a flush of light-green new growth and small green-white flower spikes appear. The flowers can reappear in fall when Indian summer warmth follows a cold snap. We can't do without pachysandra, but it can have problems in our region, especially when growing in the sun.

Other Names
Japanese Pachysandra, Pachysandra

Bloom Period and Seasonal Color
Spring; flowers are insignificant.

Mature Height × Spread
8 to 10 in. × indefinite spread

When, Where, and How to Plant
Plant rooted cuttings in the early spring and fall in the bright shade of tall trees or in day-long dappled light. In direct sun, especially where summers are hot and muggy, pachysandra has problems. Humusy, well-drained acid soil, pH 4.5 to 6.0, is best. Follow the soil preparation and planting instructions at the beginning of this chapter and mix in a 2-in. layer of peat moss or chopped leaves along with a 1-in. layer of acidic compost. Provide planting holes 6 in. deep and set the cuttings 4 to 6 in. apart. Water thoroughly. Spread a 3-in. mulch of shredded pine bark, pine needles, or rotted oak leaves.

Growing Tips
For the first season, water your planting well every week, especially where pachysandra is competing with the roots of trees and shrubs.

Care
Remove autumn leaves. In late fall or winter, apply a slow-release organic fertilizer for acid-loving plants. Maintain the mulch. Especially growing in sun, pachysandra is susceptible to volutella stem blight, and to scale and mites. For the stem blight, use a copper fungicide, and use ultrafine or horticultural oil to control scale and mites. Keep the bed airy and cool by thinning and cutting. If leaves wilt where soil is reasonably moist, treat the area with a fungicide. Cuttings of new growth taken in summer will root in damp sand tented with plastic; mist often for six weeks. Clumps of pachysandra dug with lots of soil attached transplant well in early spring; keep the transplants well watered.

Companion Planting and Design
Pachysandra is perfect as a ground cover for formal plantings anywhere, beautiful under rhododendrons, azaleas, tall trees, and in open woodlands.

Our Personal Recommendations
The most attractive variety is deep-green 'Green Carpet', which has wide, compact, rather smooth leaves. Glossy 'Green Sheen' has a more formal look. 'Variegata' and 'Silver Edge' are beautiful but tolerate less direct sun and are less vigorous. Our native Allegheny pachysandra, *P. procumbens*, is not as good an evergreen ground cover but it withstands heat and sun and has showier flowers.

Leadwort
Ceratostigma plumbaginoides

When, Where, and How to Plant
In early spring, plant rooted divisions or container plants in sun, or moderate shade. Plumbago needs a well-drained site. It does best in rich, acidic loam but tolerates other soils. Follow the soil preparation and planting instructions at the beginning of this chapter, but omit the fertilizer. Make the planting holes 6 to 8 in. deep. Set the divisions 9 to 15 in. apart: plumbago spreads rapidly. Water well. Mulch with salt hay, straw, or compost to keep weeds at bay until the plants shade the ground so completely that weeds cannot get started. That will take two or three seasons. Once established, it gives the garden a weed-free ground cover.

Growing Tips
The first three or four weeks after planting, maintain soil moisture. Overhead watering is suitable.

Care
Half an inch or so of compost applied in late fall or winter every two or three years keeps plumbago a good green. Cut plumbago back after frost wilts the leaves to keep the bed tidy and healthy, and to promote the new growth on which flowers will appear the next season. Plumbago blooms on new growth. If you do not cut it back, you will get lots of foliage but you will miss out on its really beautiful flowers. We shear the tops of plumbago growing in an all-plumbago bed in winter and then mow with a sharp rotary mower. Plumbago spreads by underground stems, rooting as it rambles. It gets matted in time, and every three or four years benefits from dividing. To multiply your holdings, in early spring cut all around rooted clumps to free them from the parent plants, then dig them and replant.

Companion Planting and Design
We like plumbago combined with other flowering ground covers, such as myrtle and lamium. It's lovely with flowering perennials. Confine it to 3-gallon pots to keep it from spreading so much that it overwhelms its neighbors.

Our Personal Recommendation
If you live in Zone 8, try *Ceratostigma willmottianum*, Chinese plumbago, a shrubby form usually 2 to 3 in. or 5 in. tall; the flowers are violet-blue, and quite beautiful.

This is a beautiful ground cover for small sunny or partly shaded areas and it bears one of the bluest of all blue flowers in late summer and fall. The plants form sprawling 6- to 8- to 12-in.-high mats of glossy leaves. The peacock-blue flowers tip new growth from midsummer to frosts, perfectly set off by rusty-red calyxes and bracts. With frost plumbago dies, leaving behind a tangle of not very attractive brown stems. Plumbago takes a year or two to get under way, but once established, it throws new growth in every direction, overwhelming lower-growing ground covers such as pachysandra and periwinkle. It handles more than the usual Mid-Atlantic cold and tolerates our high heat. Butterflies, large and small, love it.

Other Names
Plumbago, *Plumbago larpentae*

Bloom Period and Seasonal Color
Late summer and early fall; bright blue blooms.

Mature Height × Spread
8 to 12 in. × 12 to 18 in.

Lenten Rose
Helleborus orientalis

Imagine a flower blooming in the cold of February and March! That's the Lenten rose, the best of the hellebores, and one of the toughest and hardiest ground covers we have. Growing in lightly shaded areas, under rhododendrons and other tall shrubs for example, the plants develop dense stands of shining, leathery, deeply-divided foliage as beautiful in winter as it is in summer. Unique nodding flowers appear in late winter. In clear colors, or speckled, mottled, or streaked with color, these are the finest, most long lasting of any winter flower. Rather like small nodding roses, they are composed of five petal-like sepals and persist for two to three months. Undisturbed, beautiful colonies form and self-sow.

Other Name
Hellebore

Bloom Period and Seasonal Color
Late winter through mid-spring; hybrids range from green-white through rose to maroon, pink, and black maroon.

Mature Height × Spread
1 to 1^1/$_2$ ft. × 1^1/$_2$ to 3 ft.

When, Where, and How to Plant
Set out large container-grown plants in early spring or early fall. In Washington, D.C., and other warm areas the hellebores do best in light shade; in Zone 6 they tolerate morning sun. The hellebores thrive in well-drained, humusy, nearly neutral woodland soil. Follow the soil preparation and planting instructions at the beginning of this chapter and, unless you are planting in woodland soil, mix in 50 to 75 percent of humusy forest soil or decayed shredded leaves mixed with slow-release, organic, acid fertilizer. Make the planting holes twice as wide and as deep as the container. Set the rootball a little higher than the level at which it was growing in the pot. Water well. Mulch with shredded leaves or leaf compost.

Growing Tip
During the first six weeks after planting, water often enough to keep the soil damp to the touch.

Care
Fertilize in early winter and remove old foliage. Established clumps are relatively drought tolerant. Lenten rose self-sows: eventually you'll find seedlings growing. Lift them with as much soil as possible, and transplant to a similar environment. Baby the seedlings with sustained moisture and yearly feeding of an organic acid fertilizer till they are growing lustily. August to September 10th is the best time to divide the plants.

Companion Planting and Design
The hellebores are especially handsome under tall evergreen shrubs. To make sure you get to fully enjoy this rare winter flower, plant hellebores along well-used paths and where they can been seen from a window. They're especially attractive growing with narcissus, skimmia, hostas, and *Pulmonaria saccharata* 'Mrs. Moon'.

Our Personal Recommendations
There are hellebores in many strains and colors now, but the Lenten rose and its cultivars are the best of the best. Other species we plant with the Lenten rose are musty-smelling stinking hellebore, *H. foetidus*, which bears panicles of drooping, bell-like, pale apple-green flowers edged with red in Zone 7 as early as January, and in Zone 6 in April; and *H. atrorubens*, which has deep green foliage and deep purple flowers that fade to green.

Lily-of-the-Valley
Convallaria majalis

When, Where, and How to Plant

You can plant container-grown lily-of-the-valley any time. Bare-root divisions or rhizome segments are best planted in early spring or early fall. Lily-of-the-valley is most successful in sun and in dappled light. The cooler the region, the more sun it can handle. It thrives in somewhat acid soil that is well-drained, humusy, and moist. Follow the soil preparation and planting instructions at the beginning of this chapter. Set planting holes for bare root divisions 6 to 8 in. apart and place the pips just below the surface with the roots bunched up underneath. Space plants from 4- or 5-in. containers 8 to 10 in. apart. Water well. Provide a 2-in. mulch for the area.

Growing Tip

During the first six weeks after planting, water often enough to keep the soil damp to the touch.

Care

If the foliage browns in late summer, spider mites are at work, so apply a miticide, according to label directions. Fertilize in fall with a light top dressing of slow-release organic fertilizer for acid-loving plants. Water when you water your lawn. If the flowers become smaller and less fragrant, it means the roots are crowded: dig out clumps in the fall, and replant them elsewhere with space all around. Lily-of-the-valley roots go deep, so push your spading fork way down and make sure you get all the roots; fill the empty space with improved soil and the plants all around will move into the new ground.

Companion Planting and Design

Well-tended, lily-of-the-valley stays a fresh green all during the growing season and is charming as a ground cover for garden plants as well as wildflowers. Delightful in a woodland garden with columbines, primroses, Solomon's seals, trilliums, and lady's-slippers.

Our Personal Recommendations

We recommend the cultivar called 'Fortin's Giant', a tall, full-flowered white that has larger flowers than the species. If you are planting for the beauty of the flowers, plant 'Plena', a double-flowered variety, and little 'Rosea', a less fragrant variety whose flowers are lavender-pink.

One of the world's great perfumes, Joy, is derived from lily-of-the-valley, a slim stem of pure white bells topping foliage that starts out looking like a tiny furled umbrella. The leaves pop up in early spring, and the flowers rise up through them a few weeks later. Lily-of-the-valley is loved for its fragrance; it's also a great ground cover. In light woodlands and shaded wild gardens it naturalizes, and rapidly colonizes surrounding territory with deep—and hard to eradicate—underground roots. You can get lily-of-the-valley to put up flower stems tall enough to cut easily by interplanting it with pachysandra. Pre-cooled pips (pointed tips) of lily-of-the-valley can be forced into bloom early indoors. Lily-of-the-valley is listed among toxic plants.

Bloom Period and Seasonal Color

Spring; white, pink cultivars.

Mature Height × Spread

10 to 12 in. × indefinite spread

Lily-Turf
Liriope muscari

Liriope looks like a graceful clump of grass, but is in the lily family, and it produces lovely flower spikes, is as tough as any ground cover, evergreen here, and spreads rapidly. The grass-like leaves are tall, coarse, and broad, about 1/2 to 3/4 in. wide. The flowers appear in late summer and early fall. They look a little like slim stems of grape hyacinth but much taller. They bloom in shades of blue, purple, lilac, or white, and are followed by attractive shiny black fruits that persist through early winter. A tough and resistant plant, it takes several seasons of growth to fill out, but once established it's almost indestructible. It's ideal for edging and can handle the Mid-Atlantic climate in cities as well as in the suburbs.

Other Names
Blue Lily-Turf, Liriope

Bloom Period and Seasonal Color
August and September; blue, lavender, purple, white.

Mature Height × Spread
1 to 1 1/2 ft. × 1 to 2 ft.

When, Where, and How to Plant
In early spring or early fall, set out container-grown root divisions. Liriope thrives in bright shade under tall trees, but spreads even in dense shade. It is not particular as to soil pH, tolerates high-alkaline soils, and succeeds in hot, dry locations. Following the planting instructions at the beginning of this chapter, prepare a planting bed, or planting holes twice the width of the container, with well-drained, moderately fertile soil. Set the plants 12 in. apart. Water thoroughly, and provide a permanent mulch.

Growing Tips
Keep the planting watered during droughts the first summer. Liriope withstands muggy weather and high humidity, and spreads as long as the soil doesn't dry out completely.

Care
In late winter, cut the foliage down to the crown to allow for fresh growth, and replenish the mulch. In continuing wet weather slugs and snails may chew the edges of the leaves; the control is to wait until the soil dries then sprinkle diatomaceous earth around each plant. Repeat the treatment as necessary. Well-established clumps can be divided in early spring before growth begins.

Companion Planting and Design
We use liriope many different ways: we plant clumps of several together as filler for flowering borders. The white-flowered cultivar 'Monroe White' is lovely with variegated liriope, and lavender-flowered 'Gold Banded' whose leaves have a gold stripe down the middle and form a mound. 'John Burch', whose foliage is variegated, bears attractive crested lavender flowers. Dwarf mondo grass, *Ophiopogon japonicus* 'Nana', and 'Silver Mist', the variegated form, are fast-spreading dwarf lily-turfs.

Our Personal Recommendations
For edging flower beds and garden paths, we like the effect of 'Christmas Tree' which produces a large, full flower spike in lavender-lilac. Another beauty is 'Royal Purple' whose flowers are deep purple. For ground cover foliage, the best of the variegated forms is 'Variagata'. Creeping lily-turf, *L. spicata*, spreads rapidly by underground stolons and is excellent as a bank holder and to cover very large areas. It is a slightly smaller species with 1/4-in. leaves and pale violet or white flowers.

Periwinkle
Vinca minor

When, Where, and How to Plant

Set out flats of rooted cuttings of *V. minor* in early spring or fall. Vinca does best in bright shade under tall shrubs or trees and in the partial shade created by a building. It prefers well-drained soil with pH between 5.5 and 7.2 that is well-worked, fertile, and loamy. Follow the soil preparation and planting instructions at the beginning of this chapter. Provide planting holes 6 to 8 in. deep and space the plants 8 in. apart. Water thoroughly. Mulch with pine needles, or composted leaf mold.

Growing Tips

Do not allow to dry out the first season. In early spring before growth starts, use a mower or shear vinca to keep the bed thick.

Care

Scratch in a slow-release organic fertilizer in the spring. Water vinca during extended droughts. To multiply your holdings, divide and replant rooted stems as growth resumes in early spring, or during wet weather in late summer and fall. You can also bunch up root divisions or offsets and plant them.

Companion Planting and Design

For small areas we like the look of ground covers grouped in richly varied combinations rather than in single-species displays. A combination that has everything—flowers, fresh foliage, fall color—is *Viola odorata*, *Vinca minor*, pachysandra, plumbago, and ferns. It includes plants for shade, semi-shade under tall trees, and sun. In planters we sometimes combine variegated forms of *Vinca major* and *V. minor*. *V. major* has larger leaves, is a paler green, and produces 3- to 4-ft.-long branches, lovely trailing over the edges of containers. *V. major* 'Variegata' has jade-green leaves edged with creamy white. It isn't reliably winter hardy in the Mid-Atlantic, but often survives mild winters.

Our Personal Recommendations

Some of the most beautiful cultivars are: *V. minor* 'Alba', which has creamy-white flowers and is somewhat less vigorous; 'Bowlesii', which has large blue flowers; 'Miss Jekyll', which bears small white flowers; and 'Sterling Silver', which has midnight-blue flowers and beautiful white margins around the leaves.

Small-leaved Vinca minor is a low-to-the-ground flowering evergreen plant with trailing branches and dainty, shiny, dark-green leaves. It creates a beautiful green carpet for open woodlands, rocky slopes, and shrub borders. Though it tolerates only a little foot traffic, it's a handsome lawn substitute. Vinca stems root every few feet, but unlike ivy, vinca does not cling to masonry so it's ideal for edging walls and terraces. The little flowers that appear in very early spring are a real asset: almost flat, wide open, a beautiful periwinkle-blue, they're lovely against the dark green foliage. Like other rapidly-spreading ground covers, vinca can crowd out desirable natives and exotics, so plant it only where you are sure it will remain under your control.

Other Name

Myrtle

Bloom Period and Seasonal Color

March to May; shades of periwinkle blue, white.

Mature Height × Spread

3 to 6 in. × trailing stems 2 to 3 ft. long

Herbs *for the Mid-Atlantic*

In the long ago and far away our forebears grew aromatic kitchen herbs alongside the roses, cinnamon-scented pinks, spicy nasturtiums, and other perfumed flowers with which they flavored food—so the old-time herb garden was a place of beauty and fragrance. But enhancing food was just one of the ways in which herbal plants improved life. You can get a sense of the past—and present—importance of herbs by visiting the U.S. National Arboretum in Washington, D.C. There The Herb Society of America has established a beautiful two-acre herb garden planted with medicinal and dye herbs, early pioneer and Native American herbs, industrial and fragrance herbs, Oriental and beverage herbs. Herbal trees and shrubs occupy the center of this grouping.

Growing together, the herbs become an aromatic sprawl of greens. The knot garden at the National Arboretum illustrates the classical solution to herb sprawl, which is to group herbs within ribbons of low boxwood hedges. "Knot garden" originally referred to any garden with an intricate design but has become almost synonymous with the growing of herbs.

The most indispensable kitchen herbs are those on the following pages. We grow our cooking herbs in beds of ornamentals handy to the kitchen door. The lush greens of parsley and cilantro enhance the flower borders. Low-growing thyme makes an aromatic edger for the path to the kitchen steps. Basil hides the yellowing foliage of small spring bulbs. Dill adds grace to the flower-filled tub by the door.

Lavender 'Hidcote'

When to Plant, and How to Harvest and Dry

Seeds of most perennial herbs are slow to germinate and growing the seedlings on can be a challenge. So, unless we need many plants of one kind—basil for bouquets, creeping thyme for tucking between stepping stones—we buy potted plants, rooted cuttings, or seedlings and set them out usually about mid-spring. Most herbs thrive in full sun and well-drained soil with a pH between 5.5 and 7.0. A few kitchen herbs do well here in part shade, among them dill and basil. To prepare soil for herbs, see Soil Preparation and Planting in the Introduction.

Thyme

To encourage an herb to bush out and be more productive, early on pinch out the tip of the main stem. Remove herb flowers as they develop—they're edible and make charming garnishes. When the plants have filled out, you can harvest the tender tip sprigs of the youngest branches at will without harming the plant. Never strip a plant of more than a third of its foliage or it will have trouble maintaining itself. In summer's high heat—especially in a very warm summer—herbs may go into semi-dormancy. During this season, you should pick herbs sparingly, as the plants are unable to replace the missing foliage and will look awful and be slow to recover.

Herbs are most flavorful harvested in the early morning before the sun dissipates the essential oils that give them flavor. Rinse herbs only if they're muddy. You won't have to rinse the foliage if you surround your herbs with a clean mulch. We find herb foliage stays fresh for a week or so when we seal it in a vegetable bag lined with damp paper towels and store it in the crisper.

To dry herbs, harvest clean, healthy stems 12 to 14 inches long, and strip off the lower leaves. Tie them loosely in small bunches and hang them upside down in an airy, dry, preferably dark place. Direct sunlight fades the foliage. When they're crackling dry, strip off the leaves and discard the stems. Rub the leaves between your palms to break them up. Pour the leaves into jars, label, and seal them. We try to find time to renew our supply every season: old herbs lose much of their flavor.

Ornamental Herbs

Some of the many other herbs we include in ornamental gardens, mainly for their beauty and fragrance, include these:

Catmint, *Nepeta mussinii*

Fennel, *Foeniculum vulgare*

Feverfew, *Chrysanthemum parthenium*

Italian Oregano, *Origanum vulgare*

Lemon Grass, *Cymbopogon syriacus*

Rue, *Ruta graveolens* 'Jackman's Blue'

Summer and Winter Savory, *Satureja* spp.

Sweet Woodruff, *Galium odoratum*

Basil

Ocimum basilicum

The basils are vigorous, upright annuals or short-lived perennials with light-green, often slightly puckered leaves that have the cool strong bite of mint (a close relative), with hints of anise, or sweet licorice, clove, and thyme. The leaves are used to flavor Mediterranean dishes, raw tomatoes, salads, pasta sauces, and pesto, and in sauces for lamb, fish, and beef. We wouldn't be without basil for cooking, but we also plant basil for the aroma, color, and texture its colorful varieties add to garden plantings. To have fragrant fillers for bouquets we plant opal basil which has purplish leaves with green markings, and 'Dark Opal' basil which has little green markings, red stems, and a sweet, anise-like flavor. 'Red Rubin', purple leaf basil, is a European selection that holds its color well.

Bloom Period and Seasonal Color
Summer; lavender flower spikes.

Mature Height × Spread
1 to 2¹/₂ ft. × 10 to 15 in.

When, Where, and How to Plant
Pots of seedlings can be set out after the weather has warmed. You can start seeds indoors four to six weeks before that, or sow basil seeds in the garden once night temperatures stay above 50 degrees Fahrenheit. Basil prefers full sun but will tolerate some afternoon shade. It does well in well-drained humusy soils whose pH is between 6.0 and 7.0. See Soil Preparation and Planting in the Introduction. Provide planting holes 8 to 12 in. deep, and allow 6 to 8 in. between plants. Water well with diluted fertilizer. Basil wilts quickly and easily in summer heat, so apply a 3-in. layer of mulch starting 3 in. from the stem to help keep in moisture.

Growing Tips
Pinch out the central leader and harvest branch tips and flowers early and often to encourage leaf production. To promote rapid growth, water often enough to sustain the soil moisture for two or three weeks. After that, water weekly unless you have a soaking rain.

Care
Fertilize every three to five weeks through August with a liquid fertilier such as seaweed. If you have planted seeds, keep weeds away. At mid-season, cut the plants back by about half. Pick tip sprigs at will when the leaves still are young. Big harvests for making pesto can begin when flower spikes start to form. Basil will go on through Indian summer if you protect it from early frosts.

Companion Planting and Design
The purple varieties especially are beautiful tucked into flower borders and growing in containers planted with flowers in pastel colors. They're lovely with cosmos. In window boxes and for edging containers use tiny bush basils like 'Spicy Globe', which grows between 6 and 12 in. tall; the flavor is quite good.

Our Personal Recommendations
Our favorite basils for flavoring are common sweet basil and holy basil, *Ocimum sanctum*. We plant purple-leaved basils, which aren't very flavorful, for the fragrance and rich color they bring to flower beds and bouquets. The opal basils and 'Purple Ruffles', an All-America Selections winner, are our current favorites.

Chives

Allium schoenoprasum

When, Where, and How to Plant

Chives can be started from seed indoors six to eight weeks before the last frost date; they grow best at a temperature of 75 degrees Fahrenheit. The clumps enlarge over the years so unless you are planting lots for the garden display, we suggest you buy a few potted seedlings. Potted chives can be planted spring, summer, or early fall. They thrive in full sun and in soils between pH 6.0 and 7.0. Choose a well-drained site—chives hate puddles—and work the soil to a depth of 8 to 12 in. See Soil Preparation and Planting in the Introduction. For each plant, mix in a handful of either compost or composted manure. Set the plants 12 to 18 in. apart and water with diluted fertilizer. Mulch all around 2 in. deep.

Growing Tips

To promote rapid, unchecked growth, for the first two or three weeks water often enough to sustain soil moisture. After that, water deeply only during prolonged droughts. Keep weeds away: they're hard to get out of a clump once the chives are well established.

Care

In early spring, fertilize the bed with a slow-release organic fertilizer. To encourage more foliage, pinch out the flower heads. Use sharp, clean scissors to harvest chives and cut no lower than 2 in. from the crown. Never take more than a third of the plant at one time and harvest sparingly in summer's high heat. Divide chives every three to four years in early spring or early fall. In late summer, you can pot chives in a clay container and bring a clump indoors for modest winter harvests.

Companion Planting and Design

Chives are pretty little plants lovely in bloom and attractive tucked into a flowering border or edging an herb or a vegetable garden. They do well in large containers.

Our Personal Recommendations

For cooking, we recommend the variety called 'Fine Chives'. There are interesting other species. One we plant for cooking and for its flowers is *A. tuberosum*, the tall garlic, or Chinese, chives. The leaves are flat, not round, and the flowers are white.

Chives are perennials. They develop attractive mounds of perfectly round, hollow, dark-green leaves that at first glance look like grass. Beginning in June, pretty, dryish, lavender-pink globes appear and these, too, are edible. It's a charming display that continues all summer. Chive leaves impart a mild onion flavor. They're used chopped as a garnish and flavoring agent for salads, dips, stews, casseroles, and laid full size over fish or meat that will be roasted. Chopped chives put a flavorful finishing touch to one of the world's great cold soups, vichyssoise, and the flowers, pulled apart, make an elegant garnish for eggs benedict. Chives keep well frozen, or dried on a screen and sealed into airtight containers.

Bloom Period and Seasonal Color
Spring and summer; mauve/lavender-pink.

Mature Height × Spread
8 to 12. in. × 12 to 15 in.

Dill
Anethum graveolens

Dill is a willowy annual with foliage as fine as asparagus fern. It looks a lot like fennel, Foeniculum, and tastes of parsley-carrot-lemon-anise. The foliage is called "dill weed." Flower heads resembling yellowish green Queen-Anne's-lace develop as the season warms. They are edible and eventually produce seeds that can be dried and bottled for winter seasoning of casseroles and stews—and for pickling. Dill foliage dries quickly on screens and also can be bottled for later use. Snipped fresh dill weed is excellent in salads and with salmon, potatoes, green beans, salads, and in chicken soup. It's also a really pretty garnish. We use whole stems of aromatic dill weed as a garnish for platters of cold cuts, salmon, tomatoes, and cheese.

Bloom Period and Seasonal Color
Late summer; yellow-green flower heads.

Mature Height × Spread
2 to 3 ft. × 8 to 12 in.

When, Where, and How to Plant
You can start dill from seed indoors six to eight weeks before the last frost. Dill's taproot doesn't transplant easily, so sow the seeds in peat pots and transplant the seedlings in their pots. Or, sprinkle the seed over the soil surface after the ground has warmed; sow where the plants are to grow. Dill needs sun but deteriorates in prolonged, intense heat. In our area shade at noon helps keep dill going longer. Avoid growing dill where walls or white-painted surfaces intensify the heat. Dill prefers soil in the acid range, pH 5.5 to 6.5. See Soil Preparation and Planting in the Introduction. Work the soil 8 to 12 in. deep and set seedlings about 12 in. apart. Water with diluted fertilizer. Apply a 2-in. mulch starting 3 in. from the stem.

Growing Tips
To promote rapid, unchecked growth, for the first two to three weeks, water often enough to keep the soil moist. Pinch out tip sprigs regularly to encourage branching.

Care
Water deeply every week unless you have a soaking rain. Harvest sparingly in high heat. If dill deteriorates when heat comes, discard it and plant new seedlings in early September. Keep the flower heads picked until the end of the season. Dill may self-sow if the soil around the parent plants is cultivated and moist. To have dill seed for cooking, when the seedheads yellow or brown, but before they dry, shake the seeds into a paper bag and dry them on paper towels on screens.

Companion Planting and Design
Dill foliage lends grace to an herb garden, kitchen garden, or cutting garden. In choosing a place for dill, take into account that it may die out when high heat arrives. Dwarf dill varieties do well in containers.

Our Personal Recommendations
'Dukat' or 'Tetra' dill have a delicate, rather sweet flavor and are slow to bolt. 'Bouquet' has especially large seed heads. 'Fernleaf' dill, a 1992 All-America Selections winner, is a lovely, blue-green, 18-in. dwarf with excellent flavor. 'Mammoth' is an aromatic 4-ft. dill for pickling.

Lavender
Lavandula angustifolia

When, Where, and How to Plant
Lavender seed is very slow to germinate, and the seedlings are easily lost after transplanting. We recommend you set out container-grown plants. They can be planted in early spring, late summer, or early fall. Lavender requires full sun but can stand a touch of noon shade. It will grow in a large container on a patio, but isn't suited to indoor growing. Lavender does best in soil that has a pH above 6.0. It needs a well-drained site, and flourishes growing on a sandy southern slope. See Soil Preparation and Planting in the Introduction. Work the soil to a depth that is twice the height of the container to assure good drainage. Set the plants 15 to 30 in. apart. Water well. Apply a 2-in. mulch starting 3 in. from the stem.

Growing Tips
To promote rapid, unchecked growth, for the first two or three weeks water often enough to sustain soil moisture. After that, water deeply every week or ten days unless you have a soaking rain.

Care
In early spring to encourage new growth, prune 1 to 2 in. from the branch tips of established plants. Lavender often re-blooms in late summer if the first set of flowering stems has been deadheaded or harvested. Harvest lavender stems just before the buds begin to open, tie them in loose bunches and hang them upside down to air dry, then strip off the buds and store in a sealed container for later use.

Companion Planting and Design
Lavender grows well in a rock garden, and makes a wonderful ground cover for sunny orchards. In ornamental gardens we plant 'Hidcote' for its deep-purple flowers, and silvery little 'Munstead'.

Our Personal Recommendations
The lavender we recommend as a dry perfume scent and for flavoring is the English type or true lavender, *L. angustifolia* ssp. *angustifolia*. 'Lavender Lady' is a gray-green dwarf that blooms in late summer from spring-sown seed. The beautiful purple-pink French, or Spanish, lavender, *L. stoechas*, isn't reliably winter hardy in Zone 6 but it makes a pretty pot plant, and may winter over in Zone 8. Other great varieties are *L. intermedia* × 'Provence' and the dwarf *L. angustifolia* 'Blue Cushion'.

Lavender's sweet, lasting scent has been a source of fragrance for thousands of years. It's a shrubby evergreen whose every part is intensely fragrant—flower spikes, stems, and needle-like, gray-green leaves. Lavender stems are harvested before the buds open, dried, and the buds are stripped and used to scent linens and lingerie, sleep pillows, and other tools of aromatherapy. The buds, dried or fresh, are also used to add a sweet mint-anise-rosemary flavor to herbes de Provence, honey, dessert butters, savory sauces, grilled fish and steaks, marinades for game, and to stews and soups. We plant lavender near roses, and where it will sprawl across paths so we will brush against it often, releasing its wonderful aroma. Deer dislike it.

Other Name
English Lavender

Bloom Period and Seasonal Color
June and may repeat in August; lavender, deep purple, blue-gray, pink, white.

Mature Height × Spread
2 to 4 ft. × 2 to 2^1/$_2$ ft.

Mint
Mentha spicata

The mints are upright or sprawling herbs 12 to 36 in. tall with intensely aromatic, crinkly green leaves (hairy in some species) that are pungent when brushed against. In summer fuzzy mint-scented flower spikes appear. This species, M. spicata, has small, pointed, dainty leaves and a truly fine sweetish mint flavor. It is our choice for use as a culinary herb—for teas, juleps, vinaigrette, lamb sauce, desserts (use fresh tiny tips), jellies, and soups. The fresh leaves decorate and flavor desserts and confections, Middle Eastern and Indian foods, are steeped for "digestif" teas, and dried in potpourris. Stepped on, mint sprawling onto a garden path becomes a carpet of magical fragrance. Bees graze mint diligently.

Other Name
Spearmint

Bloom Period and Seasonal Color
Summer; purplish, white, pink, mauve, lilac.

Mature Height × Spread
1 to 3 ft. × 2 ft.

When, Where, and How to Plant
Mint spreads relentlessly, so gardeners are eager to share rooted divisions. But plant only a mint whose flavor you have tasted and like, or one you will use in bouquets. Garden centers offer many container-grown varieties. You can plant rooted mint at almost any season in full sun or in filtered or bright shade. It is invasive (in fact, very invasive) so unless you are planting in poor or clay soil, confine the roots to a large bottomless plastic pot or coffee tin and plant the container. Mints do best in slightly acid soil, pH 5.5 to 6.5, but any well-drained soil will do. Space the plants 12 to 15 in. apart. Water well. The sprawling mints get muddied during rainstorms, so stake a few branches to have clean leaves available for cooking. Apply a 2-in. mulch starting 3 in. from the stem.

Growing Tip
To get the plants off to a good start, for the first two or three weeks water often enough to sustain the soil moisture.

Care
Water the small-leaved mints when you water the flower beds. Harvest only sparingly in summer's high heat. Shear mint to keep it looking neat and to produce fresh new growth. Mint growing in a container should be divided every year or two in the spring or early fall. Six-inch tip cuttings root readily in damp potting soil, sand, or water.

Companion Planting and Design
Centuries of growing mint has resulted in more than 500 species and cultivars. They are diverse in appearance and aroma and make an interesting collection for garden hobbyists. As an edger along walkways and in containers we like the beautiful, variegated pineapple mint, *Mentha suaveolens* 'Variegata'; the flavor is negligible but this mint is somewhat less invasive than other species.

Our Personal Recommendations
We grow a few spearmint plants to use fresh to flavor food and to dry for making mint tea. And, because we love the aroma of mint in bouquets, we let *M. arvensis*, which has broad, hairy leaves, grow wild in our kitchen flower bed.

Parsley

Petroselinum crispum

When, Where, and How to Plant

Parsley is a biennial—that is, it lives two years. It stays green through Mid-Atlantic winters, flourishes mightily through most of spring, then when heat comes it quickly goes to seed. To have a steady supply of parsley, plant two or three parsley seedlings in early spring, and the following fall plant a new batch near the veterans. Discard the veterans when they bolt—or let them grow their greenish flower heads and enjoy watching the butterflies flocking to them. Planting time for cilantro seedlings is after the air has warmed. All three parsleys do best in full sun in well-drained neutral soil, between pH 6.0 to 7.0. See Soil Preparation and Planting in the Introduction. Dig planting holes 8 to 12 in. deep and set the plants 8 to 10 in. apart. Water well. Provide a 2-in. mulch.

Growing Tip

To promote rapid, unchecked growth, water often for the first two to three weeks.

Care

The parsleys can be harvested as soon as the plants have grown a substantial number of stems. Use scissors to harvest the outer stems and make the cut at the base. Never take more than a quarter to a third of one plant at a time. When curly and Italian parsley are growing lushly, harvest, mince, and freeze some for winter use.

Companion Planting and Design

From an ornamental point of view, the parsleys can be planted wherever a low-growing mound of bright green is desirable. Curly parsley makes a handsome edging for bright red geraniums, and it thrives in window boxes and large containers. We like to keep a little bouquet of red geraniums and curly parsley in the kitchen.

Our Personal Recommendations

'Clivi' is a mossy, dwarf curly parsley to use in window boxes. 'Krausa' parsley is a moss variety we like for flavor. 'Triple Curled' is a thickly-ruffled parsley. 'Giant Italian' is a 3-ft., deep-green parsley with a full, mellow flavor excellent fresh or dried. Cilantro labeled "slow bolt" is best for foliage. If you'd like to grow your own coriander seeds, plant varieties called just "coriander."

We plant three parsleys: curly parsley, and flat-leafed or Italian parsley, which are varieties of Petroselinum crispum; *and Chinese parsley,* Coriandrum sativum, *more often called cilantro now. All three are low, very green, leafy plants. Curly and flat-leaved parsley are pungent, winter-hardy biennials. Their earthy carrot/celery flavor blends other flavorful ingredients. Rich in chlorophyll, they kill odors and sweeten the breath. Curly parsley is the most beautiful for garnish and the quickest to mince. Flat Italian parsley,* P. crispum var. neapolitanum, *is more richly flavored. Cilantro is a cold-tolerant annual that grows to a foot or two in a season. It adds a unique flavor to Latin and Oriental recipes. Its dried ripe seed is the ancient Asian spice called coriander, which imparts a sweet lemony flavor and a hint of sage.*

Other Names

Curly Parsley, Italian Parsley, Chinese Parsley, Fresh Coriander

Bloom Period and Seasonal Color

Summer; grown for its foliage; once it flowers, its season for usable leaves is past.

Mature Height × Spread

1 to 1^1/$_2$ ft. × 1 to 1^1/$_2$ ft.

Rosemary
Rosmarinus officinalis

An age-old symbol of remembrance and beloved of bees, rosemary is a shrub-like perennial that has gloriously aromatic, needle-like, gray-green leaves. Evergreen in Zone 8, in Zones 6 and 7 it may be wintered indoors and sometimes grows well enough to be trained as a Christmas tree topiary. The pungent needles impart a sweet, hot, piney, nutmeg flavor used to flavor many foods—polenta and potatoes, fruit, cookies, breads and biscuits, grilled meats and fish. Olive oil infused with rosemary makes a delicious dipping and sautée oil. Rosemary is the base for many men's colognes and for potpourris. A circlet of rosemary branches makes a great base for an herb wreath. Sprigs of rosemary add aroma to bouquets of fresh flowers.

Bloom Period and Seasonal Color
Summer; pale lavender-blue flower spikes.

Mature Height × Spread
2 to 4 ft. × 2 to 3 ft.

When, Where, and How to Plant
In Zones 6 and 7, rosemary is grown as an annual but in Duck, North Carolina, Zone 8, it has naturalized in the sand at the Viette beach house. To germinate, the seeds need nights at 75 degrees Fahrenheit, and can take three months to sprout. We recommend starting with a container-grown plant. Plant rosemary after danger of frost in full sun. A native to the Mediterranean, it withstands high heat and drought once established, and can be grown where it will be neglected. Rosemary does best in well-drained soil, acid or neutral. See Soil Preparation and Planting in the Introduction. Work the soil 8 to 12 in. deep and set baby plants 6 to 8 in. apart, shrub sizes 12 to 24 in. apart. Water well. Provide a 2-in. mulch starting 3 in. from the stem.

Growing Tips
To promote rapid, unchecked growth, water often enough to sustain the soil moisture for the first two or three weeks. Harvest 1- or 2-in. sprigs from young branch tips often to encourage bushiness.

Care
Water established plants only during droughts. Before winter, pot the plant in sandy, humusy soil and bring it indoors to a sunny window; water regularly but don't keep the soil moist. Mist several times each week. Rosemary will last longest in bright light in a room kept at 50 degrees Fahrenheit. Put the plant out in the spring after all danger of frost is past.

Companion Planting and Design
Rosemary is a good bonsai and pot plant, and specimen to place near entrances, windows, and garden seats where you can enjoy its fragrance. In Zone 8 gardens it grows into an aromatic evergreen.

Our Personal Recommendations
For flavoring we recommend the species *Rosmarinus officinalis*. The hardiest rosemary is 'Arp', which is said to withstand winters as far north as New Jersey. Ornamental rosemaries that are lovely in the garden, though not the best for cooking, include: *R. officinalis* 'Benenden Blue' which has handsome blue flowers; 'Lockwood de Forest' which has brighter leaves and bluer flowers; 'Kenneth Prostrate' and 'Huntington Carpet' which are superior creeping forms; and variegated 'Golden Prostratus'.

Sage
Salvia officinalis

When, Where, and How to Plant

Set out container-grown plants or root divisions in early spring after all danger of frost is past. Sage does best in full sun, but tolerates afternoon shade. Provide very well-drained, ordinary, neutral soil, around pH 7.0. See Soil Preparation and Planting in the Introduction. Work the soil 8 to 12 in. deep and dig generous planting holes 2 ft. apart. Water well. Stake stems that sprawl to avoid having to rinse the foliage, robbing it of some of its flavorful oils. Apply a 2-in. mulch starting 3 in. from the stem.

Growing Tips

For the first two or three weeks water often enough to sustain the soil moisture. The flower spikes are edible and removing them improves the appearance and growth of the plant.

Care

Water deeply when you water the flower beds. Harvest tender tip sprigs at will. In the fall trim sage back to a tidy mound to avoid root rot—a problem where drainage is poor. Sage can be harvested sparingly in winter. To multiply your holdings, divide well-established older plants in spring or early fall. Sage can also be grown successfully indoors as long as it gets sun at least six hours a day and has proper drainage. The plant should be pruned to no more than 12 in. If it starts to look leggy and the leaves grow pale and are thinly spaced, the plant isn't getting enough light.

Companion Planting and Design

For their texture and beauty, we plant colorful cultivars of *S. officinalis* toward the front of flowering borders and in the herb and the kitchen gardens. Sage is pretty in a planter; set it so it droops over the edge. Several varieties of sage grouped together are striking. Sage's camphor aroma is said to deter garden insects.

Our Personal Recommendations

The species is best for flavoring food, but some of the more colorful sages also have flavor, though less than *S. officinalis*. 'Tricolor', the showiest, has leaves splattered with deep pink, silver gray, cream, and purple. *S. officinalis* 'Icterina' has beautiful gray leaves splashed with gold.

Common sage is a small, beautiful woody perennial whose grayish leaves have the texture of crepe. Some colorful varieties are beautiful enough to be grown as ornamentals. The leaves impart a subtle flavor—sweet pine, camphor, and citrus. Minced fresh sage is used to flavor bread, pasta sauces, and with roasted pork, chicken, and vegetables. Dried sage enhances fatty meats and is used in stuffing for poultry. The flavor of fresh sage becomes more potent the longer it cooks—so use it with caution in delicate sauces. Sage stays fresh for a week sealed in a vegetable bag in the crisper. The leaves dry well in a microwave oven, on screens, or tucked into a wreath.

Bloom Period and Seasonal Color
Midsummer; violet, blue, white.

Mature Height × Spread
1 to 2 ft. × 1 to 2 ft.

Tarragon
Artemisia dracunculus

Tarragon is a perennial that grows into a good-sized, rather weedy shrub in our region. The slim, delicately flavored leaves impart a heavenly aroma of sweet anise or sweet licorice, and camphor. Unique, haunting, the flavor and scent are used in vinegars, dressings, French and Southern European dishes, and in potpourris. Tarragon is what gives Béarnaise sauce its flavor and it is an essential ingredient in fines herbes for stocks, broths, and Green Goddess salad dressing. It enhances mushrooms, chicken, and fish. There are two main tarragon groups, French and Russian. French tarragon has an addictive, haunting sweet aroma, and that's what makes the plant worth looking for. Taste before buying! Russian tarragon can grow to 5 ft. tall and doesn't do much for food but is handsome in the garden.

Bloom Period and Seasonal Color
Summer; whitish-green florets.

Mature Height × Spread
1 to 2 ft. × 2 to 3 ft.

When, Where, and How to Plant
True French tarragon cannot be grown from seed, so buy a container-grown plant or rooted cutting that meets your taste test. It may not winter over in exceptional winters. One or two plants will satisfy your needs. Plant tarragon in mid-spring in full sun—it tolerates a few hours of afternoon shade. It can take a lot of heat and resists drought, so you can plant it where it may be neglected. Don't plant tarragon in a kitchen garden where rototilling might disturb it. Tarragon thrives in ordinary neutral soil between pH 5.5 or 6.0 and pH 7.0. Good drainage, especially in winter, is essential. See Soil Preparation and Planting in the Introduction. Dig planting holes 8 to 12 in. deep and 8 to 12 in. apart. Water well. Apply a 2-in. mulch starting 3 in. from the stem.

Growing Tips
Water often enough to sustain soil moisture for the first two or three weeks. Harvest tip sprigs often in spring to promote growth of tender branches—the leafy tips are the tastiest.

Care
Water established plants deeply when you water the flower beds. Cut the plants back in the summer when they begin to flower in order to promote new growth. In time tarragon's roots become crowded and tangled, resulting in a less productive plant. Renew your plant by dividing the clumps in the spring. Carefully separate 3-inch pieces with shoots intact and replant. Discard any woody roots.

Companion Planting and Design
For all of its elegant flavor, tarragon is not a very jazzy looking plant. We recommend placing it in an out-of-the-way place in your herb garden surrounded by other tall, more interesting looking plants. It's useful as a filler in a flower border or a container garden.

Our Personal Recommendations
We grow the species for flavoring, and two of its aromatic cousins for their appeal in the garden and in bouquets. One is true wormwood, *Artemisia absinthium*, and the other is southernwood, *A. abrotanum*, a beautiful foliage plant with finely divided scented leaves.

Thyme

Thymus spp. and hybrids

When, Where, and How to Plant

For an early crop, in mid-spring set out container-grown thyme. Plant it in full sun for the best flavor. A little noon shade can be helpful in the hottest parts of our region but the plant dies out if it doesn't have enough sun. Thyme tolerates considerable drought and abuse, so it can be planted where it is likely to be neglected. It does well in ordinary soil that has a pH above 6.0. See Soil Preparation and Planting in the Introduction. Provide a well-drained site and generous planting holes 8 to 12 in. deep and 12 in. apart. Water well. Mulch the area 2 in. deep.

Growing Tips

For a week or two after planting, promote rapid growth by watering often enough to sustain soil moisture.

Care

After the first few weeks, water deeply during droughts. Harvest thyme sparingly in summer's high heat. Every year in early spring shear established plants back mercilessly, and fertilize them with a handful of a slow-release fertilizer. To multiply your holdings, divide mature plants in spring or early fall.

Companion Planting and Design

Two or three thyme plants will likely meet your needs for thyme. The good culinary thymes make good edgers. Thyme's trailing stems and white-splashed pineapple mint are beautiful together in a hanging basket with white petunias and pink geraniums. Creeping thyme, *T. serpyllum*, is tough enough to be walked on and can be used between flagstones. Colorful when in bloom, varieties of the larger flowered subspecies *T. serpyllum* ssp. *serpyllum*—white-flowered 'Albus', crimson 'Coccineus', and red 'Splendens'—are suitable ground covers for sunny slopes and attractive planted where they will trail over garden walls. For edging, we plant varieties whose leaves are splashed silver or gold; the names usually include 'Argenteus' or 'Aureus'.

Our Personal Recommendations

The sweetest culinary thymes are *Thymus vulgaris* and its cultivars, such as 'Wedgewood English', an excellent taller form, and 'Orange Balsam', which has a hint of citrus. We also grow lemon thyme, *T. × citriodorus*, and caraway-flavored *T. herba-barona*.

The thymes are small prostrate evergreen perennials with graceful trailing branches 6 to 10 in. long. The tiny, dark green leaves have a sharp aroma, and an earthy mint taste. The flavor combines well with bay leaf, parsley, and onion. The leaves are used dried or fresh in stuffings for pork and lamb, and in salads, soups, stews, Creole dishes, and gumbos. Parisians sprinkle thyme on steaks before broiling. The leaves are so small they don't need to be minced, just bruised to release the flavor. Herb fans brew thyme to make an herbal tea. To dry thyme for storing, pick tip sprigs, air dry them on screens until crisp, then strip off the leaves, and bottle and cap them. The thymes are excellent basket and container plants.

Other Names
French Thyme, Summer Thyme

Bloom Period and Seasonal Color
Early summer; pale pink, white, lilac, purple.

Mature Height × Spread
2 to 8 in. × 2 to 3 ft.

Ornamental Grasses *for the Mid-Atlantic*

Windblown, untamed, graceful, 1 to 12 feet tall and more, the ornamental grasses are the signature plants of today's naturalistic landscaping, and they need little maintenance. The sight and sound of wind whispering through tall grasses is refreshing on a hot summer day—a country sound very welcome in a city garden. Airy, luminous seed heads develop late in the season and remain lovely through fall and early winter.

The low-growing ornamental grasses add texture to the front of flower beds and to pocket wild gardens. Those 6 feet tall or more can replace a high-maintenance espalier fronting a masonry wall. Planted among native trees and shrubs, grasses become part of a handsome low-maintenance screen. The mid-height ornamental grasses are the natural transition plants to woodland or water and, in combination with native wildflowers, make a beautiful flowering meadow. The recommended ratio for a meadow garden is one-third flowers to two-thirds ornamental grasses for sunny places, and one-third grasses and two-thirds flowers for shade.

The first consideration in choosing a grass is how the end-of-season height and width of the plant will fit the site. The very tall grasses must be featured as specimens and nearby plantings chosen to complement them. Then consider the overall form. Some grasses clump, some mound, some fountain. Chinese silver grass is very erect, maiden grass arches, while pennisetum fountains. The texture of the leaves and their color is important—fine, coarse, bold, bluish, greenish, reddish, gold, striped, variegated. For contrast, combine both fine- and coarse-textured grasses. When you have thought all that through, then you can consider which of the flower heads you are going to fall in love with. Grouping many plants of a few varieties is more effective than planting a few of many.

Author Carole Ottesen classes the grasses into cool-season and warm-season plants, and it's a useful concept. The cool-season grasses shoot up in late January or February, so they're cut back in late winter. Their early growth makes them the best

Ornamental grasses in autumn splendor, including Japanese Blood Grass and *Miscanthus* cultivars.

Chinese Silver Grass and Hostas

choice when you want a grass that will be highly visible, the main show, all year round. The warm-season grasses begin to grow later, so you can wait until early spring to cut them back. A warm-season grass is a good choice when you have in mind combining grasses and flowers: interplant them with big early spring-flowering bulbs that will bloom after the grasses' annual haircut and hide the bare crown while the grass is growing up. The grass will soon grow tall enough to hide the ripening bulb foliage.

When, Where, and How to Plant

Like the perennial flowers, the ornamental grasses begin to fill out the second year. They may be planted in early spring, summer, or early fall. At garden centers they are sold in containers; mail order suppliers may ship some ornamental grasses bare root. These plants must be soaked thoroughly before planting. Most of the ornamental grasses thrive in acid to neutral soil that is one-half to one-quarter humus, and most need a well-drained site. See Soil Preparation and Planting in the Introduction. Set the crowns $1/2$ to 1 inch higher than the soil surface. Surround the plants with 1 to 2 inches of mulch.

The annual haircut is just a matter of shearing low-growing grasses and new plantings of the big grasses. When a big grass begins to mature, simplify the annual haircut by using sisal twine to rope the leaves together all the way to the top so that it ends up looking like a telephone pole. Then saw the top off a few inches above the crown. (If you use a chain saw take care not to catch the twine in the teeth!) For low-growing grasses, cut off the leaves and stalks a few inches above the crown.

Most ornamental grasses need annual fertilization. The time for fertilizing is when signs of new growth appear. Apply a slow-release organic fertilizer. In prolonged droughts, water slowly and deeply.

Other Options

In addition to the grasses recommended in this chapter, we like:

Compact Pampas Grass, *Cortaderia selloana* 'Pumila'

Korean Feather Reed Grass, *Achnatherum brachytricha* (formerly *Calamagrostis brachytricha*)

Leather Leaf Sedge, *Carex buchananii*, *C. morrowii* 'Goldband'

Ravenna Grass, Plume Grass, *Erianthus ravennae*

Blue Fescue
Festuca glauca

Blue fescue forms low rounded tufts or hummocks of slender metallic-blue-green blades that are evergreen in most areas of the Mid-Atlantic. It's a cool-season grass, that is it starts to grow soon after the January haircut, which is all the maintenance it needs, and it blooms in mid- to late spring. The flowers are loose, lacy panicles on stems that reach well above the foliage. The contrast between the relatively small, stiff clump and the thin, gracefully arching and gently swaying flower stalks is charming. It's widely used in perennial borders where it adds a welcome blue accent. The genus includes familiar lawn grasses as well as big, handsome ornamentals.

Other Names
Blue Sheep's Fescue, *Festuca ovina* var. *glauca*

Bloom Period and Seasonal Color
Tan flower heads rise in mid- to late spring; the blue foliage is attractive all season.

Mature Height × Spread
8 to 12 in. × 8 to 10 in.

When, Where, and How to Plant
Set out dormant, container-grown plants as soon as the ground can be worked in late winter. Plant blue fescue in full sun or in very bright shade. Without enough light, the blue will be less intense. Avoid damp spots. The foliage has a bluish-gray, waxy coating that protects it from excessive water loss through transpiration, and wet feet can cause problems. The fescues thrive in a range of soils from pH 5.5 to 6.5. They develop the bluest color in soil that is not especially fertile, and on the dry side. See Soil Preparation and Planting in the Introduction. Provide roomy planting holes and set the plants an inch above the soil level about 2 ft. apart. Water well. Mulch 2 in. deep around and between the plants.

Growing Tips
Water a new planting every week or two the first season. Blue fescue grows rapidly during cool weather, but in hot, dry periods it sulks. Do not try to force growth by watering or fertilizing. Wait for cool weather, and it will revive.

Care
The plant is fairly drought-resistant, so once it is established, local rainfall should be enough to keep it growing except during our mid- and late-August droughts. Allow the seedheads to ripen and stand through fall and winter. Toward the end of January, prune the plant back to the crown. Replenish the mulch until the plants have spread widely enough to shade out weeds. This grass benefits from division every few years. You can divide and replant this grass in fall, but not in summer.

Companion Planting and Design
Blue fescue is attractive planted as edging for beds of shrubbery, walks, naturalized areas, and grass gardens. It is sometimes used as a ground cover, but we find the clumps too compact, and the foliage too stiff—it never seems quite comfortable in the role. It looks well, and grows well, with lavender, salvia, and Russian sage.

Our Personal Recommendation
'Elijah Blue' has the most intense blue of all the fescues.

Blue Oat Grass
Helictotrichon sempervirens

When, Where, and How to Plant

As soon as the ground can be worked in early spring, set out container-grown plants or rooted divisions. Plant blue oat grass in full sun or in bright shade. Without enough light, the blue will be less intense. Avoid damp spots. In Zone 8, our southern shore region, plant blue oat grass in high, bright shade such as there is under tall pines; it doesn't tolerate high temperatures combined with strong sun and drying winds. Blue oat grass thrives in rich soil and succeeds in a wide pH range from acid 3.0 to neutral 7.0. See Soil Preparation and Planting in the Introduction. Provide roomy planting holes and set the plants an inch above ground level and about 2 ft. apart. Water well. Mulch 2 in. deep around and between the plants.

Growing Tips

Water a new planting every week or two the first season. Once established, local rainfall should be enough to keep blue oat grass growing except during our mid- and late-August droughts.

Care

Allow the spikelets to ripen and stand through fall and winter. In late January prune the plant back to the crown. Trim the plant back earlier if storms flatten the flower stems, or if it becomes less appealing. Replenish the mulch in late winter until the plants have spread widely enough to shade weeds out. You can divide and replant this grass in fall, but not in summer. Dig the crown, cut it apart, and replant the pieces.

Companion Planting and Design

Blue oat grass has many uses in the home landscape. Planted toward the middle of a large perennial border, it makes a colorful textural accent and it is beautiful massed and naturalized. We've seen it combined very effectively in wild gardens near the shore with silvery plants like artemisia, nepeta, and stachys.

Our Personal Recommendation

Plant the species.

This is a lovely steely-blue grass a little taller than blue fescue, and it maintains its color through late winter. A cool-season grass, it starts growing very quickly after its early spring haircut, forming compact spiky tufts of striking silvery blue-green leaves. In May, delicate, golden, oat-like flowers sway far above the foliage on graceful, erect or arching stems that extend 1 ft. or more beyond the foliage, swaying and bobbing in the wind. In summer, the blue-gray flower heads turn a bright tan that contrasts beautifully with the foliage. It's a good specimen for open situations, terraces, and rock gardens.

Other Names

Avena Grass, *Avena sempervirens*

Bloom Period and Seasonal Color

Blue-gray inflorescences turn to tan in summer; the metallic-blue leaves are attractive all season.

Mature Height × Spread

2 to 3 ft. × 25 in.

Chinese Silver Grass

Miscanthus sinensis and cultivars

Chinese silver grass is one of the most desirable and versatile of the big landscape grasses, a 6- to 7-ft. grass to use boldly, in big spaces. Beautiful in fall and winter, it is a warm-season grass that grows slowly in spring and then rapidly, producing robust, open, upright clumps of gracefully arching leaves that develop into dense, effective screening. In late summer and fall silky, silvery, pale pink flower clusters open on panicles up to 1 ft. long. With cold weather, the foliage and the plumes turn to silver and tan. Long grown in Japan and China, beloved of the Victorians, who called it eulalia, the species has given rise to many cultivars considered the most beautiful of the ornamental grasses.

Other Names
Eulalia, Maiden Grass, Zebra Grass

Bloom Period and Seasonal Color
Pale pink flower clusters in late summer, fading with the foliage to silver and gold in fall.

Mature Height × Spread
6 to 8 ft. × 3 to 5 ft.

When, Where, and How to Plant

Set out container-grown plants as soon as the ground begins to warm. Most Chinese silver grass cultivars grow best in six or more hours of direct sun, but some, including the lovely cultivar 'Gracillimus', or maiden grass, make do with three to four hours of direct sun. Given a constant supply of moisture, *Miscanthus* thrives, but established plantings sustain modest growth in drier soil. *Miscanthus* is not particular as to pH, and adapts to reasonably fertile soil. See Soil Preparation and Planting in the Introduction. Provide generous planting holes and plant with 3 to 4 ft. between the centers. Water well. Mulch 2 in. deep.

Growing Tip

Water a new planting every week or two the first season.

Care

Water during droughts until the plants are fully matured. Established cultivars can do with less moisture—the leaves roll if they need more. This warm-season grass starts its growth when winter is over, so wait until early spring to cut it back to the crown. Replenish the mulch. To multiply, divide before new growth begins. Lift and carefully use an axe to cut the crown apart, giving each section at least one growing point.

Companion Planting and Design

Some cultivars are planted as specimens, others as transitional plants by water features. We think it's most beautiful growing in groups.

Our Personal Recommendations

For the smaller home garden we recommend 4- to 7-ft. maiden grass; *M. sinensis* 'Gracillimus', which has narrow arching leaves and a conspicuous white midrib; 5- to 7-ft. 'Cabaret', whose broad leaves have a silver stripe; 5-ft 'Cosmopolitan', whose wide leaves have white margins; 4-ft. 'Morning Light', which is striped green and white and has a silvery look. In larger landscapes we like 6- to 8-ft. silver zebra grass, 'Zebrinus', a striking upright grass banded horizontally; refined 6- to 8-ft. 'Silver Feather' ('Silberfeder'), which bears beautiful silver plumes. Giant silver grass, *M. floridulus*, is a wide-leaved coarse species 10 to 14 ft. tall that fills with silvery light when the wind catches it.

Feather Reed Grass

Calamagrostis × acutiflora 'Karl Foerster'

When, Where, and How to Plant

Set out dormant, container-grown plants as soon as the ground can be worked in late winter. It requires full sun: without enough light the flower heads will flop over. A pH range of between 6.0 and 7.0 suits feather reed grass. It grows well in dry or wet soil and isn't particular as to fertility. See Soil Preparation and Planting in the Introduction. Provide generous planting holes and set the plants an inch above ground level and about 2 ft. apart. Water well. Mulch 2 in. deep around and between the plants.

Growing Tips

If the plants are in dry soil, water every week or two the first month, or until you see signs of vigorous growth.

Care

Allow the seedheads to ripen and stand through fall and winter. Toward the end of January, cut the plant back to the crown. Trim it earlier if storms flatten the flowering stems. Replenish the mulch. Feather reed grass grows rapidly during cool weather, but in hot, dry periods it may sulk. Do not try to force growth by watering or fertilizing. The plants will not need dividing for eight to ten years or more. When they do, dig the crowns, and chop them apart with an axe. You can divide and replant this grass in spring, but not in summer or fall.

Companion Planting and Design

In a smaller landscape, we like this grass in mass plantings. It's beautiful as a specimen or a hedge against a masonry wall and also lovely interplanted among shrubs and evergreens. Its meadowy autumn golds are beautiful backing black-eyed Susans, sedum 'Autumn Joy', pale- and dark-purple asters, and boltonia, and fronting taller varieties of *Miscanthus*.

Our Personal Recommendation

In a very small garden, a good choice would be *C. × acutiflora* 'Overdam', which has arching, white-striped foliage about 1 ft. high. Its flowers are 3-ft. pink plumes that age to gold. It requires some shade in hot regions.

The feather reed grass 'Karl Foerster', named the Perennial Plant Association Plant of the Year in 2001, is an upright cool-season grass that shoots up after its winter haircut, and remains attractive through hot summers. The seeds are sterile, so it never is invasive. Most of the spring the plant is a solid mass of medium- to dark-green foliage. By the time the late-blooming daffodils have gone it is 4 ft. tall and producing pale, feathery, bronze-purple, foot-long panicles of florets that stand straight up on wiry green stems and gradually turn tan colored. With the coming of frost, the foliage fades to gold and platinum and, unless winter storms flatten the stems, it remains really beautiful until it is cut back.

Bloom Period and Seasonal Color

In spring purple-tinted flower heads that change to tan; with frost the foliage fades to gold and platinum.

Mature Height × Spread

5 to 6 ft. × 20 in.

Fountain Grass

Pennisetum alopecuroides

Fountain grass is a beautiful, medium-tall, finely textured grass that produces dense, graceful clumps of cascading foliage. A warm-season grass, it begins its growth at tulip time and is considered by many to be the best ornamental grass for use in perennial gardens. When fountain grass begins to fade in fall, it still maintains a real presence in the garden. In summer, flowering stems rise topped by slender, cascading rose-tan to maroon foxtails that nod and toss in the slightest breeze. Exceptionally graceful and beautiful in flower, it also is lovely in winter when it blanches to the color of silvery wheat. Fountain grass sprawls, so it needs space all around. A single plant makes an impressive show and a trio is spectacular.

Other Names
Chinese Pennisetum, Swamp Foxtail Grass

Bloom Period and Seasonal Color
Rose-tan to maroon foxtails in summer, fading with the foliage to a silvery wheat shade.

Mature Height × Spread
3 to 4 ft. × 2 to 3 ft.

When, Where, and How to Plant

Set out container-grown plants in mid-spring. Fountain grass will be fullest and most colorful growing where it receives at least six hours of sun daily; in warm Zone 8, it succeeds in bright shade. A pH range of between 6.0 and 7.0 suits it well. It thrives in a site with good drainage and moist, fertile soil. See Soil Preparation and Planting in the Introduction. For a ground cover, space the plants 2 ft. apart; to grow fountain grass as a specimen, allow 3 ft. all around. Set the plants an inch or so above ground level. Water well. Mulch 2 in. deep around and between the plants.

Growing Tips

Water a new planting every week the first season. Once established, local rainfall should be enough to keep fountain grass growing except during droughts. But if it goes dry it will be less beautiful.

Care

Allow the seedheads to ripen and stand through winter—in a moist situation they may self-sow. Wait until late winter to cut the plant back to ground level. Trim it back earlier if it becomes less appealing. Replenish the mulch in late winter. Divide and replant this grass in spring before heat comes. Dig the crown, cut it apart, and replant. Fountain grass is considered winter hardy where temperatures do not fall below 5 degrees Fahrenheit; if your winter wind-chill factor goes below that, protect the plants with a cover of ever-green branches or leaves.

Companion Planting and Design

Beautiful naturalized with asters, black-eyed Susans, sedums, and small flowering trees. You can use it in gardens of large perennials for texture and color. Position it so the new growth will camouflage yellowing bulb foliage and fill spaces left empty as poppies and other spring perennials go by.

Our Personal Recommendations

'Little Bunny' is the smallest cultivar, a graceful little fountain grass about 16 in. with green foliage and tan-gold foxtails, which can be used as a ground cover. Oriental fountain grass, *P. orientale*, is a dainty form 18-in. high, which is grown as an annual in Zones 7 and 8.

Japanese Blood Grass
Imperata cylindrica 'Red Baron'

When, Where, and How to Plant

Set out container-grown plants or root divisions in mid-spring. Japanese blood grass is most colorful when it receives direct sun at least part of the day, but it will grow well in light shade. In our hottest region, the shore near the border of North Carolina, it may do better in semi-sun. Though it needs fairly constant moisture, Japanese blood grass also requires good drainage, so avoid planting it in soggy places. Japanese blood grass prefers soils in the slightly acid to neutral range, pH 6.0 to 7.5. See Soil Preparation and Planting in the Introduction. Provide generous planting holes, space the plants 12 to 18 in. apart, and set them about an inch above ground level. Water well. Mulch 2 in. deep around and between the plants.

Growing Tips

Water a new planting every week or two the first season. To keep the grass thriving, maintain soil moisture at the roots and let the surface dry between waterings.

Care

Japanese blood grass requires moist soil, so even after the plants are established and spreading, water when late-summer drought stresses your flowers. This warm-season grass will start new growth only when winter is over, so wait until early spring to cut the plants back to the crowns. Fertilize with a light application of slow-release organic fertilizer. Replenish the mulch until the plants have spread widely enough to shade out weeds. To multiply, divide the plants before new growth begins. Lift and gently break or cut the clump apart, giving each section at least one growing point.

Companion Planting and Design

We like Japanese blood grass as edging for a bed of taller ornamental grasses. It's a nice lead-in to a naturalized area, and an excellent ground cover for an informal landscape. An interesting grouping is Japanese blood grass planted with low-growing very textural plants such as leather-leaved burgundy bergenia, and fuzzy, silvery stachys. An attractive companion is the golden-leaved meadow foxtail, *Alopecurus pratensis* 'Aureus'.

Our Personal Recommendation

'Red Baron' is our favorite cultivar.

'Red Baron' is a short, coarse grass that starts out tipped wine-red then toward fall turns blood red and almost translucent. It is gorgeous when backlit by the sun. A spiky warm-season grass, it doesn't start to re-grow until mid-spring, then heads up quickly, producing unremarkable flowers, and peaks during the dog days of late August. It can stand a lot of heat. The plants become established slowly and spread at a moderate rate. Like other grasses that start growing only as the weather warms, we like to interplant it with medium to tall spring-flowering bulbs whose foliage will screen the stubble while the grass is dormant, and in turn will be screened by the grass when it starts to grow.

Bloom Period and Seasonal Color

Insignificant flowers; in late summer the grass becomes blood red and seems translucent.

Mature Height × Spread

1 to 1 1/2 ft. × 1 to 1 1/2 ft.

Northern Sea Oats
Chasmanthium latifolium

This is a beautiful tall woodland grass that grows in narrow, upright clumps and produces fresh green leaves that, like bamboo leaves, are held perpendicular at intervals on stiff wiry stems. It is a warm-season grass. Though northern sea oats reach maximum size when they are growing in full sun, they also flourish in semi-shade at the edge of woodlands, and in the shadow of tall buildings. The flower heads are eye-catching spikelets of flat fruits with oat-like heads. As much as an inch wide and an inch long, they are green in summer and gradually mature to shades of pink and copper. Spangled over wiry drooping stems that stand well above the foliage, they rustle and shimmer in a breeze.

Other Names
River Oats, Wild Oats, *Uniola latifolia*

Bloom Period and Seasonal Color
Seed heads green in summer, gradually changing to pink and copper.

Mature Height × Spread
3 to 4 ft. × 2 to 3 ft.

When, Where, and How to Plant
Set out container-grown plants of this warm season grass in mid-spring as the ground begins to warm. It will be fullest and most colorful growing where it receives at least six hours of sun daily. It thrives in partial shade, but the less light it receives the more it will sprawl. A pH range of between 6.0 and 7.0 suits it and it does best where the soil has sustained moisture without being soggy. It does, however, tolerate dry soil. See Soil Preparation and Planting in the Introduction. If the soil is sandy, work in 25 percent compost, peat moss, chopped leaves, or other organic material. Provide generous planting holes 2 to 3 ft. apart. Set the plants about an inch above ground level and water well. Mulch 2 in. deep around and between the plants.

Growing Tips
To encourage rapid growth, water a new planting every week the first season. Once established, local rainfall should be enough to keep northern sea oats growing except during droughts, but it spreads most quickly if it doesn't dry out.

Care
Allow the seedheads to ripen and stand through fall and winter. This warm-season grass will start new growth only when the cold has ended, so wait until late winter to cut the plant back to the crown. Trim the plant back earlier if storms flatten the stems, or it becomes less appealing. Replenish the mulch in late winter until the plants have spread widely enough to shade out weeds. Sea oats self-sows in the right environment, so you may have to rogue out the volunteers.

Companion Planting and Design
Northern sea oats is an excellent transitional plant that can be positioned to create screening. It looks best planted in groups, even massed. Ornamental plants that flourish in the same environment include Japanese anemone, lobelia, and toad lily. Sea oats are especially lovely growing on a slope where the seed heads can catch the light and be seen against a darker background.

Our Personal Recommendation
Plant the species.

Switch Grass
Panicum virgatum 'Heavy Metal'

When, Where, and How to Plant
Switch grass develops from rhizomatous roots and spreads quickly. Set out container-grown plants or root divisions in mid-spring or early fall. It will be most colorful where it receives direct sun. Though it thrives with fairly constant moisture, switch grass is so deeply rooted it can withstand drought, as well as high heat and bitter cold. Any well-worked soil will do, and it is tolerant of sandy soils. See Soil Preparation and Planting in the Introduction. Provide generous planting holes and space the plants 16 to 18 in. apart. Water well. Mulch 2 in. deep around and between the plants.

Growing Tips
Water a new planting every week or two the first season. The grass will do well if you maintain soil moisture at the roots even if the surface is dry between waterings.

Care
Switch grass does best in moist soil, so even after the plants are established and spreading, water when late-summer drought stresses your flowers. This warm-season grass will start new growth only when winter is over, so wait until early spring to cut the plant back to 4 to 5 in. above the crown. Fertilize with a light application of slow-release organic fertilizer. Replenish the mulch in late winter until the plants have spread widely enough to shade out weeds. To multiply, divide the plants in early spring before new growth begins. Lift and gently break or cut the clump apart, giving each section a few growing points.

Companion Planting and Design
Naturalize switch grass with flowers that stand some neglect, such as daffodils, foxtail lilies, species tulips, Joe Pye weed, black-eyed Susan, asters, boltonia, and sedums. It is attractive planted as a specimen, and quite beautiful set out in large sweeps in transitional spaces.

Our Personal Recommendations
'Heavy Metal' is one of the most beautiful of the grasses that add a strong blue accent to the landscape—and you can plant it where the drainage isn't very good, a definite advantage! 'Rot Braun' is an excellent green foliaged cultivar.

North American switch grass, a prairie native, is an upright, narrow, arching, clump-forming warm-season grass that lifts a mist-like ethereal cloud of pale blooms on 4- to 5-ft. stalks in summer. The inflorescences are spikelets on long open panicles held high above the foliage. With frost the foliage turns a warm gold; that color and its handsome structure remain until cut back. In the garden we plant the 5-ft.-tall cultivar 'Heavy Metal' whose leaves are a beautiful metallic blue green; the flowers are tinged pink and the upright structure is useful for introducing contrast into the garden. The species itself occurs naturally in most of the country and is an excellent choice for naturalizing.

Bloom Period and Seasonal Color
In summer 'Heavy Metal' produces pink inflorescences; flowers and foliage are gold in fall and winter.

Mature Height × Spread
5 ft. × 2 to 3 ft.

Perennials *for the Mid-Atlantic*

Perennial flower and foliage plants give our gardens continuity. Annuals live one season. Some perennials come back for just a few years, but many live ten to fifteen, and peonies can go on for more than 100 years. When we're planning a garden, our first selections are hardy perennial flowers whose sequence of bloom will carry color through the bed all season long. Within most species' stated bloom period, you can find varieties that come into flower early, midseason, or late. To avoid late spring frostbite in cool regions, choose late-blooming varieties of spring-flowering species; where frosts can come early in fall, choose early-blooming varieties of perennials that bloom in late summer. Most hardy perennials are resistant to frosts unless temperatures go below freezing, 32 degrees Fahrenheit.

Once we've chosen the flowers for a garden, we look for foliage plants that will complement or contrast with the flowers. Colorful foliage—silver, blue, yellow, or red—placed to reinforce, or to contrast with, the colors of nearby flowers, add depth to the design. Think of the effect of spiky globe thistle and furry lamb's ears. Two lovely blue foliage plants are the blue-green rue 'Jackman's Blue', and blue oat grass. Variegated foliage lightens the greens. At a distance, white variegated foliage appears jade green or soft gray; yellow looks like a splash of sunshine or a flower. We add ferns for the romance they lend to shaded

Summer perennial border, with Daylilies, Monarda, Baby's Breath, and Statice.

spots. And ornamental grasses tall and
small that dance, whisper, and bring sound
and movement as well as contrasting texture to the garden.

In a large mixed border we include
the big leaves and striking architectural
forms of a few bold-foliaged perennials,
like the big hostas, brunnera, and
rodgersia. Giant tropical foliage plants—
dwarf canna and the hardy banana—add a
hint of mystery. These "tender perennials"
won't winter over, but the effect they
create is worthwhile. We also like to set

Poppy 'Pinnacle'

two or three dwarf needled evergreens in strategic places. Their solid forms and strong color anchor
flower beds in early spring and, with the ornamental grasses, they maintain a sense of life when the
garden falls asleep.

Finally, we look for places to tuck in a few aromatic herbs and very fragrant flowers. Low-growing,
fuzzy, white-splashed pineapple mint and silver variegated thyme lighten the bed and release their
fragrance as you brush by. Aggressive plants like the mints can be set out in buried containers. Some
flowering bulbs and many important perennials have fragrant varieties. The most fragrant of the spring
flowers are the hyacinths. The Oriental lilies, especially pure white 'Casa Blanca', spread a fantastic
perfume. 'Myrtle Gentry' is a scented peony. Many tall bearded irises are fragrant, as are some daylilies
including 'Fragrant Light'.

When, Where, and How to Plant

If you are interested in experimenting with a flowering meadow or a wild garden, you'll need hundreds
of plants. Try your hand at starting the perennials indoors from seed. (See Starting Seeds Indoors, in the
Introduction.) Plants that are the species, rather than an improved or named variety, will come true from
seed. But when you want named varieties, we strongly recommend you choose container-grown perennials
grown from root divisions and rooted cuttings. Here's why: the named varieties (hybrids and cultivars)
are superior flowers selected from among thousands planted. Growers propagate them from cuttings or
root divisions and so they bloom true to the parent plants. André's motto is, "plant less and grow the
best." Buy one plant, divide it into three plants, repeat for three years and you will have twenty-seven
plants, in five years 243 plants ad infinitum . . . so a perennial bed of the best can be inexpensive.

Perennials in 1-quart containers planted in the spring produce some blooms the first season; those
sold in 2- to 3-gallon containers will make a bigger show. Most container-grown plants can be set out
spring, summer, or fall. In the spring growers ship some perennials bare root—astilbes, for instance. These

often flower fully only the second or third season. A perennial that blooms early in the spring—columbine, for example—gives the best show its first year when it is planted the preceding late summer or early fall.

In clay and sandy soil the surest way to provide soil in which perennials will thrive for many years is to create a raised bed. In the Soil Preparation section of the Introduction you'll find instructions for creating a raised bed and for bringing the soil to pH 5.5 to 7.0, the range for most flowers. André's recipe for a raised bed includes long-lasting organic fertilizers. See the Appendix for more information on fertilizers.

The spacing of perennials depends on the size the mature plant will be; we've offered suggestions with each plant. Always provide a generous planting hole, one twice the width and as deep as the rootball. Before you plant a container-grown perennial, unwind roots that may be circling the rootball, or make shallow vertical slashes in the mass, and cut off the bottom $1/2$ inch of soil and rootball. Soak the rootball in a big bucket containing starter solution. Then set the plant in the hole, fill the hole with soil, and tamp firmly. Water slowly and deeply, then mulch around the planting following our suggestions in the Introduction. Staking protects very tall flowers like lilies in a storm. But most others, if correctly fertilized and given plenty of space all around, won't need it. Tall, weak growth is often the result of force-feeding with non-organic fertilizers. Wide spacing also improves air circulation, reducing the risk of disease and mildew! Water a new planting slowly and deeply, every week or ten days for a month or so unless you have soaking rains. And water any time the plants show signs of wilting.

Care

After summer, we like to leave in place seed-bearing perennials with woody upright structures, like black-eyed Susans, because they look interesting in winter, and to feed the birds. Some self-sow and will refurnish the planting. In late fall we clear away collapsed foliage that will grow slimy after frost. When you remove dead foliage, cut it off, don't pull it off because that may damage the crown beneath. In late winter or early spring, after the soil has dried somewhat, it is time to clear away the remains of last year's dead foliage; watch out for tender burgeoning new stems while raking through perennials such as lilies. Every year in spring, and again in September to October, we fertilize established perennial beds, not individual plants, by broadcasting a slow-release organic fertilizer in sunny areas, and a similar fertilizer for acid-loving plants in shaded areas.

Dividing for Productivity

To remain productive and showy, some perennials should be divided and replanted every four or five years. Dividing also gives you plants for the development of new gardens and to give away as gifts. On the plant pages that follow we explain when each is likely to need dividing. But the perennials themselves indicate when the time has come: the stems become crowded and leggy, the roots become matted, and there are fewer and smaller blooms. As to timing, the rule of thumb is to divide spring-flowering perennials a month before the ground will freeze in the fall, or before new growth begins in early spring; divide autumn-flowering perennials, such as chrysanthemums, in spring before any sign of growth appears. More specific instructions are given with each plant.

Other Choices

The perennials described in this chapter are the best of the best for Mid-Atlantic gardens. Other perennials that we think very highly of include:

Adam's Needle, *Yucca filamentosa* 'Bright Edge'

Bellflower, *Campanula carpatica, C. persicifolia, C. poscharskyana*

Blazing Star, Gayfeather, *Liatris spicata* 'Kobold'

Brunnera, *Brunnera macrophylla*

Butterfly Weed, *Asclepias tuberosa*

Candytuft, *Iberis sempervirens* hybrids

Catmint, *Nepeta faassenii*

Foxglove, *Digitalis* spp. and hybrids

Geranium, *Geranium* spp. and cultivars

Goatsbeard, *Aruncus dioicus*

Goldenrod, *Solidago* spp. and hybrids

Heliopsis, *Heliopsis helianthoides* cultivars

Lungwort, *Pulmonaria* spp. and hybrids

Meadow Rue, *Thalictrum aquilegifolium, T. flavum* ssp. *glaucum, T. rochebrunnianum*

Mist Flower, Hardy Ageratum, *Eupatorium coelestinum*

Southernwood, *Artemisia abrotanum*; Silver King Artemisia, *A. ludoviciana* var. *albula*

Speedwell, *Veronica* spp. and hybrids

Spurge, *Euphorbia epithymoides, E. dulcis, E. griffithii*

Stokes' Aster, *Stokesia laevis* cultivars

Tickseed, *Coreopsis* spp. and cultivars

Hostas beside a woodland pond.

Astilbe
Astilbe × arendsii

The shade-loving astilbes are beautiful plants whose flowers are tall, graceful plumes composed of masses of small florets in mostly pastel shades. The deeply cut, fernlike, green or bronzed foliage is attractive both before and after flowering; with the years, plantings spread to make large, dense mats. Cut, the flowers are lasting, and they dry well. Although most astilbes flower from June through the middle of July, you can achieve a lasting show of color by planting early, midseason, and late bloomers. For instance: plant the white early-blooming favorite 'Deutschland', red 'Fanal', and pink 'Europa', with mid-season 'Ostrich Plume' ('Straussenfeder'), and late bloomers such as the lilac 'Superba' and 'Pumila'.

Bloom Period and Seasonal Color
Late spring and early summer; creamy white, pale pink, lilac, coral, red.

Mature Height × Spread
1 to 3 and 5 ft. × 2 to 3 ft.

When, Where, and How to Plant
Catalogs ship bare-root astilbe crowns in early spring. Follow their planting instructions and be patient. For a quick show, set out container-grown astilbe plants in mid-spring or late summer. Astilbe grows best in light shade in well-drained, rich, moist humusy soil. In full sun, it can succeed if the soil never dries out. Although *A. chinensis* tolerates drought, most astilbes need adequate moisture, but they suffer if soil is soggy in winter. Slightly acid pH is best. See Soil Preparation in the Introduction. Follow the planting instructions at the beginning of this chapter, spacing the plants about 18 in. to 3 ft. apart, according to the size of the variety. Water well. Mulch 2 to 3 in. deep starting 3 in. from the crown.

Growing Tips
Water astilbes deeply every week to ten days unless you have a soaking rain. The keys to success—particularly in the warmer reaches of the Mid-Atlantic—are sustained moisture and summer mulches.

Care
Fertilize the bed between late winter and early spring, and again in September to October, with a slow-release organic fertilizer for acid-loving plants. We don't deadhead since the drying flower spikes are attractive. In spring replenish the mulch. You can divide astilbe crowns every three years if you wish, between early spring and August.

Companion Planting and Design
Astilbes are excellent fillers for the middle or back of the border and lovely edging a woodland path, stream, or pond. Massed, astilbes in a range of colors make a lovely low tapestry of color. In summer and early fall the little Chinese astilbes, *A. chinensis* 'Pumila', raise tall mauve-pink flower heads; they spread rapidly by underground stolons and are very attractive as edging or ground cover in part shade.

Our Personal Recommendation
Our favorite is little *A. simplicifolia* 'Sprite', the 1994 Perennial Plant Association Plant of the Year. It has much-divided, bright green foliage, masses of light-pink florets borne on slightly pendulous panicles, followed by attractive rust-colored seed-heads. The total height of the plant is 12 in. It begins blooming in midsummer and continues for several weeks.

Balloon Flower
Platycodon grandiflorus 'Mariesii'

When, Where, and How to Plant
Sow balloon flower seeds following the instructions on the seed packet in early to mid-spring, mark the place, and be patient. Balloon flower is one of the last plants to come up from seed. For more immediate results, set out container-grown plants or root divisions any time after the ground can be worked in spring. Balloon flower succeeds in full sun in the cooler regions of Zone 6, and in semi-sun in Zones 7 and 8. It needs well-drained soil, tolerates almost any pH, and does well in dry city conditions and by the shore. See Soil Preparation in the Introduction. If you are setting out container-grown plants, follow the planting instructions at the beginning of this chapter, spacing the plants about 2 ft. apart. Water well. Provide a permanent 2-in. mulch starting 3 in. from the crown.

Growing Tips
Water new plants deeply every week the first season unless you have a good soaking rain. Balloon flower is drought resistant, so once it's established, local rainfall will be enough to keep it growing.

Care
Fertilize the bed between late winter or early spring, and again in September to October, with a slow-release organic fertilizer for acid-loving plants. In spring replenish the mulch. Deadhead to promote flowering. Balloon flower rarely needs dividing.

Companion Planting and Design
Use balloon flower to keep blue in the perennial bed all summer. We use it in place of the somewhat similar campanula, which fails regularly in our hot summers.

Our Personal Recommendations
We are very taken with an 8-in.-high dwarf balloon flower, *P. grandiflorus* 'Sentimental Blue', which is perfect for a rock garden or the front of the flower border. Others we like are *P. grandiflorus* 'Apoyama', which bears violet flowers on plants 15 to 18 in. tall, and is very attractive planted with herbs. The Fuji series, a Japanese strain, is one of the best for the cutting garden; the cut flowers are long-lasting if the stems are seared before they're put in water.

Old-fashioned balloon flower is a graceful, easy perennial, one of the best summer bloomers. This outstanding 1- to 2-ft.-tall variety produces distinctive balloon-shaped buds along wand-like stems that open to starry flowers up to 2 in. across. There are double varieties. An excellent cut flower, fresh or dried, it blooms freely from early summer to early fall and has glossy foliage. In a test conducted in Zones 7 and 8 over a five-year period, both at the shore and 600 ft. from the ocean, the balloon flower gave an excellent performance. It was grown in pure sand with Osmocote® and fertilized once yearly. The plantings were deeply watered 3 times each month, June through October, but not at all November through May.

Other Name
Chinese Bellflower

Bloom Period and Seasonal Color
Early summer to early fall; blue, white, or lilac-pink.

Mature Height × Spread
1 to 2 ft. × 2 to 3 ft.

Bleeding Heart
Dicentra spp. and cultivars

The bleeding hearts are old-fashioned, shade-loving plants named for the shape of the blossom—pretty pink, white, or red heart-shaped flowers that dangle from arching stems above beautiful lacy foliage. The loveliest flower is borne by the Asian species D. spectabilis, a shrub-like, spring flowering perennial that grows to 36 in. across and bears up to twenty or more arching racemes from which dangle perfect little pink or white hearts. It is long-lived, a true aristocrat, though the foliage dies back when heat comes. The native fringed, or wild, bleeding hearts, D. formosa from the Western U.S., and D. eximia from the East, are smaller ever-blooming species that flower throughout the summer and until frost; they are a better choice where summers are really hot.

Bloom Period and Seasonal Color
Spring, or summer to fall, depending on the species; D. spectabilis—cherry red and white; D. formosa and D. eximia—pink, cultivars white.

Mature Height × Spread
D. spectabilis—2 ft. × 3 ft.
D. formosa and D. eximia—9 to 24 in. × 18 in.

When, Where, and How to Plant
The best time for planting bleeding hearts, container grown, is just as active growth begins in early spring. Bright shade is ideal. In cool areas where soil moisture is retained evenly, bleeding hearts accept some exposure to full sun. They do best in well-drained, rich, moist, humusy soil in the pH range of 5.0 to 6.0. See Soil Preparation in the Introduction. Follow the planting instructions at the beginning of this chapter. Space planting holes for old-fashioned bleeding hearts 2 ft. apart; space holes for wild bleeding hearts 15 to 18 in. apart. Water well. Provide a permanent 3-in. mulch starting 3 in. from the crown.

Growing Tips
Water bleeding hearts deeply every week to ten days for a month or so unless you have a soaking rain. The keys to a long bloom period—particularly in the warmer reaches of the Mid-Atlantic—are sustained moisture and mulch.

Care
Fertilize the bed between late winter and early spring, and again in late September to October, with a slow-release, organic, acid fertilizer. In spring, replenish the mulch. When the foliage of the old-fashioned species looks ragged, cut the plant back to the ground. Cutting flowering stems of wild bleeding heart that have finished blooming prolongs flowering; wait for several killing frosts before cutting back the foliage entirely. In spring, if late frosts threaten, cover bleeding hearts with Remay cloth, old blankets, or burlap. The roots are brittle so divide bleeding hearts only if needed. Established plants resent being disturbed but with care they can be successfully divided in early spring.

Companion Planting and Design
Delightful massed in shady gardens, especially *D. spectabilis*, among ferns, hostas, and Solomon's seal, with wildflowers, and in rock gardens.

Our Personal Recommendations
For its lasting foliage, we recommend *D. formosa*. Our favorite cultivars are 12-in. white 'Aurora'; 15-in. pink 'Bountiful'; 15-in. deep pink 'Luxuriant'; and 'King of Hearts', a clear deep pink.

122

Blue False Indigo
Baptisia australis

When, Where, and How to Plant

Baptisia seeds are fresh when they first start to rattle around in the pod; plant fresh seeds in late summer if you want to start from scratch. Setting out root divisions of young plants in early spring is recommended because baptisia is slow to establish itself and doesn't transplant easily. Baptisia does best in full sun, but it can take a little filtered shade and still be productive. In partial shade it probably will require staking, or support from a peony ring. It tolerates drought but cannot stand soil that is soggy in winter. Blue false indigo thrives in humusy, somewhat acid soil, pH range 5.5 to 6.5, but can tolerate higher pH. See Soil Preparation in the Introduction. Follow the planting instructions at the beginning of this chapter, spacing the plants about 3 ft. apart. Water well. Mulch 1 in. deep starting 3 in. from the crown.

Growing Tip

Water new plants deeply every week to ten days the first month or so unless you have a soaking rain.

Care

Fertilize the bed between late winter and early spring, and again in September to October, with a slow-release, organic, acid fertilizer. In spring replenish the mulch. If you cut the plant back by a third after flowering, it will fill in a few weeks later and become a handsome background "shrub" for the flower bed. But you lose the seed pods. Removing spent flowers may encourage a few more blooms, but we like to let the end-of-season flower spikes remain for a fall and winter show. Cut baptisia to the ground when frosts blacken the foliage. You needn't divide it for ten years or more unless you want to multiply your holdings.

Companion Planting and Design

Baptisia's medium-tall mound of foliage and its indigo-blue flowers create strong vertical lines at the middle or back of a large flowering border. It's one of those very substantial plants used to anchor other flowers, and an excellent meadow plant.

Our Personal Recommendation

Plant the species.

Baptisia is a bold, 3- to 4-ft. plant that in early spring produces multiple stems of beautiful gray-green foliage. By mid-spring the foliage is topped by 1- to 2-ft. flowering spikes that are a magnificent indigo-blue. The flowers last about a month. The leaves and the individual blossoms resemble those of the pea vine but they are much larger, showier, and more substantial. Handsome blue-black seed pods, 1 or 2 in. long, follow the flowers and usually remain handsome until at least the first hard frost. They're lovely in dried arrangements. Baptisia is a long-lived perennial—a little slow to get under way but it seems to go on practically forever. And it's a great indigo-blue flower for climates too hot to grow delphinium. A related species, B. pendula, has white flowers, and a cross between the two, called 'Purple Smoke', has purplish flowers and lavender-gray stems.

Other Names
Plains False Indigo, Wild Blue Indigo, Baptisia

Bloom Period and Seasonal Color
Mid-spring; indigo blue.

Mature Height × Spread
3 to 4 ft. × 4 ft.

Chrysanthemum
Dendranthema spp. and hybrids

For André, fall is not about potted mums sold for instant fall color. It's about pumpkins and gourds, ornamental grasses, trees and shrubs changing color, berries and witches and goblins, Halloween and Thanksgiving—and real chrysanthemums. For wherever color will be needed in September and October, André plants long-lived hardy mums like 'Ryan's Pink', the semi-double pink 'Mei Kyo', 'Pumpkin Harvest', pale pink 'Venus', and 'Viette's Apricot Glow'. For summer bouquets, the Viettes plant green-eyed Nippon daisies, Nipponanthemum nipponicum (Chrysanthemum nipponicum), *and sparkling white shasta daisies,* Leucanthemum × superbum (C. maximum). *Nippon daisies are great border flowers with handsome rhododendron-like foliage. Shastas are big, beautiful, single or double daisies. For edging, plant 12-in. tall* Dendranthema pacificum, *a ground cover mum whose leaves are edged thinly with silver.*

Other Names
Mum, Daisy, Shasta Daisy

Bloom Period and Seasonal Color
Nippon daisies bloom from September or October until frost; shasta daisies bloom in early summer; hardy mums bloom September and October. White and many colors.

Mature Height × Spread
Nippon Daisies—3 to 5 ft. × 3 ft.
Shasta Daisies—2 to 4 ft. × 3 to 4 ft.
Garden Mums—15 in. to 3 ft. × 3 to 5 ft.

When, Where, and How to Plant
Set out container-grown plants in early spring, in summer, or in early fall. Nippon daisies and single-flowered shastas need full sun; shasta doubles do well in light shade. The hardy mums tolerate some drought and cannot stand soil that is soggy in winter. A wide range of soil types are suitable but a slightly acid pH is best. See Soil Preparation in the Introduction. Follow the planting instructions at the beginning of this chapter, spacing the plants about 2 ft. apart. Water well. Mulch 2 in. deep starting 3 in. from the crown.

Growing Tip
For a month or so after planting, water deeply every week to ten days unless you have a good soaking rain.

Care
Fertilize the bed with a slow-release organic fertilizer for acid-loving plants between late winter and early spring, and again in early summer. Replenish the mulch. After the first flush of bloom, deadhead shastas back to the nearest side buds; when these have bloomed, cut the plants down to the basal foliage, which will remain attractive until frost. Mums need to be divided every two or three years to remain fully productive; the best time is early spring or after the plants become dormant in fall.

Companion Planting and Design
Nippon and shasta daisies are handsome in perennial beds and flowering borders. For edging, plant the beautiful 12-in. high ground cover mum, silver-edged *D. pacificum*. It spreads rapidly to make a 3 1/2 ft. mat, and bears very small tansy-like flowers in October. For glorious fall color, interplant perennials with hardy garden mums for September-October color.

Our Personal Recommendations
André's favorite shasta daisies are 2-ft. 'Switzerland', a big, long-lived beautiful Viette introduction that blooms in June and July; and long-blooming 'Ryan's White' which flowers from June to September. 'Becky' is another good single shasta.

Columbine
Aquilegia spp. and hybrids

When, Where, and How to Plant
Fresh seed gathered from plants and sown in late spring or early summer produces plants the following year. For bloom this year, in early spring set out container-grown plants or root divisions any time after the ground can be worked. In cool areas you can plant columbine in the fall. Columbines succeed in sun in areas where the climate is moderate, and prefer some noon shade in warm regions. They do well in shade gardens in Washington, D.C. *Aquilegia* needs well-drained, rich, evenly moist soil. See Soil Preparation in the Introduction. Follow the planting instructions at the beginning of this chapter, spacing the plants 12 to 15 in. apart in groups of at least 3 to 5. Taller varieties may need staking. Water well. Mulch 2 in. deep starting 3 in. from the crown.

Growing Tip
Water new plants deeply every week to ten days for a month or so unless you have a soaking rain.

Care
Fertilize the bed between late winter and early spring, and again in late September to October, with a slow-release organic fertilizer for acid-loving plants. Replenish the mulch. After the flowers have bloomed, cut the foliage way back, almost to the crown: it will grow back and make a beautiful low foliage filler for the rest of the season. Columbines generally live only four or five years, and need no dividing. They often self-sow; dig out those you don't want and transplant elsewhere.

Companion Planting and Design
The columbines do well in part shade, so they are often naturalized along sun-dappled paths through woodlands. The old-fashioned garden columbine, *A. vulgaris*, granny's bonnet, is a favorite cottage garden flower. The native eastern wild columbine, *A. canadensis*, can be resistant to the leaf minor that defaces the foliage of less hardy breeds; it self-sows so it's a good choice for naturalizing.

Our Personal Recommendations
Among our favorites are varieties of *A. flabellata*, the fan columbine, which grows to 8 to 10 in., needs no staking, and is longer lived than other species. 'Nora Barlow' is a beautiful dark-pink and white, double-flowered columbine.

The columbine is one of the most beautiful of our mid- to late spring and early summer flowers, loved as much for its foliage as for its long-lasting, intricate blossoms. These nodding or upright flowers, usually in two shades, end in graceful spurs, and they stand out against the fresh blue-green scalloped foliage. Superb hybrids are available in a variety of heights, and in many colors and amazing bi-colors. Some have huge spurs—'Spring Song', for example, and the Music series. There are double-flowered strains of columbine for perennial beds, and dwarfs, which are charming in a rock garden. The leaves make a beautiful addition to the foliage plants in a perennial border.

Bloom Period and Seasonal Color
Mid-spring to early summer; white, yellow, blue, rusty pinks, lavenders, purples, reddish orange, bi-colors.

Mature Height × Spread
1 to 3 ft. × 1 1/2 ft.

Coneflower

Rudbeckia fulgida var. *sullivantii* 'Goldsturm'

The showy perennial 'Goldsturm' is probably the finest of the yellow black-eyed Susan types. André's father, nurseryman Martin Viette, imported it from Germany forty years ago and André still loves it. It blooms freely throughout the midsummer and well into fall on compact, bushy plants 18 to 30 in. high. The ray florets are deep yellow and the cone-shaped centers bronze-black. The foliage stays in good condition no matter how hot it gets. 'Goldsturm' is such a superior performer it was chosen as the 1999 Plant of the Year by the Perennial Plant Association. It self-sows aggressively so it's a good choice for wild gardens. Removing spent blooms early in the flowering season encourages repeat flowering. The flowers dry well. Leave a few for the birds, for winter interest, and to reseed.

Other Name
Black-Eyed Susan

Bloom Period and Seasonal Color
Summer into fall; dark gold with a sooty eye.

Mature Height × Spread
$1^1/_2$ to $2^1/_2$ ft. × 2 to $2^1/_2$ ft.

When, Where, and How to Plant
You can plant coneflower from seedlings started indoors, or as seed in the open garden, any time after the ground can be worked in spring. But you will have bigger plants sooner if you set out container-grown plants or root divisions (friends often have coneflowers to share). *Rudbeckia* withstands high heat and thrives in full sun; in bright or partial shade it blooms well but tends to grow toward brighter light. A well-drained, light, and fertile soil is best, pH 5.0 to 6.5. See Soil Preparation in the Introduction. Follow the planting instructions at the beginning of this chapter, spacing the plants 8 to 12 in. apart. Water well. Mulch 2 in. deep starting 3 in. from the crown.

Growing Tip
Water a new planting deeply every week to ten days the first season unless you have a good soaking rain.

Care
Fertilize the bed between late winter and early spring, and again September to October, with a slow-release, organic, acid fertilizer. *Rudbeckia* is drought resistant, so once it's established, local rainfall will be enough to keep it growing. After the first flush of bloom, deadhead down to the next pair of buds. The cut stems last a few days in water. The plants are rhizomatous and spread, creating large colonies. Divide the planting in early spring every four years to keep the bed full and flowery.

Companion Planting and Design
'Goldsturm' self-sows and is a good naturalizer. A very tough plant that glows gold throughout the summer, it's an excellent edger for stands of ornamental grasses, for meadow gardens, and for hot, sunny flower borders. Let the sooty black seedheads stand when flowering begins to wind down as cold weather approaches, and you will be providing food for birds, and adding interest to the garden in the winter months.

Our Personal Recommendations
'Goldsturm' is our first choice. Mark has introduced a new coneflower edger, *R. speciosa* 'Viette's Little Suzy', just 12 to 14 in. tall whose foliage turns a lovely mahogany in cold weather.

Coral Bells
Heuchera spp. and hybrids

When, Where, and How to Plant
Set out container plants or root divisions any time after the ground can be worked in spring. Plants that are still near-dormant or just beginning to grow will give the best performance. 'Palace Purple' can stand more direct sun in the cool reaches of Zone 6, but it needs noon protection from hot sun in Zones 7 and 8. *Heuchera* is drought-resistant, but the leaves scorch if the plant dries out. It needs well-drained slightly acid soil, pH 5.5 to 6.5. See Soil Preparation in the Introduction. Follow the planting instructions at the beginning of this chapter, spacing the plants 12 to 18 in. apart. Water well. Mulch 2 to 3 in. deep starting 3 in. from the crown.

Growing Tip
The first month or so water new plants deeply every week to ten days unless you have a good soaking rain.

Care
In cold climates, mulch with branches of evergreens after the first solid frost. Fertilize the bed between late winter and early spring, and again in September to October, with a slow-release organic fertilizer for acid-loving plants. *Heuchera* is fairly drought-resistant, so water when you water the other perennials. Deadhead if you want to prolong the flowering. If your main interest is the foliage, removing the flowers before they grow makes for a better-looking plant. In late summer cut off leaves that are less than perfect and allow the new foliage to develop and stay for winter. Divide every four or five years in early spring.

Companion Planting and Design
Heuchera foliage is low to the ground, so the plant is used at the front of a flower border, or to edge a path, whether the plant is being grown for its foliage or its flowers.

Our Personal Recommendations
'Palace Purple' is our favorite for foliage, but *H. villosa* 'Purpurea' comes close. July to October, panicles of blush pink bells sway in every breeze above the glowing purple foliage. 'White Cloud' blooms May to July, and bears white flowers. Other wonderful varieties are 'Cathedral Windows' and 'Pewter Veil'.

In late spring and early summer, coral bells' dainty, eye-catching panicles of tiny bell-shaped flowers sway on 1- to 2-ft. wiry stalks arching high above the foliage. The Bressingham hybrids bloom in shades of coral to deep red, pink, and white. The leaves of the species are low-growing, evergreen, dark green scalloped clusters that remain attractive most of the year. But these days the excitement generated by Heuchera has to do with cultivars with colorful foliage. In 1991 H. micrantha 'Palace Purple' was named Plant of the Year by the Perennial Plant Association. It introduced a Heuchera planted primarily for its foliage. 'Palace Purple' has ivy-shaped leaves that are mahogany-red above, beet-red below, and is especially handsome with the tans and reds that dominate in the fall. The flowers are off-white.

Other Name
Alumroot

Bloom Period and Seasonal Color
May to July; coral, deep red, pink, white.

Mature Height × Spread
15 to 20 in. × 18 to 20 in.

Daylily
Hemerocallis spp. and hybrids

Daylilies, André's favorite summer flower, bloom July through August in the gardens surrounding the Viette home in the Shenandoah Valley, and thousands more flower in the trial fields below the nursery. Enhanced performance has given rise to a whole new breed of these easy-care, long-lived flowers. The blossoms range from 2¹/₂ in. to huge 8-in. trumpets. Large-flowered daylilies typically open one to three blossoms per stem every day; the miniatures open three to seven blossoms per stem every day. The daylilies classed as tetraploids have intense color, heavily textured petals, and strong stems—'Viette's Cranberry Red' and 'Viracocho' are examples. Those labeled as diploids are showy but smaller—'Stella de Oro', the miniature famous for its everblooming quality, is a diploid.

Bloom Period and Seasonal Color
June through September; near white, creamy yellows, oranges, golds, purples, pinks, fiery reds, lavenders, bi-colors.

Mature Height × Spread
Standards: 2 to 4 ft. (a few reach 5 ft.) × 2 to 4 ft.
Miniatures: 12 to 14 in. (some reach 40 in.) × 1¹/₂ to 2 ft.

When, Where, and How to Plant
The best planting time is spring. Soak tuberous roots for two to six hours before planting. You can plant container-grown daylilies any time, but early spring is best. Daylilies are adaptable. They will bloom most fully in full sun but also bloom well in bright shade. They thrive in clay, loam, or sandy soils, and tolerate heat, wind, cold, and seashore conditions. See Soil Preparation in the Introduction. If you are planting bare-root plants, fan the roots out in the planting hole, and set the crown so it is about 1 in. below the soil surface. Plant container-grown daylilies following the planting instructions at the beginning of this chapter. Space daylilies 24 in. apart. Water well. Mulch with pine needles, pine bark, or hardwood bark 2 to 3 in. deep starting 3 in. from the crown.

Growing Tips
Water deeply every week for the first two weeks. Once the plants are growing well, water deeply in lasting droughts.

Care
After a couple of hard frosts, remove the foliage. In mid-fall and again in late winter fertilize established beds with a slow-release organic fertilizer. Maintain the mulch. Water in prolonged periods of drought. Divide in mid-spring or early fall every four to five years.

Companion Planting and Design
With daylilies André likes *Rudbeckia,* ornamental grasses, sunny *Heliopsis* and *Helianthus*, *Crocosmia*, and poppies. Other good companion plants are fall-blooming asters and mums that take over as the daylilies begin to fade away.

Our Personal Recommendations
For a long season of bloom, look for "re-bloomer" daylilies which flower early, and again in late summer or early fall, or from summer into frost, such as 'Happy Returns'. For a small garden, André recommends little 'Stella de Oro' that bears somewhat fragrant 2³/₄-in. gold flowers with green throats. A three-year-old plant produces literally hundreds of blooms. Among daylilies with a marked fragrance are 'Fragrant Light', 'Hyperion', 'Lemon Cap', and the species *H. citrina*. The daylilies billed as evergreen are most successful in the frost-free areas of the South.

Globe Thistle
Echinops ritro 'Taplow Blue'

When, Where, and How to Plant
Set out container-grown plants in spring. Globe thistle blooms fully given six hours of full sun, and benefits from afternoon shade, especially in warmer regions. *Echinops* is not particular as to soil pH, as long as the soil is well drained. It spreads in moist, rich soil, which may or may not be a blessing. See Soil Preparation and Planting in the Introduction. Follow the planting instructions at the beginning of this chapter, spacing the plants 20 to 24 in. apart. Water well. Mulch 2 to 3 in. deep starting 3 in. from the crown.

Growing Tip
Water new plants deeply every week or ten days for the first month or so unless you have a soaking rain.

Care
Established globe thistles tolerate drought. To encourage reblooming, deadhead flowering stems back by a third or half, to a pair of basal leaves; if cut back twice they often bloom a third time. At the end of the season leave the flower heads for the birds. In early spring cut back to the crown. Fertilize the bed between late winter and early spring, and again in late September to October, with a slow-release organic fertilizer for acid-loving plants. Maintain the mulch. Division is usually not needed—and difficult—but can be successful undertaken in early spring. If you let the flower heads remain over the winter, globe thistle may self-sow.

Companion Planting and Design
The globe thistles are handsome massed in a wild garden, and fronting tall shrubs. We grow a stand with ferns, astilbe, and Japanese iris as a backdrop to rocks encircling a small water garden. Attractive companion plants are ornamental grasses, Siberian iris, peonies, yucca, and coneflowers.

Our Personal Recommendations
'Taplow Blue' is a favorite. The flower heads produced by 'Veitch's Blue' are a deeper blue; if flowers are your main interest, this one is also a good choice because it often re-blooms.

When you are looking for a plant that will add texture and variety to the perennial border, consider the globe thistle. It is a stately, erect, thistle-like plant, 2 to 4 ft. tall with big, beautiful spiny leaves that are gray-green and hairy on the underside. The foliage is spectacular, reason enough for growing the plant. From June through August the globe thistle raises handsome, spiky, perfectly round flower heads that last for a couple of months. An added benefit is that they attract goldfinches and nocturnal moths. The flower heads of 'Taplow Blue' are steel blue, and about 2 in. across. They add interesting texture and color to arrangements of fresh flowers, dry easily, and look great in dried winter arrangements. 'Taplow Blue' is the most popular of the cultivars.

Bloom Period and Seasonal Color
June to August; steel blue.

Mature Height × Spread
3 to 4 ft. × 2 to 3 ft.

Hosta

Hosta spp. and hybrids

The hostas are clump-forming foliage plants—the finest of all foliage plants for shaded places. From low mounds of bold leaves, hostas raise slender flower stems studded with bell-like blooms in summer. The flowers of some are fragrant. Newer hybrids, like 'Aphrodite', have remarkably beautiful double flowers. There are dwarfs 7 in. across, giants 5 ft. across, leaves that may be narrow or broad, smooth textured, quilted, puckered, or semi-twisted. The colors range from rich or muted shades of blue-green to yellow-white. The countless colorful variegations light up dim corners. There are green leaves with narrow or broad, white or gold edges, or interior splotches, and yellow-green leaves with dark-green splotchings and edgings. Deer, alas, love hostas as much as we do, as do voles. Plant hostas with VoleBloc™ to prevent losing them to these short-tailed little field mice.

Other Names
Plantain Lily, Funkia

Bloom Period and Seasonal Color
Summer to early fall; white, lavender, purple flowers, and foliage that may be green, chartreuse, blue, blue-green, gold, or white or gold variegated.

Mature Height × Spread
4 to 36 in. × 7 to 56 in.

When, Where, and How to Plant
Catalogs ship hostas bare root in early spring but they're slow to develop. Container-grown plants can be set out anytime after the ground has warmed. Hostas thrive in filtered light; yellow foliaged and variegated forms tolerate more sun. Where there are late frosts, hostas are safer under tall trees. Adaptable as to pH, hostas need well-drained, moist, humusy, fertile soil. See Soil Preparation in the Introduction. Follow the planting instructions at the beginning of this chapter, setting the plants an inch or two below ground level. Space small-leaved varieties 18 to 24 in. apart, and large-leaved forms 24 to 36 in. apart. Water deeply, and mulch well.

Growing Tips
Water a new planting every week or ten days for a month or two unless you have a good soaking rain. Don't overdo: moisture encourages slugs.

Care
In fall clean the beds since fallen leaves can harbor slugs. In early spring and mid-fall fertilize with a slow-release, organic, acid fertilizer. If late frosts threaten, cover hostas with Remay cloth, old blankets, or burlap. Maintain soil moisture the first two or three years; established plants tolerate drought. Harvest the flowers for bouquets. Hostas need three years to mature and the older they get the more impressive they become. Divide them if you wish in early spring or fall. In prolonged rainy weather slugs attack hostas—sprinkle diatomaceous earth, silica gel, or Sluggo® around the plants. You also can trap them with small saucers of beer.

Companion Planting and Design
Mass hostas in a woodland garden using a single type. Or, combine contrasting colors and sizes. Small white variegated hostas make a neat edging for shaded paths. The hostas start up rather late, so they're good companion plants for spring bulbs.

Our Personal Recommendations
André was one of the original charter members of the American Hosta Society. He loves all hostas, especially big, bold 'Sum and Substance', and new 'Blue Mammoth', which has 4-ft. foliage; and perfumed *H. fortunei* 'Fragrant Bouquet', and *H. plantaginea*.

Japanese Anemone
Anemone × hybrida

When, Where, and How to Plant
Plant a container-grown Japanese anemone after the ground has warmed in spring—April in Zone 8, mid-May in Zones 6 and 7. In the warmer areas Japanese anemone does best in morning sun or all-day bright shade. The Japanese anemone needs well-drained soil, and does well in pH 5.5 to 6.0. See Soil Preparation in the Introduction. Follow the planting instructions at the beginning of this chapter, spacing the plants at least 24 in. apart. The tallest cultivars will need staking. Water well. Mulch 2 in. deep starting 3 in. from the crown.

Growing Tip
For the first month to six weeks, water a new plant every week to ten days unless there's a soaking rain.

Care
Deadhead to keep the plant attractive. When the foliage dies down, cut the plant back to the crown. In Zone 6, it's a good idea to cover hybrids with a winter mulch. Fertilize the bed between late winter and early spring with a slow-release organic fertilizer for acid-loving plants. Replenish the mulch. Established clumps are fairly drought resistant, but best results are obtained when plants are well watered during dry periods. These plants need two or three seasons to become established and resent disturbance; divide every ten years to refresh the clump.

Companion Planting and Design
The Japanese anemones are lovely growing at the edge of a woodland with ferns, hostas, and epimediums. We've seen white Japanese anemones blooming as follow-on plants in a bed for spring bulbs with a formal gray stone wall in the background, and that was quite a sight! Anemones are lovely backed by a tall ornamental grass.

Our Personal Recommendations
Historic 'Honorine Jobert' is a gleaming white, single-flowered anemone 3 to 4 ft. tall. 'Margarette' is smaller and produces masses of double or semi-double bright rose-pink blooms on stems 2 to 3 ft. tall. 'Queen Charlotte' is an exquisite pink semi-double.

Fall-flowering anemones are late summer and early fall's most beautiful tall flowers. Low, attractive clusters of divided leaves that are crimson on the reverse side appear first. Then multi-branched stems develop, and toward late summer the plants climb to 2 or 3 ft. and for many weeks silvery buds open to airy flowers 2 to 3 in. in diameter. The single-flowered types have five rounded petals surrounding a central heart of bright yellow stamens. There are also doubles. Anemone hupehensis is covered in fall with attractive seedheads rather like cotton balls. The stems withstand whipping winds. A. × hybrida varieties are larger and more beautiful, and have been bred to many forms and colors, but they don't have the cottony seedballs.

Other Name
Windflower

Bloom Period and Seasonal Color
August to September; white, pink, deep rose.

Mature Height × Spread
2 to 4 ft. × 2 ft.

Lamb's Ears
Stachys byzantina

Lamb's ears is included in flowering borders for the unusual texture and the striking silvery light it brings to the dominant greens. The plant develops a mound of long, oval, semi-evergreen leaves that are so furry they invite stroking, and so luminous they catch moonlight. From midsummer until frosts lamb's ears produces fuzzy, semi-upright spikes of small flowers that are usually violet or white. Most gardeners remove the flowering spikes as they begin to develop to keep the mound low, and the focus on the leaves. The plant has been a favorite long enough to have acquired a number of common names, including lamb's tongue and lamb's tails, which describe the shape of the leaves.

Other Name
Woolly Betony

Bloom Period and Seasonal Color
Furry, silvery foliage all season long; in summer, violet or white flower spikes.

Mature Height × Spread
12 to 15 in. × 12 to 18 in.

When, Where, and How to Plant
Set out container plants or root divisions in early spring or in early fall. Lamb's ears grows well in full sun in cool Zone 6, but in hot zones 7 and 8 it can do with protection from noon sun, and from hot late afternoon sun. It is not particular as to soil pH, but requires a very well-drained site and light, fertile, humusy soil. See Soil Preparation in the Introduction. Follow the planting instructions at the beginning of this chapter, spacing the plants 12 to 24 in. apart and 1 in. above ground level. Water slowly and deeply. Mulch an inch deep with something fine textured, like cocoa hulls or pine needles, starting 3 in. from the outer leaves.

Growing Tips
Water a new planting three times during every thirty days, slowly and deeply. Lamb's ears tolerates drought once established, but wetting the foliage, especially in hot weather, may encourage disease. Avoid overhead sprinkling and frequent shallow watering.

Care
Remove the flower spikes to keep the plants tidy; if you let the flowers open and go to seed that will cause the foliage to deteriorate. Cut out leaves and stems that are showing signs of rot. Leave healthy foliage in place for the winter, and remove it before growth begins in spring.

Companion Planting and Design
Lamb's ears is a good container plant, and gives pleasure wherever you plant it. It's a delight as an underplanting for sedums 'Ruby Glow' and 'Vera Jameson', and lovely nestled in fallen leaves. To make a show, you need to plant lamb's ears in groups of at least three plants. The leaves dry well and can be included in tussie mussies and dried wreaths.

Our Personal Recommendations
André loves 'Helen von Stein' whose silvery leaves are twice the size of other varieties and better able to withstand heat and humidity. The non-flowering 8-inch high 'Silver Carpet' spreads rapidly and is choice for cooler regions.

Marsh Rose Mallow

Hibiscus moscheutos

When, Where, and How to Plant

Set out container-grown or dormant roots (bare root) in early spring in full sun; in part shade, it won't produce as many big flowers. Rose mallow does well in moist situations, and in a wide range of soils. It does best where the pH is between 5.5 and 7.0. See Soil Preparation in the Introduction. Follow the planting instructions at the beginning of this chapter; provide a hole twice the size of the rootball and deep enough to set the crown 2 in. below the soil surface. If you plant more than one, space plants on 4- to 5-ft. centers. Rose mallow doesn't have to be staked, but it benefits from the support of a wall, or a fence corner where it also gets air. Water deeply. Mulch 2 to 3 in. deep with pine needles or decayed leaves starting 3 in. from the crown.

Growing Tip

Water a new plant deeply every week to ten days the first season unless you have a good soaking rain.

Care

The blooms, like tropical hibiscus, last a day then turn to brown mush. Removing them keeps the plant more attractive. Late in the season we allow seedheads to form and stay on the plant through winter. Rose mallow resists some drought once it's established, so local rainfall should be enough to keep it growing. Fertilize the bed in fall and again between late winter and early spring with a slow-release, organic, acid fertilizer. Cut the stems to the ground in early spring and in late spring new stems will appear. To keep the plant groomed, author Tracy DiSabato-Aust recommends cutting the stems back by half when they are 18 in. high.

Companion Planting and Design

Rose mallow is handsome in a corner, and beautiful blooming through and over a low metal fence.

Our Personal Recommendations

The red 'Lord Baltimore' strain bears masses of flowers and has beautifully lobed leaves. 'Appleblossom' has light pink flowers with deeper rose margins. 'Turn of the Century' is a bi-color with soft pink-on-white flowers.

The most familiar hibiscus used to be the tropical H. rosa-sinensis, a gorgeous funnel-shaped flower that lasts just a day. And, the lovely old-fashioned rose-of-Sharon, shrub althea, H. syriacus, a woody flowering plant or small tree described in the chapter on Shrubs. But in recent years, the huge blooms of the marsh rose mallow have captured the imagination of gardeners. It's a shrubby perennial that in midsummer bears funnel-shaped flowers 7 and 10 and 12 in. across. In late spring, the plant's new growth shoots up 3 to 6 ft. The canes eventually sprawl but the plant does not need staking— just lots of sprawl space. When in bloom, it's eye-catching even at some distance. The dried pods are handsome.

Other Names

Common Rose Mallow, Swamp Rose Mallow

Bloom Period and Seasonal Color

Midsummer to frost; red, white, pink, bi-color.

Mature Height × Spread

3 to 8 ft. × 5 ft.

Monarda
Monarda didyma

We call it "monarda" now and grow modern varieties with perennials and in wild and meadow gardens for their beauty and long season of bloom. But in the past monarda was called "bee balm" and grown primarily for its herbal properties. The tips of young shoots were—still are—used as garnishes for drinks and salads. An herb tea was, and is, made of the pointed, bright green leaves which have the scent of mint-bergamot. Middling tall, the attractive globelike flowers are made up of whorls of shaggy tubular petals surrounded by red-tinted bracts. They bloom throughout the summer on stiff stems above neat plants and are wildly attractive to hummingbirds, butterflies, and bees. Monarda is a native American plant. It makes an excellent cut flower.

Other Names
Bee Balm, Bergamot, Oswego Tea

Bloom Period and Seasonal Color
July and August; scarlet, pink, cerise, red, white, violet.

Mature Height × Spread
2 to 4 ft. × 2 to 4 ft.

When, Where, and How to Plant
Set out container plants or root divisions in spring, summer, or fall. Monarda blooms fully in direct sun, or with afternoon shade, even in cooler regions. It thrives in well-drained, moist, humusy soil that is slightly acid, pH 5.0 to 6.5. See Soil Preparation in the Introduction and follow the planting instructions at the beginning of this chapter. The plant is susceptible to mildew so plant it where it has plenty of space and good air circulation all around; it will fill its space quickly. Water well. Mulch 2 to 3 in. deep starting 3 in. from the crown.

Growing Tip
Water new plantings of monarda deeply every week to ten days for a month or so unless you have a soaking rain.

Care
Fertilize the bed between late winter and early spring with an organic slow-release fertilizer at the rate of 4 pounds per 100 sq. ft. In spring, replenish the mulch. Maintain soil moisture during dry spells. Deadheading lengthens the period of bloom. If the plant shows signs of mildew after flowering, cut the stems back to just above the fresh new foliage at the base. Monarda spreads thanks to creeping stems that can quickly fill a considerable area; planting it in 3- to 5-gallon containers keeps it under control. You can divide the planting every two to three years in late summer; just pull individual rooted stems from the center of the clump and replant them with space all around.

Companion Planting and Design
Monarda provides splashes of subtle color throughout midsummer. We like it in perennial borders, meadow and wild gardens, anywhere that we get to see the wildlife it attracts in action. It's a good cut flower, but when you are harvesting bee balm, watch out for bees who may think it belongs to them.

Our Personal Recommendations
We recommend mildew-resistant varieties, such as 48-in. 'Jacob Kline', which has large, dark red flowers; 36-in. 'Marshall's Delight', a compact pink-flowered variety; and an exciting new dwarf, 15-in. 'Petite Delight', which has lavender-pink flowers.

Oriental Poppy
Papaver orientalis

When, Where, and How to Plant

Set out sturdy container-grown plants in early spring. Poppies need full sun, but can be productive in filtered shade. In Zone 8 they succeed in bright shade under tall trees. Poppies tolerate a range of soils, pH 6.0 to 7.5, as long as it is well-drained, deeply dug, light, somewhat sandy, but humusy enough to hold moisture. See Soil Preparation in the Introduction. Follow the planting instructions at the beginning of this chapter. Set the crowns $1^1/2$ in. below the soil level and space the plants about 2 to 3 ft. apart. Water deeply. Mulch 2 to 3 in. deep starting 3 in. from the crown.

Growing Tips

Maintain moisture during the growing and flowering period, but don't force watering during the dormant period that follows. The big, decorative seedheads should be removed: it's better for the plant.

Care

When poppies die the foliage deteriorates; allow it to yellow and brown, then gently remove it from the crown. When the foliage begins to re-grow in the fall, fertilize with a slow-release, organic, acid fertilizer. In late winter replenish the mulch. Oriental poppies have a fleshy taproot that is difficult to dig and transplant. They're very long lived and rarely need dividing; the best time to dig a poppy is after it becomes dormant. These are gorgeous cut flowers and will last longer if you sear the bottom of the stem with a hot flame before putting it into water.

Companion Planting and Design

Don't plant poppies with flowers requiring moist soil in summer. Since the Orientals are unsightly as the foliage is dying, they belong toward the back of the border, fronted by plants that will grow big as they fade away—dahlias, asters, chrysanthemums, for example.

Our Personal Recommendations

Oriental poppies are cold hardy but difficult south of Zone 7. The most beautiful and easy to grow are 'Cedar Hill', light pink; 'Maiden's Blush', a ruffled white poppy with a blush-pink edge; brilliant 'Raspberry Queen'; and fringed 'Turkenlouis', a fiery orange red.

Poppies come in all sizes. Silky, shiny, and colorful, they're a mainstay of sunny gardens everywhere. The stars of the poppy domain are the big, crinkled-silk Oriental poppies. A spangle of these brilliant, beautiful blossoms lifts a garden from ordinary to extraordinary. The blossoms measure between 5 and 8 to 10 in. across, and they unfold in spring and early summer in vibrant colors and color combinations. The petals of some are splotched at the base in a contrasting color, usually black or mahogany, and others have contrasting edges. Though the wiry stems bend to even a little wind, the flowers withstand storms of amazing proportions. The fuzzy pods are attractive in dried arrangements. The deeply cut foliage dies after the flowers have bloomed and new foliage appears in the fall.

Bloom Period and Seasonal Color

Spring and early summer; red, orange, salmon, pink, white, bi-colors.

Mature Height × Spread

2 to 4 ft. × 2 ft.

Peony
Paeonia hybrids

There are two types of peonies—the familiar herbaceous perennials, and woody forms that are classed with shrubs. The herbaceous peonies often outlive the gardeners who plant them. The showy flowers bloom in April and May for four to six weeks, producing huge heads of crinkled silk—single, semi-double, fully double—that make awesomely luscious bouquets. The doubles are the most popular, but interest is growing in the exotic single flowered and Japanese peonies. Peonies must have a chilling period at below 40 degrees Fahrenheit to flower. The best bets for Zone 8 are herbaceous types that flower early and in midseason, and the Japanese and single herbaceous peonies.

Bloom Period and Seasonal Color
Spring; white, shades of pink and rose, coral, deep crimson, and bi-colors.

Mature Height × Spread
3 ft. × 3 ft.

When, Where, and How to Plant
In our area we plant container-grown peonies between early September and early December. They require a minimum of six hours of the strongest sun and are most successful in well-drained, fertile, humusy, neutral or slightly alkaline soils, pH 6.0 to 7.5, but tolerate mildly acid soils. See Soil Preparation in the Introduction. Do not use barnyard or composted manure with peonies. Provide a hole 24 in. wide and 18 in. deep and follow the planting instructions for container-grown plants at the beginning of this chapter. Space peonies 36 in. apart. Water well. Do not mulch.

Growing Tips
Water plants every week or ten days for the first month or so, unless you have a soaking rain, then water as needed.

Care
In fall and in early spring, fertilize the bed with a slow-release organic fertilizer. Water established peonies during droughts. Remove invasive ground covers and weeds by hand. Harvest slow-to-open side blooms: they may open in vase water. In early September to October cut the stems to the ground and burn them. That's the moment to divide or transplant peonies. Provide each piece of the crown with three to seven eyes, and plant so the eyes are 2 in. below ground level. Transplanted peonies need a year or two to re-establish themselves.

Companion Planting and Design
Plant peonies in groups of four to eight in lawns, and in groups of two or three to anchor large flowering borders. In snow country they are planted in rows to hedge walks, and even driveways, because the foliage dies away in fall, leaving space for snow removal.

Our Personal Recommendations
Peonies were the favorite flowers of André's father, the late nurseryman Martin Viette. A world-famous peony grower, he once won seventeen out of nineteen blue ribbons at the International Peony Show. André still grows Martin Viette's favorites—here they are in the order of his preference: 'Gay Paree', 'Sword Dance', 'Sea Shell', the Lobata hybrids, 'Jan Van Leuven', 'Tomate Boku', 'Nick Shaylor', and fragrant 'Philippe Revoire'.

Phlox

Phlox paniculata 'David'

When, Where, and How to Plant

Set out container-grown plants in early fall or spring. Will bloom most fully in full sun, but also flowers in partial shade or bright filtered light. 'David' tolerates a wide pH range, but to be all it can be it requires well-drained, moist, fertile soil rich in compost and humus. See Soil Preparation in the Introduction. Follow the planting instructions at the beginning of this chapter, spacing the plants 24 in. or more apart; good air circulation deters mildew. Water deeply. Mulch 2 in. deep starting 3 in. from the crowns.

Growing Tips

For the first two months water new plantings weekly unless you have a soaking rain; keeping phlox growing is part of the program that keeps it healthy. To prolong the flower display, early on pinch back one or two weaker stems in each clump so secondary flowers will be growing as the main stems fade.

Care

Rogue out seedlings and remove seeded flower heads so the plants will bloom again and won't self sow. Cut them down to the crown at the end of the season or in early fall, and destroy the stems. Fertilize the bed between late winter and early spring with a slow-release, organic, acid fertilizer. Maintain soil moisture to keep the plants growing lustily. Keep them vigorous by dividing the crowns every three years in spring before growth begins. Discard the center of the crown, and provide each piece with three to four vigorous shoots.

Companion Planting and Design

Plant phlox near asters that will come into bloom as the phlox flowers fade in late summer, or with fall-flowering Japanese anemone. In mid-fall, tuck in potted cushion mums in white and lavender.

Our Personal Recommendations

In 1920-1922, Martin Viette hybridized 'Katherine', a light lavender-blue with white eyes. It was lost until the great horticulturist Fred McGourty found it in an old Connecticut garden. André has reintroduced it, and says it's still the best blue. 'Flamingo Pink' is one of the most mildew resistant. André also loves the little creeping phloxes *P. divaricata*, *P. stolonifera*, and the moss pink, *P. subulata*.

The full flower heads of P. paniculata filled old-time mid-summer gardens with luscious pastels, and homes with their sweet scent. An American native, the species bears big rounded heads of open-faced, silky-soft florets. This was the backbone of summer borders until its vulnerability to mildew—and a strong tendency to self-sow and come back in magenta—caused gardeners to forget about it. Now it's making a comeback in healthy and beautiful hybrids such as 'David', named Plant of the Year for 2002 by the Perennial Plant Association. It is praised for the bright white, delightfully fragrant flowers that bloom from mid-July to September. Its resistance to powdery mildew, according to PPA, is better than that of other phloxes.

Other Names

Summer Phlox, Perennial Phlox, Fall Phlox

Bloom Period and Seasonal Color

July to September; white.

Mature Height × Spread

35 to 40 in. × 2 ft.

Pinks

Dianthus spp. and hybrids

Pinks are dainty members of the genus Dianthus, which includes carnations and sweet Williams. Annuals, biennials, and perennials, they are loved for their sweet, spicy clove scent. The perfume is strong in the big florists' carnations and in the little grass or cottage pinks that fill gardens with sparkling colors spring, summer, and fall. Pinks range in size from 6 to 24 in. and the fresh, grassy foliage, evergreen in most, is an all-season asset. Some we plant for the perfume, some for their colorful flowers, and some for both flowers and foliage. Many varieties of pinks will bloom for months if they are deadheaded, or sheared, after the first flush of bloom. There are double-flowered forms.

Other Name
Miniature Carnation

Bloom Period and Seasonal Color
Spring, summer, early fall; pink, red, salmon, white, yellow (*D. knappii*), often with a contrasting eye, bi-colors.

Mature Height × Spread
6 to 24 in. × 8 to 12 in.

When, Where, and How to Plant
Flats of dianthus varieties and container-grown plants are available in early spring, in summer, and early fall. Full sun is best, but in Washington, D.C., pinks bloom in part sun, too. They do best in well-drained, even sandy, soil whose pH is between 6.0 and 7.5. Excellent drainage in winter is essential. In unimproved clay and where humidity is high, the pinks are short-lived. See Soil Preparation in the Introduction, and for the pinks, be a little stingy with the humus. Annuals are often sold in flats; cut the plants apart with a sharp, clean knife for planting. For container-grown plants follow the planting instructions at the beginning of this chapter. Space pinks 12 to 15 in. apart and set them a little higher than the soil level. Water well. Spread a light, fine mulch such as cocoa hulls 2 to 3 in. deep starting 3 in. from the crown.

Growing Tips
Water new plantings every week or ten days unless you have rain. After the first flush of bloom, deadhead or shear off the faded flowers. If the plants show brown tips in August, cut them off, and make sure the plants don't go dry. They will freshen when fall comes, and can go on blooming until frost.

Care
Fertilize the bed between late winter and early spring with a slow-release organic fertilizer at the rate of 6 pounds per 100 sq. ft. Replenish the mulch. Pinks are drought resistant once established and they don't like wet feet. The little pinks divide and transplant easily in spring or early fall.

Companion Planting and Design
We use pinks as edgers, and position them where the fragrance is a frequent experience.

Our Personal Recommendations
André recommends the cheddar pink, *D. gratianopolitanus* 'Bath's Pink', which can take a lot of heat. 'Tiny Rubies' is a very popular double-flowered, deep pink variety. The Zing group—'Zing Rose' for example—are 6-inchers that bloom all summer. The old-fashioned annual sweet William, a great cutting flower, is nicely scented, too.

Purple Coneflower

Echinacea purpurea 'Magnus'

When, Where, and How to Plant

To have plants the first season, set out container-grown plants or root divisions any time after the ground can be worked in spring. Purple coneflower really needs full sun, but it can take a little filtered shade and still be productive, especially in the warmer parts of the Mid-Atlantic. It tolerates drought and can't stand soil that is soggy in winter. The ideal soil is in the somewhat acid range, pH 5.5 to 6.0. Over-fertilized soil makes for tall, leggy plants that need staking. See Soil Preparation in the Introduction, and reduce the fertilization recommendations by half. Follow the planting instructions at the beginning of this chapter, spacing the plants 18 in. to 24 in. apart. Water well. Mulch 2 to 3 in. deep starting 3 in. from the crown.

Growing Tips

The first six weeks, water purple coneflower every week unless you have a soaking rain; given time to become established, it will tolerate drought.

Care

In reasonably fertile soil, spring fertilization may not always be necessary. Deadheading keeps the plants from self-seeding and reverting to inferior forms. Whether you deadhead or not, new blossoms keep coming. André recommends keeping some stands of purple coneflower deadheaded, and allowing some to form seedheads to feed the birds that relish the seeds; next year you can rogue out the self-sown plantlets that will appear in abundance in the spring. When harvesting flowers for bouquets, cut the stem just above the next flower bud so the stem can produce more blooms.

Companion Planting and Design

Purple coneflower is the backbone, showpiece, and eye catcher, of a meadow garden! Lovely in groups of five to seven planted in the center or toward the back of a formal border it keeps color there throughout midsummer. Virtually pest- and disease-free and tolerant of considerable drought, the purple coneflower is an excellent choice for naturalizing.

Our Personal Recommendations

For the cutting garden, plant 'Bright Star', which is a rosy-pink coneflower with a maroon center. The cream-white varieties with orange centers, like 'White Lustre', are attractive growing with black-eyed Susans.

This big bold coneflower with huge, mauve, daisy-like blooms is one of the showiest, toughest, and longest-lived natives for meadow gardens. It grows 2 to 4 ft. tall, and has coarse dark green foliage. In 1998, 'Magnus' was named Plant of the Year by the Perennial Plant Association. The petals sweep back from a deep orange-bronze cone and are a rich, dusky rose-purple. Purple coneflower blooms in late spring and early summer; deadheaded, it goes on intermittently into fall. There are white varieties but they don't have the eye-catching appeal of the purple. Purple coneflowers last well as cut flowers, and they dry easily and the cones look terrific in dried winter flower arrangements. Butterflies love purple coneflower.

Bloom Period and Seasonal Color

Late spring, early summer; magenta petals surround an orange cone.

Mature Height × Spread

2 to 4 ft. × 2 ft.

Red Hot Poker Plant

Kniphofia spp. and hybrids

Now that we are eager for more drought-resistant plants, the red hot poker plant is getting the attention it deserves for its color, style, and for its ease of maintenance. In late spring and summer, eye-catching 18- to 36-in. flower spikes appear, yellow on the bottom and bright red on the top. They stand straight as a poker, several spikes per plant. The yellow lower portion of the "pokers" is where early-blooming florets are aging; the red at the top is where new florets are just opening. The arching sword-shaped, gray-green, semi-evergreen or evergreen foliage is attractive when new. There are many new cultivars, and they're more compact than the old-fashioned varieties and have attractive softer colors.

Bloom Period and Seasonal Color
Late spring and summer; yellow and red, cream, orange.

Mature Height × Spread
2 to 4 ft. × 3 ft.

When, Where, and How to Plant
In the cool uplands, set out container-grown plants in early spring. In Zones 7 and 8, red hot poker plant can be set out in early fall. It can stand a lot of direct sun, but in the hotter regions it benefits from protection from noon sun. Good drainage for the planting site is essential. Red hot poker plant tolerates drought but can't stand soil that is soggy in winter and does best when it's not constantly buffeted by strong winds. It does best in neutral to alkaline soils, pH 6.0 to 7.5. See Soil Preparation in the Introduction. Follow the planting instructions at the beginning of this chapter, spacing the plants 24 in. apart. Water well. Mulch 2 in. deep starting 3 in. from the crown.

Growing Tips
Water new red hot poker plants every week unless you have a soaking rain. Once established they are tolerant of drought.

Care
Fertilize the bed between late winter and early spring, with a slow-release organic fertilizer at the rate of 6 pounds per 100 sq. ft. In spring, replenish the mulch. Keep fading flower spikes removed until the end of the season. The plants rarely set seed. In spring before growth begins, cut the plants back to about 3 in. above the crown. Red hot poker plant dislikes being disturbed and rarely needs dividing. If you want to multiply your plants, divide in early spring.

Companion Planting and Design
A flower for dry places, xeriscapes, and modernistic gardens fronting stark modern architecture.

Our Personal Recommendations
We like 'Springtime', whose colors are coral and a muted yellow. The colors of 2- to 2$\frac{1}{2}$-ft. 'Earliest of All' include a soft coral rose.

Russian Sage
Perovskia atriplicifolia

When, Where, and How to Plant
Set out container-grown plants anytime; set out rooted softwood cuttings in early spring or fall. Russian sage requires full sun to do its best, and a very well-drained site. It thrives in moderately fertile soil in the neutral range. See Soil Preparation in the Introduction. Follow the planting instructions at the beginning of this chapter, spacing the plants 24 in. apart. Water well. Mulch 2 to 3 in. deep starting 3 in. from the crown.

Growing Tips
For the first two months, water deeply and thoroughly every week to ten days, unless you have a good soaking rain, then water as needed.

Care
Russian sage is a sub-shrub with a woody base. Cut the stems back to about 6 in. above the ground in the spring and new buds will start from these stems. In cooler regions the stems may die to the ground; as long as your winters are no colder than Zone 5, the plant will likely re-grow. If unusually late frosts damage the stems, trim off the spoiled branch tips. In very warm areas where Russian sage blooms early, cutting the branches back by two-thirds after they have flowered will produce a new flush of bloom in fall. Russian sage hardly ever needs dividing.

Companion Planting and Design
We like Russian sage at the back of a perennial border in groups of three, backed by evergreens that will show off its winter color. It is beautiful massed with boltonia and ornamental grasses in naturalized settings. It's also a great shore plant.

Our Personal Recommendation
André's choice is 'Filigran', which is just 40 in. tall and blooms from July to October.

Russian sage keeps a cloud of that coveted color, blue—a beautiful, soft, powdery lavender blue—in the garden for a long time in summer and early fall—July, August, and most of September. In Zone 8 it starts to bloom in June. Very tall, so airy they're cloudlike at a distance, the silvery stems and the grayish foliage are topped by spikes of tiny florets a lovely, subtle shade of blue. When the foliage is crushed, you get a whiff of the clean, warm scent of sage. In winter the branches are a cloud of silvery white. One of the most heat- and drought-resistant of all the perennials, in 1995 Russian sage was named Plant of the Year by the Perennial Plant Association.

Bloom Period and Seasonal Color
June through September; powder blue.

Mature Height × Spread
3 to 4¹/₂ ft. × 3 ft.

Salvia 'May Night'

Salvia × sylvestris 'May Night'

This perennial salvia is a tough plant that winters over even in Zone 3. Square-stemmed like its kissin' cousin Salvia splendens, *described in the chapter on Annuals, perennial salvia has a whole other look, more that of a small upright shrub with dark green, pointy leaves. The slim flowering spikes of 'May Night' are a rich, wonderful, midnight violet-blue. Growing in full sun the flower spikes rise straight up like a candelabra and they bloom for weeks, followed by reddish bracts that are attractive in their own right. In less light, 'May Night' grows taller and sprawls so widely you'd hardly recognize it. Deadheading extends the flowering period. 'May Night' was chosen Plant of the Year by the Perennial Plant Association in 1997.*

Other Names
Perennial Salvia, *Salvia × sylvestris* 'Mainacht', *Salvia nemorosa* 'May Night'

Bloom Period and Seasonal Color
June to August; midnight blue.

Mature Height × Spread
1 1/2 to 3 ft. × 2 ft.

When, Where, and How to Plant
Set out container-grown plants anytime; set out rooted divisions in early to mid-spring or late summer. Salvia needs full sun to stay trim looking, but, while it sprawls widely in partial shade, it still blooms well. Perennial salvia is tolerant as to pH, but needs a site that is well drained, and soil that is fertile and humusy. See Soil Preparation in the Introduction. Follow the planting instructions at the beginning of this chapter, spacing the plants 24 to 30 in. apart. Water well. Mulch 2 to 3 in. deep starting 3 in. from the crown.

Growing Tips
For the first two months, water newly planted perennial salvia every week to ten days unless you have a soaking rain. Deadhead down to a pair of lateral leaves, and perennial salvia re-blooms beautifully. If the plant falls open and gets stringy looking after blooming, you can cut it down to the crown and it will usually re-grow and, depending on your climate, may have time to re-bloom. After such radical treatment it's a good idea to fertilize the plant and make sure the soil doesn't go dry.

Care
André has seen salvia re-bloom three and four times when the flowers are deadheaded right after blooming. Fertilize the bed between late winter and early spring with a slow-release, organic, acid fertilizer at the rate of 4 pounds per 100 sq. ft. In spring, replenish the mulch. Water only as needed. Dividing, which isn't often necessary, is best undertaken in early spring.

Companion Planting and Design
Perennial salvia is the perfect plant for the middle of the border between airy summer flowers like boltonia, sturdy yarrow, and dainty coreopsis 'Moonbeam'. We like it anchoring clumps of flowers with light variegated foliage.

Our Personal Recommendations
'May Night' is André's favorite but there are other perennial salvias and more are coming because it is a very useful border plant. Recently introduced 'Rose Wine' is the rose-pink version of 'May Night'. And now there's a white perennial salvia that comes to us from Germany called 'Snow Hill' that makes a striking plant in part shade.

Scabiosa

Scabiosa columbaria 'Butterfly Blue'

When, Where, and How to Plant

In early spring set out container-grown plants or root divisions. In cooler regions, scabiosa does best in full sun but in warm regions it flowers well with noon or afternoon shade. Scabiosa thrives in soil close to neutral, pH 7.0, and very well drained. Excellent drainage in winter is essential. See Soil Preparation in the Introduction. Follow the planting instructions at the beginning of this chapter, spacing the plants 15 to 18 in. apart. Water well. Mulch 2 to 3 in. deep starting 3 in. from the crown.

Growing Tip

For the first two months, water new plantings of scabiosa every week to ten days unless you have a soaking rain.

Care

In cool regions, provide a light, dry winter mulch of pine boughs or hay. Fertilize the bed between late winter and early spring, and again in September with a slow-release, organic, acid fertilizer. In spring, replenish the mulch. Water only as needed. Deadheading prolongs bloom, but is complicated by the fact that the fading blooms can be mistaken for the emerging flower buds. If the stems do not branch, just cut down to the crown. With time scabiosa begins to put up just one central leader; when that happens, cut it down to the basal foliage. Before winter, cut back old flowering stems but leave the basal foliage in place; in spring before growth begins, remove dead foliage. Every three to four years, if the plants seem crowded, divide the crowns anytime in early to mid-spring, until active growth begins. The flowers last longer harvested half open.

Companion Planting and Design

Plant scabiosa toward the front of the perennial bed with space all around.

Our Personal Recommendations

'Butterfly Blue' is the best. Another lovely scabiosa is *S. caucasica*, which has very large flowers and is grown specifically for cutting. It has grayish ferny foliage and pale blue, white, or lavender flowers summer to frost. 'Fama' is the clear intense sky blue version, and 'Alba' is the white form. 'Pink Mist' is a lavender-pink version of 'Butterfly Blue'.

Scabiosa, the "pincushion" flower, is an old-time favorite—and the blossoms do look like sweet little pincushions surrounded by curving petals. Actually, the blooms are domed heads composed of tiny flowers surrounded by leafy bracts. It's an excellent flower for cutting and for drying. 'Butterfly Blue' can take the cold all the way to Zone 3 and keep flowers into fall if it is consistently sheared, or deadheaded. A heavy-blooming dwarf, it produces 2-in. flowers in amazing abundance from mid-spring until mid-fall. The color is beautiful, the plant itself a neat compact mound, and the masses of flowers are amazing. 'Butterfly Blue' was named Plant of the Year for 2000 by the Perennial Plant Association.

Other Name

Blue Pincushion Flower

Bloom Period and Seasonal Color

May to October; blue.

Mature Height × Spread

1 to 1 1/2 ft. × 1 ft.

Sedum

Sedum spp. and hybrids

Indestructible, heat- and drought-resistant, sedums are valued for their succulent, evergreen foliage and for the beautiful fall flower color of some tall hybrids. The flowers are tiny, star-shaped and in taller forms cluster in showy flat-topped flower heads. The little ground-hugging sedums are used in rock gardens, between stepping stones, in wall crannies, and by steps. Taller types, like 'Autumn Joy', are considered by perennial experts including André Viette, to be among the top fifteen perennials. Its jade green foliage is evergreen. In spring new stems rise, followed in early summer by fresh, apple green broccoli-like flower heads. These change to rich pink, then rose, salmon, bronze, and finally to rosy russet. Deer sometimes eat sedum foliage but leave the flowers.

Other Name
Stonecrop

Bloom Period and Seasonal Color
Summer to fall; yellow, pink, white, red.

Mature Height × Spread
1 to 24 in. × 1 to 2 ft.

When, Where, and How to Plant

Set out container-grown plants spring, summer, or fall. Plant root divisions anytime after the ground can be worked in spring, or in late summer. Many smaller sedums are invasive, and even tall varieties, if not deadheaded, self-sow. The plants flourish in full sun in cold Zone 6 and all the way to Zone 3; in warmer areas they are at their best during cool weather. The ideal soil is pH 6.0 to 7.5, very well drained, humusy, and fertile. Most seem to prefer dry soil, but tolerate moisture. See Soil Preparation in the Introduction. Follow the planting instructions at the beginning of this chapter, spacing the plants according to the size at maturity. Water well. Mulch 2 to 3 in. deep starting 3 in. from the crown.

Growing Tips

Sedum withstands heat and drought even in sand and by the sea. Watering if there's no rain is a good idea but necessary only until you see vigorous new growth.

Care

Fertilize the bed between late winter and early spring, with a slow-release organic fertilizer and replenish the mulch. Sedums need average moisture during active growth but can stand a lot of drought later. Don't deadhead the taller sedums, like 'Autumn Joy'—the flowers change color as they go to seed and provide a beautiful color accent in the garden throughout fall and winter; cut them off just above the basal foliage in late winter. Divide clumps to multiply your holdings any time; to refresh the plants divide clumps in early spring every six to ten years.

Companion Planting and Design

The taller cultivars are superb growing with ornamental grasses in naturalized plantings that include *Rudbeckia* 'Goldsturm', purple coneflowers, and Russian sage.

Our Personal Recommendations

'Autumn Joy' is the favorite. Another handsome sedum is 'Ruby Glow', a slightly smaller plant whose flower heads are iridescent ruby-red. *Sedum spurium* 'John Creech', an excellent evergreen ground cover, was introduced by André Viette who named it for the horticulturist who first collected it.

Siberian Iris

Iris sibirica

When, Where, and How to Plant

You can plant container-grown Siberian irises anytime; growers ship rhizomes bare root in early spring. The irises are successful growing in full sun in cold wet climates; in warmer regions they tolerate light shade or late afternoon shade. They adapt to pH 5.0 to 7.5, but prefer moderately acid soils. They tolerate poor, dry soil but bloom best in well-drained, rich, evenly moist garden loam with good drainage. Once established, they can stand some drought. See Soil Preparation in the Introduction. For container-grown plants follow the planting instructions at the beginning of this chapter, allowing a good 18 in. between crowns. Plant rhizomes with the roots on the underside, and the tops just below the soil surface, and space them 18 to 24 in. apart depending on the size of the iris; they soon grow into a solid, deep-rooted clump. Water well. Mulch 2 to 3 in. deep starting 3 in. from the outer edges of the planting.

Growing Tip

Water the planting every week for a month to six weeks, unless you have a soaking rain.

Care

Fertilize the bed between late winter and early spring with a slow-release organic fertilizer for acid-loving plants, 4 pounds per 100 sq. ft. Water as needed. Deadhead, leaving a third of the handsome seedheads in place to extend the plant's high season. Remove dead foliage in spring before growth begins. Divide and transplant Siberian iris late summer to early fall, or in early spring. Get the rhizomes into the ground as soon as possible; keep them moist until planted.

Companion Planting and Design

One or two slim, elegant Siberian irises are beautiful beside a water garden and are among the few flowers allowed into a Japanese water garden. Clumps of Siberians add grace to mixed perennial borders. Siberian iris, *Sedum* 'Autumn Joy', and a bramble of coreopsis give the garden form while the earth rests.

Our Personal Recommendations

Good hybrids include deepest purple 'Tealwood', yellow and white 'Butter and Sugar', and blue 'Ego'.

We love the Siberian irises—they're easy to maintain and have few problems. Breeders agree, and are enhancing the colors, range, and bloom times of these exceptionally graceful plants. Depending on the zone, Siberian irises bloom in late spring to early summer. Clusters of two or three flowers top tall slender stems above slim grassy leaves that turn lovely shades of rust in winter. The flowers stand a little taller than the bearded irises, from 24 in. to 40 in., and come in as many colors and forms as anyone could want—from white to yellow, blues, some edged with silver, and there's a pansy purple with white lines. Some are ruffled, some have huge flaring blossoms. It's an excellent flower for cutting and very lovely massed in a large border. The dried pods are handsome.

Bloom Period and Seasonal Color

In late spring; blue-purple, lavender, maroon, white, off-pink, yellowish tones.

Mature Height × Spread

24 to 40 in. × 10 to 24 in.

Solomon's Seal
Polygonatum spp. and cultivars

Solomon's seal is a superb flower and foliage plant for woodland gardens and naturalized corners of the landscape. The North American, Asian, and European species gardeners grow are graceful spring-bloomers that originated in damp light woodlands, so they're reliable performers for a shade garden. Polygonatum biflorum, a native aristocrat, is now propagated and sold by nurseries. In spring, rows of dangling bell-shaped green or cream-white flowers, usually in pairs, line the arching stems and are followed by blue-black berries. Pretty if not spectacular, and the flowers of some are fragrant. The foliage turns an appealing yellow-brown in fall and persists. Solomon's seal thrives in domesticity as long as it is provided with light and soil approximating its native haunts.

Other Name
King Solomon's Seal

Bloom Period and Seasonal Color
Mid- to late spring; creamy white flowers.

Mature Height × Spread
2 to 3 ft. × 18 to 20 in.

When, Where, and How to Plant
Set out nursery-grown root divisions in fall or spring; do not dig Solomon's seal growing in the wild as it is protected. *Polygonatum* volunteers in full sun where there is moisture in cool Zones 5 and 6, and in quite deep shade in woodlands, so it is adaptable. In regions where summers are very hot, a partially shaded site is best. Solomon's seal thrives in well-drained, deeply dug, rich, humusy, somewhat acid soil, about pH 5.0 to 6.0. See Soil Preparation in the Introduction. Follow the planting instructions at the beginning of this chapter, spacing the plants 18 to 20 in. apart. Water well. Mulch 2 to 3 in. deep starting 3 in. from the outer stems.

Growing Tips
Keep the soil moist while the plant is establishing itself, and water deeply during droughts.

Care
Fertilize the bed between late winter and early spring with a slow-release organic fertilizer for acid-loving plants at the rate of 4 pounds per 100 sq. ft. Once a planting is established you can dig and transplant the rhizomes while still dormant in late winter; divide the rhizomes with a knife, allowing each section at least one healthy bud. Set the rhizomes 2 to 3 in. deep with the bud facing upward in the direction in which you want the plant to grow.

Companion Planting and Design
Plant Solomon's seal along a woodland path with columbines, fragrant lily-of-the-valley, primroses, trilliums, and hostas. *P. commutatum*, a magnificent 5-footer at maturity, belongs in a large wild garden.

Our Personal Recommendations
André's favorite is *Polygonatum multiflorum*, a beautiful, graceful, deep green, European Solomon's seal. Martin Viette introduced 30-in. *P. odoratum* 'Variegatum', a superb variegated Solomon's seal that is fragrant, to American gardeners just before World War II. André introduced the 6-in. dwarf species *P. humile*. It was a gift received from a friend.

Yarrow

Achillea spp. and hybrids

When, Where, and How to Plant
In spring or late fall set out container-grown plants or root divisions. Yarrow really needs full sun, even in hot regions. It is excellent for very well-drained sandy soils, and poor soils. Very rich or moist soils encourage lax growth and cause *A. millefolium* cultivars to become invasive. Yarrow handles drought but can't stand soggy soil, especially in winter. See Soil Preparation in the Introduction but halve the fertilization recommendations. Follow the planting instructions at the beginning of this chapter. Yarrow is a wide-spreading plant, so space the plants 18 to 24 in. apart. Water well. Mulch to keep weeds down 2 to 3 in. deep starting 3 in. from the crown

Growing Tips
Yarrow requires watering for the first few weeks after planting; once it shows signs of vigorous growth, it should do well with ordinary rainfall.

Care
Prune spent flowers down to the first pair of buds, and these will bloom. Yarrow, especially fern-leaved yarrow, *A. filipendulina*, makes a delightful dried flower, so harvest the last round of blooms for winter bouquets. Fertilize the bed lightly between late winter and early spring, applying a slow-release organic fertilizer for acid-loving plants at the rate of 2 pounds per 100 sq. ft. In spring, replenish the mulch. Before growth begins in spring, gently remove the dead foliage. Every four or five years—or if the plant becomes less productive—divide in early spring before growth begins.

Companion Planting and Design
Yarrow's beautiful ferny foliage adds texture to perennial beds and is very attractive in naturalized plantings.

Our Personal Recommendations
Beautiful cultivars of fern-leaved yarrow, *A. filipendulina*, which has deeply divided silvery foliage, are golden 'Coronation Gold', and 'Moonshine'. Varieties of *A. millefolium*, a slightly smaller species that self-sows, come in many attractive shades: 'Cerise Queen' is cherry red; 'Paprika' is brick red; 'Red Beauty' is rose red. André loves the new 'Terra Cotta', which starts out peach colored and matures to a rich terra-cotta hue.

Yarrow is a flower for all seasons and all locations, from the formal perennial border to the herb garden. From spring through midsummer, the large, flat-topped flower heads of modern cultivars stand in strong yellows, gold, off-pink, cerise, and off-white above woolly gray-green foliage 8 to 36 in. high. The ferny foliage of this ancient herb is strongly scented and makes a great filler. Yarrow is showy naturalized with ornamental grasses in meadow gardens, and a wonderful textural accent in perennial borders. The cut flowers are very long-lasting in fresh bouquets. They also dry quickly, preserve excellent color and much of their volume, and are a mainstay of winter arrangements.

Other Name
Milfoil

Bloom Period and Seasonal Color
June through August; yellow, gold, off-pink, cerise, red, rust, salmon, off-white.

Mature Height × Spread
1 to 4 ft. × 2 to 3 ft.

Roses *for the* Mid-Atlantic

The rose was designated the nation's floral emblem in 1987. Roses thrive here—and gardeners fall in love with the beautiful form and seductive fragrance of varieties like green-eyed white 'Madame Hardy' and David Austin's 'Graham Thomas'. Fall in love, but confine your passion to roses billed as "disease resistant." Those we recommend are resistant, as are those that receive awards from All-America Rose Selections and the American Rose Society.

Planting and Pruning

For roses to produce a dazzle of flowers and fragrance, nearly all need eight hours of morning sun, or six hours of afternoon sun, all day sun, or very bright filtered light. They need a well-drained site, and for most a pH of between 5.5 and 7.0. See Soil Preparation in the Introduction. The key to success is thorough and deep soil preparation—deeply dug planting holes 24 inches wide and 24 inches deep, and humusy, fertile soil. André applies an organic fertilizer three times a year: in late winter or early spring, in early midsummer, and in early fall.

You can plant a container-grown rose in early or late spring, in summer, or fall before Indian summer. If the rootball is encircled by roots, untangle them gently. If they can't be unwound, make four shallow vertical cuts in the wall of roots and slice off the matted roots on the bottom. Half fill the planting hole with improved soil, and pack it down very firmly. Set the rootball into the hole so it is about an inch above the ground level. For grafted or budded roses, set the plant so that the bud union is 2 to 3 inches above ground level. Roses on their own roots do not have a bud union. See the Appendix for a list of sources for roses grown from cuttings rather than grafts. Half fill the hole again with improved soil, and pack it down firmly. Finish filling the hole with improved soil, and pack it down firmly. Make a saucer around the plant, and water it slowly and deeply. You plant bare-root roses the same way, but soak the roots for twelve hours before planting, and drape them over a firm mound in the center of the hole.

'Double Delight'

Deadheading, and harvesting, big-flowered show roses keeps them blooming. When cutting roses for bouquets, leave a five-leaf sprig on each shoot as a base for new flowering shoots. Make all pruning cuts $1/2$ inch above an outside bud eye or sprig. Do not prune roses after the wood has hardened for the winter. Before growth begins in early spring, cut out diseased and damaged canes. Prune roses that bloom on new wood to the desired shape in early spring. Prune roses that bloom on wood from the previous season—some shrub and climbing roses—after they have flowered. Cut the oldest canes of recurrent bloomers back to two or three bud eyes, and remove twiggy ends. As new canes grow, tie them to fencing or trellising. To encourage growth of flowering laterals, cut side branches to short spurs.

Some roses, especially the hybrid teas and miniatures, may require winter protection. Cover the plants with pine boughs, or hill soil over the lower stems. Don't mulch with leaves or anything that creates a cozy habitat for field mice (voles): they'll girdle the roses and kill them.

Bush and Climbing Roses in a cottage garden.

Rose Problems

If you run into *Rosa*'s big three problems—Japanese beetles, blackspot, and powdery mildew—what we have learned may help. One way to deal with Japanese beetles is to spray plants under attack with rotenone, an OK spray. Another is to apply milky disease spores to the gardens and the lawn. Effective the second year, this natural deterrent kills the larvae. In early morning the beetles are sluggish, and you can knock them into a pot of soapy water. Loosing native parasitic wasps and flies that go for the beetles helps. Do not crush the beetles as that releases pheromones that will draw more Japanese beetles to the garden.

For blackspot, which loves hybrid teas, floribundas, and grandifloras, try the spray recommended by Cornell University research: 1 tablespoon of baking soda (sodium bicarbonate) and 1 tablespoon of ultra-fine horticultural oil to 1 quart of water. And, remove infected vegetation from the plant and the ground.

Powdery mildew may be minimized by spraying with the Cornell University research solution. Ask your garden center about new, environmentally safe controls.

Deer—well, sprays containing very bitter Bitrex® may keep deer away for a time. The only sure protection is to screen the bushes with chicken wire. It isn't noticeable at a distance. Or put up a 10-foot deer fence.

Climbing Rose

Rosa spp. and hybrids

The roses we call "climbers" put forth long canes that can be trained to cover an arch, an arbor, a trellis, a wall, a fence, or to climb a tree. "Training" means being tied— roses don't climb on their own. The showiest climbers are ramblers that bear clusters of small blooms on pliant canes that rise annually from the base. Climbers that are tall shrubs with stiff, not pliant, canes bear large flowers singly or in clusters. There are large climbing roses (CL) and miniature climbing roses (MCL). The large types are usually included as backdrops for rose gardens—trained to an arch, a pergola, or a wall. The miniatures require little space at the base and succeed in containers with winter protection; they are ideal for small condominium patios and porches.

Other Name
Pillar Rose

Bloom Period and Seasonal Color
Bloom period depends on the variety; hues of all colors, except true blue.

Mature Height × Spread
6 to 20 ft. × 3 to 6 ft.

When, Where, and How to Plant
Plant bare-root roses before the last frost in spring. Plant container-grown roses in early to mid-spring, summer, or early to mid-fall. Most roses need full sun, but climbers whose branches are in the sun will bloom with their roots in shade. Climbers attach themselves with their thorns but they must be trained (tied) in the direction they are to grow, unless climbing a tree. Plant a rose meant to climb a tree so prevailing winds blow the branches toward the tree. Leave 12 in. between a climber and a house wall, and provide a trellis for support. The ideal planting soil is well-drained, fertile, humusy, with pH between 5.5 and 7.0. See Soil Preparation in the Introduction. Follow the planting instructions at the beginning of this chapter. For grafted roses, set the plant so that the bud union is 2 to 3 in. above ground level. Water well. Apply a 3-in. mulch beginning 3 in. from the main stem.

Growing Tips
The first year, unless there's a soaking rain, in spring and fall pour a bucketful of water slowly and gently around the roots every two weeks; in summer every week or ten days. Maintain the mulch throughout the summer.

Care
Apply a slow-release organic rose fertilizer in late winter or early spring, again in early midsummer, and again in early fall. Renew the mulch. Every year remove one of the oldest canes, and save two or three of the new canes for next year; five or six heavy canes is all a climbing rose can support.

Companion Planting and Design
A climbing, or pillar, rose can be trained into a 10- to 12-ft. pillar. Climbing roses trained to grow horizontally along fences tend to flower more. To hide a climber's bare legs, plant a bushy companion, catmint or lavender for example.

Our Personal Recommendations
For pillar roses with recurrent bloom, we recommend fragrant 'Golden Showers', an AARS winner; fragrant blush-pink 'New Dawn'; and 'White Dawn'. Very fragrant climbers include 'Don Juan', 'Golden Artie', and 'Paul's Lemon Pillar'.

Garden Rose

Rosa spp. and hybrids

When, Where, and How to Plant

Plant bare-root roses before the last frost; plant container-grown roses in early to mid-spring or early to mid-fall. Most roses need full sun; when a rose can do well with less, that is stated in the grower's description. Leave 12 in. between a rose-bush and a house wall because the ground there tends to stay dry even in hard rain. The ideal planting soil is well drained, fertile, humusy, with a pH between 5.5 and 7.0. See Soil Preparation in the Introduction. Follow the planting instructions at the beginning of this chapter. For grafted roses, set the plant so that the bud union is 2 to 3 in. above ground level. Water well. Mulch 2 to 3 in. deep starting 3 in. from the main stem.

Growing Tips

The first year, unless there's a soaking rain, in spring and fall slowly and gently pour a bucketful of water around the roots every two weeks; in summer every week or ten days. Maintain the mulch throughout the summer.

Care

Apply a slow-release organic rose fertilizer in late winter or early spring, again in early midsummer, and again in early fall. Renew the mulch. If an English rose sends out an excessively long shoot, cut it back hard any time. As the buds swell in spring, prune English roses back by about a third of their height, and cut polyanthas and floribundas back a third of their size. Remove the oldest flowering canes and leave the plants open in the center, creating a vase-shaped framework.

Companion Planting and Design

English roses are most effective planted in groups of three or more of one variety. The floriferous little polyantha roses grow into dense impenetrable low hedges, so you may need only one or two. The pretty, slightly fragrant, seashell pink 'The Fairy' makes a dense flowery hedge. A floribunda favorite for edging fences is 'Betty Prior', a vivid pink whose emerald foliage stays fresh all summer.

Our Personal Recommendations

Among our favorite David Austin English roses are the pink 'Cottage Rose' and pristine white 'Fair Bianca'. In warm regions pink 'Gruss an Aachen' blooms in high shade.

The English roses, the polyanthas, and the floribundas (meaning many-flowered) are cluster-flowering garden roses whose beauty rivals hybrid teas. Modern disease-resistant plants, they produce blooms almost all season long and many are fragrant. The many-petaled David Austin English roses bear 2½- to 5-in. blooms that recall the full, fragrant roses our grandparents grew, but the shrubs are compact and easily managed. The polyanthas are 2 to 3 ft. tall, and bear clusters of charming little seashell-like flowers under 2 in. across. The floribundas are 4 or 5 ft. tall with 2- to 5-in. blooms which, like the polyanthas, are borne in clusters. Some have blooms in the form of hybrid tea roses. In Europe, they landscape many roadsides and parks.

Other Names

English Rose, Polyantha Rose, Floribunda Rose

Bloom Period and Seasonal Color

Recurrent all-season bloom; hues of all colors, except true blue.

Mature Height × Spread

English Roses—3 to 8 ft. × 4 to 5 ft.
Polyanthas—2 to 3 ft. × 2 to 3 ft.
Floribundas—2 to 5 ft. × 2 to 5 ft.

Ground Cover Rose

Rosa spp. and hybrids

Ground cover roses spread outward rather than upward to carpet slopes, edge shrub borders and gardens of shrub roses, and they are grown as low hedges. Best known are the Meidilands, which reach 2 to 3 ft. high. They bloom from early summer until fall, have natural resistance to rose blights and the only maintenance they need is pruning in late winter. The flower colors are white, cherry pink, scarlet, and there is a pearly-white blushed with pink called 'Pearl Sevillana'. Recently introduced, the new "carpeting" roses grow on their own roots. They add coral to the colors available. Just 2 to 2¹/₂ ft. tall, they can spread in a season to 4 ft. across.

Other Names
Landscape Rose, Carpet Rose

Bloom Period and Seasonal Color
All season; white and hues of pink, rose, coral.

Mature Height × Spread
2 to 3 ft. × 4 to 5 ft.

When, Where, and How to Plant
Ground cover roses are generally offered growing in containers. They are best planted a few weeks before the last frost, but will succeed planted anytime in early to mid-spring to mid-fall. They produce the most blooms in full sun but will bloom in some shade. The ideal planting soil is well-drained, fertile, humusy, with pH between 5.5 and 7.0. See Soil Preparation in the Introduction. Follow the planting instructions at the beginning of this chapter. For grafted roses, set the plant so that the bud union is 2 to 3 in. above ground level. Water well. Mulch 2 to 3 in. deep starting 3 in. from the main stem.

Growing Tips
The first year, unless there's a soaking rain, in spring and fall slowly and gently pour a bucketful of water around the roots every two weeks; in summer every week or ten days. Maintain the mulch throughout the summer.

Care
Apply a slow-release organic rose fertilizer in late winter or early spring, again in early midsummer, and again in early fall. Renew the mulch. Deadheading isn't necessary. As buds begin swelling in spring, shear the plants back to 1¹/₂ to 2 ft. high.

Companion Planting and Design
The modern ground cover roses are just what they are called: excellent ground cover. Some sprawling/trailing miniature roses can serve as ground cover roses. Some leggy shrub roses, like the bourbons, are trained as ground cover by pegging the sprawling branches to the ground with a forked stick or a bent wire—an interesting but a high-maintenance endeavor!

Our Personal Recommendations
The best-known ground cover rose is 'Flower Carpet' whose flowers are lavender-pink, and slightly perfumed. 'Jeepers Creepers' is a white version, and there's a light pink called 'Baby Blanket'. The native Virginia rose, spring-blooming rose-magenta *R. virginiana*, can be used as ground cover for sandy gardens and slopes along the coast. The autumn foliage is brilliant.

Hedge Rose
Rosa spp. and hybrids

When, Where, and How to Plant

Plant bare-root roses before the last frost; set out container-grown plants in early to mid-spring, summer, or early to mid-fall. They need full sun. Leave 12 in. between the bush and a house wall because the ground there tends to stay dry. The ideal planting soil is well drained, fertile, humusy, with pH between 5.5 and 7.0. See Soil Preparation in the Introduction. Follow the planting instructions at the beginning of this chapter. For grafted roses, set the plant so that the bud union is 2 to 3 in. above ground level. Water well. Mulch 2 to 3 in. deep starting 3 in. from the main stem.

Growing Tips

The first year, unless there's a soaking rain, in spring and fall slowly and gently pour a bucketful of water around the roots every two weeks; in summer every week or ten days. Maintain the mulch throughout the summer.

Care

Apply a slow-release organic rose fertilizer in late winter or early spring, again in early midsummer, and again in early fall. Renew the mulch. As the buds swell in spring, remove diseased and damaged canes. Beginning the fourth season for a rugosa rose, in early spring remove all canes that have flowered to encourage vigorous new growth.

Companion Planting and Design

If space allows, plant several different roses for a longer season of interest, including colorful hips in the fall.

Our Personal Recommendations

'Madame Hardy', a fragrant old white rose with a green-button eye, is one of the world's most beautiful roses. For brilliant rose hips in fall, plant *R. rugosa* 'Alba', 'Rubra', and 'Belle de Provins', which has almost double, pink flowers. The 4-ft. light pink cultivar 'Fru Dagmar Hastrup' can be pruned repeatedly without diminishing the production of flowers. 'Therese Bugnet' grows to 5 or 6 ft. and bears large, flat, slightly fragrant deep-pink flowers, with some repeat. Almost thornless 'Linda Campbell' grows 5 to 8 ft. and produces large clusters of crimson flowers in six to seven flushes of blooms.

For hedging and impressive specimen planting, we recommend the repeat-blooming hedge and shrub roses, along with the old garden and rugosa roses (as well as the cluster-bearing polyanthas and floribundas described on preceding pages). Many varieties have flowers shaped like hybrid teas. The shrub roses and the old garden ("romantica") species are robust growers, and bear gorgeous flowers. The romantica species tend to bloom profusely but only in spring; modern shrub roses may repeat bloom. The modern rugosa, or Japanese roses, hybrids of R. rugosa, bear clove-scented single or double flowers in spring with some repeat blooming, followed in fall by colorful foliage and shiny coral-orange rose hips high in vitamin C. Tall, stiff, and spiny, they're effective as hedges and known for success by the sea.

Other Names
Shrub Rose, Old Garden Rose, Rugosa Rose

Bloom Period and Seasonal Color
Profuse bloom in spring, modern hybrids repeat; colors are white, and all hues of pink, rose, red.

Mature Height × Spread
4 to 8 ft. × 3 to 6 ft.

Hybrid Tea Rose
Rosa hybrids

The hybrid tea roses are long-stemmed cutting flowers, with blooms that are large, high-centered, pointed, and semi- or double-flowered. The best, like the exquisite and enduring yellow-and-rose 'Peace', are perfumed. Most bloom in June, throw a few flowers throughout summer, and bloom well from September through October. Though the shrubs are leggy, need attention, and are not always hardy here, these are the most popular roses. The tea rose form appears in small polyantha roses, large-flowered floribunda roses, miniature roses, and climbing roses. To set the florist's single-stemmed, large-flowered hybrid tea rose apart, its classification has recently been changed to Large-flowered Bush Rose; but time will pass before most nurseries and catalogs call them anything but hybrid tea roses.

Other Name
Large-Flowered Bush Rose

Bloom Period and Seasonal Color
Spring, and sporadically through the season; many colors.

Mature Height × Spread
3 to 6 ft. × 3 to 6 ft.

When, Where, and How to Plant
Plant bare-root hybrid teas before the last frost; set out container-grown teas in early to mid-spring, summer, or before mid-fall. They need full sun. Leave 12 in. between the bush and a house wall because the ground there tends to stay dry. The ideal planting soil is well drained, fertile, humusy, with a pH between 5.5 and 7.0. See Soil Preparation in the Introduction. Follow the planting instructions at the beginning of this chapter. For grafted roses, set the plant so that the bud union is 2 to 3 in. above ground level. Water well. Mulch 2 to 3 in. deep starting 3 in. from the main stem.

Growing Tips
The first year, unless there's a soaking rain, in spring and fall slowly and gently pour a bucketful of water around the roots every two weeks; in summer every week or ten days. Maintain the mulch throughout the summer.

Care
Apply a slow-release organic rose fertilizer in late winter or early spring, again in early midsummer, and again in early fall. Renew the mulch. As the buds swell in spring, remove diseased and damaged canes, and the oldest flowering canes, leaving an open structure of four to five strong canes 5 or 6 in. long with the uppermost buds pointing outward. Remove spent flowers, fallen petals and leaves, and suckers as they occur. Cut roses and spent blossoms at a point just above a five-leaf stem. Every seven to ten days, and after heavy rainfalls, apply an all-purpose rose spray that controls insects and disease.

Companion Planting and Design
Hybrid teas are most often grown in a bed of their own with lavender, or full-foliaged annuals, to disguise their legginess.

Our Personal Recommendations
Some fragrant favorites are: beautiful orange 'Tropicana', AARS 1963; 'Miss All-American Beauty', AARS 1968, a deep-pink rose; 'Fragrant Cloud', a vivid coral-red; 'Double Delight', AARS 1977, whose white flowers are blushed a rich red; and 'Touch of Class', AARS 1986, a slightly fragrant pink, coral, and cream rose usually raised for show.

Miniature Rose
Rosa spp. and hybrids

When, Where, and How to Plant
Miniature roses are usually sold growing in containers. They may be planted anytime in early to mid-spring, summer, or early to mid-fall. They produce the most blooms in full sun but will bloom in some shade. The ideal planting soil is well drained, fertile, humusy, with pH between 6.5 and 7.0. Space the plants 2 ft. apart. See Soil Preparation in the Introduction. Follow the planting instructions at the beginning of this chapter, but make the holes twice the width of the rootball and 12 in. to 15 in. deep. Set the roses so they are at ground level. For grafted roses, set the plant so that the bud union is 2 to 3 in. above ground level. Water well. Mulch 2 to 3 in. deep starting 3 in. from the main stem.

Growing Tips
The first year, unless there's a soaking rain, in spring and fall slowly and gently pour a bucketful of water around the roots every two weeks; in summer every week or ten days. Maintain the mulch throughout the summer.

Care
Apply a slow-release organic rose fertilizer in late winter or early spring, again in early midsummer, and again in early fall. Renew the mulch. Deadheading isn't necessary. As buds begin swelling in spring, remove dead, weak, and discolored canes and canes that cross. Trim all the branches back by about a third, enough to maintain a pleasing form.

Companion Planting and Design
We like miniature roses as edging for beds of leggy shrub roses. Those sold as climbers make beautiful tree form roses, and are lovely dripping from containers. Some of the very dense miniature roses make delightful edgers for paths and driveways.

Our Personal Recommendations
For fragrance we recommend yellow 'Rise 'N Shine', a recipient of the American Rose Society Award for Excellence. 'China Doll' makes a sweet 18-in. hedge covered with pink, semi-double blooms. For hanging baskets we like 'Red Cascade', a vigorous miniature with cascading branches, and 'Starina', a fragrant, orange-red miniature, which also has an award for excellence from the ARS.

The miniature roses are offspring of 'Rouletii', a selection of the China rose 'Minima', the fairy rose, which blooms all season. Those sold as climbers can also be trained as tree form, basket, and container plants. The minis flower modestly from June to frost, and bear flowers less than 1 3/4 in. in diameter, often shaped like hybrid teas or cabbage roses. Too small to be effective as specimen plantings, they're delightful as edging plants and in rock gardens and containers. Miniature roses will bloom for a time indoors on very sunny windowsills. They also flourish in containers set in sun on patio or porch, but to be safe for the winter they need to be in a spot protected from the wind.

Bloom Period and Seasonal Color
Spring, or repeat bloom; white, and all hues of yellow and pink through red.

Mature Height × Spread
1 to 1 1/2 ft. × 1 1/2 to 2 ft.

Shrubs *for the Mid-Atlantic*

Shrubs wed the other elements of the landscape to the buildings and the trees. Given a minimum of maintenance they provide flowers, foliage, fragrance, fruit, and interesting structures—pyramidal, columnar, arching, rounded, upright, or sprawling.

The leaf-losing flowering shrubs bring color to the garden early in the year. Forsythia turns to gold in March and the beautiful quinces follow. The spicily fragrant viburnums bloom later. In mid-spring, mature mock oranges perfume our gardens and the roses described in the Roses chapter come out full force. Summer has its stars, among them shore-loving hydrangeas, and butterfly bush—a prime attraction for these beautiful insects. Daphne fills summer afternoons with perfume. The foliage of some deciduous flowering plants also contributes to the beauty of the garden. When shrub borders are a mass of dark green in summer, the colorful foliage of *Weigela florida* 'Variegata' lightens the overall effect. In cold weather spirea and the silver-backed leaves of willowleaf cotoneaster, *Cotoneaster salicifolius* 'Autumn Fire', take on a purplish cast that blends beautifully with autumn's russet tones. The structure of the deciduous shrubs is an important winter asset, especially very twiggy plants like the barberries.

Many beautiful broadleaved evergreens flourish here, and we recommend them highly because they not only add color, they green the garden at other seasons. Bright and beautiful azaleas and rhododendrons, some deciduous, some evergreen, peak in late April and early May. Evergreen mahonia's fragrant

Oakleaf Hydrangea

spring flowers are followed by blue berries that
attract bevies of birds. In fall and winter nandina
adds lipstick-red berries and red-tipped leaves to
perennial beds and shrub borders. The favorite
hedge and accent plant in the Mid-Atlantic is
English boxwood. It can be sheared for centuries,
literally, so it's ideal for low hedges and to edge
formal beds. Have a look some time at the most
complete living collection of boxwood—at the
National Arboretum in Washington, D.C. The
needled evergreen shrubs we find most beautiful
and valuable are included in the Conifers chapter.

Beautyberry

When, Where, and How to Plant

When we are choosing shrubs, our first concern is
whether the places we have in mind will suit them as they mature. To develop well a shrub needs air and
space. Small young shrubs may look cozy in a deep, airless corner but they become cramped as they
mature, and might fall prey to certain insects and diseases under the stressful conditions. Light isn't usually a problem. Many are "understory" plants that developed in partial shade of taller trees, so they thrive
in partial sun.

Early spring and fall before Indian summer are the best planting seasons; early spring is best for
shrubs that don't transplant easily. Container-grown plants can be set out any time, spring, summer, or
fall. Mail order suppliers deliver some shrubs bare root and in time for spring planting—the roots need to
be soaked six to twelve hours before planting. Young shrubs tend to be more vigorous than bigger, older
plants that may have been in their containers for some time. Before buying a bargain plant, make sure the
rootball has a healthy, earthy smell and is vigorous looking, not irretrievably locked in wound-around
roots. When the color of a shrub's blossoms or its foliage is important to you, buy a plant whose flower or
leaf color is evident.

A generous planting hole is the best send-off you can give a plant. Make the hole three times as
wide and twice as deep as the rootball and plant the shrub so the crown will be an inch above the ground
level. Loosen the soil on the sides, and blend the soil taken from the hole with the organic amendments
described in Soil Preparation in the Introduction. Never replace existing soil with potting soil. Half fill
the bottom of the hole with the improved soil, and tamp it down to make a firm base for the shrub to
rest on. Then proceed with the planting.

Before placing a bare-root shrub in its planting hole, make a firm mound in the center of the hole. Drape the plant roots over and around the mound and proceed with the instructions for planting a container-grown shrub. To free a containerized shrub, tip the container on its side and roll it around until the rootball loosens, or slit the pot open. If roots wrap a rootball, before planting make four deep vertical cuts in the sides and slice the matted roots off the bottom 1 to 2 inches. Set the shrub in the hole and half fill with amended soil. Tamp it down firmly. Fill the hole with improved soil and once more tamp it down firmly. Shape the soil around the crown into a wide saucer. Water the soil slowly, gently, and thoroughly with a sprinkler, a soaker hose, a bubbler, or by hand. You need to put down $1^1/2$ inches of water measured in a regular sized coffee can, or 10 to 15 gallons of water poured slowly from a bucket. Mulch newly planted shrubs 2 to 3 inches deep (for bigger shrubs) starting 3 inches from the main stem. Replenish the mulch as needed to maintain it 2 to 3 inches deep.

Care

For a shrub's first season, unless there's a soaking rain, in spring and fall slowly and gently pour two to three bucketsful of water around the roots every two weeks; in summer every week or ten days. Even after cold sets in, roots continue to develop, so during fall droughts continue the watering program sufficiently to keep the soil from drying out. Once established, most shrubs will require less extra watering than perennials; they slow their growth in high heat so they adapt unless forced by shallow watering and inappropriate fertilizing to grow when the weather isn't supporting growth. Fertilize shrubs twice a year. Late winter is the best time to apply the slow-release, natural, organic fertilizers we recommend (see the Appendix), but early spring is OK; repeat in fall. Avoid fertilizing flowering shrubs with chemical fertilizers shortly before blooming: that stimulates growth at a time when you want the plants to direct their energy into flowering. After the winter or early spring fertilization, renew the mulch. For shrubs that do best in a soil with a low pH, apply fertilizers for acid-loving plants. Nourish the soil as the forest does with fallen leaves—gather, shred, allow to age, and return them to the garden in the form of leaf mold or compost.

Japanese Kerria

Pruning

You can reduce the amount of pruning your shrubs will need by selecting dwarf and slow-growing varieties. But even dwarfs grow, albeit slowly, and they need some pruning to maintain their size. Pruning—reducing leaf surfaces—limits the sugar synthesized and sent to the roots, and that limits next year's growth. Pruning also stimulates growth. Pruning young, just-developing shrubs when they are growing actively encourages growth and makes growth bushier. Fresh, young shoots that are cut back by half

Witch-Hazel in fall color.

immediately begin to grow lateral shoots.

The season to prune flowering shrubs depends on their bloom habit: in late winter or early spring, well before growth begins, it is time to prune shrubs that bloom on the current season's wood. Prune a shrub that blooms in summer on current growth—butterfly bush for example—shortly before growth begins in spring. Those that bloom on last season's wood, such as azaleas, flowering quince, and forsythia, should be pruned as soon after their flowering period as possible, usually spring, because the next thing they do is to initiate buds for the following season. To encourage branching that produces more foliage in broadleaf evergreens like nandina, cut succulent new shoots in half while they are actively growing.

By pruning drastically in late winter you can rejuvenate leggy flowering shrubs that bloom on new wood. Make the cut 6 to 10 inches from the ground. To rejuvenate a multi-stemmed shrub, before growth begins in spring, take out a third to a quarter of the oldest of the branches and the suckers crowding young branches. Repeat the process for the next three to four years.

More Options

Other beautiful shrubs that flourish here include:

Beautybush, *Kolkwitzia amabilis*

Bush Cinquefoil, *Potentilla fruticosa*

Privet, *Ligustrum vulgare*

California Privet, *Ligustrum ovalifolium*

Golden Privet, *L.* 'Vicary'

Japanese Stewartia, *Stewartia pseudocamellia*

Korean Stewartia, *S. koreana*

Prostrate Broom, *Cytisus decumbens*

Scotch Broom, *C. scorparius*,

  C. 'Moonlight'

Warminster Broom, *C.* × *praecox*

Spicebush, *Lindera benzoin*

Virginia Sweetspire, *Itea virginica*;

  I. 'Henry's Garnet'

Blue Spirea
Caryopteris × *clandonensis*

Blue spirea is a small, easy deciduous shrub or subshrub that in August produces spikes of airy flowers in delightful shades of blue. The long arching branches are covered with silvery foliage and the leaves, stems, and flowers are delicately aromatic. The plant grows quickly to 2 or 3 ft., and develops an open, airy, twiggy shape very appealing in flowering borders, and attractive edging walks and paths. The flowers bloom on new wood at or after midsummer when most other flowering shrubs have gone out of bloom, and they attract hordes of butterflies. Both foliage and flowers are used in bouquets, fresh and dried. This hybrid is superior to the common bluebeard, C. incana, and some first-rate cultivars are offered by nurseries and garden centers.

Other Names
Blue-Mist Shrub, Bluebeard

Bloom Period and Seasonal Color
Midsummer; shades of blue.

Mature Height × Spread
2 to 3 ft. × 3 to 4 ft.

When, Where, and How to Plant
Container-grown blue spirea transplants easily in early spring or in early fall. The flowering will be most satisfactory in full sun but it also will do well in some shade. Almost any soil will do as long as it is well drained, loose, or loamy, with enough humus to maintain moisture. See Soil Preparation in the Introduction, and the planting instructions at the beginning of this chapter. Provide a planting hole three times the width of the rootball and twice as deep. Set the shrub so the crown will be an inch or two above ground level. Shape the soil around the crown into a wide saucer. Water slowly and deeply. Apply mulch 3 in. deep starting 3 in. from the crown.

Growing Tips
The first year, unless there's a soaking rain, in spring and fall slowly and gently pour two to three bucketsful of water around the roots every two weeks; in summer every week or ten days. Maintain the mulch.

Care
Using a slow-release organic fertilizer, fertilize lightly in fall and again in late winter or early spring. Replenish the mulch. The bluebeards bloom on new wood: to improve flowering, in spring, just as the buds are breaking, prune back to within an inch of the living wood growth that starts from the short woody branches at the base of the plant. Severe pruning in early spring improves the flowering.

Companion Planting and Design
Include blue spirea in your butterfly plantings. Its late blooming habit makes it an excellent addition to flowering borders.

Our Personal Recommendations
We recommend 'Longwood Blue', a small blue spirea between $1^1/2$ and 2 ft. tall, for its heavy crop of deeper blue flowers and silver foliage; 'Dark Knight', a 3-footer with a spread of 3 to 4 ft., for the very fragrant dark purple-blue flowers that attract butterflies and hummingbirds and silvery-green foliage; 'Blue Mist', which is about the same height, and has fringed blue flowers; and 'Worcester Gold', which has blue flowers and bright yellow to chartreuse foliage.

Boxwood
Buxus sempervirens

When, Where, and How to Plant
Plant a container-grown boxwood in spring, summer, or fall. Transplant established box just before growth begins in mid-March, but spray it with wilt-proofing first. Mature plants thrive in full sun or light shade. Boxwood doesn't tolerate salt or wet feet; established plants tolerate some drought. They need well-drained, humusy, loose soil, pH 6.0 to 7.0. See Soil Preparation in the Introduction, and planting instructions at the beginning of this chapter. Dig a hole three times the width of the rootball and twice as deep. Set the shrub so the crown will be an inch or two above ground level. Shape the soil around the crown into a wide saucer. Water slowly and deeply. Apply mulch 3 in. deep starting 3 in. from the crown.

Growing Tips
Shade newly transplanted boxwoods from summer sun. The first year, unless there's a soaking rain, in spring and fall slowly and gently pour two to three bucketsful of water around the roots every two weeks; in summer every week or ten days. Maintain the mulch to keep the temperature even around the roots.

Care
Using a slow-release organic fertilizer, fertilize lightly in early fall and again in spring. Replenish the mulch as needed. Boxwood's very fibrous roots are close to the surface, so weed by hand—not with a cultivator. Prune elongated shoots in late spring after new growth is complete to keep boxwood bushy and beautiful. To reshape overgrown shrubs, in February or early March, cut the plants back to within 18 in. of the ground. They may take several years to fully recover.

Companion Planting and Design
Boxwood thrives in both city gardens and country estates. It is used with foundation plants, as a specimen, in group plantings, for hedges, and to edge knot gardens.

Our Personal Recommendations
André recommends the species, and var. 'Arborescens' for shade; the 3 to 4 ft. little-leaf boxwood, *B. microphylla*; and 'Kingsville Dwarf', a smaller variety. Where winters are hard, Korean little-leaf box, *B. microphylla* var. *koreana* is best; var. *japonica* is another good boxwood.

Boxwood is more than just a shrub to the Mid-Atlantic: it's a link to the clipped hedges that defined our ancestors' gardens and the great estates in their European homelands. It is the most popular subject for garden topiary work. The trim hedges outlining the parterres at the Palace of Versailles are clipped box. The species has dainty evergreen leaves, grows very slowly, is long lived, and can be clipped and pruned to almost any shape. Clippings are used to make Christmas roping and imitation Christmas tree topiaries. Historically, boxwood was used as edging, and for tailored hedges. The most popular variety is true English box, B. sempervirens 'Suffruticosa', a slow-growing shrub with us since colonial times. Plants 150 years old have been kept to below 3 ft. by pruning. The next most popular is the variety 'Arborescens', true tree boxwood. Deer avoid boxwood: chewing the leaves has caused the death of animals.

Other Name
Box

Bloom Period and Seasonal Color
Spring blooms are insignificant.

Mature Height × Spread
4 to 5 ft. × 4 to 5 ft.

Butterfly Bush

Buddleja davidii

Butterflies and hummingbirds—and bees—really do love this shrub, but that's not the only reason we recommend butterfly bush. The species grows to between 6 and 8 ft. in a single season, and from July until frost produces slim arching canes that sweep the ground and in late summer are tipped with 4- to 10-inch spikes of delicately scented florets. The flowers are a rich source of nectar and a magnet for hummingbirds and bees as well as butterflies. The leaves range from green to gray-green to gray, and are narrow, 4 to 10 in. long, and silvery on the underside. Many beautiful cultivated varieties are available in a wide range or colors.

Other Name
Summer Lilac

Bloom Period and Seasonal Color
August through September; species flowers are lilac; cultivars are white, pink, lavender, dark purple, purple-red.

Mature Height × Spread
5 to 8 ft. × 4 to 7 ft.

When, Where, and How to Plant
Container-grown butterfly bush transplants easily in early spring or in early fall. It flowers best in full sun but tolerates some shade. It thrives in humusy, fertile, well-drained soil with a pH of 5.5 to 7.0. See Soil Preparation in the Introduction, and the planting instructions at the beginning of this chapter. Provide a planting hole three times the width of the rootball and twice as deep. Set the shrub so the crown will be an inch or two above ground level. Shape the soil around the crown into a wide saucer. Water slowly and deeply. Apply mulch 3 in. deep starting 3 in. from the crown.

Growing Tips
The first year, unless there's a soaking rain, in spring and fall slowly and gently pour two to three bucketsful of water around the roots every two weeks; in summer every week or ten days. Maintain the mulch.

Care
Using a slow-release organic fertilizer, fertilize lightly in fall and again in late winter or early spring. After the winter fertilization, replenish the mulch. To get the best flowering from butterfly bush, prune the shrub to 12 to 18 in. in early spring while the plant is still dormant. It blooms on new wood and will recover quickly.

Companion Planting and Design
For a small garden, dwarf butterfly bush is the better choice. *B. davidii* var. *nanhoensis* 'Mongo', 'Petite Indigo', and 'Petite Plum' are 4-ft. dwarfs with attractive grayish foliage; they are small enough to plant next to the kitchen steps where you can watch the butterflies. For a large garden, or for the back of a flowering border, consider *B. alternifolia*, a graceful 20-ft. *Buddleja* with long, pendulous branches and flower spikes that are neat clusters of lilac-purple florets. It blooms early, in June.

Our Personal Recommendations
The species offers a range of attractive colors we enjoy seeing planted together: 'White Profusion', which bears white trusses 8 to 12 in. long; 'Pink Delight', whose trusses are up to 15 in. and a true pink; and 'Black Knight', which has very dark purple-violet flowers.

Camellia
Camellia japonica and hybrids

When, Where, and How to Plant
Spring or fall, plant a dormant container-grown camellia in semi-sun, or in dappled or bright shade. In Zones 6 and 7, choose hardy camellias, and site them out of wind and direct western sun. Camellias prefer well-drained, humusy, acid soil, pH 4.5 to 6.5. See Soil Preparation in the Introduction, and planting instructions at the beginning of this chapter. Provide a planting hole three times the width of the rootball and twice as deep. Set the shrub so the crown will be an inch or two above ground level. Shape the soil around the crown into a wide saucer. Water slowly and deeply. Apply mulch 3 in. deep starting 3 in. from the crown.

Growing Tips
The first year, unless there's a soaking rain, in spring and fall slowly and gently pour two to three bucketsful of water around the roots every two weeks; in summer every week or ten days. Maintain the mulch. Deadhead, including a couple of leaves below the flower to keep the shrub from growing straggly.

Care
In fall, make a light application of a slow-release organic fertilizer for acid-loving plants. Protect for winter with a 5- to 6-in. winter mulch and burlap barriers, or a Remay wrap. Annual pruning is usually not needed. However, you can improve the flowering of a straggly camellia by shortening long shoots back to sturdy outward-facing side-shoots or buds after it has flowered. To rejuvenate older plants, remove a third of the played-out branches before the shrub blooms every year for three years.

Companion Planting and Design
Camellias are used as foundation plants, grouped in a center island, planted as a flowering allée.

Our Personal Recommendations
When cold cost the National Arboretum its large collection of camellias, 12-ft. sasanqua camellia, *C. sasanqua*, survived and William Ackerman crossed it with hardy *C. oleifera*, the fragrant tea oil camellia. The hybrids are as pretty as the sasanquas and hardy in Zone 6, to -10 degrees Fahrenheit. The Ackerman hybrids have names like 'Winter's Charm'. Even Ackerman hybrids suffer in exposed, windy areas, especially facing western sun.

The camellia is a tall Southern belle with lustrous olive green evergreen leaves and spectacular flowers that appear fall and winter in the Mid-Atlantic's warmest region, and in early spring in cooler areas. The blossoms are truly beautiful, sometimes fragrant, and many-petaled, semi-double and double in many colors and bi-colors. The widely grown Japanese camellia is a rather formal plant that bears flowers as much as 5 in. across in late winter and early spring. Temperatures below 32 degrees Fahrenheit can brown the buds and ruin the flowers. Select winter-hardy camellias with the assistance of a reliable local nursery such as Merrifield, in Merrifield and Fairfax, VA; Hill's in Arlington; Betty's Azalea Ranch in Fairfax; or Behnke's in Beltsville, MD.

Other Name
Japanese Camellia

Bloom Period and Seasonal Color
In warm regions, fall and winter; in cold regions, late winter and spring; flower shades range from white to pink, rose, crimson, purple-red, bi-colors.

Mature Height × Spread
10 to 15 ft. × 5 to 10 ft.

163

Cotoneaster
Cotoneaster horizontalis

The cotoneasters are fine-textured, evergreen or semi-evergreen shrubs with layered branches and small white or pinkish flowers in spring and summer. The big show is the fall display of bright red or orange-red berries. There are tall and very low-growing members of the clan. Mid-size rockspray cotoneaster, C. horizontalis, is the most commonly planted species. It's a wide-spreading, semi-evergreen tiered mound of branches that creates a herringbone pattern. The light pink flowers are followed in late summer by masses of persistent red fruits. The leaves are shiny dark green and usually turn scarlet-orange in the fall. Cotoneasters are good shore plants, and the fruits attract birds.

Other Name
Rockspray Cotoneaster

Bloom Period and Seasonal Color
Spring and summer; white or pinkish flowers; bright red berries; colorful fall foliage.

Mature Height × Spread
2 to 3 ft. × 5 to 8 ft.

When, Where, and How to Plant
Set out a container-grown cotoneaster in early spring or early fall. It flowers well in full sun, four to six hours of sun, or all-day filtered light. Cotoneaster doesn't tolerate wet feet, but handles some drought. It succeeds in well-drained, humusy soil, acid or alkaline. See Soil Preparation in the Introduction, and planting instructions at the beginning of this chapter. Provide a planting hole three times the width of the rootball and twice as deep. Set the shrub so the crown will be an inch or two above ground level. Shape the soil around the crown into a wide saucer. Water slowly and deeply. Apply mulch 3 in. deep starting 3 in. from the crown.

Growing Tips
The first year, unless there's a soaking rain, in spring and fall slowly and gently pour two to three bucketsful of water around the roots every two weeks; in summer every week or ten days. Maintain the mulch.

Care
In late winter or early spring fertilize with a slow-release organic fertilizer. Replenish the mulch. Fertilize again in the fall. Rockspray cotoneaster blooms on old wood. Minimal pruning is needed, and it's best undertaken after the berries are over. If the plant is growing against a wall, retain a few widely separated main branches and allow these to develop side branchlets. Keep an informal hedge in bounds by light selective pruning during the growing season. A formal hedge may be lightly sheared as needed.

Companion Planting and Design
Use cotoneaster for hedges, to clothe slopes, steps, and rocky places with attractive foliage, interesting branching, and bright berries.

Our Personal Recommendations
In addition to the popular rockspray cotoneaster, for ground cover in rocky places we recommend cranberry cotoneaster, C. apiculatus, which bears larger, bright red berries; creeping cotoneaster, C. adpressus, a very compact dwarf form; bearberry cotoneaster, C. dammeri, a low, prostrate evergreen ground cover; and spreading upright cotoneaster, C. divaricatus, a pink-flowered shrub, 6 to 7 ft. tall, which has smaller red berries and foliage that colors reddish purple in fall.

Daphne 'Carol Mackie'

Daphne × burkwoodii 'Carol Mackie'

When, Where, and How to Plant

Plant a container-grown daphne in early spring, and handle with care until new growth is evident. Choose a site with some protection from hot noon sun, and cold north winds. By the shore it may be able to take full sun. Daphne will do best in well-drained, sandy loam, with lots of leaf mold added, in the pH range between 6.0 and 7.0. See Soil Preparation in the Introduction, and the planting instructions at the beginning of this chapter. Provide a planting hole three times the width of the rootball and twice as deep. Set the shrub so the crown will be an inch or two above ground level. Shape the soil around the crown into a wide saucer. Water slowly and deeply. Apply mulch 3 in. deep starting 3 in. from the crown.

Growing Tips

The first year, unless there's a soaking rain, in spring and fall slowly and gently pour two to three bucketsful of water around the roots every two weeks; in summer every week or ten days. Maintain the mulch.

Care

Where snow cover is uncertain, protect for the winter with a cover of evergreen boughs. Using a slow-release organic fertilizer, fertilize lightly in fall and again in late winter or early spring. Replenish the mulch. To maintain daphne's shape, when it finishes blooming and before July, prune the branches back to outward-facing buds. This also stimulates growth, and encourages the formation of flowering buds for the next season.

Companion Planting and Design

Valued for rock gardens and small flowering borders. Plant daphne where its fragrance can be appreciated.

Our Personal Recommendations

Daphne 'Carol Mackie' is a superb plant, but there are two others we recommend: lilac daphne, *D. genkwa*, a 3- to 4-ft. deciduous plant; and the taller semi-evergreen February daphne, *D. mezereum*, which blooms earlier than 'Carol Mackie'—late March and April—and bears long clusters of rose-purple blooms followed in late summer by bright red berries.

The daphnes are deciduous, semi-evergreen, or evergreen shrubs, low, wide, slow-growing, and they bear wonderfully fragrant flowers followed by brightly colored fleshy fruits. They are native to Europe, Asia, and northern Africa. One of the hardiest of the daphnes is the semi-evergreen D. × burkwoodii variety 'Carol Mackie'. 'Carol Mackie' is a very beautiful bushy shrub about 3 ft. tall by 3 ft. and a little more wide, whose narrow leaves are delicately edged with a band of cream or pale gold. In late spring, it opens masses of star-shaped, light pink flowers that are extremely fragrant. These are superb garden plants, with a dense, round, mounded form that works particularly well in a small garden. They are not particularly easy to get established, but well worth the effort.

Other Name

Carol Mackie Daphne

Bloom Period and Seasonal Color

May; pale pink flowers; foliage is variegated cream or pale gold.

Mature Height × Spread

3 ft. × 3 ft. or more

Deciduous Azalea

Rhododendron mucronulatum

If we grow only one flowering shrub in the Mid-Atlantic, it is likely to be an azalea. Azaleas are botanically distinct members of the Rhododendron genus. Those that are evergreen are discussed elsewhere in the chapter. The first azaleas to bloom are leaf-losers, and the earliest of these is the Korean azalea, R. mucronulatum, whose rose-magenta flowers appear well before the leaves. There are thousands of azalea hybrids, including some that bloom again in fall. The blooms may be single, semi-double, or double and the colors include hues of white, yellow, pink, orange, purple, and red.

Other Names
Korean Rhododendron, Korean Azalea

Bloom Period and Seasonal Color
March and early April; pink, rose, white.

Mature Height × Spread
4 to 8 ft. × 4 to 8 ft.

When, Where, and How to Plant

Azaleas are shallow-rooted and transplant well even when quite large. Plant a balled-and-burlapped azalea in early spring or early fall; plant a container-grown azalea in spring, summer, or fall. Azaleas do best in bright dappled light, but they tolerate full sun if the soil is moist. Provide soil that is well drained, rich in humus, and between pH 4.5 and 6.0. See Soil Preparation in the Introduction, and the planting instructions at the beginning of this chapter. Provide a planting hole three times the width of the rootball and twice as deep. Set the shrub so the crown will be an inch or two above ground level. Shape the soil around the crown into a wide saucer. Water slowly and deeply. Apply mulch 3 in. deep starting 3 in. from the crown.

Growing Tips

The first season, unless there's a soaking rain, every two weeks in spring and fall slowly and gently pour two to three bucketsful of water around the roots; in summer every week or ten days. Maintain the mulch.

Care

Using a slow-release organic fertilizer for acid-loving plants, fertilize an azalea in late winter or early spring, and in the fall. Replenish the mulch. To keep an azalea shapely, stimulate growth, and encourage the formation of flowering buds, after blooming prune the branches back to outward-facing buds.

Companion Planting and Design

We like deciduous azaleas with broadleaved evergreen shrubs—rhododendrons, mountain laurels, and evergreen azaleas. The Korean azalea is especially nice with early blooming forsythia.

Our Personal Recommendations

André's father Martin Viette's favorites were a white and 'Cornell Pink' Korean azalea. André recommends the showy, fragrant, pink royal azalea, *R. schlippenbachii*; the native, fragrant, white sweet azalea, *R. arborescens*, for its red fall foliage; the native flame azalea, *R. calendulaceum*, for its showy flowers in shades of yellow, apricot, orange, and scarlet; the pinkshell azalea, *R. vaseyi*, which is native to the Blue Ridge Mountains of North Carolina. And for their rhododendron-like blooms, the Knap Hill and Exbury hybrids, and the Mollis group, *R. × kosteranum*.

166

Dwarf Burning Bush
Euonymus alatus 'Compactus'

When, Where, and How to Plant
Container-grown euonymus can be planted spring, summer, or fall. It succeeds even on dry, rocky slopes. The dwarf burning bush and the winged spindle tree color most brilliantly in full sun, but succeed in shade or part shade. Any soil that isn't swampy will do, pH 6.0 to 8.0. See Soil Preparation in the Introduction, and the planting instructions at the beginning of this chapter. Provide a planting hole three times the width of the rootball and twice as deep. Set the shrub so the crown will be an inch or two above ground level. Shape the soil around the crown into a wide saucer. Water slowly and deeply. Apply mulch 2 in. deep starting 3 in. from the crown.

Growing Tips
The first year, unless there's a soaking rain, in spring and fall slowly and gently pour two to three bucketsful of water around the roots every two weeks; in summer every week or ten days. Maintain the mulch.

Care
Fertilize with a slow-release organic fertilizer for acid-loving plants in fall and again in late winter or early spring. Replenish the mulch periodically. Burning bush is most attractive when it is allowed to develop naturally with some thinning to keep the plant structure open. To keep a hedge of evergreen euonymus to 4 to 6 ft., cut back branch tips of older wood in April or May.

Companion Planting and Design
Dwarf winged spindle tree is used in informal hedges and as a featured lawn specimen. On the grounds of the U.S. Capitol, winged spindle tree grows with evergreens, forsythias, and other shrubs, unnoticed until fall—then the color draws the eye for weeks.

Our Personal Recommendations
While all euonymus are subject to scale, there's very little problem with *E. alatus*, either the dwarf or the species. A cultivar of the European euonymus, *E. europaeus* 'Aldenhamensis', bears bright pink capsules and is more fruitful than the species. *E. fortunei*, the wintercreeper euonymus planted for its silver-veined foliage, is a beautiful ground cover or vine, but has too many problems.

Euonymus is a member of the bittersweet family, a group that includes both leaf-losing and evergreen shrubs, small trees, and vines that have beautiful foliage and colorful fall fruits. Dwarf burning bush is a slow-growing shrub with outreaching branches, a compact version of the winged spindle tree, Euonymus alatus, whose flaming fall color rivals the sugar maple. When cold comes, every leaf on the winged spindle tree, and on the dwarf burning bush, turns a glowing rosy crimson before falling. The show is enhanced by small clusters of tiny fruits that turn lipstick red. The birds love the fruits and usually pick the branches clean. "Winged" in the common name refers to corky ridges edging the branches. The ridges are most pronounced in the tree, enough to have textural interest.

Other Name
Dwarf Winged Spindle Tree

Bloom Period and Seasonal Color
Fall foliage is a glowing crimson.

Mature Height × Spread
8 to 10 ft. × 8 to 10 ft.

Dwarf Fothergilla

Fothergilla gardenii

Fothergilla is native to the Alleghenies and is rated as one of the top ten to twenty native American shrubs. Like witch-hazel, to which it is related, fothergilla blooms early, has fragrant somewhat similar blossoms, and the foliage colors brilliantly in fall. Dwarf fothergilla is a small bushy shrub, just as wide as it is high. In April and early May it bears rounded tufts of whitish bottlebrush flowers that have the sweet scent of honey. The flowers and the crinkly dark green foliage are reason enough to plant fothergilla, but the brilliant fall foliage is the star attraction. The leaves turn to yellow gold, orange, and scarlet, and usually with all three colors on the same bush.

Other Name
Witch Alder

Bloom Period and Seasonal Color
April to early May; white flowers in spring; fall foliage is yellow gold, orange, and scarlet.

Mature Height × Spread
2 to 4 ft. × 2 to 4 ft.

When, Where, and How to Plant
Plant a balled-and-burlapped fothergilla in early spring or early fall. If it's container-grown, it can be planted spring, summer, or fall. Fothergilla flowers best and produces the brightest fall colors growing in full sun, but in hot areas it benefits from protection from noon sun in summer. To succeed, fothergilla must have soil with an acid pH, under 6.0. It is not suited to alkaline or limey soil. See Soil Preparation in the Introduction, and the planting instructions at the beginning of this chapter. Provide a planting hole three times the width of the rootball and twice as deep. Set the shrub so the crown will be an inch or two above ground level. Shape the soil around the crown into a wide saucer. Water slowly and deeply. Apply mulch 2 in. deep starting 3 in. from the crown.

Growing Tips
The first year, unless there's a soaking rain, in spring and fall slowly and gently pour two to three bucketsful of water around the roots every two weeks; in summer every week or ten days. Maintain the mulch.

Care
Using a slow-release organic fertilizer for acid-loving plants, fertilize lightly in fall and again in late winter or early spring. Replenish the mulch. Before growth begins in spring, cut back to the ground old branches that are crowding others, taking care not to harm young shoots coming up from the base.

Companion Planting and Design
Fothergilla lights up shrub borders planted with azaleas, rhododendrons, and evergreens. We like to place them near the house and along paths where the sweet honey scent of the flowers can be appreciated.

Our Personal Recommendations
The dwarf fothergilla is the best choice for most gardens, but where there's space for a larger plant, choose faster-growing *F. major*, the large fothergilla: it is similar to the dwarf but grows more upright and matures at 6 to 10 ft.

Evergreen Azalea
Rhododendron cultivars and hybrids

When, Where, and How to Plant
Azaleas are fibrous-rooted and transplant well even when quite large. The best times to plant them are early fall and early spring. An azalea tolerates full sun here as long as the soil is moist, but it will do best in bright, dappled light. Provide soil that is well drained, rich in humus (we add leaf mold to the hole), and between pH 4.5 and 6.0. See Soil Preparation in the Introduction, and planting instructions at the beginning of this chapter. Provide a planting hole three times the width of the rootball and twice as deep. Set the shrub so the crown will be about an inch above ground level. Shape the soil around the crown into a wide saucer. Water slowly and deeply. Apply mulch 3 in. deep starting 3 in. from the crown.

Growing Tips
The first year, unless there's a soaking rain, in spring and fall slowly and gently pour two to three bucketsful of water around the roots every two weeks; in summer every week or ten days. Maintain the mulch.

Care
Using a slow-release organic fertilizer for acid-loving plants, fertilize in spring and again in fall. Replenish the mulch. To maintain the shape of an azalea, as soon as it finishes blooming prune the branches back to outward-facing buds. Shearing to remove flowering tips when the blooms fade improves the next season's flowering; pruning too long after flowering cuts off next year's blooms.

Companion Planting and Design
Evergreen azaleas are especially useful for fronting a border of rhododendrons, andromeda, mountain laurel, and deciduous azaleas.

Our Personal Recommendations
In addition to the Glenn Dale evergreen azaleas that do so well here, we recommend the Gable hybrids, which come in many colors and are hardy even in Zone 5. The Yodogawa azalea, *R. yedoense*, has fragrant, fully double, lavender flowers and is hardy in Zone 5. The lovely Kurume azaleas, which derive from *R. obtusum*, 'Hino-Crimson' and vivid red 'Hinodegiri', are hardy in Zones 5 and 6.

Evergreen azaleas, like the deciduous azaleas described earlier in the chapter, belong to the genus Rhododendron. The flowers of the evergreen azaleas are funnel-shaped rather than bell-shaped, like the leaf-losing azaleas, and the plant is smaller and more refined. The foliage of some varieties acquires a plum or maroon tint in fall and others turn to gold. You can have evergreen azaleas in flower from early spring to late summer. The hundreds of medium-tall R. kaempferi cultivars, which are hardy in Zones 5b to 9, are usually evergreen. An evergreen group that does well here is the Glenn Dale type, developed by B. Y. Morrison, first director of the U.S. National Arboretum. You can see hundreds of varieties in bloom there in May.

Bloom Period and Seasonal Color
April to September; white, shades of coral, pink, rose, red, purple, bi-colors.

Mature Height × Spread
2 to 6 ft. × 4 to 6 ft.

Firethorn

Pyracantha coccinea

Firethorn is a big, thorny, wide-branching evergreen or semi-evergreen shrub that produces fine foliage and white, lightly scented flowers in mid-spring. It is grown primarily for the clusters of brilliant orange or scarlet fruits that mature in the fall. The species is susceptible to scale, but in recent years several improved varieties have been introduced. When you buy pyracantha, insist on having a scale- and fireblight-resistant specimen.

Other Name
Scarlet Firethorn

Bloom Period and Seasonal Color
Late spring; white, somewhat scented flowers; bright, persistent, orange or red berries in the fall.

Mature Height × Spread
8 ft. × 8 ft.

When, Where, and How to Plant
Firethorn transplants with difficulty, so plant a container-grown shrub in early spring before growth begins. Firethorn flowers best and produces the brightest fruits growing in full sun. However, like most shrubs, it succeeds with four to six hours of sun, or all-day filtered light. It thrives in any well-drained soil in a broad pH range, 5.5 to 7.5. See Soil Preparation in the Introduction, and planting instructions at the beginning of this chapter. Provide a planting hole three times the width of the rootball and twice as deep. Set the shrub so the crown will be an inch or so above ground level. Shape the soil around the crown into a wide saucer. Water slowly and deeply. Apply mulch 3 in. deep starting 3 in. from the crown.

Growing Tips
The first year, unless there's a soaking rain, in spring and fall slowly and gently pour two to three bucketsful of water around the roots every two weeks; in summer every week or ten days. Maintain the mulch.

Care
Using a slow-release organic fertilizer, fertilize lightly in the fall and again in late winter or early spring. Replenish the mulch. Firethorn becomes very wide-spreading if left unpruned. If you wish to maintain the shape of this spring flowering shrub, shortly after it finishes blooming, prune the branches back to outward facing buds. Flower buds—and the fruit—form on old wood; as you prune, keep in mind that the flowers you don't prune off will provide you with a lovely show of berries in the fall.

Companion Planting and Design
Firethorn can be used as a freestanding specimen, and in hedges, but is most striking espaliered against a blank masonry or wooden wall, or grown on a trellis where the asymmetrical branching and bright fall fruits stand out.

Our Personal Recommendations
One we can recommend is 'Mohave', an upright shrub 8 to 10 ft. tall that bears masses of bright orange-red berries. It isn't hardy near the West Virginia border, but 'Fiery Cascade', another resistant hybrid that bears an abundance of bright fruits, withstands winters even in Zone 6.

Flowering Quince
Chaenomeles speciosa

When, Where, and How to Plant
Plant a balled-and-burlapped quince in early spring or fall. Plant a container-grown quince spring, summer, or fall. Quince does best growing in full sun but succeeds with four to six hours of sun, or all-day filtered light. It thrives with pH 5.5, but can succeed in a broad range of soil types and pH as high as 7.5. See Soil Preparation in the Introduction, and the planting instructions at the beginning of this chapter. Provide a planting hole three times the width of the rootball and twice as deep. Set the shrub so the crown will be an inch or two above ground level. Shape the soil around the crown into a wide saucer. Water slowly and deeply. Apply mulch 3 in. deep starting 3 in. from the crown.

Growing Tips
The first year, unless there's a soaking rain, in spring and fall slowly and gently pour two to three bucketsful of water around the roots every two weeks; in summer every week or ten days. Maintain the mulch.

Care
Using a slow-release organic fertilizer for acid-loving plants, fertilize lightly in fall and again in late winter or early spring. Replenish the mulch. Quince flowers on wood grown the previous season and on a system of spurs. To keep the center open, when the blossoms fade and before May, cut back older canes and suckers to the ground. As new wood hardens in summer, remove branches that cross or are badly positioned, and thin out older woody spurs. After the leaves fall, take the main branches back to two or three buds.

Companion Planting and Design
Flowering quince branches develop an elegant asymmetrical sprawl that is attractive in an informal hedge. In spite of its beauty, flowering quince is a single season plant, and in a small landscape shouldn't be given space that could go to a plant with appeal in three or four seasons.

Our Personal Recommendations
There are innumerable named varieties, such as 'Cameo', 'Jet Trail', and 'Toyo Nishiki'. The single flowered forms have a kind of purity common to all singles—more drama, perhaps. The double-flowered forms appeal to us less but that's not the common experience.

Flowering quince in bloom is one of spring's most beautiful flowering shrubs. The blossoms appear to sprout from the bark, like apple blossoms, and are perfectly arranged on the branches. There are exquisite single or double flowering forms that come in white and many beautiful coral and rose-red shades. The shrub is broad spreading, and produces a twiggy mass of rather thorny branches, quite extraordinary trained as an espalier, a pruned hedge, or in a Japanese structured, stylized form. The branches are easy to force into early bloom and are remarkably lovely. The new foliage is red-rose-bronze that changes to glossy green leaves. The quince grown for making preserves is the common quince, Cydonia oblonga, a large shrub or small tree, but flowering quince also bears fruit—waxy, yellowish, 2-in. fruits that are fragrant.

Other Name
Chinese Flowering Quince

Bloom Period and Seasonal Color
Early spring; flowers may be white, peach, pink, coral, rose, orange, red, ruby red.

Mature Height × Spread
6 to 10 ft. × 6 to 10 ft.

Forsythia

Forsythia × intermedia 'Spectabilis'

Forsythia is the herald of spring everywhere. It pops a few golden blooms before the plum trees have even budded. Forsythia flower buds open before the leaves appear, covering the wide-spreading, arching branches with small, showy, vivid yellow flowers. The small blooms last well, as long as we don't have a heat spell. When the cold comes in fall, the leaves take on an orangey-plum hue before they fall. This is a fast-growing arching shrub that roots where it touches the ground. It develops dense thickets unless it is pruned annually, and is used as a tall ground cover for slopes. Branches pruned in late winter as the buds swell are easily forced into bloom indoors.

Other Name
Border Forsythia

Bloom Period and Seasonal Color
March and April; pale to deep yellow flowers.

Mature Height × Spread
8 to 10 ft. × 10 to 12 ft.

When, Where, and How to Plant
Container-grown forsythia transplants easily spring, summer, and fall; a balled-and-burlapped shrub, and rooted plantlets, transplant best in very early spring or in fall after the leaves drop. Forsythia flowers best in full sun but blooms in part shade. It thrives in almost any soil that is well drained, loamy, and has enough humus to maintain moisture, with a pH range of 6.0 to 8.0. See Soil Preparation in the Introduction, and the planting instructions at the beginning of this chapter. Provide a planting hole three times the width of the rootball and twice as deep. Set the shrub so the crown will be an inch or two above ground level. Shape the soil around the crown into a wide saucer. Water slowly and deeply. Apply mulch 3 in. deep starting 3 in. from the crown.

Growing Tips
The first year, unless there's a soaking rain, in spring and fall slowly and gently pour two to three bucketsful of water around the roots every two weeks; in summer every week or ten days. Maintain the mulch.

Care
Using a slow-release organic fertilizer, fertilize lightly in fall and again in late winter or early spring. Replenish the mulch from time to time. To keep forsythia in bounds, when it finishes blooming, prune the branches back to outward facing buds and remove the oldest canes down to the ground. Branches that touch the ground root over time and can be transplanted.

Companion Planting and Design
Fast-growing border forsythia is used for screening, in informal hedges, as tall ground cover, and as a bank holder. It can stand a lot of shearing, and can be espaliered. It is attractive featured as a specimen in the middle of a large lawn, or in a group with evergreens and other flowering shrubs.

Our Personal Recommendations
The named variety 'Lynwood' ('Lynwood Gold') is a more upright plant that has perhaps the most beautiful flowers—they're more open and slightly lighter. 'Primulina', which has pale yellow flowers and golden fall foliage that turns to mahogany, was a favorite of André's father, Martin Viette. 'Spring Glory' is a sulfur yellow.

Glossy Abelia
Abelia × *grandiflora*

When, Where, and How to Plant

The time to plant a container-grown abelia is in the fall before Indian summer, and in early spring while the shrub is still dormant. Abelia flowers best growing in full sun. However, like most shrubs, it succeeds with four to six hours of sun, or all-day filtered light. The ideal soil is well drained, humusy, sandy, and in the acid range, pH 5.5 to 6.5, but pH can be variable. See Soil Preparation in the Introduction, and planting instructions at the beginning of this chapter. Provide a planting hole three times the width of the rootball and twice as deep. Set the shrub so the crown will be about an inch or two above ground level. Shape the soil around the crown into a wide sauce. Water slowly and deeply. Apply mulch 3 in. deep starting 3 in. from the crown.

Growing Tips

The first year, unless there's a soaking rain, in spring and fall slowly and gently pour two to three bucketsful of water around the roots every two weeks; in summer every week or ten days. Maintain the mulch.

Care

Using a slow-release organic fertilizer for acid-loving plants, fertilize lightly in fall and again in spring. Replenish the mulch. Glossy abelia blooms on side branches of the previous year's growth, and on new wood, so in late winter prune back dead branch tips to outward facing buds. Prune winterkilled tips in early spring. Once the shrub has attained a size that is pleasing, you can keep it at that size by removing up to a third of the branch tips in a year. Prune to restrict its size when flowering is over.

Companion Planting and Design

Abelia is used as a bank cover. 'Edward Goucher' makes an informal hedge and is handsome enough on its own to be a featured specimen.

Our Personal Recommendations

For the foliage, André also recommends the cultivar 'Prostrata', a compact, low-growing shrub with smaller leaves that turn burgundy-green in winter.

Glossy abelia's great asset is a summer-long show of flowers. The plant is a rounded, multi-stemmed, semi-evergreen shrub about 5 ft. tall, with twiggy branches, dainty foliage, and small, slightly fragrant, funnel-shaped pink flowers. It comes into bloom in June or July and goes on blooming until frost. The leaves take on a purplish-bronze cast in late fall and persist until early winter. There are many varieties. A tried and true favorite is 3- to 6-ft. 'Edward Goucher', a dense, arching shrub with orange-throated, lilac-pink flowers. In warmer areas of the Mid-Atlantic, glossy abelia is an evergreen. In the cool uplands the leaves may eventually fall. Either way, the shrub's twiggy structure is an asset to the garden.

Other Name
Abelia

Bloom Period and Seasonal Color
June till frost; pink flowers, purplish foliage in fall.

Mature Height × Spread
3 to 6 ft. × 5 ft.

Hydrangea
Hydrangea arborescens 'Annabelle'

The hydrangeas are fast-growing deciduous shrubs with cane-like branches, large handsome leaves, and a mid- to late summer show of often huge flower heads composed of dozens of florets. The hortensia, or mophead, types have rounded flower heads of basically sterile florets; lacecaps are composed of both showy (sterile) flowers around the outer edge, and tiny (fertile) florets in the center, and may be cone-shaped or flattened. H. arborescens 'Annabelle' was selected for the 1995 Georgia Gold Medal Award. It's a superb plant that blooms fully every year, with white flower heads up to 12 in. across that turn a beautiful pale green with age. The blossoms dry so easily you can't resist making winter arrangements with them. Another favorite is the bigleaf hydrangea, H. macrophylla, which includes both lacecap and hortensia varieties in cream, rose, pink, and light or dark blue: the color depends on soil acidity. It needs winter protection in Zone 6.

Bloom Period and Seasonal Color
Mid- to late summer; white, and shades of pink and blue.

Mature Height × Spread
3 to 5 ft. × 3 to 5 ft.

When, Where, and How to Plant
Plant container-grown hydrangeas in early spring. They bloom in full sun, and in bright or dappled shade; in hot areas they benefit from noon or afternoon shade. *H. arborescens* 'Annabelle' and *H. quercifolia* (oakleaf hydrangea) are tolerant as to pH. *H. macrophylla* requires acid soil. It will color blue or pink according to soil pH: acid soil assures blue; pH 5.0 to 5.5 results in a soft blue; 6.0 to 6.5, or slightly higher, maintains pink. Hydrangeas need a well-drained site, and loose or sandy soil with enough humus to maintain moisture. See Soil Preparation in the Introduction, and the planting instructions at the beginning of this chapter. Provide a planting hole three times the width of the rootball and twice as deep. Set the shrub so the crown will be an inch or two above ground level. Shape the soil around the crown into a wide saucer. Water slowly and deeply. Apply mulch 2 in. deep starting 3 in. from the crown.

Growing Tips
The first year, unless there's a soaking rain, in spring and fall slowly and gently pour two to three bucketsful of water around the roots every two weeks; in summer every week or ten days. Maintain the mulch.

Care
Using a slow-release organic fertilizer, fertilize lightly in fall and again in late winter or early spring. Replenish the mulch. *H. arborescens* flowers on new wood. To maintain flowering and form, cut out the oldest canes between late fall and early spring; deadhead to prolong flowering. Bigleaf hydrangea, *H. macrophylla*, must be pruned in spring since it blooms on new growth from buds from the previous season. Cut back to a live bud.

Companion Planting and Design
Hydrangeas are great seashore plants. They deserve a bed of their own.

Our Personal Recommendations
André recommends 'Annabelle'. He also likes oakleaf hydrangea, *H. quercifolia*, a magnificent plant with elegant cone-shaped flower heads in early summer and striking foliage that colors red-purple in the fall; especially nice are 'Snowflake', a double-flowered form, and 'Snowqueen', which bears enormous flower trusses.

Japanese Andromeda
Pieris japonica

When, Where, and How to Plant
A young container-grown or balled-and-burlapped andromeda transplants easily in early spring. The andromedas are known as shrubs for shady places, two to six hours of sun a day, but some growers recommend full sun for modern hybrids. The ideal site is out of the wind, well-drained, with humusy, moist soil that is acid, pH 4.5 to 6.0. See Soil Preparation in the Introduction, and planting instructions at the beginning of this chapter. Provide a planting hole three times the width of the rootball and twice as deep. Set the shrub so the crown will be an inch or two above ground level. Shape the soil around the crown into a wide saucer. Water slowly and deeply. Apply mulch 3 in. deep starting 3 in. from the crown.

Growing Tips
The first year, unless there's a soaking rain, in spring and fall slowly and gently pour two to three bucketsful of water around the roots every two weeks; in summer every week or ten days. Maintain the mulch. Removing spent blooms when the plant is young encourages growth and flower production.

Care
Using a slow-release organic fertilizer for acid-loving plants, fertilize lightly in fall and again in spring. Replenish the mulch. Ideally, andromeda's cascading branches are allowed to develop naturally. Damaged wood should be pruned back in March before new growth begins.

Companion Planting and Design
Andromeda has a rather formal appearance and is an excellent foundation plant. We like it in shrub groups with rhododendrons and azaleas whose need for acid soil it shares.

Our Personal Recommendations
There are some beautiful named varieties of Japanese andromeda. Among our favorites are 'Flamingo', whose flowers are deep rose-red bells; the semi-dwarf 'Variegata', whose foliage is flushed pink when new, then margined with white; and 'White Cascade', which bears long, large panicles of pure white flowers that last weeks longer than the species. The native mountain andromeda, *P. floribunda*, is a better choice for naturalized situations and cooler, more exposed sites.

The andromedas are handsome evergreen shrubs that do well in sun and in part shade and the acid soils that suit azaleas and rhododendrons. They're the first of the evergreen shrubs to bloom. In late winter and early spring they are covered with large clusters of waxy, cream white buds that open into small urn-shaped flowers. The leaves are shiny green year round, and the new foliage is a gleaming rose-bronze. Japanese andromeda is a beautiful species, whose branches cascade almost to the ground. The tips are dense with clusters of rather fragrant flowers in strands 3 to 6 in. long that last two to three weeks. The new foliage is bronze to wine red, and very showy in the newer hybrids.

Other Name
Japanese Pieris

Bloom Period and Seasonal Color
February to April; white flowers, with pink buds in some varieties.

Mature Height × Spread
6 to 8 ft. × 6 ft.

Japanese Aucuba
Aucuba japonica

Aucuba is a tall, beautiful, shade-loving, drought-resistant, broadleaved evergreen that makes a great foundation plant, screen, or hedge. Though it produces berries, the leaves are its glory—large, leathery, and bright green, they clothe the plant's many succulent branching stems, usually all the way to the ground. A planting becomes increasingly dense because shoots touching the ground root and produce new plants. Male and female flowers are produced on different plants. When pollinated by a male, a female aucuba produces large, persistent, red berries. The variety 'Variegata', the gold-dust tree, is a female plant whose leaves are beautifully marked with flecks of gold. A suitable pollinator is the male plant 'Maculata', which is handsomely blotched yellow-white.

Bloom Period and Seasonal Color
March and April; purple blooms are not very obvious.

Mature Height × Spread
6 to 10 ft. × 3 to 4 ft.

When, Where, and How to Plant
Aucuba survives droughts, urban situations, is pest- and disease-resistant, and thrives even under heavy-rooted trees where grass won't grow. In Zone 6 it needs a location protected from freezing winds and western sun. Plant a container-grown aucuba in early spring or late summer. It thrives in partial shade and handles deep shade; direct sun facing south or west may result in leaf damage. Provide a site that is well drained, with humusy soil that has a high organic content so that the roots are kept moist. Aucuba is pH tolerant. See Soil Preparation in the Introduction, and planting instructions at the beginning of this chapter. Provide a planting hole three times the width of the rootball and twice as deep. Set the shrub so the crown will be an inch or two above ground level. Shape the soil around the crown into a wide saucer. Water slowly and deeply. Apply mulch 3 in. deep starting 3 in. from the crown.

Growing Tips
The first year, unless there's a soaking rain, in spring and fall slowly and gently pour two to three bucketsful of water around the roots every two weeks; in summer every week or ten days. Maintain the mulch.

Care
Using a slow-release organic fertilizer, fertilize lightly in fall and again in late winter or early spring. Replenish the mulch. Late winter and late summer are the best seasons to prune aucuba. To control the shoots that sprawl outward from the central stems, cut them out below ground level; to control the height, cut the tallest stems back to just above a pair of leaves.

Companion Planting and Design
Groups of aucuba soften bare shaded walls and light up dim corners. You can use it as a background hedge for small flowering shrubs, such as azaleas, and for perennials. In cold regions, it is grown in tubs and used as a screen and background plant in patio and terrace gardens; it winters indoors successfully in a bright, cool room.

Our Personal Recommendations
'Variegata' is our favorite, but we also like 'Crotonifolia', whose leaves are dusted with white spots.

Japanese Kerria
Kerria japonica 'Pleniflora'

When, Where, and How to Plant

You'll find balled-and-burlapped kerria transplants well in early spring or early fall. Container-grown kerria can be planted spring, summer, or fall. Kerria blooms well in sun and in part shade, even in dry urban gardens. Light shade is the best situation in our hotter regions. Kerria also isn't difficult about soil—it will flourish in almost any well-drained soil that is moderately moist and fertile. See Soil Preparation in the Introduction, and the planting instructions at the beginning of this chapter. Provide a planting hole three times the width of the rootball and twice as deep. Set the shrub so the crown will be an inch or two above ground level. Shape the soil around the crown into a wide saucer. Water slowly and deeply. Apply mulch 3 in. deep starting 3 in. from the crown.

Growing Tips

The first year, unless there's a soaking rain, in spring and fall slowly and gently pour two to three bucketsful of water around the roots every two weeks; in summer every week or ten days. Maintain the mulch.

Care

Using a slow-release organic fertilizer, fertilize lightly in fall and again in late winter or early spring. Replenish the mulch periodically. Kerria tolerates summer heat and drought. To keep 'Pleniflora' shapely, as flowers fade, trim old flowering stems back to strong young shoots or to ground level. Remove suckers that rise around the variegated cultivar 'Picta': they tend to revert to plain green.

Companion Planting and Design

A traditional wall plant in cottage gardens, kerria is attractive massed in naturalistic plantings, on slopes, anywhere you have room for a good sized shrub and would like to see a sunny color in early spring and wonderful green foliage in summer heat.

Our Personal Recommendation

'Pleniflora' is our choice.

Like forsythia, Japanese kerria covers itself for two or three weeks in April or May with small flowers as bright and cheerful as sunshine. There's one species in cultivation and it comes from Central and Western China, though we call it Japanese kerria. A 3- to 6-ft. shrub that was once so popular you still find it in all the older parks in the East, it bears masses of little, flat-faced, five-petaled flowers. Sometimes it repeats its bloom in summer. The variety 'Pleniflora', which is taller than the species, is the best for landscaping. It's a tough, vigorous, upright, bushy plant that bears masses of double golden yellow flowers. Cut, kerria lasts well in a vase.

Bloom Period and Seasonal Color
April to May; bright yellow.

Mature Height × Spread
6 to 8 or 10 ft. × 6 to 8 ft.

Lilac
Syringa vulgaris and hybrids

Lilacs are multi-stemmed shrubs or small trees that bear panicles of single or double florets in late spring. The one most famous for fragrance is the 20-foot common lilac, Syringa vulgaris, which came to America with the colonists. It was being hybridized in France to improve the flowers by the late 1700s, so many of today's most beautiful double-flowered forms and unusual colors are known as French lilacs; not all are fragrant. If perfume is what you love, look for hybrids advertised as very fragrant, like 'Charles Joly', a double flowered form with deep wine-red flowers, and 'Ludwig Spaeth', a heavily fragrant, dark purple, single-flowered hybrid. Lilacs are subject to mildew, so look for hybrids advertised as mildew-resistant.

Other Name
Common Lilac

Bloom Period and Seasonal Color
May; white to lilac, blue, lavender, purple, pink, wine red.

Mature Height × Spread
5 to 20 ft. × 8 to 20 ft.

When, Where, and How to Plant
Lilacs transplant easily in early spring and in early fall. They succeed in open, airy sites in full sun or light shade. The ideal soil is well drained, moist, and neutral—pH 7.0 to 7.5; an annual sprinkling of wood ashes or lime keeps soil neutral. See Soil Preparation in the Introduction, and the planting instructions at the beginning of this chapter. Provide a planting hole three times the width of the rootball and twice as deep. Set the shrub so the crown will be an inch or two above ground level. Shape the soil around the crown into a wide saucer. Water slowly and deeply. Apply mulch 3 in. deep starting 3 in. from the crown.

Growing Tips
The first year, unless there's a soaking rain, in spring and fall slowly and gently pour two to three bucketsful of water around the roots every two weeks; in summer every week or ten days. Maintain the mulch.

Care
Using a slow-release organic fertilizer, fertilize lightly in fall and again in late winter or early spring. Replenish the mulch. Established lilacs tolerate some drought. Deadhead to encourage flowering. Regularly prune out the oldest branches and all but two or three strong suckers. The taller lilacs can be pruned to grow as single-stem or multi-stemmed plants.

Companion Planting and Design
A staple of Victorian shrub borders, lilacs are now featured lawn specimens, or used in tall hedges, and in allées called "lilac walks." Smaller forms do well in containers.

Our Personal Recommendations
André's father Martin Viette hybridized lilacs on the Havemeyer estate Cedar Hill on Long Island; it later became Lilacland. André's favorites are fragrant: compact, mildew-resistant, very flowery, violet-purple Meyer lilac, *S. meyeri* 'Palibin', which blooms before the leaves appear; the small pale flowered Persian lilac, *S. × persica*, which blooms in mid-May, a beautiful old hybrid; and the 20- to 30-foot Japanese tree lilac, *S. reticulata*, which blooms last with big plumes of creamy white florets, (alas, sharply scented as a privet hedge). 'Ivory Silk' is a lovely cultivar that will grow in acid soil.

Mock Orange
Philadelphus coronarius

When, Where, and How to Plant
To guarantee your mock orange will be as per-fumed as you hope, buy a container-grown plant already in bloom. Plant a container-grown mock orange in spring, summer, or fall. It will flower most fully in full sun, but can handle some shade during the day. Mock orange succeeds in most any soil, but does best in a moist, well-drained site, pH 6.0 to 7.0. See Soil Preparation in the Introduction, and the planting instructions at the beginning of this chapter. Provide a planting hole three times the width of the rootball and twice as deep. Set the shrub so the crown will be an inch or two above ground level. Shape the soil around the crown into a wide saucer. Water slowly and deeply. Apply mulch 3 in. deep starting 3 in. from the crown.

Growing Tips
The first year, unless there's a soaking rain, in spring and fall slowly and gently pour two to three bucketsful of water around the roots every two weeks; in summer every week or ten days. Maintain the mulch.

Care
Using a slow-release organic fertilizer, fertilize lightly in fall and again in late winter or early spring. Replenish the mulch. An established mock orange tolerates some drought. The mock oranges flower on growth made on branches developed the previous year. Giving older branches a light annual pruning after they have bloomed helps keep mock orange productive and well shaped. Woody stems that are more than five years old should be removed in winter or early spring.

Companion Planting and Design
Mock orange is a big shrub that needs a large gar-den to show off its beauty. It's usually grown as a specimen plant in the middle of the lawn. It's also attractive in a border for big shrubs such as weigela, forsythia, spirea, and deutzia.

Our Personal Recommendations
Among the most fragrant modern mock oranges are named varieties of *P.* × *lemoinei*, which André's father Martin Viette worked with, including 8-ft. 'Innocence', which is single flowered and perhaps the most fragrant, and 4-ft. 'Avalanche', a very fragrant single-flowered form.

Mock orange is a big old-fashioned shrub with crisp white flowers whose beauty and perfume recall orange blos-soms. It's a large, rather dull plant with stiff branches until May and early June when it opens clusters of five to seven beautiful little 1- to 2- in. pure white flowers that have showy golden anthers. The perfume of fully fragrant plants permeates a garden. The modern varieties with old-fashioned fragrance are preferred. One of the best is P. × virginalis with semi-double or double flowers, which will quite often bloom for a second time in the summer. 'Glacier' has double flowers. 'Minnesota Snowflake' is a tall—9 ft.—plant with arching branches whose big double flowers are fragrant.

Bloom Period and Seasonal Color
May to June; white.

Mature Height × Spread
10 to 12 ft. × 12 to 16 ft.

Mountain Laurel

Kalmia latifolia

The mountain laurel is a tall, exceptionally handsome evergreen shrub with shiny, leathery leaves that make beautiful Christmas roping. In mid- to late spring, mountain laurel bears clusters of white, pink, or red-variegated cup-shaped florets. The blooms of the species are pale pink; modern hybrids are showier, blooming in brighter pinks, reds, and bi-colors. 'Elf' is a slow-growing smaller mountain laurel, which grows 4 to 6 ft. tall eventually, and whose showy clusters of light pink buds open to white. The buds of 'Ostbo Red' are an intense crimson that open to pink. 'Bullseye' is one of several forms whose flowers are banded red inside. (By the way, every part of the plant is toxic to people but not to wildlife—deer will nibble leaves.)

Other Name
Laurel

Bloom Period and Seasonal Color
Spring; white, pink, red, bi-colors.

Mature Height × Spread
7 to 8 ft. × 5 to 6 ft.

When, Where, and How to Plant

In poor, dry soil and full sun, mountain laurel develops leaf spot and dies. Plant a container-grown laurel in the fall before Indian summer, or in early spring while the shrub is still dormant. It needs a half-day of sun or bright shade all day to flower well and does best in light, open woodlands. It needs well-drained soil, one-third to one-half humus or leaf mold, and pH 4.5 to 6.0. See Soil Preparation in the Introduction, and planting instructions at the beginning of this chapter. Provide a planting hole three times the width of the rootball and twice as deep. Set the shrub so the crown will be an inch or two above ground level. Shape the soil around the crown into a wide saucer. Water slowly and deeply. Apply mulch 3 in. deep starting 3 in. from the crown.

Growing Tips

The first year, unless there's a soaking rain, in spring and fall slowly and gently pour two to three bucketsful of water around the roots every two weeks; in summer every week or ten days. Maintain the mulch.

Care

Using a slow-release organic fertilizer for acid-loving plants, fertilize lightly in fall and again in late winter or early spring. Replenish the mulch as needed. Remove flower heads as they fade. Kalmia recovers slowly from pruning, and it is unnecessary in healthy plants. To restore an overgrown mountain laurel, wait till flowering is over, and remove one or two of the less attractive branches each year over a period of three to five years.

Companion Planting and Design

Mountain laurel is used at the back of shaded shrub borders and is ideal for naturalizing at the edge of an open sunny woodland fronted by rhododendrons and azaleas. Nothing is more beautiful than a shaded bank on the edge of a woodland with well-grown, fully flowered mountain laurels in bloom.

Our Personal Recommendation

'Elf' is used as a landscape accent, to create an informal low hedge, and toward the front of an evergreen shrub border.

Nandina
Nandina domestica

When, Where, and How to Plant
Plant a container-grown nandina in fall before Indian summer, or in early spring while the shrub is still dormant. Nandina produces its bright red fruits whether it is growing in full sun or part shade. The shrub flourishes in well-drained, moist, fertile soil, but it is tolerant of other situations and not particular about soil pH. See Soil Preparation in the Introduction, and planting instructions at the beginning of this chapter. Provide a planting hole three times the width of the rootball and twice as deep. Set the shrub so the crown will be an inch or two above ground level. Shape the soil around the crown into a wide saucer. Water slowly and deeply. Apply mulch 3 in. deep starting 3 in. from the crown.

Growing Tips
The first year, unless there's a soaking rain, in spring and fall slowly and gently pour two to three bucketsful of water around the roots every two weeks; in summer every week or ten days. Maintain the mulch.

Care
Using a slow-release organic fertilizer, fertilize lightly in fall and again in late winter or early spring. Replenish the mulch. To keep the plant compact, every year in early spring, before your nandina blooms, cut crowded or gangling canes back all the way to the ground; if only partially cut back, they sometimes don't break into new growth.

Companion Planting and Design
Nandinas are excellent in a shrub border, as a hedge, in containers, and compete successfully with tree roots. Stems of nandina provide lasting greenery for bouquets.

Our Personal Recommendations
A favorite nandina for the vivid red of its winter foliage is big 'Moyers Red'. 'Umpqua Chief' is another—a vigorous plant that makes a fine 5- to 6-ft. hedge and has leaves that turn fully red in winter. A superior dwarfish cultivar is 'Harbour Dwarf', a graceful plant that forms a dense mound 18 to 24 in. tall. The foliage is touched with pink or bronze in spring, and turns reddish purple in the fall.

Nandina is a tall, airy, graceful, unbranched, semi-evergreen or evergreen shrub whose dainty painted leaves are edged and splashed with real red in winter. In spring it produces loose clusters of small whitish florets that are followed in fall by small, perfectly round, lipstick-red berries in beautiful drooping clusters—great for Christmas decorations! The clusters are shaped like bunches of grapes, and they last until mid-spring. The new leaves are copper-toned and turn bluish green as they mature. The species is native to China and Japan, and has been grown widely in the South where the leaves are reliably evergreen and the berries color well and stay on the bushes for months.

Other Name
Heavenly Bamboo

Bloom Period and Seasonal Color
May; pinkish in bud, then white; followed in September by drooping panicles of bright red berries.

Mature Height × Spread
6 to 8 ft. × 5 to 6 ft.

Oregon Grape Holly
Mahonia aquifolium

The mahonias are shade-loving broadleaved evergreen shrubs with shiny, spiny, holly-like leaflets and small yellow flowers. The new leaves of the very upright Oregon grape holly start out red-bronze-green in spring, are dark green in summer, and turn a beautiful bronze-plum in winter. It has another asset we value: in late winter and early spring it bears clusters of small, sweetly scented, yellow flowers that are followed in summer by blue-black fruits. Another beautiful species thrives here, leatherleaf mahonia, M. bealei. It's more massive, with arching stems and big, gorgeous, blue-green, toothed leaflets that hold their color all winter. In late February and early March, drooping clusters of very fragrant yellow flower spikes appear, followed by blue changing to grapelike blue-black fruits the birds adore.

Bloom Period and Seasonal Color
April; yellow flowers followed by blue changing to blue-black berries.

Mature Height × Spread
3 to 6 ft. × 3 to 4 ft.

When, Where, and How to Plant
Plant a container-grown mahonia in early spring while the shrub is still dormant. The mahonias do best in partial shade. Oregon grape holly can stand more sun, but prefers shade. Avoid dry, hot spots, and windy, unprotected locations. The mahonias require soils that are slightly acid, pH 6.0 to 7.0, well drained, with enough humus to maintain moisture around the roots. See Soil Preparation in the Introduction, and planting instructions at the beginning of this chapter. Provide a planting hole three times the width of the rootball and twice as deep. Set the shrub so the crown will be an inch or two above ground level. Shape the soil around the crown into a wide saucer. Water slowly and deeply. Apply mulch 3 in. deep starting 3 in. from the crown.

Growing Tips
The first year, unless there's a soaking rain, in spring and fall slowly and gently pour two to three bucketsful of water around the roots every two weeks; in summer every week or ten days. Maintain the mulch.

Care
Using a slow-release organic fertilizer for acid-loving plants, fertilize lightly in fall and again in late winter or early spring. Replenish the mulch. If Oregon grape holly gets straggly, when blooming is over cut the tallest stems back to the ground; to keep it from expanding, root out suckers as they arise. To keep leatherleaf mahonia fresh and productive, after it has bloomed cut the oldest canes back to the ground.

Companion Planting and Design
Use the upright Oregon grape holly as a textural backdrop for shaded shrub and perennial borders, to anchor corners, and to mark entrances. Massive leatherleaf mahonia is ideal anchoring a large shaded area planted in hellebores, rhododendrons, azaleas, and low trailing evergreen ground covers such as bearberry.

Our Personal Recommendation
For a smaller garden we recommend the dwarf form of the Oregon grape holly, *M. aquifolium* 'Compactum', which grows to just 2 or 3 ft. tall and has very glossy leaves that turn to bronze in winter.

Purple Beautyberry
Callicarpa dichotoma

When, Where, and How to Plant
Plant container-grown beautyberry in spring, summer, or fall. The berries will be most effective if the plant is growing in full sun but it can make do with less light and still be productive. Almost any soil will do as long as it is well-drained, loose, or loamy soil with enough humus to maintain moisture. See Soil Preparation in the Introduction, and the planting instructions at the beginning of this chapter. Provide a planting hole three times the width of the rootball and twice as deep. Set the shrub so the crown will be an inch or two above ground level. Shape the soil around the crown into a wide saucer. Water slowly and deeply. Apply mulch 3 in. deep starting 3 in. from the crown.

Growing Tips
The first year, unless there's a soaking rain, in spring and fall slowly and gently pour two to three bucketsful of water around the roots every two weeks; in summer every week or ten days. Maintain the mulch.

Care
Fertilize beautyberry in late winter or early spring, and again in the fall. Replenish the mulch from time to time. In spring before growth begins, tip prune and thin, but if the shrub is old and woody, you can prune 6 to 12 in.; beautyberry produces its flowers and fruit on the current year's growth.

Companion Planting and Design
Attractive planted in a shrub border where the berries will add color and texture in fall.

Our Personal Recommendations
Our favorite is purple beautyberry, but there are other valuable varieties. *C. bodinieri*, bodinier beautyberry, is popular in Britain where it grows to 6 to 10 ft. and bears lavender flowers and glossy purple-blue fruits. The variety 'Profusion' is grown in Holland and imported into the U.S. *C. japonica* has lilac-violet berries and is rather similar to bodinier beautyberry but taller; the variety 'Alba' is a white-berried form that keeps producing fresh, clean, new flowers July to September. The native *C. americana* is a courser shrub with larger berries.

Purple beautyberry is a multi-stemmed shrub valued for its late season appeal. Beautyberry's flowering period is summer but its biggest contribution is for the beauty of the berries that follow the flowers in fall. The shrub has other assets, however—the long slender branches arch over gracefully and touch the ground at their tips, and in spring medium gray-green leaves array themselves in tidy pairs all along the stems. The flowers are pinkish lavender and stand above the foliage, so the small, luminous lilac-violet fruits that follow are nicely displayed against the foliage. The fruit is very dependable and makes an appealing show. When the leaves turn purplish and fall off, the fruits really stand out.

Other Name
Beautyberry

Bloom Period and Seasonal Color
June to August; pinkish lavender flowers; deep lilac-violet berries in fall.

Mature Height × Spread
4 to 5 ft. × 6 to 8 ft.

Purple Japanese Barberry

Berberis thunbergii 'Atropurpurea'

The barberries are low deciduous and evergreen shrubs whose twiggy branches are so thorny they make almost impenetrable hedges. Deciduous barberries, like Berberis thunbergii, have pinkish or reddish new leaves in late spring and glowing shades of orange, yellow, and scarlet in fall. The winter silhouette is very textural, a real asset. In mid-spring, they bear small, attractive yellow flowers rather hidden by the foliage, followed by red, purplish, or bluish black fruits in late summer. 'Atropurpurea' has reddish purple leaves, and 'Atropurpurea Nana' is its dwarf form. The named variety 'Crimson Pygmy' has better color than the species, and is often the first to leaf out in spring. It is a low-growing, dense, rounded plant 2 to 3 ft. wide by 3 to 5 ft. tall, whose foliage emerges a rosy crimson in spring, fades a little in summer, and turns dark crimson in the fall.

Bloom Period and Seasonal Color
Flowers are insignificant; new foliage is pinkish or reddish in late spring, paler red in summer, and glowing shades of orange, yellow, and scarlet in fall.

Mature Height × Spread
2 to 3 ft. × 3 to 5 ft.

When, Where, and How to Plant
Plant a bare-root shrub while it is still dormant, anytime between late fall and early spring, before the buds start to break. A container-grown barberry can be planted in spring, summer, or fall. The barberries display the brightest fall color when growing in full sun. However, like most shrubs, they succeed with four to six hours of sun, or all-day filtered light. They do well in most any soil, but prefer soil that is slightly acid, well drained, loose or loamy, with enough humus to maintain moisture. See Soil Preparation in the Introduction, and the planting instructions at the beginning of this chapter. Provide a planting hole three times the width of the rootball and twice as deep. Set the shrub so the crown will be an inch or two above ground level. Shape the soil around the crown into a wide saucer. Water slowly and deeply. Apply mulch 3 in. deep starting 3 in. from the crown.

Growing Tips
The first year, unless there's a soaking rain, in spring and fall slowly and gently pour two to three bucketsful of water around the roots every two weeks; in summer every week or ten days. Maintain the mulch.

Care
Using a slow-release organic fertilizer for acid loving plants, fertilize lightly in fall and again in late winter or early spring. Replenish the mulch. Barberries bloom on old wood. Pruning to control the height or shape of a hedge should be undertaken shortly after the shrubs have flowered. You can remove up to a third of the branch tips in a year.

Companion Planting and Design
The barberries are used a great deal for hedges because the spiny leaves and thorns are wicked enough to discourage pets and wildlife. And gardeners as well, should you forget to wear gauntlet type garden gloves when handling barberries.

Our Personal Recommendations
'Crimson Pygmy' is our favorite. 'Rose Glow' is an excellent reddish-purple barberry that is a little larger. Another appealing variety is 3- to 4-ft. 'Aurea', whose foliage is bright yellow.

Rhododendron

Rhododendron spp. and hybrids

When, Where, and How to Plant

Plant a balled-and-burlapped or container-grown rhododendron in early fall or in early spring. To be sure of the flower, buy one already blooming, or labeled with its cultivar name. Rhododendrons do best in the bright dappled light of tall trees with protection from high winds. Ideal soil is well drained, humusy, and acid, pH 4.5 to 6.0. See Soil Preparation in the Introduction, and planting instructions at the beginning of this chapter. Dig the hole three times the width of the rootball and twice as deep. Set the shrub so the crown will be an inch or so above ground level. Shape the soil around the crown into a wide saucer. Water slowly and deeply. Apply mulch 3 in. deep starting 3 in. from the crown.

Growing Tips

The first year, unless there's a soaking rain, in spring and fall slowly and gently pour two to three bucketsful of water around the roots every two weeks; in summer every week or ten days. Maintain the mulch.

Care

Apply a slow-release organic fertilizer for acid-loving plants lightly in fall and in late winter or early spring. Replenish the mulch. As each flower truss withers, pinch or cut it off, taking care not to damage the tiny leaf buds just behind it. Prune a rhododendron after it has bloomed, removing individual branches that have grown ragged or as required to achieve the desired shape.

Companion Planting and Design

Use rhododendrons for the transitional area to a woodland, backing a border of acid-loving shrubs, for screening, and rural hedges.

Our Personal Recommendations

Showy, large-leaved, super hardy evergreen rhododendron hybrids that handle winters in our area include Catawba rhododendrons: 5- to 7-ft. bright red 'America'; compact 4- to 5-ft. white 'Boule de Neige'; 6-ft. white Catawba rhododendron, 'Catawbiense Album'; 6- to 10-ft. rose-lilac 'Roseum Elegans', which does well in the sun; 6-ft. rosy pink 'English Roseum'; and 5-ft. red 'Nova Zembla'. André likes the Dexter hybrids 8-ft. pink 'Scintillation' and 'Wyandanch Pink', and the small-leaved lavender-pink PJM hybrids for fall color.

In the Mid-Atlantic these big shrubs with their huge, airy globes of exquisite flowers are among the most valued of spring and early summer flowering shrubs. Native species growing in the wild reach 20 ft. and more, but in cultivation most reach 6 or 8 ft. Mature specimens of the popular large-leaved evergreen rhododendrons provide spectacular displays of their huge blossoms in mid-spring—providing you have planted a variety suited to your climate, your site, and your soil. The large-leaved evergreen rhododendrons you can count on to survive winters everywhere in the Mid-Atlantic are the Catawba rhododendrons, from R. catawbiense; the one yellow rhododendron, dwarfish R. keiski; our native rosebay rhododendron, R. maximum; and the 3-ft. by 3-ft. Yakushima rhododendron, R. yakusimanum.

Bloom Period and Seasonal Color

May to June; white, pink, rose, lavender, purple-red, yellow flowers that may be flushed, splotched, or spotted with another shade or color.

Mature Height × Spread

3 to 8 ft. × 3 to 8 ft.

Rose-of-Sharon

Hibiscus syriacus

This is an old-fashioned, tall, spreading shrub, or small upright tree, that bears a profusion of flowers in July and goes on blooming until the end of September. The blossoms are trumpet shaped, like its relative the exotic tropical hibiscus, and about 4 to 6 in. across with ruffled petals crinkled on the margins. The usual colors are white, pink, crimson, and purple, most with an eye in a vivid contrasting color. Look for one of the new cultivars introduced through the U.S. National Arboretum by the late, great Dr. Donald Egolf. They are sterile triploids that have a longer blooming season and set less fruit, which can be a nuisance.

Other Name
Shrub Althea

Bloom Period and Seasonal Color
July to September; pure luminous white, pink, lavender blue, lilac, deep red.

Mature Height × Spread
8 to 12 ft. × 6 to 10 ft.

When, Where, and How to Plant
Choose a young—under 6 ft.—container-grown shrub, and plant it in fall before Indian summer, or in early spring. Rose-of-Sharon flowers best growing in full sun. It thrives in a wide variety of soils, and pH ranging between 5.5 and 7.0. Provide a site that is well-drained and has about 50 percent leaf mold, peat moss, or acid humus. See Soil Preparation in the Introduction, and the planting instructions at the beginning of this chapter. Provide a planting hole three times the width of the rootball and twice as deep. Set the shrub so the crown will be an inch or two above ground level. Shape the soil around the crown into a wide saucer. Water slowly and deeply. Apply mulch 3 in. deep starting 3 in. from the crown.

Growing Tips
The first year, unless there's a soaking rain, in spring and fall slowly and gently pour two to three bucketsful of water around the roots every two weeks; in summer every week or ten days. Maintain the mulch.

Care
Using a slow-release organic fertilizer for acid-loving plants, fertilize lightly in fall and again in late winter or early spring. Replenish the mulch. In early spring before the buds break, prune the branches back heavily to a pair of outward-facing buds. If you want larger flowers, prune the branches all the way back to three or four outward-facing buds. Water at the same time you water flower borders during prolonged droughts.

Companion Planting and Design
Rose-of-Sharon looks great anchoring a corner of a mixed border fronting a building. It can be used for screening and to create a tall hedge.

Our Personal Recommendations
'Diana' bears big, beautiful, pure white flowers that last more than a day. 'Blue Bird' produces beautiful lavender blue flowers.

Spirea

Spiraea japonica

When, Where, and How to Plant

Plant a balled-and-burlapped spirea in fall or in early spring; a container-grown plant can be set out spring, summer, or fall. Spirea flowers best in full sun and an airy site but it tolerates shade a portion of the day. It handles all but very wet soil; ideal pH is 6.0 to 7.0. See Soil Preparation in the Introduction, and the planting instructions at the beginning of this chapter. Provide a planting hole three times the width of the rootball and twice as deep. Set the shrub so the crown will be an inch or two above ground level. Shape the soil around the crown into a wide saucer. Water slowly and deeply. Apply mulch 3 in. deep starting 3 in. from the crown.

Growing Tips

The first year, unless there's a soaking rain, in spring and fall slowly and gently pour two to three bucketsful of water around the roots every two weeks; in summer every week or ten days. Maintain the mulch.

Care

Using a slow-release organic fertilizer, fertilize lightly in late fall and again in late winter or early spring. Replenish the mulch. To maintain the shape and to increase flowering of low, shrubby spireas, snip off stem tips before growth begins. Bridal wreath spireas need little attention, except to remove dead interior wood after the shrub has bloomed.

Companion Planting and Design

Shrubby spireas are used to cover sloping beds and planted banks. Their twiggy mass adds texture as well as flower power to perennial beds.

Our Personal Recommendations

Other compact spireas we recommend are *S. japonica* 'Alpina', 'Goldmound', and 'Little Princess', plants between 15 and 30 in. tall. We still love the old-fashioned, 5-ft. bridal wreath spirea, *S. prunifolia*, whose graceful branches arch to the ground, and are covered with showy, small white flowers in mid-spring. Not all gardens today are big enough to accommodate *S. × vanhouttei*, which grows up to 8 ft. tall and 8 to 10 ft. wide. *S. nipponica* 'Snowmound' is replacing the bridal wreath your grandmother planted.

Japanese spirea is a low, very wide, twiggy shrub with dainty leaves and arching branches that literally cover themselves with rounded clusters of exquisite flowers in the summer. Undemanding, and one of the most successful of the spireas, it has been much hybridized. A long-time favorite variety is 3- to 4-ft. 'Anthony Waterer', whose 4- to 6-in. wide rose-pink flower heads open in July and remain in bloom into August. The new foliage has a pink tinge, and in fall the leaves turn to wine red. Several pink-flowered varieties with colorful foliage have been introduced. 'Goldflame' is our favorite. It's a smaller plant, 2 to 3 ft. high, with compact pink flowers, whose foliage is a fiery gold in spring and in fall turns to red, copper, and orange. 'Bumald' spirea is dwarf, with dark pink flowers.

Other Names
Japanese Spirea, Pink Spirea

Bloom Period and Seasonal Color
July and August; rose pink flowers; pink tinted foliage in spring, that turns to wine red.

Mature Height × Spread
2 to 4 ft. × 3 to 5 ft.

Sweet Pepper Bush

Clethra alnifolia

If you love fragrance in the garden, then consider planting summersweet. It's a tall shrub native to the Eastern U.S. that naturalizes readily in shady, damp places and coastal gardens. The dense, rather shiny leaves are an attractive green, and have a nice yellow-orange glow in the fall. The plant's shrubby silhouette is a winter asset. But summersweet's best gift is the masses of scented flowers it produces in July and August. The flowers are fuzzy little 6-in. spikes so fragrant just one or two plants can perfume a whole garden. Bees love them. For André, the 2- to 3½-ft. 'Hummingbird' is one of the finest compact deciduous shrubs available to the gardener. 'Rosea', 'Pink Spires', and 'Fern Valley Pink' are compact pink-flowered varieties. And they say deer don't like Clethra!

Other Name
Summersweet

Bloom Period and Seasonal Color
July and August; white or pink flowers.

Mature Height × Spread
3 to 8 ft. × 4 to 6 ft.

When, Where, and How to Plant

Like so many of our native plants, summersweet takes a little time to get established in the garden. Choose a young container-grown plant and plant it in early spring, summer, or early fall. *Clethra* does well in either sun or shade. The ideal soil is rich, moist, mixed with 50 percent humus or leaf mold, and somewhat acid. But it tolerates wet feet, dryish soil, and salty seashore conditions. See Soil Preparation in the Introduction, and the planting instructions at the beginning of this chapter. Provide a planting hole three times the width of the rootball and twice as deep. Set the shrub so the crown will be an inch or two above ground level. Shape the soil around the crown into a wide saucer. Water slowly and deeply. Apply mulch 3 in. deep starting 3 in. from the crown.

Growing Tips

If the planting site is ordinary garden soil, unless there's a soaking rain, the first spring and fall slowly and gently pour two to three bucketsful of water around the roots every two weeks; in summer every week or ten days. If the planting site is rather moist, the extra watering may not be needed. But keep in mind that sweet pepper bush needs moisture at the roots. Maintain the mulch.

Care

Using a slow-release organic fertilizer for acid-loving plants, fertilize lightly in fall and again in late winter or early spring. Replenish the mulch. In winter, cut bare older branches back to ground level, and remove the weakest suckers. In ideal conditions, *Clethra* will colonize in its environment.

Companion Planting and Design

Clethra grows wild in moist places, so if you have a wild spot or a wet place, *Clethra* is a candidate. Summersweet's foliage makes it useful as a foundation plant, and we include it in large shrub borders and look for spots along paths and much frequented places where its perfume will be enjoyed.

Our Personal Recommendations

We recommend both the full size sweet pepper bush, and compact 'Hummingbird', and like them growing together.

Viburnum
Viburnum spp. and hybrids

When, Where, and How to Plant
Plant container-grown and balled-and-burlapped viburnums in fall before Indian summer, or in early spring. Viburnums thrive in full sun but they also do well in bright, all-day filtered light. Most species prefer well-drained, humusy soils that are slightly acid, pH 6.0 to 7.0. See Soil Preparation in the Introduction, and the planting instructions at the beginning of this chapter. Provide a planting hole three times the width of the rootball and twice as deep. Set the shrub so the crown will be an inch or two above ground. Shape the soil around the crown into a wide saucer. Water slowly and deeply. Apply mulch 3 in. deep starting 3 in. from the crown.

Growing Tips
The first year, unless there's a soaking rain, in spring and fall slowly and gently pour two to three bucketsful of water around the roots every two weeks; in summer every week or ten days. Maintain the mulch.

Care
With viburnums, be sure to use low-analysis, natural organic fertilizers that don't force or stimulate excessive growth. Fertilize lightly in fall and again in late winter or early spring. Maintain the mulch. To keep the shape of this spring-flowering shrub, shortly after it finishes blooming, prune protruding branches back to outward-facing buds, and cut old branches to the ground.

Companion Planting and Design
Plant fragrant viburnums by a porch, patio, and near house windows, or along a well-traveled path near the house. The doublefile viburnum needs plenty of space all around; it's a choice plant for the entrance to a property, by a stone wall, or cloaking a garage corner.

Our Personal Recommendations
Our favorite variety of Koreanspice viburnum, *V. carlesii*, is 'Aurora'. In a flowering border we like another hybrid, *V.* × *carlcephalum*, a tall, open shrub whose flowers change from pink bud to white when open. For hot areas of the Mid-Atlantic a very similar hybrid is the best choice, *V.* × *juddii*. Our doublefile viburnum favorites are 'Shasta', a spectacular National Arboretum introduction by Donald Egolf, and 'Mariesii', which is lovely in bloom and spectacular in fruit.

The viburnums are magnificent spring-flowering shrubs. Two distinctly different forms are popular: the scented viburnums planted for their fragrance, and the large, strikingly handsome doublefile viburnums planted for their flower display. Both develop colorful berries and fall foliage. Our favorite fragrant viburnums are the cinnamon-scented Koreanspice viburnum, V. carlesii, whose fall foliage is a cheerful red, and V. × *burkwoodii 'Mohawk', a National Arboretum introduction whose fall foliage is red-plum. In early spring both bear beautiful rounded clusters of deep pink buds that open to a cream pink. The perfume is intoxicating. The doublefile viburnum, V. plicatum, is different altogether—a big, handsome bush with beautifully layered branches that are covered in mid-spring with a snowfall of white blossoms. Michael Dirr has called it "possibly the most elegant of flowering shrubs."*

Bloom Period and Seasonal Color
Spring; pure white or pink or scarlet; summer and fall fruits are red or black.

Mature Height × Spread
6 to 15 ft. × 9 to 12 ft.

Weigela

Weigela florida 'Variegata'

The weigelas are foolproof members of the honeysuckle family, dense-flowering shrubs with spreading branches that arch to the ground in maturity. Their gift to the gardener is late color and a disposition to thrive no matter what the conditions. The flowers are showy clusters of 1-in. long tubular blooms that cover the plant in late spring and early summer. Some have a slight fragrance, and some repeat a few blooms later in the season. The most ornamental form is old-fashioned Weigela florida 'Variegata', whose leaves are edged with a creamy white margin. It's a tidy 4- to 6-ft. shrub whose flowers are a deep rose. For smaller gardens the 3-ft. dwarf, 'Variegata Nana', is a good choice.

Other Name
Old-Fashioned Weigela

Bloom Period and Seasonal Color
Mid-May and June; rosy shades of pink and crimson, and white varieties.

Mature Height × Spread
3 to 10 ft. × 8 to 12 ft.

When, Where, and How to Plant
A container-grown weigela transplants easily in spring, summer, or fall. Growing in full sun it will flower most satisfactorily, but it also will bloom in partial shade. The ideal soil is well drained and has a nearly neutral pH, between 6.0 and 7.5. But almost any soil will do as long as it is fertile and contains enough humus to maintain moisture around the roots. See Soil Preparation in the Introduction, and the planting instructions at the beginning of this chapter. Provide a planting hole three times the width of the rootball and twice as deep. Set the shrub so the crown will be an inch above ground level. Shape the soil around the crown into a wide saucer. Water slowly and deeply. Apply mulch 3 in. deep starting 3 in. from the crown.

Growing Tips
The first year, unless there's a soaking rain, in spring and fall slowly and gently pour two to three bucketsful of water around the roots every two weeks; in summer every week or ten days. Maintain the mulch.

Care
Using a slow-release organic fertilizer, fertilize lightly in fall and again in late winter or early spring. Replenish the mulch periodically. A weigela flowers mostly on old wood. Wait until the branches leaf out to cut back tips that have died during the winter. 'Variegata' is somewhat compact and should be allowed to develop freely. Branches that fail to show the variegation should be cut back to older wood.

Companion Planting and Design
We like weigela 'Variegata' planted in an evergreen shrub border where the flowers and foliage will really stand out. It's a good choice when you are looking for a shrub that will do well almost anywhere without much help.

Our Personal Recommendations
Three varieties whose colors we especially like are 'Bristol Ruby', which bears ruby red flowers; 'Mont-Blanc', a big shrub with somewhat fragrant white flowers; and 'Wine & Roses', which has three-season appeal—the new foliage that is a fresh green, pink-rose flowers, and in fall glossy burgundy-purple foliage.

Witch-Hazel
Hamamelis × intermedia

When, Where, and How to Plant
Plant a balled-and-burlapped witch-hazel in early spring or early fall. Plant a container-grown specimen in spring, summer, or fall. It may be a few years before it blooms. Witch-hazel does well in full sun or partial shade. It prefers moist loam that is well drained and somewhat acid, in the pH range between 6.0 and 7.0. See Soil Preparation in the Introduction, and the planting instructions at the beginning of this chapter. Provide a planting hole three times the width of the rootball and twice as deep. Set the shrub so the crown will be an inch or so above ground level. Shape the earth around the crown into a wide saucer. Water slowly and deeply. Apply a 3-in. mulch starting 3 in. from the stem.

Growing Tips
The first year, unless there's a soaking rain, in spring and fall slowly and gently pour two to three bucketsful of water around the roots every two weeks; in summer every week or ten days. Maintain the mulch.

Care
Apply a slow-release organic fertilizer for acid-loving plants in late winter or early spring. Water it in. Replenish the mulch. After a witch-hazel has bloomed, cut away sprigs that will grow into the center of the shrub or that will rub against other branches.

Companion Planting and Design
Witch-hazels are successful in the light shade of deciduous woods. Their picturesque form is well suited to naturalized settings. They do very well in city conditions and are attractive as container plants, and as specimens in small gardens.

Our Personal Recommendations
We like *H. × intermedia* 'Diane', which has copper-red blossoms and rich orange-red fall color. The Chinese witch-hazel, *H. mollis*, blooms later, in March usually, and it is the most fragrant; however the blooms can be lost when temperatures go below -10 and -15 degrees Fahrenheit. Japanese witch-hazel, *H. japonica*, is a 10- to 15-ft. tree, with somewhat fragrant, yellow flowers and foliage that turns yellow, red, and purple. The winter hazels, *Corylopsis* species, are beautiful shrubby relatives that bear fragrant flowers in April.

The witch-hazels are tall shrubs and small picturesque trees that flower in the winter or very early spring and turn lovely shades of yellow, orange, and carmine red in the fall. The blossoms, which consist of four twisted ribbon-like petals dangling on bare branches, survive temperature drops by curling up. The leaves appear later. The best known witch-hazels are varieties of H. × intermedia, a classification which includes a number of hybrids resulting from crossing H. japonica and H. mollis. They bear wonderfully fragrant flowers that are a soft yellow or a bronzed red, and the fall foliage is rich yellow with red tints. Each has its special appeal. 'Arnold Promise', one of the last to bloom, has large flowers that are a clear yellow and have a rich fragrance. It is considered one of the best.

Bloom Period and Seasonal Color
Late January to Mid-March; yellow or bronzed red; fall foliage is rich yellow with red tints.

Mature Height × Spread
15 to 20 ft. × 15 to 20 ft.

Trees *for the Mid-Atlantic*

A tree is such a large presence in a landscape; its every aspect—habit, color, and texture—can contribute to your pleasure in fall and winter as well as in spring and summer. In this chapter we have included deciduous and broadleaved evergreen trees, and trees we plant for their flowers. Needled evergreen trees and shrubs can be found in the Conifers chapter.

In choosing a tree, beauty is the first thing we look for, and we think of foliage. A maple's flaming fall color can be breathtaking. But when the leaves go, it's the bark, bole, and branch structure that lend beauty to your garden view. Imagine white birches against a stand of evergreens. A tree's silhouette, whether columnar, pyramidal, oval, vase-shaped, round, clumping, or weeping, also makes a deep impression. By repeating the same silhouette, color, and texture—the symmetry of paired blue spruces flanking an entrance, or an allée of columnar flowering apple trees—you create an air of gracious formality. By combining a variety of forms, such as a symmetrical incense cedar and a stylized Serbian spruce with a wide-branching maple and a clump of birches, you create a natural, informal effect, add a hint of mystery, a little excitement.

When it's shade we need, we look to wide-branched trees whose silhouettes are oval, pyramidal, vase-shaped, or round. Maples and oaks are excellent shade trees, and some evergreens make good shade trees, too—hollies and magnolias for example. Limbed up, small flowering trees can provide all the shade a small urban garden needs—the dogwoods and some flowering fruit trees, for example.

For style and for the fun of something different, we look to columnar trees. Many species now are offered in this form—red maple, European hornbeam, beech, and apple. 'Princeton Sentry'® is a

Kousa Dogwood

An allée of interlocking trees.

beautiful columnar ginkgo. Small columnar forms even grow well in big tubs, adding style to patios, roof gardens, and decks.

For romance, grace, and movement, weeping trees are tops. They're especially effective planted where their drooping branches will be reflected in water. The graceful weeping willow loves wet places but the roots invade underground water pipes too regularly for us to recommend it. A weeping birch or a weeping beech, or the gorgeous weeping crabapple 'Red Jade' can be very beautiful. And weeping varieties of the flowering and the kousa dogwoods are lovely.

To create a seasonal parade that is a true delight, we plant small flowering trees. The shrubby witch-hazels open the season at the National Arboretum with fragrant ribbon-like blossoms, followed by the flowering fruit trees—almond, plum, cherry, pear, crabapple, apple. Some flowering trees bear colorful fruits—the fruits of the dogwoods and flowering crabapples are among many that attract birds. Most small flowering trees developed in the bright shade of taller trees, so, while they can stand full sun, they also do well in a partly shaded city garden. A few big trees rival the show staged by the small flowering trees. In early spring the maples are outlined in tiny garnet-red buds. In summer a mature Japanese pagoda tree bears showy panicles of creamy-white, fragrant, pea-like flowers followed in September by beautiful showers of winged, yellow-green seedpods.

Size can be an asset, or a debit. A tree that will grow out of scale with a dwelling is a debit. The heights we give in this chapter are for trees in cultivation—in the wild and in arboreta they can often be twice as big.

When, Where, and How to Plant

Young trees knit into their new environments quickly: trees 7 to 8 feet tall can overtake the growth of 15-foot trees set out at the same time. Early fall and early spring are the best planting seasons for trees. Choose early spring for trees difficult to transplant. Most large trees need full sun; many small flowering trees are understory plants that developed in the partial shade of a forest, and do well in partial shade.

Make the planting hole for a tree three times as wide as the rootball and twice as deep. Mix into the soil from the hole the amendments described in Soil Preparation in the Introduction. Half fill the bottom of the hole with improved soil, and tamp it down to make a firm base for the tree to rest on.

Sugar Maples in autumn.

Trees are sold balled and burlapped, or growing in containers. To free a containerized tree, tip the container on its side and roll it around until the rootball loosens, or slit the pot open. If roots wrap the rootball, before planting make four deep vertical cuts in the sides and slice the matted roots off the bottom 2 inches. A balled-and-burlapped tree goes into the hole in its wrapping, then you cut the rope or wires and remove as much of the burlap as you can. Set the tree in the hole so the crown will be 1 to 2 inches above ground level (the weight on unsettled soil will cause it to sink some after planting). Half fill the hole again with improved soil and tamp it down. Fill the hole to the top with improved soil and tamp it down firmly. Shape the soil around the trunk into a wide saucer. Water slowly and gently with a sprinkler, a soaker hose, a bubbler, or by hand. Put down $1^1/2$ inches of water measured in a regular sized coffee can, or pour 10 to 15 gallons of water slowly from a bucket.

Apply 3 inches of mulch starting 3 inches from the trunk and extending to the edge of the saucer. Stake a young tree so the trunk will grow up straight, and wrap the lower trunk to protect the bark from sunscald and deer rubbing. Remove the stake and wrapping as the trunk fills out. Or, paint the trunk with whitewash, which is calcium carbonate with resins in it.

Care

The first year, unless there's a soaking rain, in spring and fall slowly and gently pour two to three bucketsful of water around the roots every two weeks; in summer every week or ten days. Maintain the mulch. The slow-release organic additives mixed into the soil at planting time are sufficient fertilizer for that year (see the Appendix for more information on fertilizers). For flowering trees, use a slow-release organic fertilizer for acid-loving plants. For trees whose flowers are not the show, use a complete, slow-release, long lasting, organic lawn fertilizer. In the following years, in late winter or early spring apply one of these fertilizers from the drip line outward to a distance that equals the height of the tree, plus half again its height. And compost the leaves you rake up in the fall. The nutrients they contain should go to enriching your soil, not clogging a landfill!

Pruning Trees

Most new trees require periodic light pruning. The first few years are the most important times to prune and shape a new tree. When needed, remove branches growing into the center of the tree, or crossing other branches. Never remove more than 25 percent: such "dehorning" causes "water sprout" growth. Before cutting a branch, find the collar or ring at the base where it springs from the trunk. Taking care not to damage the ring, make the cut just to the outside of it. From the collar an attractive, healthy covering for the wounded area can develop. Current wisdom says "no" to painting or tarring these cuts. That said, André prefers to paint with orange shellac any wounds caused by removing big branches: it disinfects and seals the cuts.

The best time to prune is when the tree is dormant in late winter, just after the coldest part of the season. If sap starts to flow, never mind. It will stop when the tree leafs out. Light pruning in summer is not harmful, and you can see what you're doing. Pruning stimulates growth and you can use that to encourage bushier growth and more flowering stems. Prune a spring-flowering tree that blooms on last year's wood after the flowers fade. Prune a summer-flowering tree that blooms on current growth shortly before growth begins.

Nurturing a beautiful tree for years and then losing it leaves a gap in the heart as big as the gap in the garden. For an extra fee, nurseries will plant your purchase and guarantee replacement if it fails. Still, the best protection against loss or disappointment is to choose disease-resistant trees and to plant, water, and feed them wisely.

Other Choices

While the trees in this chapter are the very best for Mid-Atlantic gardens, here are a few others we like:

Small Flowering Trees

Carolina Silverbell, *Halesia tetraptera*,
 H. monticola

Chaste Tree, *Vitex negundo* (Zones 7 to 10),
 V. agnus-castus (Zones 6 to 9)

English Hawthorn, *Crataegus laevigata*

Washington Hawthorn, *C. phaenopyrum*

Winter King Hawthorn, *C. viridis*
 'Winter King'

Large Deciduous Trees

American Hornbeam, Blue Beech Ironwood,
 Carpinus caroliniana

European Hornbeam, *C. betulus*
 'Fastigiata'

Kentucky Coffee Tree, *Gymnocladus dioicus*

Thornless Honeylocust, *Gleditsia triacanthus*
 var. *inermis*; cultivars 'Moraine', 'Ruby
 Lace', 'Shade Master', 'Sunburst'

Yellowwood, American Yellowwood,
 Cladrastis kentukea (*C. lutea*)

American Beech
Fagus grandifolia

The American beech is a grand tree, a magnificent pyramidal native species that needs plenty of space all around and belongs in a park-like setting. It has silky silver-gray bark and beautifully symmetrical branches that reach to the ground, shading out weeds and creating a hiding place for nut-loving squirrels, and children. The shimmery green leaves appear late in spring, turn russet-gold-brown in fall and cling to lower branches well into winter. The big oily seeds appeal to many species of birds and animals. This species is slow growing and rather difficult to transplant. The European beech, F. sylvatica, and its cultivars transplant more readily and are successful in all but the warmest parts of the Mid-Atlantic.

Bloom Period and Seasonal Color
April to early May; fall foliage is russet-gold-brown; bark is silky gray.

Mature Height × Spread
50 to 70 ft. × 60 ft.

When, Where, and How to Plant
Transplant a young container-grown or balled-and-burlapped tree with great care in early spring. Take care not to break the rootball—American beech does not transplant easily. It needs space all around and full sun, though it can handle dappled shade when young. The brow of a low hill, and toward the top of a slope is a likely site. It does best in soil in the somewhat acid range, pH 5.0 to 6.5, well drained, loose, and humusy enough to hold moisture. See Soil Preparation in the Introduction, and the planting instructions at the beginning of this chapter. Provide a planting hole three times the width of the rootball and twice as deep. Set the tree so the crown will be an inch or so above ground level. Staking might help the tree grow straighter, but remove it once the tree is established. Shape the earth around the crown into a wide saucer. Water slowly and deeply. Apply mulch 3 in. deep starting 3 in. from the stem.

Growing Tips
The first year, unless there's a soaking rain, in spring and fall slowly and gently pour two to three bucketsful of water around the roots every two weeks; in summer every week or ten days. Maintain the mulch.

Care
Apply a complete, slow-release, long lasting, organic lawn fertilizer in late winter or early spring from the drip line out to a distance equal to $1^1/2$ times the tree's height. Water it in. Replenish the mulch.

Companion Planting and Design
The American beech has high surface roots that are hard to cover, but are attractive when interplanted with small flowering bulbs.

Our Personal Recommendations
The European beech is smaller and easier to transplant than the American species, and many fine cultivars are available. 'Pendula' is a striking weeping form. The young leaves of the purple beech, 'Atropunicea' ('Purpurea'), are an extraordinary black-red that changes to purple-green. The purple leaves of the tricolor beech, 'Purpurea Tricolor' ('Roseo-marginata'), have an irregular edge of rose, and pinkish white.

Birch

Betula spp. and cultivars

When, Where, and How to Plant

The birches transplant easily in early spring or fall. They thrive in full sun, but accept bright shade. Most cultivated varieties grow well in somewhat wet or dry soils and are not particular as to pH. Provide soil that is well drained, fertile, and humusy. See Soil Preparation in the Introduction. Follow the planting instructions at the beginning of this chapter. Staking might help the tree grow straighter, but remove it once the tree is established. Water well. Mulch 3 in. deep starting 3 in. from the main stem.

Growing Tips

The first year, unless there's a soaking rain, in spring and fall slowly and gently pour two to three bucketsful of water around the roots every two weeks; in summer every week or ten days. Maintain the mulch.

Care

Apply a complete, slow-release, long lasting lawn fertilizer in late winter or early spring from the drip line out to a distance equal to $1^1/2$ times the tree's height. Water it in. Replenish the mulch. In summer or fall prune out limbs that threaten to cross others or grow in the wrong direction.

Companion Planting and Design

Beautiful, resistant birches are at their best standing alone as specimens with a background of evergreens.

Our Personal Recommendations

'Whitespire' may be the most resistant of the white barked birches but there are others: Chinese paper birch, *Betula albo-sinensis*, is one of the whitest of all the birches—but not easy to find; the handsome bark of *B. nigra* 'Heritage', river birch, peels to expose inner bark that may be salmon-pink to grayish, cinnamon, or reddish brown. The older bark of monarch birch, *Betula maximowicziana*, is white, and it is represented as exceptionally resistant. Weeping birch, *B. pendula* 'Youngii', has a graceful habit, but may be vulnerable to the bronze birch borer.

As a group, the birches are fast growing, tall, slender trees known for beautiful bark. They have graceful crowns of dainty pointed leaves that move in every breeze and turn to yellow and yellow-green in fall. In our mild climate birches are especially susceptible to birch leaf miner and bronze birch borer, so choosing a resistant cultivar is a wise move, such as Himalayan birch, B. utilis var. jacquemontii, which has beautiful, strikingly white bark. One of the most beautiful resistant birches is a single-trunk cultivar, the Japanese white birch, B. platyphylla var. japonica 'Whitespire'. Introduced by John L. Creech, late director of the U.S. National Arboretum, it has chalk-white bark enhanced by contrasting triangles of black at the base of the branches. The bark doesn't peel off, like that of the canoe birch, and the structure of the tree is very appealing.

Bloom Period and Seasonal Color
April; 2- to 3-in. catkins; chalk-white bark patterned with black triangles.

Mature Height × Spread
30 to 40 ft. × 12 to 15 ft.

Callery Pear
Pyrus calleryana

The flowering pear is a beautiful, pyramidal tree bigger than most of the flowering fruit trees. In very early spring, before the leaves appear, it covers itself with clusters of small, white blooms. In fall, the glossy, green leaves turn an attractive wine red and stay on the tree into late October and November. The fruits are small and russet-colored and attract birds. The flowering pear has been widely planted as a street tree. The first flowering pear was 'Bradford', a beautiful tree that unfortunately tends to split as it matures. It is being replaced with stronger varieties such as 'Aristocrat', which we planted years ago when it was first introduced: it is now a very large, magnificent tree that never has broken a branch. The flowering pear is a little too big for a small city garden, but handsome in a larger suburban landscape.

Other Name
Flowering Pear

Bloom Period and Seasonal Color
Early spring; white; foliage turns wine red in fall.

Mature Height × Spread
30 to 50 ft. × 15 to 20 ft.

When, Where, and How to Plant
Plant a balled-and-burlapped tree in late winter or early spring before the plant leafs out. A flowering pear flowers most fully and produces the brightest fruits when growing in full sun. However, like most small flowering trees, with four to six hours of sun or day-long bright, filtered light, it will perform well. The callery pears succeed in soils with a broad pH range, 5.5 to 7.5. See Soil Preparation in the Introduction, and the planting instructions at the beginning of this chapter. Provide a planting hole three times the width of the rootball and twice as deep. Set the tree so the crown will be an inch or so above ground level. The tree might grow straighter if it's staked, but remove the stake once the tree is established. Shape the earth around the crown into a wide saucer. Water slowly and deeply. Apply mulch 3 in. deep starting 3 in. from the trunk.

Growing Tips
The first year, unless there's a soaking rain, in spring and fall slowly and gently pour two to three bucketsful of water around the roots every two weeks; in summer every week or ten days. Maintain the mulch.

Care
Apply a slow-release organic fertilizer for acid-loving plants in late winter or early spring to just beyond the drip line, at half the recommended rate and water it in. Replenish the mulch. In late winter or early spring cut away branches that will grow into the center of the tree or rub against other branches—keep it open and airy.

Companion Planting and Design
The callery pear is tolerant of urban conditions, and a superb street tree and park specimen.

Our Personal Recommendations
'Chanticleer' (which may be the same as 'Select' and 'Cleveland Select') has a distinctive conical form ideal for street planting. 'White House', a larger National Arboretum introduction, André recommends for boulevards and parks: it has a strongly developed central stem, produces masses of pure white flowers, and colors red-purple early in the fall.

198

Crape Myrtle
Lagerstroemia indica and hybrids

When, Where, and How to Plant
Plant a balled-and-burlapped crape myrtle in early spring or early fall. Plant a container-grown specimen spring, summer, or fall. Crape myrtles leaf out late, especially when young. Full sun is best but four to six hours of sun or all-day dappled light will do. Moist, fertile, heavy loam and clay soils in the acid range, pH 5.0 to 6.5, are best. See Soil Preparation in the Introduction, and the planting instructions at the beginning of this chapter. Provide a planting hole three times the width of the rootball and twice as deep. Set the tree so the crown will be an inch or so above ground level. To encourage a single trunk, prune out all but the main stem; cut back a shrubby crape myrtle to the desired height. Shape the soil around the crown into a wide saucer. Water slowly and deeply. Apply mulch 3 in. deep starting 3 in. from the crown.

Growing Tips
The first year, unless there's a soaking rain, in spring and fall slowly and gently pour two to three bucketsful of water around the roots every two weeks; in summer every week or ten days. Maintain the mulch.

Care
In colder areas of Zone 6 a crape myrtle may die back and re-grow from the base. If that happens, thin the suckers to three, five, or seven stems and they will grow and bloom. Apply a slow-release, organic, acid fertilizer lightly in fall and again in late winter or early spring. Replenish the mulch. Water during dry spells. To maintain the height you wish, and to have lots of flowers, prune the plant back every year in early spring.

Companion Planting and Design
Underplant with small spring bulbs, wood hyacinths, and mixed flowering ground covers such as ajuga and periwinkle.

Our Personal Recommendations
Choose the color and height that will do the most for your landscape. A miniature crape myrtle with mildew resistance has been introduced by the National Arboretum: named 'Chickasaw', it is pink-lavender, and will remain between 20 and 30 in. tall.

The crape myrtles are flowering trees and shrubs that light up July and August with sprays of blooms that look like lilacs and last for months. The crape myrtles you see in gardens and parks all over the Mid-Atlantic are likely to be disease- and mildew-resistant hybrids developed by the late, great hybridizer Don Egolf, and introduced by the National Arboretum. Named for Native American tribes, these new varieties have cinnamon-colored, exfoliating bark, and the foliage of pink varieties turns showy colors in fall. There are dwarfs, low shrubs, shrubs, and small and large tree forms. Most grow relatively quickly, but they can be kept to shrub-size by cutting the plants back to the ground before they leaf out.

Other Name
Southern Summer Lilac

Bloom Period and Seasonal Color
July and August; warm raspberry, melting shades of rose, pink, melon, mauve, red, purple, white; colorful foliage; colorful bark.

Mature Height × Spread
20 in. to 25 ft. × 30 in. to 25 ft.

Common Smoke Tree
Cotinus coggygria

A favorite of the Victorians, beautiful in every season, the smoke tree can be counted on for beautiful foliage, romantic effect, and intense fall color. In June and early July tiny, inconspicuous, yellowish flowers appear, then in midsummer clouds of long, pink-gray fruiting panicles envelop the branches in misty halos that create a smoky effect. The source is thousands of tiny hairs attached to the developing fruit that dangles in clusters at the ends of the branches. Rounded, bluish purple or wine colored to dark green in summer, the leaves change in fall to yellow, red, and purple. The fall color is most pronounced in the hybrids. Medium to slow growing, as the tree matures the bark becomes corky and quite beautiful.

Other Names
Venetian Sumac, Wig Tree

Bloom Period and Seasonal Color
Smoky effect July and August; yellow, red, purple fall foliage.

Mature Height × Spread
10 to 15 ft. × 10 to 15 ft.

When, Where, and How to Plant
The smoke tree transplants readily in spring while the plant is still dormant, and in fall before Indian summer. It achieves the best color growing in full sun but grows well in part shade. Almost any soil will do; it can handle dry rocky soils, but in well-drained loam it thrives. See Soil Preparation in the Introduction, and the planting instructions at the beginning of this chapter. Provide a planting hole three times the width of the rootball and twice as deep. Set the tree so the crown will be an inch or so above ground level. Shape the earth around the crown into a wide saucer. Water slowly and deeply. Apply mulch 3 in. deep starting 3 in. from the trunk.

Growing Tips
The first year, unless there's a soaking rain, in spring and fall slowly and gently pour two to three bucketsful of water around the roots every two weeks; in summer every week or ten days. Maintain the mulch.

Care
Apply a slow-release organic fertilizer for acid-loving plants in late winter or early spring, at half the recommended rate, from the drip line out to a distance equal to $1^1/2$ times the tree's height. Water it in. Replenish the mulch. The flowers appear on new growth, so you can cut the plant back in late winter or early spring to keep it small, and to encourage greater flowering.

Companion Planting and Design
Smoke tree is a lovely addition to any shrub grouping, and makes a beautiful hedge.

Our Personal Recommendations
We like several of the colorful named varieties: 'Royal Purple' unfolds from a rich maroon red to a rich purple that doesn't fade; 'Velvet Cloak' is a luminous dark purple; 'Black Velvet' has dark purple foliage. 'Notcutts' Variety' is a strikingly rich dark maroon purple. Where a larger plant can be used, the 20- to 30-ft. native American smoke tree, *C. obovatus*, would be our choice because the color is more spectacular. Michael Dirr says, "It may be the best of all American shrub trees for intensity of color."

When, Where, and How to Plant

Plant a young, container-grown or balled-and-burlapped dogwood in early spring while it's still dormant, and handle the rootball with care. Dogwoods do best in partial or dappled light though they can handle full sun if the soil is humusy and moist. Ideal is a well-drained site with acid pH, 5.5 to 6.5, and about 40 percent humus. See Soil Preparation in the Introduction, and the planting instructions at the beginning of this chapter. Provide a planting hole three times the width of the rootball and twice as deep. Set the tree so the crown will be an inch or so above ground level. Staking might help the tree grow straighter, but remove it once the tree is established. Shape the earth around the crown into a wide saucer. Water slowly and deeply. Apply mulch 3 in. deep starting 3 in. from the trunk.

Growing Tips

The first year, unless there's a soaking rain, in spring and fall slowly and gently pour two to three bucketsful of water around the roots every two weeks; in summer every week or ten days. Maintain the mulch.

Care

Apply a slow-release, organic, acid fertilizer in late winter or early spring from the drip line out to a distance equal to $1^1/2$ times the tree's height. Water it in. Replenish the mulch.

Companion Planting and Design

Dogwoods are beautiful at the edge of a woodland, centering a lawn, or by a stone wall.

Our Personal Recommendations

'Cloud 9' is one of the best large-flowering white cultivars of *C. florida*; 'Multibracteata' and 'Pluribracteata' have double white flowers; 'Rubra' has pinkish red flowers and the foliage colors well in the fall. The kousa dogwood 'Milky Way', a broad bushy tree, produces quantities of white blooms; the bracts of the hybrid 'Summer Stars' stay beautiful for up to six weeks. Two other dogwood species with great appeal are 20- to 25-ft. *C. mas*, cornelian cherry, a yellow-flowered tree with showy, edible, acid-scarlet fruits that attract birds; and 30- to 40-ft. *C. controversa* variety 'Variegata', the variegated giant dogwood whose foliage has an irregular yellowish-white border.

The dogwood is a graceful tree whose layered branches are covered in mid-spring with sparkling white, star-shaped flowers (actually bracts), followed in fall by bright red fruits that attract birds. Cold turns the foliage red-plum. The wild dogwood that blooms with the redbuds at the edges of our woodlands is the 20- to 30-ft. Cornus florida, Virginia's state tree. Dr. Elwin Orton of Rutgers University has crossed C. florida with the Chinese dogwood, C. kousa, and produced C. × rutgeriensis, and a group of hybrids resistant to anthracnose and borers; patented, they're marketed as the Stellar series. The other dogwood we recommend is the late-blooming, disease-resistant Chinese dogwood, C. kousa var. chinensis, whose flowers perch on branches that droop a little. The bark exfoliates attractively as the plant matures.

Bloom Period and Seasonal Color
Spring; white, pink, and pink-red; in fall foliage colors red-plum and red fruits ripen.

Mature Height × Spread
20 to 30 ft. × 20 to 25 ft.

Eastern Redbud
Cercis canadensis

When the wild dogwoods are just ready to bloom at the edge of the woodlands here, the slim branches of little red-buds growing nearby are covered with showy, red-purple or magenta buds opening into rosy pink flowers. Usually after it blooms, but sometimes before, this multistemmed or low-branching native tree puts forth reddish purple leaves that change to dark, lustrous green, which often turn to gold in the fall. A mature redbud reaches 20 to 30 ft. in the wild but is likely to be half that size in cultivation. The fruit is a brown beanlike pod. Some lovely cultivated varieties are available but the excitement these days is generated by a beautiful white form, C. canadensis 'Alba'—not to be confused with a white subspecies of C. texensis.

Bloom Period and Seasonal Color
Early spring; red-purple, lavender-pink, magenta, white.

Mature Height × Spread
20 to 30 ft. × 25 to 35

When, Where, and How to Plant
Plant a balled-and-burlapped redbud in early spring or early fall. Plant a container-grown tree in spring, summer, or fall. Redbuds flower most fully growing in full sun but do well in open woodlands as long as they receive four to six hours of sun or all day dappled light. Redbud succeeds in well-drained sites in either alkaline or acid soil, but not in a permanently wet location. See Soil Preparation in the Introduction, and the planting instructions at the beginning of this chapter. Provide a planting hole three times the width of the rootball and twice as deep. Set the tree so the crown will be an inch or so above ground level. The tree might grow straighter if it's staked, but remove the stake once the tree is established. Shape the earth around the crown into a wide saucer. Water slowly and deeply. Apply mulch 3 in. deep starting 3 in. from the trunk.

Growing Tips
The first year, unless there's a soaking rain, in spring and fall slowly and gently pour two to three bucketsful of water around the roots every two weeks; in summer every week or ten days. Maintain the mulch.

Care
Apply a slow-release organic fertilizer for acid-loving plants in late winter or early spring from the drip line out to a distance equal to $1^1/2$ times the tree's height. Water it in. Replenish the mulch.

Companion Planting and Design
The redbud is small enough to use at the back of a shrub or a flower border; well grown, it will be large enough at maturity to be a specimen tree for a small yard. It is especially charming naturalized at the edge of a woodland.

Our Personal Recommendations
'Royal White' is another beautiful white-flowered cultivar. The flowers of 'Wither's Pink Charm' are a clear pink. 'Forest Pansy' is a favorite—a strikingly colorful, purple-leaved redbud. 'Flame' is an attractive, double-flowered form. The showy, shrubby, multistemmed Chinese redbud, *C. chinensis*, is smaller and is an option for gardeners in our warmer regions.

Flowering Cherry

Prunus spp. and hybrids

When, Where, and How to Plant

Transplant a balled-and-burlapped tree in early spring; a container-grown flowering fruit tree can be planted spring, summer, or fall. Flowering fruit trees bloom best in full sun. The ideal soil is well-drained, sandy loam, pH 6.0 to 7.5. See Soil Preparation in the Introduction, and the planting instructions at the beginning of this chapter. Provide a planting hole three times the width of the rootball and twice as deep. Set the tree so the crown will be an inch or so above ground level. The tree might grow straighter if it's staked, but remove the stake once the tree is established. Shape the soil around the crown into a wide saucer. Water slowly and deeply. Apply mulch 3 in. deep starting 3 in. from the trunk.

Growing Tips

The first year, unless there's a soaking rain, in spring and fall slowly and gently pour two to three bucketsful of water around the roots every two weeks; in summer every week or ten days. Maintain the mulch.

Care

Apply a slow-release organic fertilizer for acid-loving plants in late winter or early spring from the drip line out to a distance equal to $1^1/2$ times the tree's height. Water it in. Replenish the mulch. After the tree has bloomed, remove any sprigs that will become branches headed for the center of the tree or that will ultimately cross other branches.

Companion Planting and Design

Cultivars of the sargent cherry are excellent street trees, and beautiful set out as specimens in lawns, large or small.

Our Personal Recommendations

P. subhirtella 'Autumnalis' is a double-flowered pink cherry that blooms fully in early spring and repeats some in fall. The weeping cherry, *P. subhirtella* 'Pendula', blooms early; 'Pendula Plena Rosea', a double-flowered form, blooms later and holds its flowers even in bad weather.

After the witch-hazel's early show the flowering fruit trees come into bloom—and most are species and hybrids of the genus Prunus. The most celebrated are the flowering cherries, but there are plums, apricots, peaches, almonds, and nectarines. Bred for their blooms, they produce rudimentary fruit appealing to birds. The Higan cherry, P. subhirtella, is a beautiful species, which has given rise to numerous cultivars and forms. The four-season appeal of the sargent cherry, P. sargentii, makes it the most useful of the cherries: it bears showy clusters of single, deep-pink flowers; is big enough to provide shade for a small garden; has bronzy leaves that turn a nice red in fall; and the polished mahogany bark is handsome in winter. It blooms later than the Yoshino cherries, P. × yedoensis, that flower at the Tidal Basin in Washington, D.C., often just in time to catch the last winter snow storm. Various lovely hybrids also have been developed by crossing these and other cherry species.

Other Names

Sargent Cherry, Yoshino Cherry, Higan Cherry

Bloom Period and Seasonal Color

April to May; pink flowers; leaves turn bronze-red in fall.

Mature Height × Spread

40 to 50 ft. × 40 to 50 ft.

Flowering Crabapple
Malus spp. and cultivars

Apple orchards thrive in the Shenandoah Valley near the West Virginia border, where summers aren't quite so hot and fall is crisp and lingers—but the apple tree found in most gardens is the flowering crabapple. These small, spreading trees are covered in spring with exquisite apple blossoms, fragrant in some hybrids, and the brilliant fall fruits attract birds. Older varieties have problems, but there are new and beautiful disease-resistant hybrids. One of the best is 'Donald Wyman', a showy crab with soft pink buds opening to white. The magnificent 18-ft. Japanese crab, M. floribunda, which does well in warm regions, has much to recommend it: a branch spread of 25 ft., a lovely silhouette in winter, buds that are deep pink opening to white, fragrant flowers, and yellow-red fruits.

Other Name
Flowering Crab

Bloom Period and Seasonal Color
Mid-spring; pink or carmine buds opening to white; colorful fruits follow.

Mature Height × Spread
10 to 25 ft. × 10 to 25 ft.

When, Where, and How to Plant
A young container-grown or balled-and-burlapped crabapple transplants in early spring or fall. The best light is full sun. Eastern red cedar, *Juniperus virginiana*, is the alternate host of the cedar apple rust, so be sure to plant a rust-resistant crabapple. Crabs flourish in well-drained, heavy, loamy soil on the acid side, pH 5.0 to 6.5. See Soil Preparation in the Introduction, and the planting instructions at the beginning of this chapter. Provide a planting hole three times the width of the rootball and twice as deep. Set the tree so the crown will be an inch or so above ground level. Staking may help the tree grow straighter, but remove it once the tree is established. Shape the earth around the crown into a wide saucer. Water slowly and deeply. Apply mulch 3 in. deep starting 3 in. from the stem.

Growing Tips
The first year, unless there's a soaking rain, in spring and fall slowly and gently pour two to three bucketsful of water around the roots every two weeks; in summer every week or ten days. Maintain the mulch.

Care
Apply a slow-release, organic, acid fertilizer in late winter or early spring from the drip line out to a distance equal to $1^{1}/_{2}$ times the tree's height. Water it in. Replenish the mulch. Remove branches heading to the center of the tree, or crossing others. Prune after the tree has bloomed, or in summer; orchardists are now pruning dwarf fruit trees in summer.

Companion Planting and Design
A flowering crabapple should be set out as a featured specimen. 'Narragansett', an introduction of the National Arboretum, is recommended for small gardens. Striking weeping forms included red-berried 'Red Jade', and white-flowered 'Sugar Tyme' and 'White Cascade'.

Our Personal Recommendations
Disease-resistant crabs that André's father Martin grew include: *M. hupehensis*, the picturesque tea crab with wandlike branches; 'Katherine', a double-flowered hybrid; 'Sargentii', the Sargent crab, which is just 5 to 8 ft. high and twice as wide; the Asiatic apple, *M. spectabilis*, a 30-ft. tree with double flowers.

Franklin Tree

Franklinia alatamaha

When, Where, and How to Plant
The Franklin tree is not always easy to transplant, so start with a young container-grown or balled-and-burlapped tree from a reliable nursery. Set the tree out in early spring while still dormant. The flowers and fall color are most remarkable when the tree is growing in full sun. It thrives in well-drained soil that is fertile, loose, humusy enough to hold moisture, and in the acid range, pH 5.0-6.0, although it adapts to mildly alkaline soils. See Soil Preparation in the Introduction, and the planting instructions at the beginning of this chapter. Provide a planting hole three times the width of the rootball and twice as deep. Set the tree so the crown will be an inch or so above ground level. Staking might help the tree grow straighter, but remove it once the tree is established. Shape the earth around the crown into a wide saucer. Water slowly and deeply. Apply mulch 3 in. deep starting 3 in. from the stem.

Growing Tips
The first year, unless there's a soaking rain, in spring and fall slowly and gently pour two to three bucketsful of water around the roots every two weeks; in summer every week or ten days. Maintain the mulch.

Care
Apply a slow-release organic fertilizer for acid-loving plants in late winter or early spring from the drip line out to a distance equal to $1^{1}/_{2}$ times the tree's height. Water it in. Replenish the mulch.

Companion Planting and Design
The Franklin tree is an exceptionally lovely plant that belongs out in the open where its flowers and fall color can be appreciated.

Our Personal Recommendation
Plant the species.

This lovely little flowering tree with a romantic history bears fragrant, 3-in., white flowers from late July through August with some bloom in fall. New growth at the tips of the upright spreading branches gives the plant an airy, open look. The long, lustrous leaves appear late in the spring; in summer they turn bright green; then in fall they color bronze, orange, and red. The bark is interestingly ridged. The tree is native but no longer found in the wild. In 1765 John Bartram discovered it growing near Fort Barrington along Georgia's Altamaha River, and he collected seeds. Bartram planted his seeds and grew the first cultivated trees at his home near Philadelphia. He named it for Benjamin Franklin. As a child André remembers a planting of a dozen or so specimen trees that grew by the office window at his father's nursery.

Other Name
Ben Franklin Tree

Bloom Period and Seasonal Color
July and August into fall; white with showy yellow stamens; fall foliage is bronze, orange, red.

Mature Height × Spread
15 to 20 ft. × 6 to 15 ft.

Ginkgo
Ginkgo biloba

A tall, stately tree ideal for city parks, the ginkgo has easily recognized, fan-shaped leaves and turns a truly luminous butter-yellow-gold in fall, and the color lasts. It forms a rounded crown near the top of the tall, straight trunk. Because it tolerates pollution and salt it has been used as a street tree but that isn't its best use. Though it bears these broad, triangular leaves, it is more closely related to conifers (cone bearing trees and shrubs). This ancient species is estimated to have been growing on the planet for 150 million years: a Korean ginkgo has been documented as 1,100 years old. The strain we have now comes from China, but at one time it grew wild on this continent. Several beautiful specimens are growing on the grounds of the Capitol in Washington, D.C.

Other Name
Maidenhair Tree

Bloom Period and Seasonal Color
March and April; gold fall foliage.

Mature Height × Spread
30 to 50 ft. × 30 to 50 ft. and more with age

When, Where, and How to Plant
Gingkos transplant readily in spring while the plant is still dormant, and in fall before Indian summer. The ginkgo requires full sun, at least six hours a day. It does well in almost any soil, but thrives in sandy, deeply dug, well-drained, moist soil with a pH 5.5 to 7.5. See Soil Preparation in the Introduction, and the planting instructions at the beginning of this chapter. Provide a planting hole three times the width of the rootball and twice as deep. Set the tree so the crown will be an inch or so above ground level. Staking might help the tree grow straighter, but remove it once the tree is established. Shape the earth around the crown into a wide saucer. Water slowly and deeply. Apply mulch 3 in. deep starting 3 in. from the stem.

Growing Tips
The first year, unless there's a soaking rain, in spring and fall slowly and gently pour two to three bucketsful of water around the roots every two weeks; in summer every week or ten days. Maintain the mulch.

Care
Apply a complete, slow-release, long lasting lawn fertilizer in late winter or early spring from the drip line out to a distance equal to $1^1/2$ times the tree's height. Water it in. Replenish the mulch. Cut away any young branches that will grow into the center of the tree or rub against other branches.

Companion Planting and Design
A mature ginkgo is a tall, stately, handsome tree at its best growing in a large landscape or park setting. Several beautiful examples are growing on the grounds of the Capitol in Washington, D.C. Its open form is not that attractive as a young tree, and it's too tall to look well in a small garden when it begins to mature.

Our Personal Recommendations
Ask for and make sure you get a male ginkgo. The female tree produces a messy, plum-like fruit/seed that, in André's words, "is vile, stinky, not just bad." One of the best-looking cultivars is a broad-headed male called 'Autumn Gold'. The male clone 'Princeton Sentry'® has a narrow, upright form.

Golden Rain Tree
Koelreuteria paniculata

When, Where, and How to Plant
The golden rain tree transplants well when it is purchased as a *young* container-grown plant. Plant it in early spring while still dormant. The best location is a well-drained site with space all around and in full sun. However, it adapts to less light and a wide range of soils. It is tolerant of wind, pollution, drought, heat, and alkalinity. See Soil Preparation in the Introduction, and the planting instructions at the beginning of this chapter. Provide a planting hole three times the width of the rootball and twice as deep. Set the tree so the crown will be an inch or so above ground level. Staking might help the tree grow straighter, but remove it once the tree is established. Shape the earth around the crown into a wide saucer. Water slowly and deeply. Apply mulch 3 in. deep starting 3 in. from the trunk.

Growing Tips
The first year, unless there's a soaking rain, in spring and fall slowly and gently pour two to three bucketsful of water around the roots every two weeks; in summer every week or ten days. Maintain the mulch.

Care
Apply a complete, slow-release, long lasting, organic fertilizer in late winter from the drip line out to a distance equal to $1^1/_2$ times the tree's height and water it in. Replenish the mulch. In winter while the plant is still dormant, prune out young branches that will grow into the center of the tree or rub against other branches.

Companion Planting and Design
The golden rain tree is used as a street tree, along interstate highways, and is featured in parks in our region.

Our Personal Recommendations
André recommends 'September', a late-blooming cultivar. Another exceptionally lovely species, the Chinese flametree, *K. bipinnata*, bears pink to rose-pink flowers, but it is reliably hardy only in the Zones 7b and 8 of the Mid-Atlantic.

This tree deserves its romantic name. Small to medium in height, open-branched and flat-topped, it's a shade tree that from early to midsummer bears showy 12- to 15-in. panicles of yellow flowers half an inch long. But this is only the opening show: the flowers are followed in late summer by cascades of segmented papery capsules that look like tiny Chinese lanterns. As autumn advances they change from green to gold-buff to a vivid cinnamon-brown while the feathery and very graceful foliage turns a lovely yellow. The tree is fast growing, pest- and disease-resistant, a lovely specimen for the middle of a large lawn. The common name sometimes is confused with the laburnums, whose common name is golden-chain tree.

Other Name
Varnish Tree

Bloom Period and Seasonal Color
July; long panicles of yellow flowers followed by cascades of decorative seed capsules; yellow fall foliage.

Mature Height × Spread
30 to 40 ft. × 25 to 35 ft.

Holly

Ilex spp. and hybrids

Hollies thrive in our gardens. There are three types: evergreen trees and evergreen shrubs, both planted for their foliage, form, and berries; and the shrubby, leaf-losing hollies, whose berry display in fall is the main show. Evergreen Ilex opaca, American holly, which is native to the Eastern United States, grows into a handsome pyramidal tree 40 to 50 ft. tall, and ripens single red berries in October that persist through winter—unless the birds get them. It is practically indestructible here. Female plants bear lots of berries if there's a male pollinator in the neighborhood; if there isn't one, plant a male American holly. There are shrubby hollies for almost every landscape purpose and climate.

Bloom Period and Seasonal Color
Insignificant flowers in spring; red, white, yellow, inky blue berries in fall and winter.

Mature Height × Spread
Tree and shrub sizes.

When, Where, and How to Plant
Plant a container-grown shrub or a balled-and-burlapped tree holly in early spring. Hollies do well in full or part sun. It needs protection from strong winds and well-drained, humusy, acid soil, pH 5.0 to 6.0. See Soil Preparation in the Introduction, and planting instructions at the beginning of this chapter. Provide a planting hole three times the width of the rootball and twice as deep. Set the plant so the crown will be an inch or so above ground level. Shape the soil around the crown into a wide saucer. Water slowly and deeply. Apply mulch 3 in. deep starting 3 in. from the crown.

Growing Tips
The first year, unless there's a soaking rain, in spring and fall pour a bucketful of water around the roots every two weeks; in summer every week or ten days. Maintain the mulch.

Care
Apply a slow-release, organic, acid fertilizer lightly in fall and again in late winter or early spring. Replenish the mulch. To keep the plants trim, you can shear them when their spring growth is complete.

Companion Planting and Design
For hedges, varieties of the boxwood-like, shearable Japanese holly, *I. crenata*, are excellent, especially 'Convexa', 'Microphylla', and 'Stokes' holly. 'Helleri' matures at 3 ft. and makes a hedge tough enough to walk on. The 8- to 10-ft. Meserve holly, *I. × meserveae* 'Blue Girl' and its pollinator 'Blue Boy', are also excellent hedge and specimen plants. Burford's Chinese holly, *I. cornuta* 'Burfordii', is a 10-ft. cultivar that bears some berries even without a pollinator. For the wild garden and mixed shrub borders, use deciduous hollies such as compact inkberry *I. glabra* 'Compacta', 'Leucocarpa', and white-berried 'Ivory Queen'. *I. verticillata* 'Sparkleberry', a female, and its pollinator, 'Apollo', make beautiful berries together.

Our Personal Recommendations
André's favorite varieties of American holly trees are 'Merry Christmas', 'George Hart', 'Xanthocarpa', and 'Old Heavy Berry'. Other good tree hollies are longstalk holly, *I. pedunculosa*; English holly, *I. aquifolium*; slender 25-ft. 'Foster's Holly #2', *I. × attenuata*.

Japanese Maple
Acer palmatum

When, Where, and How to Plant
Japanese maples benefit from special care in transplanting. In early spring set out a container-grown plant, or a young balled-and-burlapped specimen. The Japanese maple needs four to seven hours of sun to color well, but it may burn if it is without some protection from the hot noon to afternoon sun in summer. It does best in a well-drained site and humusy, slightly acid soil but it is fairly adaptable, so almost any well-drained, rich, moist soil will do. See Soil Preparation in the Introduction, and the planting instructions at the beginning of this chapter. Provide a planting hole three times the width of the rootball and twice as deep. Set the shrub so the crown will be an inch or two above ground level. The taller Japanese maples may grow straighter if staked for the first year—don't leave a stake on after the tree is growing strongly. Shape the soil around the crown into a wide saucer. Water slowly and deeply. Apply mulch 3 in. deep starting 3 in. from the crown.

Growing Tips
The first year, unless there's a soaking rain, in spring and fall slowly and gently pour two to three bucketsful of water around the roots every two weeks; in summer every week or ten days. Maintain the mulch.

Care
In droughts water a Japanese maple slowly and deeply every two weeks. Japanese maples rarely require pruning to develop a beautiful form.

Companion Planting and Design
André has used vinca and ajuga as ground covers under a Japanese maple; if the shade cast is dense, you can thin a few branches.

Our Personal Recommendations
'Bloodgood', whose vivid color André remembers from his childhood at the Martin Viette Nursery, and the threadleaf Japanese maple, are our recommendations. Another of André's favorites is the full moon Japanese maple, *A. japonicum*, a 10- to 20-ft. tree whose foliage in spring is a soft glowing green and in fall turns to luminous yellow and crimson.

The most elegant foliage tree used in landscaping is the Japanese maple, A. palmatum. *It comes in various sizes, shapes, and colors—weeping, upright, tall shrub, or small tree, and the foliage may be green, pink, red, or black-red. The best upright deep red variety is probably* A. palmatum *'Bloodgood', which is about 8 to 10 ft. tall. The leaves hold their brilliant spring red and in fall become a rich scarlet. The most beautiful of the smaller forms is the threadleaf Japanese maple,* A. palmatum *'Dissectum Atropurpureum', which is 6- to 8-ft. tall, and has exquisite, deeply cut leaves and a picturesque weeping form. The ferny foliage is a rich purple-red in spring, fades toward green-plum in summer, then turns a spectacular orange in the fall.*

Bloom Period and Seasonal Color
Spring foliage is red, fading toward green in summer, and fiery shades in the fall.

Mature Height × Spread
6 to 15 or 20 ft. × 6 to 15 or 20 ft.

Japanese Pagoda Tree
Sophora japonica

An airy, exceptionally beautiful tree for parks, the Japanese pagoda tree bears showy panicles of creamy white, somewhat fragrant, pea-like flowers for several weeks in summer. The flowers are followed by drooping clusters of fruits—showers of pale-green, winged pods that look like beads and are persistent, and just as beautiful as the flowers. Gardeners who have planted the species often are disappointed to discover that the flowers don't begin to appear until the tree is ten to fourteen years old—but the display is worth waiting for. The bark is pale gray and the foliage handsome. A rapid grower, the Japanese pagoda tree thrives under heat and tolerates drought and difficult city conditions; it's a good specimen plant for large lawns, parks, and golf courses.

Other Name
Chinese Scholar-Tree

Bloom Period and Seasonal Color
July through mid-August; panicles of creamy white flowers followed by drooping clusters of pale-green, winged pods.

Mature Height × Spread
40 to 50 ft. × 30 to 40 ft.

When, Where, and How to Plant
Plant a *young* balled-and-burlapped or container-grown tree in spring while it is still dormant. The Japanese pagoda tree is somewhat tender to cold when young, but when it matures it will withstand more cold than it's likely to encounter in our region. The Japanese pagoda tree flowers most fully when growing in full sun. Provide a well-drained site with space all around. It adapts to a wide range of soils, tolerates poor soil, pollution, and, once mature, drought. See Soil Preparation in the Introduction, and the planting instructions at the beginning of this chapter. Provide a planting hole three times the width of the rootball and twice as deep. Set the tree so the crown will be an inch or so above ground level. Staking might help the tree grow straighter, but remove it once the tree is established. Shape the earth around the crown into a wide saucer. Water slowly and deeply. Apply mulch 3 in. deep starting 3 in. from the stem.

Growing Tips
The first year, unless there's a soaking rain, in spring and fall slowly and gently pour two to three bucketsful of water around the roots every two weeks; in summer every week or ten days. Maintain the mulch.

Care
Apply a complete, slow-release, long lasting, organic fertilizer in late winter before growth begins to just beyond the drip line at half the recommended rate, and water it in. Replenish the mulch. Repeat in November. In the fall after the leaves go, prune to create a strong central leader.

Companion Planting and Design
The tree is lovely underplanted with a living mulch of any one of the drought-tolerant ground covers, such as periwinkle or ajuga. Hostas, liriope, mondo grass, and small spring-flowering bulbs such as wood hyacinths are also acceptable ground covers.

Our Personal Recommendation
Princeton Nurseries has introduced a cultivar, 'Regent', that has a large oval crown of glossy, dark-green leaves; it comes into bloom at six to eight years of age.

Japanese Snowbell

Styrax japonicum

When, Where, and How to Plant

Plant a young, dormant, container-grown or balled-and-burlapped Japanese snowbell in early spring while it's still dormant. The site can be in full sun or partial shade. The ideal soil is moist, acid—pH 5.5 to 6.5—and well drained, with about 30 percent humus. See Soil Preparation in the Introduction, and the planting instructions at the beginning of this chapter. Provide a planting hole three times the width of the rootball and twice as deep. Set the tree so the crown will be an inch above ground level. Staking may help the tree grow straighter, but remove it once the tree is established. Shape the earth around the crown into a wide saucer. Water slowly and deeply. Apply mulch 3 in. deep starting 3 in. from the trunk.

Growing Tips

The first year, unless there's a soaking rain, in spring and fall slowly and gently pour two to three bucketsful of water around the roots every two weeks; in summer every week or ten days. Maintain the mulch. If the tree is in an exposed location and you are in Zone 6, provide winter protection from sweeping winds for the first few years.

Care

Apply a slow-release organic fertilizer for acid-loving plants in late winter or early spring from the drip line out to a distance equal to $1^1/2$ times the tree's height. Water it in. Replenish the mulch.

Companion Planting and Design

Plant a Japanese snowbell where you will pass underneath it because the yellow stamens of the flowers are so decorative. It is lovely in partial shade as a patio or shrub border specimen, and at the edge of an open woodland planted with azaleas, mountain laurels, and rhododendrons.

Our Personal Recommendations

The Japanese snowbell is considered the most useful and beautiful of the species in cultivation. *S. obassia*, the fragrant snowbell, grows more slowly, blooms earlier, and the flowers are more noticeably scented. The flowers are followed by beautiful clusters of grape-like green fruits. The flowers are partly hidden by the leaves, which do not color in fall.

One of the last flowers to bloom in spring is the beautiful Japanese snowbell. The blossoms are clusters of drooping, yellow-centered, bell-shaped, white flowers that have a faint perfume. The petals arch backward as the flowers mature to show off their colorful centers and the effect is striking. The leaves are glossy, a rich green in summer and in fall they turn toward yellow or red. The leaves perch on the topside of the branches, which makes the flowers easier to see. Green-white, egg-shaped fruits follow the flowers. A charming little tree, it develops a spreading crown that casts light shade. An interesting structure and smooth gray-brown bark add texture to the garden in winter.

Bloom Period and Seasonal Color

June and July; white blossoms.

Mature Height × Spread

15 to 30 ft. × 15 to 30 ft.

Japanese Stewartia
Stewartia pseudocamellia

The stewartias are small trees and tall shrubs that bear 2½- to 3½-in. camellia-like flowers in mid- to late summer when little else blooms. Japanese stewartia is a beautiful small tree with many assets—exquisite flowers, colorful foliage, and peeling bark that shows cinnamon red, gray, and shades of orange. The blossoms are small, cup shaped, and the color is a beautiful creamy white, set off by a prominent mass of orange anthers at the center. When the leaves emerge in early spring they are purple-bronze. In summer they turn green, and, with cold weather, they change to yellow, purple-orange, and bronze-red. As the plant matures, the bark sheds in striking patterns of cinnamon red-gray and orange. The stewartias belong to the tea family, and are related to Franklinia *and* Camellia.

Bloom Period and Seasonal Color
Mid- to late summer; white petals with orange anthers; fall foliage is yellow, purple-orange, and bronze-red; mature trees have colorful exfoliating bark.

Mature Height × Spread
30 to 40 ft. × 20 to 30 ft.

When, Where, and How to Plant
Plant a small, young, container-grown or balled-and-burlapped tree in early spring while still dormant. The flowers and fall color are most remarkable when the tree is growing in full sun but it benefits, especially in warmer regions, from some shade at noon. It thrives in soil that is fertile, moist, contains a third to a half leaf mold or peat moss, and is in the acid range, pH 4.5 to 5.5. See Soil Preparation in the Introduction, and the planting instructions at the beginning of this chapter. Provide a planting hole three times the width of the rootball and twice as deep. Set the tree so the crown will be an inch above ground level. Staking may help the tree grow straighter, but remove it once the tree is established. Shape the earth around the crown into a wide saucer. Water slowly and deeply. Apply mulch 3 in. deep starting 3 in. from the stem.

Growing Tips
The first year, unless there's a soaking rain, in spring and fall slowly and gently pour two to three bucketsful of water around the roots every two weeks; in summer every week or ten days. Maintain the mulch.

Care
Apply a slow-release, organic, acid fertilizer in late winter or early spring from the drip line out to a distance equal to 1½ times the tree's height. Water it in. Replenish the mulch.

Companion Planting and Design
Stewartia is beautiful as a lawn specimen, grouped in a shrub border with low-growing azaleas, and at the edge of an open woodland.

Our Personal Recommendations
Our favorite is Japanese stewartia, but for small gardens the very similar Korean stewartia, *S. koreana*, may be a better fit. The flowers are larger and flatter than those of the species above, and tend to appear over a longer period. The leaves turn to red and purple in the fall, and the bark flakes to show gorgeous patches of soft silvery-buff streaked with cinnamon and orange-brown. Chinese stewartia, *S. sinensis*, is smaller still in every way; the flowers are scented but the foliage does not take on the rich autumn hues of the other species.

Katsura Tree
Cercidiphyllum japonicum

When, Where, and How to Plant

The katsura tree is not easy to transplant. Set out a *young*, dormant, container-grown or balled-and-burlapped tree from a reliable nursery in early spring. The color is remarkable when the tree is growing in full sun and in soil in the acid range, pH 5.0 to 6.5. Provide a well-drained site and soil that is rich, loose, and humusy enough to hold moisture. The brow of a low hill, and toward the top of a slope is a likely situation. See Soil Preparation in the Introduction, and the planting instructions at the beginning of this chapter. Provide a planting hole three times the width of the rootball and twice as deep. Set the tree so the crown will be an inch or so above ground level. Staking might help the tree grow straighter, but remove it once the tree is established. Shape the earth around the crown into a wide saucer. Water slowly and deeply. Apply mulch 3 in. deep starting 3 in. from the trunk.

Growing Tips

The first year, unless there's a soaking rain, in spring and fall slowly and gently pour two to three bucketsful of water around the roots every two weeks; in summer every week or ten days. Maintain the mulch.

Care

Apply a complete, slow-release, long lasting, organic fertilizer in late winter from the drip line out to a distance equal to $1^1/2$ times the tree's height, and water it in. Replenish the mulch. The first two or three seasons, water the tree deeply as often as the flower beds need watering. Prune in late winter to feature the main stem and create a broad-spreading crown.

Companion Planting and Design

The best use of this tree is as a specimen, set out where it can be seen throughout the seasons. Make a point of buying a single-stemmed plant.

Our Personal Recommendations

For its beauty, we recommend planting the species. But, if you would like to add a weeping tree to your landscape, consider the weeping form of the katsura tree, 'Pendula', a lovely small tree 15 to 25 ft. tall in cultivation.

"If I could use only one tree, this would be my first tree." We are quoting noted plantsman and author Michael Dirr. This is a fast- to medium-fast-growing, very beautiful, refined shade tree planted for its foliage. The new leaves are a bronze or reddish purple, changing to blue-green in summer, then in fall transformed into a spectacular, glowing, apricot-orange and golden yellow—a show described as very well worth traveling to see. The aging leaves give off a faint spicy scent. The tree has a dense rounded form and shaggy brown bark that add interest to the winter landscape. The katsura is an excellent tree for medium-sized landscapes and parks, and it also is useful for street planting.

Bloom Period and Seasonal Color
Foliage changes from bronze or reddish purple, to blue-green, to apricot-orange and gold.

Mature Height × Spread
40 to 50 ft. × 20 to 30 ft.

Maple

Acer spp. and cultivars

For the home garden perhaps the most valuable shade tree is the majestic maple. In spring, it covers itself with colorful buds, and in fall the leaves turn to yellow, orange, and bright red. The species renowned for fall color is the big, beautiful, slow-growing sugar maple, A. saccharum, the source of maple syrup. A mature sugar maple has a pyramidal shape, great strength and character, and wide branches that provide dappled shade. In the wild, it reaches 100 ft. and more. Though smaller in cultivation it's a magnificent tree for parks and large landscapes. For home gardens and in our climate, the faster-growing, smaller, swamp or red maple, A. rubrum, is grown; its fall color is often a more intense red. But it has more root problems than the sugar maple. The maples withstand some pollution.

Bloom Period and Seasonal Color
March to April; greenish yellow to red buds in the sugar maple and garnet red buds in the swamp maple and its cultivars; foliage turns in fall to yellow, orange, and bright red.

Mature Height × Spread
60 to 75 ft. × 40 ft.

When, Where, and How to Plant
Choose a container-grown or balled-and-burlapped tree and plant it in fall before Indian summer, or in early spring while the tree is still dormant. Most maples do best in slightly acid soil and full sun, but almost any well-drained, rich, moist soil will do. Very young saplings of the swamp maple and its cultivars transplant readily bareroot; this species does best in slightly acid soil and moist conditions. See Soil Preparation in the Introduction, and the planting instructions at the beginning of this chapter. For all maples provide a planting hole three times the width of the rootball and twice as deep. Set the tree so the crown will be an inch or so above ground level. Staking may help the tree grow straighter, but remove it once the tree is established. Shape the earth around the crown into a wide saucer. Water slowly and deeply. Apply mulch 3 in. deep starting 3 in. from the stem.

Growing Tips
The first year, unless there's a soaking rain, in spring and fall slowly pour two to three bucketsful of water around the roots every two weeks; in summer every week or ten days. Maintain the mulch.

Care
Do not let the soil around a young maple go dry at any time; in dry spells, water even mature maples deeply, since they have a very shallow root system. In late winter before growth begins apply a complete, slow-release, long lasting, organic lawn fertilizer from the drip line out to a distance equal to $1^1/_2$ times the tree's height and water it in. Replenish the mulch.

Companion Planting and Design
Most large maples are better in large landscapes, and as park trees rather than street trees unless watered in droughts. The roots of a vigorous maple will buckle cement sidewalks and patios.

Our Personal Recommendations
The sugar maple cultivar 'Green Mountain' is heat tolerant and can handle more drought than some others; 'Bonfire' may grow faster than the species and has more reliable fall color. The outstanding red maple cultivar for our region is 'Red Sunset', which has orange-red fall color. Others are 'Autumn Flame', which colors earlier than the species and 'October Glory', which holds its leaves later.

Oak

Quercus spp.

When, Where, and How to Plant

Plant an oak while it is still dormant in early spring. Buy a young container-grown or balled-and-burlapped tree and handle it with TLC: most oak species have taproots that can be damaged. The pin oak has a shallow, fibrous root system that transplants more easily. Most species do best growing in full sun and in slightly acid soil, but they are tolerant of other soils. The willow oak succeeds even in poorly drained clay soil; the shumard oak withstands moist soil. See Soil Preparation in the Introduction, and the planting instructions at the beginning of this chapter. Provide a planting hole three times the width of the rootball and twice as deep. Set the tree so the crown will be an inch or so above ground level. Staking can help the tree grow straighter, but remove it once the tree is established. Shape the earth around the crown into a wide saucer. Water slowly and deeply. Apply mulch 3 in. deep starting 3 in. from the trunk.

Growing Tips

The first year, unless there's a soaking rain, in spring and fall slowly and gently pour two to three bucketsful of water around the roots every two weeks; in summer every week or ten days. Maintain the mulch.

Care

Apply a complete, slow-release, long lasting, organic lawn fertilizer in late winter from the drip line out to a distance equal to $1^1/2$ times the tree's height. Water it in. Replenish the mulch. Water deeply during droughts until the plant is growing well. In late winter, prune to develop a strong central leader.

Companion Planting and Design

The oaks mentioned all do well in urban situations.

Our Personal Recommendation

For a large landscape we also recommend the majestic white oak, *Q. alba*, which has an arresting silhouette and is considered by many the finest of all our native oaks; it develops slowly and attains heights of 80 to 90 ft.

The oaks are magnificent spreading shade trees suited to parks, large landscapes, and city streets—long-lived, symmetrical, and handsome. In Washington, D.C., there are well-grown examples of some that excel as street trees. The finest of the oaks for fall color is Quercus coccinea, the scarlet oak; Q. rubra, the Northern red oak, is not quite as showy but grows more quickly; Q. shumardii, the shumard or Southern scarlet oak, is the largest of the native red oaks and has deeply cut, lustrous leaves that turn scarlet in the fall. Many midtown Washington, D.C., areas are lined with willow oak, Q. phellos, an elegant smaller native oak with willow-like leaves that turn yellow, yellow brown, and russet red in the fall.

Bloom Period and Seasonal Color

Fall foliage turns yellow or nut brown, or various shades of red and russet.

Mature Height × Spread

40 to 75 ft. × 40 to 60 ft.

Red Horse Chestnut
Aesculus × carnea 'Briotii'

The beautiful European and Asian horse chestnuts are cousins to our native buckeyes. The horse chestnuts are admired for their showy spring flowers, but they are planted mainly for the wide branching and dense foliage that makes these superior shade trees. The red horse chestnut is a hybrid resulting from crossing the North American native red buckeye, A. pavia, with the European horse chestnut, A. hippocastanum. The cultivar 'Briotii' is a beautiful pyramidal tree that bears showy, upright panicles of flowers 8 to 10 in. long in rosy shades. The leaves have the shape of a hand and retain their rich dark green well into October. The fruit of the horse chestnut is inedible and prickly.

Bloom Period and Seasonal Color
Early to mid-May; rose-red or salmon-red flowers.

Mature Height × Spread
45 to 60 ft. × 35 to 45 ft.

When, Where, and How to Plant
Transplant container-grown or balled-and-burlapped horse chestnuts in early spring. The horse chestnuts thrive in full sun, but they also do well in bright shade. The most successful plants are growing in moist, well-drained soil whose pH is around 6.5, but they are tolerant of other soils. See Soil Preparation in the Introduction, and the planting instructions at the beginning of this chapter. Provide a planting hole three times the width of the rootball and twice as deep. Set the tree so the crown will be an inch or so above ground level. Staking may help the tree grow straighter, but remove it once the tree is established. Shape the earth around the crown into a wide saucer. Water slowly and deeply. Apply mulch 3 in. deep starting 3 in. from the stem.

Growing Tips
The first year, unless there's a soaking rain, in spring and fall slowly and gently pour two to three bucketsful of water around the roots every two weeks; in summer every week or ten days. Maintain the mulch.

Care
In late winter to early spring apply a complete, slow-release, long lasting, organic fertilizer from the drip line out to a distance equal to $1^1/2$ times the tree's height. Water it in. Replenish the mulch. Even after the plant is established and growing well, water deeply during droughts. Prune out any young branches that will grow into the center of the tree or rub against other branches.

Companion Planting and Design
'Briotii' is an excellent choice for a large yard, and it is used extensively for shade in street plantings, in parks, golf courses, and campuses.

Our Personal Recommendations
'Briotii' is our first choice for the home garden, but its big and beautiful cousin, A. *hippocastanum* 'Baumannii', whose flowers are white and double, is an inspired choice for the larger landscape.

Sour Gum
Nyssa sylvatica

When, Where, and How to Plant
The sour gum has a taproot, which makes it difficult to transplant. Choose a thriving, *young*, container-grown plant, and set it out with TLC. In cultivation it does best in full sun or bright, dappled shade. It requires moist, well-drained, acid soil, pH 5.5 to 6.5, and needs some protection from wind. See Soil Preparation in the Introduction, and planting instructions at the beginning of this chapter. Provide a planting hole three times the width of the rootball and twice as deep. Set the tree so the crown will be an inch or so above ground level. Staking might help the tree grow straighter, but remove it once the tree is established. Shape the earth around the crown into a wide saucer. Water slowly and deeply. Apply mulch 3 in. deep starting 3 in. from the stem.

Growing Tips
The first year, unless there's a soaking rain, in spring and fall slowly and gently pour two to three bucketsful of water around the roots every two weeks; in summer every week or ten days. Maintain the mulch.

Care
Apply a complete, slow-release, long lasting, organic fertilizer for acid-loving plants in late winter before growth begins from the drip line out to a distance equal to 1¹/₂ times the tree's height. Water it in. Replenish the mulch. In late fall, cut away any branches that might grow into the center of the tree or rub against other branches.

Companion Planting and Design
The black gum looks its best featured at the edge of a lawn or near a stream or a pond where its autumn foliage will be seen. It is also successful at the shore.

Our Personal Recommendations
We recommend the species but for water sites there is a handsome swamp species of the sour gum, *N. aquatica*, the water tupelo. The national champion of the species is 100 ft. tall and 55 ft. wide, and is growing in Southhampton County, VA.

In fall, this is one of the most beautiful of all our native trees—the leaves change to fluorescent yellow, orange, scarlet, and purple. The tree is pyramidal in form, with somewhat drooping branches. The usual height is 30 to 50 ft., but it grows taller in the wild, especially near water. Bees visit the small, nectar-rich, greenish white flowers that appear in spring, and an exceptionally flavorful honey is made from it. The flowers are followed by bluish fruits that are somewhat hidden by the leaves and are relished by bears and other wildlife. The bark is dark charcoal gray, broken into thick blocky ridges, giving the plant winter appeal. It tolerates pollution well enough to be used as a street tree in the suburbs.

Other Names
Black Gum, Black Tupelo

Bloom Period and Seasonal Color
Spring; small greenish white flowers; fall foliage is fluorescent yellow to orange to scarlet to purple.

Mature Height × Spread
30 to 50 ft. × 20 to 30 ft.

Sourwood
Oxydendrum arboreum

This lovely native tree of modest height veils itself in drooping racemes of fragrant, white, urn-shaped flowers in summer. Then in fall, large, dark green leaves turn yellow, orange, red, and purple. Attractive seedpods follow the flowers and persist through fall, and deeply furrowed bark makes an attractive winter feature. Sourwood is a slow-growing tree that takes a dozen years to reach 15 ft. or so. It is attractive to bees and is a source of a superb honey. Sourwood grows wild along the banks and streams of coastal Virginia, a beautiful tree that naturalizes fairly easily and is well worth the effort needed to establish it in the home landscape. It does not transplant easily nor does it tolerate urban pollution.

Other Names
Lily-of-the-Valley Tree, Sorrel Tree

Bloom Period and Seasonal Color
Late June, early July; white flowers; yellow, orange, red, and purple foliage in fall.

Mature Height × Spread
25 to 30 ft. × 20 ft.

When, Where, and How to Plant
In early spring buy a still-dormant container-grown plant from a reliable nursery, and handle the transplanting with great care. Sourwood does well in full sun, but it tolerates bright filtered light all day or partial bright shade. It requires a well-drained site, and acid soil, pH 5.5 to 6.5. See Soil Preparation in the Introduction, and the planting instructions at the beginning of this chapter. Provide a planting hole three times the width of the rootball and twice as deep. Set the tree so the crown will be an inch or so above ground level. Staking may help the tree grow straighter, but remove it once the tree is established. Shape the earth around the crown into a wide saucer. Water slowly and deeply. Apply mulch 3 in. deep starting 3 in. from the stem.

Growing Tips
The first year, unless there's a soaking rain, in spring and fall slowly and gently pour two to three bucketsful of water around the roots every two weeks; in summer every week or ten days. Maintain the mulch.

Care
Spread a compete, slow-release, long lasting, organic fertilizer for acid-loving plants in late winter before growth begins out to a distance equal to $1^1/2$ times the tree's height. Water it in. Replenish the mulch.

Companion Planting and Design
It's known as the lily-of-the-valley tree—and considered second only to one other native flowering tree, the dogwood. So make it a feature of your landscape in a spot where it will be seen year round.

Our Personal Recommendation
Plant the species.

Southern Magnolia

Magnolia grandiflora

When, Where, and How to Plant

Transplant a young container-grown or balled-and-burlapped magnolia with care, before new growth begins in early spring. Full sun is best but four to six hours of sun, or all-day filtered light will do. The ideal soil is acid, pH 5.0 to 6.5, fertile, humusy, and well drained, but not dry. See Soil Preparation in the Introduction, and follow the planting instructions at the beginning of this chapter. Make the hole three times as wide and twice as deep as the rootball. Set the tree so the crown will be about 1 or 2 in. above ground level. Staking may keep the tree growing straight, but remove it once the tree is established. Shape the soil around the crown into a wide saucer. Water slowly and deeply. Apply mulch 3 in. deep starting 3 in. from the trunk.

Growing Tips

The first year, unless there's a soaking rain, in spring and fall slowly pour two to three bucketsful of water around the roots every two weeks; in summer every week or ten days. Maintain the mulch.

Care

Apply a slow-release, organic, acid fertilizer in late winter or early spring from the drip line out to 1 1/2 times the tree's height. Water it in. Replenish the mulch. Magnolias are most beautiful allowed to develop without pruning; any pruning should be done after the tree has bloomed.

Companion Planting and Design

This majestic tree belongs as a specimen in the middle of a large lawn, or flanking a formal entrance, or as foundation plant for grounds around large buildings.

Our Personal Recommendations

André's favorite Southern magnolia is pyramidal 'Majestic Beauty', with large, lustrous green leaves and cup-shaped, white, 12-in. flowers. Outstanding half-size varieties are 'Little Gem', which bears 6-in. flowers in spring, and 'St. Mary's', which produces full-size flowers while still young. He also likes *M. × soulangiana* 'Lennei' whose blooms are rich deep purple outside, pure white inside. They appear late and so escape late frosts. The star magnolia, *M. stellata*, another beautiful, small, deciduous magnolia, blooms before the leaves appear; 'Waterlily' is a lovely variety.

The majestic 80-ft. bullbay magnolia, a very ancient evergreen tree, is a symbol of the Southern plantation. The foot-long leaves are oblong, glossy, stiff, almost indestructible, and are enhanced by cinnamon-brown undersides. The flowers are fragrant, immense, shaped like a saucer or a water lily, and appear intermittently in summer. Dark red, cone-shaped fruits with bright red decorative seeds follow the flowers and are staples for Christmas arrangements in Williamsburg. There are magnificent specimens on Capitol Hill in Washington, D.C. For small gardens and cold Zone 6, the Chinese, or saucer magnolia, M. × soulangiana, is a wise choice. A 20- to 30-ft. deciduous tree, the blooms are purplish pink on the outside and cream or white inside, and they appear before the leaves.

Other Name
Bullbay Magnolia

Bloom Period and Seasonal Color
Intermittent summer bloom; flowers are cream white; evergreen foliage has handsome cinnamon reverse.

Mature Height × Spread
60 to 80 ft. × 30 to 50 ft.

Sweet Gum
Liquidambar styraciflua

The American sweet gum is a tall, handsome shade tree with large, five-pointed leaves that in fall turn to true yellow, red, and purple—a spectacular show most years. In summer, the leaves are a deep, attractive, glossy green. The bark is grayish brown and interestingly corky. A big tree, in moist soil it grows rather quickly, 2 to 3 ft. a year. In dry soil, the growth is a little slower. The common name refers to the sap, which is rather sweet and gummy. Male and female flowers are produced in dense clusters and mature into prickly, woody seedpods that litter. It makes a superb lawn tree as long as the means exist to remove the prickly fruit before mowing.

Other Name
American Sweet Gum

Bloom Period and Seasonal Color
April to May; flowers are inconspicuous; fall foliage is true yellow, red, purple.

Mature Height × Spread
50 to 60 ft. × 35 to 45 ft.

When, Where, and How to Plant
Plant a young container-grown or balled-and-burlapped tree in early spring while the tree is still dormant. Handle the rootball with care; under the best of circumstances it takes a while to recover from the move. Sweetgum requires full sun, tolerates part shade, but not pollution. Set the tree where there will be lots of space all around for the development of its root system. It does best in well-drained, moist, acid soil, pH 5.5 to 6.5. See Soil Preparation in the Introduction, and planting instructions at the beginning of this chapter. Provide a planting hole three times the width of the rootball and twice as deep. Set the tree so the crown will be an inch or so above ground level. Staking may help the tree grow straighter, but remove it once the tree is established. Shape the earth around the crown into a wide saucer. Water slowly and deeply. Apply mulch 3 in. deep starting 3 in. from the stem.

Growing Tips
The first year, unless there's a soaking rain, in spring and fall slowly and gently pour two to three bucketsful of water around the roots every two weeks; in summer every week or ten days. Maintain the mulch.

Care
Apply a complete, slow-release, long lasting, organic lawn fertilizer in late winter before growth begins to a distance equal to $1^1/2$ times the tree's height. Water it in. Replenish the mulch. Repeat in November. If any pruning is required, do it in late winter before the buds swell.

Companion Planting and Design
Sweet gum is an excellent choice for a large, open landscape that was previously forested wetland, for example. It's a superb lawn tree, but its prickly fruit must be removed before mowing.

Our Personal Recommendations
'Rotundiloba' does not produce the prickly balls that are such a nuisance. 'Burgundy' has dark red to maroon fall color and holds its color late.

Tuliptree
Liriodendron tulipifera

When, Where, and How to Plant
The tuliptree requires care in transplanting. Plant a young, container-grown or balled-and-burlapped tree in early spring while it is still dormant. The tulip tree requires full sun. It does well in almost any soil, but thrives in sandy, deeply dug, well-drained, moist soil that is slightly acid, pH 5.5 to 6.5. See Soil Preparation in the Introduction, and planting instructions at the beginning of this chapter. Provide a planting hole three times the width of the rootball and twice as deep. Set the tree so the crown will be an inch or so above ground level. Staking may help the tree grow straighter, but remove it once the tree is established. Shape the earth around the crown into a wide saucer. Water slowly and deeply. Apply mulch 3 in. deep starting 3 in. from the stem.

Growing Tips
The first year, unless there's a soaking rain, in spring and fall slowly and gently pour two to three bucketsful of water around the roots every two weeks; in summer every week or ten days. Maintain the mulch.

Care
Spread a complete, slow-release, long lasting, organic lawn fertilizer in late winter from the drip line to a distance equal to 1 1/2 times the tree's height. Water it in. Replenish the mulch. In periods of drought water even well-established trees deeply every week. Any pruning should be done in winter; remove young branches that will grow into the center of the tree or rub against other branches.

Companion Planting and Design
This majestic, long-lived native tree is suited to large parks and landscapes and should be allowed enough space all around to be seen. If seeing the flowers is part of the purpose of planting the tree, you will have to place near an observation point that looks toward or down onto the top of the tree. The tulip tree can tolerate city conditions and is handsome in a park, but can be too big for street planting.

Our Personal Recommendations
Plant the species. A variegated form, 'Aureo-marginatum', has leaves edged with yellow.

The tulip poplar is a tall, majestic, native shade tree that probably is the tallest and straightest hardwood in America. There's a beautiful specimen on the grounds of the Capitol in Washington, D.C., and a wonderful tree at Mount Vernon, supposedly planted by George Washington. The tuliptree grows wild from Massachusetts to Florida, and westward to Wisconsin and Mississippi. It is named for the greenish yellow, tulip-like flowers that appear in late spring or early summer. Unfortunately, they're borne high in the branches, and aren't readily visible from below. The seeds in the conelike fruits, which resemble those of the large magnolias, to which it is related, attract finches and cardinals. The leaves are quite distinctive—blue-green and rather like a maple leaf with its end squared off. In fall, the leaves turn a rich, handsome, canary yellow that makes a very nice show.

Other Name
Tulip Poplar

Bloom Period and Seasonal Color
Late May or early June; chartreuse blossoms touched at the base with bright orange; leaves are canary yellow in fall.

Mature Height × Spread
70 to 90 ft. × 35 to 50 ft.

White Fringe Tree
Chionanthus virginicus

In mid-spring, just as the leaves are filling in, this lovely little tree is wrapped in a mist of delicate, 6- to 8-in. long panicles of lightly scented, greenish white flowers that consist of drooping, fringe-like petals. With the first real cold in autumn, the leaves turn luminous yellow-gold and hang on as long as the weather stays fairly moderate. The female plants bear bloomy, purple fruits the birds relish. The petals of the flowers on male trees are larger and showier, but the fruit is smaller and somewhat hidden by the foliage. The fringe tree is slow growing and tolerates urban pollution. It's often found in the Blue Ridge Mountains growing wild. It is very pretty seen at a distance—across a lawn for example, or near a pond or a stream.

Bloom Period and Seasonal Color
Mid-spring; white; foliage turns pure yellow in fall.

Mature Height × Spread
15 to 25 ft. × 15 to 25 ft.

When, Where, and How to Plant
Set out a young container-grown or a balled-and-burlapped tree in early spring while the tree is still dormant. Handle the rootball with care. The fringe tree flowers best in full sun but makes do with four to six hours of sun or bright, filtered light all day. The ideal site is near water in slightly acid soil, pH 5.5 to 6.5. See Soil Preparation in the Introduction, and the planting instructions at the beginning of this chapter. Provide a planting hole three times the width of the rootball and twice as deep. Set the tree so the crown will be an inch or so above ground level. Staking might help the tree grow straighter, but remove it once the tree is established. Shape the earth around the crown into a wide saucer. Water slowly and deeply. Apply mulch 3 in. deep starting 3 in. from the trunk.

Growing Tips
The first year, unless there's a soaking rain, in spring and fall slowly and gently pour two to three bucketsful of water around the roots every two weeks; in summer every week or ten days. Maintain the mulch.

Care
Apply a slow-release organic fertilizer for acid-loving plants in late winter or early spring from the drip line out to a distance equal to $1^1/2$ times the tree's height. Water it in. Replenish the mulch. The white fringe tree flowers on the previous season's growth; after flowering, cut out young branches that will grow into the center of the tree or rub against other branches.

Companion Planting and Design
Beautiful as a specimen in the center of a lawn. An underplanting of periwinkle, ajuga, and small, spring-flowering bulbs such as wood hyacinths set the tree off nicely.

Our Personal Recommendations
André also likes the Chinese fringe tree, *C. retusus*: it's a smaller, multistemmed plant that blooms two or three weeks before the American species. It bears male and female flowers on the same plant and has a more formal appearance. The Chinese fringe tree flowers on the current season's new growth, so it should be pruned in late winter before growth begins.

Zelkova

Zelkova serrata

When, Where, and How to Plant

Plant a container-grown or balled-and-burlapped tree in early spring while the tree is still dormant. You can also set a zelkova out in fall, well before Indian summer, but in that case protect it with burlap for winter, because young trees are susceptible to frost damage. The zelkova grows best in full sun but tolerates bright, filtered light when young. It adapts to a broad pH range and prefers soil that is deeply dug and moist. See Soil Preparation in the Introduction, and planting instructions at the beginning of this chapter. Provide a planting hole three times the width of the rootball and twice as deep. Set the tree so the crown will be an inch or so above ground level. Staking might help the tree grow straighter, but remove it once the tree is established. Shape the earth around the crown into a wide saucer. Water slowly and deeply. Apply mulch 3 in. deep starting 3 in. from the trunk.

Growing Tips

The first year, unless there's a soaking rain, in spring and fall slowly and gently pour two to three bucketsful of water around the roots every two weeks; in summer every week or ten days. Maintain the mulch.

Care

Broadcast a complete, slow-release, long lasting, organic lawn fertilizer in late winter before growth begins from the drip line out to a distance equal to $1^1/2$ times the tree's height and water it in. Replenish the mulch. In fall prune out limbs that threaten to cross others or grow in the wrong direction. Zelkova is drought tolerant once established.

Companion Planting and Design

Zelkovas are excellent lawn and street trees, well suited to taking the place of lost elms.

Our Personal Recommendations

Two excellent varieties resistant to Dutch elm disease are: 'Green Vase', a rapidly-growing cultivar with bronze-red fall color; and 'Village Green', a very resistant Princeton Nursery selection that grows more rapidly than the species, and has foliage that turns a warm rusty red in fall.

A tall, stately, Asian shade tree that recalls our native elms in many ways and thrives under similar conditions, the zelkova is being planted to replace the American elm in streets, parks, and on large properties. It is low-branched, somewhat vase-shaped, has a straight trunk, and grows quickly—2 to 3 ft. a year. The leaf rather resembles the leaf of the American elm and turns yellow-orange-buff toward the end of fall when cold weather comes. Some years the foliage colors red or maroon-red. The bark resembles that of a cherry tree: it is smooth and reddish when the tree is young, and later develops an attractive corky character. Zelkova tolerates some urban pollution.

Other Names

Japanese Zelkova, Saw Leaf Zelkova

Bloom Period and Seasonal Color

April; blossoms are insignificant; fall foliage is yellow-orange-buff.

Mature Height × Spread

60 to 70 ft. × 50 to 55 ft.

Vines *for the Mid-Atlantic*

Vines create lush vertical accents, invaluable when you want a real visual impact taking up little space in the ground. The leafy greens soften, beautify, transform, hide problems. You can create an (almost) instant shade garden by training a leafy vine—trumpet vine, for example— to cover a pergola or a trellis. A climbing rose romances a balcony. Ivy greens ugly stumps. Vines climbing wires between the railing and the roof of a porch make a privacy screen. A vine can frame an attractive view and draw your eye to it. You can clothe a barren slope with a waterfall of vines by planting several at the top of a slope and training the runners to grow down. Fragrant vines belong where you can enjoy the scent. Sweet autumn clematis is especially fragrant—it grows like a tidal wave all summer then covers itself with a foam of small, sweetly fragrant white flowers in fall.

Vines grow rapidly—up or down, or sideways, according to how you train the leading stems, and the supports you provide. When choosing a vine consider how you are going to prune it when it gets to the top of its support. How a vine climbs dictates what it needs as support. Vines that climb by twining

Carolina Jessamine

stems require a narrow support such as a wooden post, a pipe, wires, or strings. Vines that climb by twining tendrils or leaf petioles—clematis, for example—require a structure of wires, or wire mesh. Vines that climb by aerial rootlets that secrete an adhesive glue, like English ivy, need only a rugged surface, such as a brick or stucco wall, or a rough, unpainted fence. Vines that eventually will be very heavy—climbing hydrangea, and wisteria—need the support of heavy timbers, or a dead tree, to hold them up.

Vines hold moisture: make sure the lumber that will support a vine is pressure-treated. Don't set a vine to growing up a wooden wall, because its moisture can cause rot. Allow 3-in. or more air space between foliage and a house wall—vines need air circulation all the way around. Avoid planting vines that climb by tendrils near trees, large shrubs, windows, or shutters.

Clematis

Planting and Care

You plant a container-grown vine the same way you plant a shrub: see Soil Preparation and Improvement in the Introduction, and planting instructions in the Shrubs chapter. The first year, slowly and gently pour two to three bucketsful of water around the roots every week or ten days unless there's a soaking rain. Maintain the mulch throughout the year. If the vine is sheltered from rain, hose it down now and then in summer—but don't hose it when it is coming into, or already in, bloom as it will spoil the blossoms. In late winter or early spring before growth begins, broadcast a slow-release organic fertilizer around the plant and scratch it in. Replenish the mulch if necessary. Repeat in the fall.

Pruning Vines

We can't give instructions for pruning vines that will apply to all. Wisteria requires special handling, as do some others. But to keep all vines healthy and good-looking, be sure to remove dead, extraneous, or weak wood. Monitor the growth of large, fast-growing vines and prune them severely every year. When your vine will need to be pruned depends on the plant itself. The rule of thumb is, prune flowering vines that bloom on wood that grows in the current year in late winter. A good time is any time just after the coldest part of the winter season, and before growth begins. Prune spring flowering vines that bloom on wood produced the year before right after the flowers fade. That gives the plant time to mature the wood that will flower the following year. Prune in the summer those vines that do not flower. The best time is right after the major thrust of seasonal growth is over. Generally, it is best to avoid pruning in fall. The wounds heal more slowly during that season. And pruning stimulates growth, which may come too late to harden off before the first frosts. It isn't necessary to paint, tar, or otherwise cover a pruning cut.

Other Options

If you want to try the effect of a vine without making it a permanent fixture in your landscape, plant one of the fast-growing annual climbers. The three best are the lovely purple-podded, scented hyacinth bean, *Lablab purpureus* (also known as *Dolichos lablab*); white-flowered moonvine, *Ipomea alba* (formerly *Calonyction aculeatum*); or morning glory, *Ipomea tricolor* 'Heavenly Blue'.

Carolina Jessamine
Gelsemium sempervirens

A fast-growing native woodland vine with dainty foliage, in late winter Carolina jessamine covers itself with masses of fragrant, funnel-shaped golden flowers, very welcome at that time of the year. The stems are reddish and wiry, and the plant climbs by twining around anything handy, including fencing, porches, or trellises. It is often used for screening mailboxes and downspouts. It makes a good ground cover for slopes if you pin the stems to the ground to prevent them from twining around each other. It's evergreen in the Deep South, but in our area severe cold damages the leaf tips. It is not reliably winter hardy in the uplands near West Virginia. And don't chew on it! It's considered toxic.

Bloom Period and Seasonal Color
Late winter to early spring; golden yellow.

Mature Length
10 to 20 ft.

When, Where, and How to Plant
The best times for planting Carolina jessamine are in fall before Indian summer, and in late winter and very early spring before the vine blooms. It blooms lavishly planted in full sun, but it also produces flowers in partial shade. It tolerates slightly acid and slightly alkaline soil. Provide a planting hole twice the size of the rootball with soil that is well drained, humusy, and moist. See Soil Preparation in the Introduction, and planting instructions in the Shrubs chapter. Provide a planting hole three times the width of the rootball and twice as deep. Set the vine so the crown will be an inch or two above ground level. With soft twine, tie the longer branches to whatever you want the vine to grow over. Shape the soil around the crown into a wide saucer. Water slowly and deeply. Apply mulch 3 in. deep starting 3 in. from the crown.

Growing Tips
The first year, unless there's a soaking rain, in spring and fall slowly and gently pour two to three bucketsful of water around the roots every two weeks; in summer every week or ten days.

Care
In late winter before growth begins, broadcast a slow-release organic fertilizer over the area and water it in. Replenish the mulch if necessary. Repeat in fall. When flowering is over for the season, prune out all the stems twining around each other, and any heading in unwanted directions.

Companion Planting and Design
If the vine is to climb, it will in time become woody, like a small tree, and is attractive underplanted with a living mulch of periwinkle, ajuga, or a slow-growing, small-leaved variegated ivy. Don't let the periwinkle crowd, or the ivy climb, the jessamine.

Our Personal Recommendation
The cultivar called 'Pride of Augusta' is a beautiful, double-flowered form.

When, Where, and How to Plant

Set out healthy, vigorously growing container plants in spring after the soil has begun to dry and warm. Clematis vines need to be in the sun, but the roots need to be cool. If the roots aren't shaded, mulch heavily. A site with protection from strong winds is best; avoid hot, dry, airless sites. Soils with a pH between 6.0 and 7.5 are recommended, but clematis tolerates somewhat acid soils. See Soil Preparation in the Introduction, and planting instructions in the Shrubs chapter. Provide a planting hole three times the width of the rootball and twice as deep. Set the vine so the crown is at ground level. Provide a structure of twine or wire for support, or to lead the vines to a fence, a tree, or other support. Make a saucer of earth around the plant. Apply and maintain a 3-in. mulch starting 3 in. from the stem.

Growing Tips

The first year, unless there's a soaking rain, in spring and fall pour a bucketful of water around the roots every two weeks; in summer every week or ten days. Check the vines often and prune to train them in the desired direction.

Care

Using a slow-release organic fertilizer, fertilize lightly in fall and again in spring. Prune clematis that bloom in spring on last year's wood lightly right after the vines finish blooming; prune clematis that bloom on new wood just as the leaf buds begin to swell, by cutting the flowering stems back to buds within 4 to 6 in. of the main branches.

Companion Planting and Design

The big-flowered hybrids are lovely paired with open-branched shrubs or roses.

Our Personal Recommendations

For spectacular flowers in summer, plant 'Duchess of Edinburgh', a double white; 'Henryi', a large single white; 'Jackmanii Superba', dark purple; 'Nelly Moser', mauve pink. For masses of small fragrant flowers in spring plant anemone clematis, rosy-red *C. montana* var. *rubens*, and white 'Alba'. For fall fragrance, plant (and control) sweet autumn clematis, *C. terniflora* (formerly *C. maximowicziana* and *C. paniculata*), a rampant vine that produces a froth of tiny, fragrant, whitish flowers.

The striking beauty of the flowers of the clematis hybrids has made this the most popular—and most hybridized—of all the climbers. Deciduous vines with attractive dark green foliage, clematis climbs by attaching leaf petioles (stalks) to the support provided. In time a clematis will sprawl over other vegetation, walls, trellises, posts, fences, and arbors. Most clematis hybrids bloom in spring or summer; some bloom twice and others bloom in fall. Clematis isn't a difficult plant, but pruning affects the way it blooms—timing is important. To help the plant do its best, before you buy a clematis, make sure you will be able to acquire the pruning information you need. The vines expand at a rate of 5 to 10 ft. in a single season.

Bloom Period and Seasonal Color
Spring, summer, or fall; white, shades of blue, mauve, pink, red, lavender, purple, yellow, and bi-colors.

Mature Length
8 to 20 ft.

Climbing Hydrangea

Hydrangea anomala var. *petiolaris*

This slow-growing, climbing vine with its lustrous, dark-green leaves is probably the most beautiful, massive, and formal climber we have. A mature specimen is magnificent in late spring and early summer when it opens clusters of small, fragrant florets backed by showy white bracts. Clinging by means of root-like attachments, the branches extend 2 to 3 ft. outward, which gives the vine a full, rich silhouette. Though not evergreen, the leaves are a fine green, and they stay that color until late fall. In time, the central stem thickens and becomes woody, and the cinnamon-colored bark exfoliates in an attractive way. It will grow up brick, stucco, and stone walls, chimneys, arbors, and trees. It becomes massive and must have strong support.

Bloom Period and Seasonal Color
Spring and early summer; white bracts.

Mature Length
60 to 80 ft.

When, Where, and How to Plant

Set out a container-grown plant in early spring, disturbing the rootball as little as possible. It will be slow to re-establish and show new growth. The climbing hydrangea flowers best in full sun, and does well in shade, but won't flower as bountifully. It tolerates salt air. Provide deeply dug, rich, moist, loamy soil. See Soil Preparation in the Introduction, and planting instructions in the Shrubs chapter. Provide a planting hole three times the width of the rootball and twice as deep. Set the vine so the crown is at ground level. With soft twine, tie the vine to the structure that will support it. Shape the soil around the crown into a wide saucer. Water slowly and deeply. Apply mulch 3 in. deep starting 3 in. from the crown.

Growing Tips

The first year, unless there's a soaking rain, in spring and fall slowly and gently pour two to three bucketsful of water around the roots every two weeks; in summer every week or ten days.

Care

Using a slow-release organic fertilizer for acid-loving plants, fertilize in fall and again in spring. Replenish the mulch. Prune after flowering; though it's slow growing, once a climbing hydrangea matures, it can become invasive and will need to be controlled.

Companion Planting and Design

Climbing hydrangea becomes a massive many-layered, strong, structural landscape element used to enhance a brick or stone wall, trees, arbors, and other free-standing structures.

Our Personal Recommendation

Plant the species.

Goldflame Honeysuckle
Lonicera × heckrottii

When, Where, and How to Plant
The best times for planting honeysuckle are in fall before Indian summer and in early spring while the plant is still dormant. Honeysuckle is most happy, and fragrant, growing in full sun, but with four to six hours of sun, or all-day filtered light, goldflame performs well. It does best when its roots are shaded and cool, and the vine is in the sun. Honeysuckles thrive in moist, loamy soils in the neutral range, pH 6.0 to 7.5, but tolerate other soils. See Soil Preparation in the Introduction, and planting instructions in the Shrubs chapter. Provide a planting hole three times the width of the rootball and twice as deep. Set the vine so the crown is at ground level. Prune back to the main two or three stems and tie these to the structure that will support the vine. Shape the soil around the crown into a wide saucer. Water slowly and deeply. Apply mulch 3 in. deep starting 2 to 3 in. from the crown.

Growing Tips
The first year, unless there's a soaking rain, in spring and fall slowly and gently pour two to three bucketsful of water around the roots every two weeks; in summer every week or ten days.

Care
Using a slow-release organic fertilizer, fertilize lightly in fall and again in spring. Before growth begins in late winter cut out weak, crowded, or dead growth, and trim long shoots back to a pair of buds near the main stem.

Companion Planting and Design
Goldflame is perfect in a cottage garden, and shows well climbing archways, fences, arbors, mailboxes, and lampposts. Combined with a climbing rose and clematis, it makes a beautiful flowering pillar.

Our Personal Recommendations
Goldflame is our favorite, but we also like yellow trumpet honeysuckle, *L. sempervirens* 'Sulphurea'; the flowers aren't fragrant but they and the foliage are beautiful. *L. × brownii* 'Dropmore Scarlet' is hardy in Zones 3 to 9.

The honeysuckles are fast-spreading, climbing, twining vines or tall shrubs that often bear sweetly scented flowers followed by bright, berry-like fruits attractive to many types of birds. The birds disperse the seeds, so some types of honeysuckle (such as Japanese honeysuckle and Japanese bush honeysuckle) turn up as weeds in your garden, making it a sweetly scented jungle—uncontrolled, they will take over the property. Goldflame, or coral honeysuckle, is a cross between two native honeysuckle species, which do not possess the same aggressive habits of their Asian counterparts, and is considered the most beautiful of the twining, climbing types. It bears carmine buds that open to yellow and then change to pink, and it stays in bloom from late spring to fall. The fruit is red and not borne as profusely as other species, nor is the vine as vigorous, which keeps it well behaved. Although scented, it does not possess the same intensity of fragrance as the invasive Japanese species so familiar along the roadsides.

Other Name
Coral Honeysuckle

Bloom Period and Seasonal Color
Late spring to fall; carmine buds opening to yellow and changing to pink.

Mature Length
10 to 20 ft.

Japanese Wisteria
Wisteria floribunda

Dreamy, romantic, seductive, irresistible, a wisteria in full bloom is everything a flowering vine can be! Picture long drooping clusters of lightly scented, pastel-colored, single or double blooms dripping from gnarly vines and sprays of dainty new leaves. That said, wisteria should be approached with caution. You can plant it to climb pillars and arbors, as "green roofing" for porches, and to soften the harsh lines of stone walls. But do not plant where it can reach windows, doors, shutters, or gutters, or near a live tree. It can invade and damage attics, and it destroys trees. As it matures, the weight is considerable, so you must provide a strong support. The cultivars tend to be less invasive than the species. And there are native species with smaller flower clusters. But if you're a romantic at heart . . .

Bloom Period and Seasonal Color
April, May, or June; in pink, white, or lilac.

Mature Length
30 to 50 ft.

When, Where, and How to Plant
Set out a container-grown plant in spring, summer, or fall. Plant it in full sun. Wisteria is said to do better in soil with a high pH, but it is adaptable to soil that is somewhat acid too. Provide soil that is deeply dug and well drained. See Soil Preparation in the Introduction, and planting instructions in the Shrubs chapter. Provide a planting hole three times the width of the rootball and twice as deep. Set the vine so the crown is at ground level. Prune the vine to one main stem, or more according to your plan for it. With soft twine, tie the stem, or stems, to a support. Shape the soil around the crown into a wide saucer. Water slowly and deeply. Apply mulch 2 in. deep starting at the crown.

Growing Tips
The first year, unless there's a soaking rain, in spring and fall slowly and gently pour two to three bucketsful of water around the roots every two weeks; in summer every week or ten days.

Care
Using a low-nitrogen slow-release fertilizer, fertilize in early spring. Prune the vine ruthlessly to restrict it to the branching structure you want. When it reaches the desired height, prune the main stem, or the several stems, back so the laterals will develop, and tie the laterals to supports leading them in the direction you want them to grow. Japanese wisteria blooms on old wood and last season's growth; to keep it blooming, cut back all big, old shoots, leaving only three to four buds on each shoot. This is called spur pruning.

Companion Planting and Design
Plant the area around the vine with a living mulch of drought-tolerant ground covers, like periwinkle, ajuga, or a slow-growing, small-leaved ivy. Hostas, liriope, mondo grass, and small, spring-flowering bulbs, are also good.

Our Personal Recommendations
We plant 'Longissima Alba', which bears fragrant white flowers in clusters 15 to 24 in. long; 'Issai', a blue-violet with 24- to 30-in. racemes; 'Macrobotrys', with violet to red-violet flowers in 18- to 36-in. racemes; and 'Rosea', a lovely pale rose with 18-in. racemes.

Trumpet Vine
Campsis radicans

When, Where, and How to Plant

Set out container-grown plants in early spring, or in early fall. Trumpet vine grows almost anywhere in almost any soil and almost any light, but it flowers best growing against a warm wall and in full sun. See Soil Preparation in the Introduction, and planting instructions in the Shrubs chapter. Provide a planting hole three times the width of the rootball and twice as deep. Set the vine so the crown is at ground level. With soft twine, tie or lead the vine to the structure that will support it. Shape the soil around the crown into a wide saucer. Water slowly and deeply. Apply mulch 3 in. deep starting 1 to 2 in. from the crown.

Growing Tips

The first year, unless there's a soaking rain, in spring and fall slowly and gently pour two to three bucketsful of water around the roots every two weeks; in summer every week or ten days.

Care

Do not allow the roots to dry out in summer. In late winter, replenish the mulch. The colorful trumpets are produced on new growth, so early every spring prune the secondary stems back to a few buds—really, do it!—to encourage new flowering spurs. After the first year or two, when the vine is filling its space, in late fall or in early spring, prune leafy young shoots to within a few buds of old wood. Remove any out-of-control stems at any time during the growing season.

Companion Planting and Design

Trumpet vine really doesn't need companion plants. It grows into a floriferous, beautiful (heavy!) green roof for a pergola or a terrace; give it solid supports and you can also use it to soften corners, hide drain pipes, and to screen ugly structures.

Our Personal Recommendations

We love *C. radicans* 'Flava', which has been popular for more than a century, for its rich yellow, or yellow-orange, blossoms; and 'Crimson Trumpet', whose blossoms are a velvety red. 'Madame Galen', a form of *C.* × *tagliabuana*, is a superior plant that thrives in our region and bears larger orange flowers.

The trumpet vines are woody, vigorous (read: rampant), indomitable, and fast-growing deciduous climbing vines that will quickly provide you with a dense, leafy "green roof" for arbors and pergolas. The delightful bonus is a long-season crop of fresh, showy, trumpet-shaped flowers that appeal mightily to hummingbirds. You can also use a trumpet vine to cover fence posts and to soften bleak corners and bare stone and masonry walls. The vines climb by means of aerial rootlets, and grow at a run to 30 to 40 ft. As trumpet vine matures, it becomes woody and very heavy, so provide a strong support. You must be prepared to prune this vine often: although it is native to the United States, do not plant it where it can escape and invade wild areas.

Bloom Period and Seasonal Color

From spring through early fall; shades of orange, yellow, red.

Mature Length

10 to 25 ft.

Water Plants *for the Mid-Atlantic*

A water garden is a small, beautiful world, a microcosm of tumbling water, undulating fronds, perfumed flowers, butterflies and dragonflies, and shimmering goldfish. From the moment the first warmth of spring brings goldfish lazing to the surface until the last of the water lilies shuts down in fall, something interesting is always going on. Each of the water garden's living components, plants and animals, plays a role in the health of the pond. The fish eat mosquitoes, other insects, and their larvae, and their waste provides nutrients that help sustain the pond plants. The aquatic plants are chosen for their ornamental value and they also contribute to the clarity and health of the water by taking up nutrients that can encourage undesirable algae.

This is the "magic formula" for keeping a pond in balance, developed by Charles Thomas, former President of Lilypons Water Gardens, Buckeystown, Maryland:

For every 1 to 2 square feet of pond surface, provide:

1 bunch (6 stems) submerged/oxygenating plants

1 black Japanese snail

2 inches of fish, for fish up to 6 inches long

$^1/_{10}$ of a small, or medium-size, water lily (that is, 1 lily per 10 to 20 square feet)

$^1/_3$ of a marginal or a small, floating-leaved plant (that is, 1 bog or marginal plant or 1 small-leaved floater for every 3 to 6 square feet)

Taro

The Aquatic Plants

Like land plants, the aquatics need sun to bloom well, respond to fertilizing, have active and dormant seasons, and are or are not winter hardy. The small leafy submerged, or oxygenating, plants, contribute oxygen. The large-leaved floating plants, the water lilies and lotus, float round pads and blossoms like many-petaled stars over the surface of the water and provide a cool refuge for the fish. The small floating-leaved plants spread delicate green patterns between the lily pads and the lotus and give a pond a natural look. The upright narrow-leaved (irises, for example) and broad-leaved (taro, for example) marginals, or bog plants, frame the water garden and create contrast with the horizontal planes of the floating aquatics.

Altogether, water garden plants should cover no more than $^1/_3$ to $^1/_2$ of a 20- by 40-foot pond, and 60 to 70 percent of a pond measuring 10 by 10 feet. A small water lily covers 90 percent of a tub 2 feet square. The aquatics are grown in pans or pails without drainage. They rest on shelves or platforms (bricks, stones, cement blocks) on the bottom or shelves of the water garden.

Additions of plants and fish to naturally wet places are now subject to laws enforced by environmental protection agencies. So plan to install your garden in an excavation, waterproofed by a man-made pre-formed container or a plastic liner. For site, don't choose the obvious: a wet place in a dip or hollow that will flood often and where the liner will be heaved by storms. For a garden under 14 feet long, consider a preformed fiberglass liner, which is easy to install. For larger, or different, ponds, you will need a flexible rubber sheet for a liner; the best last up to twenty-five years.

Water Lily 'St. Louis'

The sound and movement of a water garden is created by a pump that pulls the water through a filter, and returns it to the pond through a fountain or along a stream bed or waterfall, which aerates it. You can assist the filtering system in keeping the water clear by pumping the pond water through a bog garden and returning it to the pond through a creek planted in bog plants. If your pond or pool lacks clarity and is filled with algae, use a pond clarifier, such as Nature's Green-Releaf™. The larger the pond, the farther the water has to be pushed, the more powerful the pump needs to be, and the more costly to buy and to operate. Small floating fountains powered by the sun are the easiest to install and maintain. They rest on islands of wiring encased in watertight containers, and they turn themselves on and send up sprays or showers 8 to 24 inches high, depending on the power of the unit. The largest solar fountains can move 60 gallons an hour!

Anacharis
Egeria densa

Anacharis is one of the submerged plants—or "oxygenating plants"—whose role is to contribute oxygen and to use up nutrients that would encourage the algae that can make a water garden murky. A small, leafy perennial with fern-like fronds, it extends from a container set at the bottom of the pond right up to the top of the water and bears tiny white flowers at the tips of thin stems. Each tiny, three-petaled, white flower is half the size of a shirt button and has a yellow dot in the middle. Moving gently with the rhythm of wind and water, anacharis adds grace and charm to the pond, and fish spawn among the fronds.

Other Name
Elodea

Bloom Period and Seasonal Color
Summer; tiny white blossoms.

Mature Spread
Indefinite

When, Where, and How to Plant
For every 1 to 2 sq. ft. of pond surface, you should plant one bunch (six stems) of submerged/oxygenating plants; they can be placed in the pond as soon as it has been filled. Water garden plants are grown in containers called pans, which have no drainage holes. Anacharis is sold in bunches of six stems secured by a rubber band. Each stem with foliage is about 6 in. high, and from $1/4$ to 1 in. across. Like the other oxygenating plants, anacharis is set out in pans 4 in. deep, one bunch of submerged plants for every 6 sq. in. of container surface. Fill the pans with clean sand to within 1 in. of the rim. Rinse the submerged plants. Cut the rubber bands and press each bunch 2 in. into the sand. Cover the sand with $1/2$ to $3/4$ in. of rinsed gravel and fill the containers with water. Distribute the containers of submerged plants evenly over the bottom of the pond with 1 or 2 ft. of water overhead. Choose locations where the containers will receive at least six hours of sun and avoid places that will be shaded later by floating-leaved plants such as water lilies. If the strands start to grow long and skinny, they need more sun.

Growing Tips
To multiply your holdings, during the growing season take 5- or 6-in. cuttings of submerged plants 8 in. or longer, press the ends into containers filled with wet sand, and place them in the pond.

Care
Do not add fertilizer.

Companion Planting and Design
In a water basin or barrel garden one pan of submerged plants will be enough. A large pond will need more, and will be more interesting if you use a variety of oxygenating plants. Four others recommended for the Mid-Atlantic are: Washington grass, *Cabomba caroliniana*; dwarf sagittaria, *Sagittaria subulata*; wild celery, *Vallisneria americana*; and several species of *Myriophyllum*. Do not plant water hyacinth or water lettuce, which are beautiful but very invasive plants, and illegal here and everywhere they survive winter cold.

Our Personal Recommendation
Plant the species.

Black Princess Taro

Colocasia affinis var. *jenningsii*

When, Where, and How to Plant

Planting time is when the pond water reaches 69 degrees Fahrenheit. In Zones 6 and 7, we set out potted plants, or start tubers indoors, four to six weeks before planting time. Each tuber is at least 7 to 9 in. in diameter and needs a $3^1/2$ quart pan that is 5 in. across. The best soil for colocasia is heavy, slightly acid, and contains a little humus. Plant black princess taro tubers 1 in. deep and cover the soil with rinsed $^1/2$ to $^3/4$ in. of gravel. Before placing the plants in the water garden, fill the containers with water. Set them in part or full shade with up to 5 in. of water over the crowns.

Growing Tip

The colocasias do not need fertilizing.

Care

Throughout the growing season remove dead foliage. After the first few freezes some pond owners cut all the verticals down to clear the water at once of decaying vegetation. It's a healthy practice. But in Zone 8 colocasia might grow on if you lift it in the fall, and store it in a sunny greenhouse.

Companion Planting and Design

Most broad-leaved marginals don't take up much more surface space than the narrow-leaved upright plants, allowing room for plants with contrasting foliage colors and textures.

Our Personal Recommendation

For smaller water gardens we like *C. esculenta* 'Hilo Beauty', a slightly smaller taro with green leaves mottled with ivory; it is planted with 2 in. of water over the crown.

The colocasias are huge, frost-tender perennials that produce 2-ft. long, heavily veined leaves shaped like an arrowhead or an elephant's ear. The way the leaf is held at a sharp angle at the top of its stalk, and its size and coloring, are tropical and exotic. In summer small, pale yellow flowers like calla lilies bloom among the leaves on short stems. Black princess taro is a bold, shade-loving variety that has dark green leaves overlaid with black. Taro, or dasheen, is another superb species, C. esculenta, whose velvety green leaves often display brilliant white veins; the leaves of a new variety, 'Black Magic' elephant's-ear, are wine-purple and reach to 5 ft. In Hawaii and the South Sea Islands taro root is pounded and cooked to make a starchy staple called poi.

Other Names
Taro, Dasheen

Bloom Period and Seasonal Color
Foliage is the ornamental feature.

Mature Height × Spread
2 to $3^1/2$ ft. × 2 to 3 ft.

Lotus
Nelumbo spp. and hybrids

The lotus is a breathtakingly big and beautiful, 2- to 6-ft.-tall relative of the water lily. Lotus needs full sun to flower, but the foliage and its growth habit are so interesting we plant it even where there isn't enough sun to bring it into bloom. The lotus starts the season by floating leaves that look like 12-in. lily pads; then it puts up magnificent, wavy-edged aerial leaves, and the floating leaves come together. Then the perfumed lotus flowers rise. As big as a man's head, for three days they open mornings and close at tea time. The seed pods that follow look like the spout of a watering can, and are handsome in dried arrangements.

Other Name
Sacred Lotus

Bloom Period and Seasonal Color
Late July to August; hues and combinations of white, pink, red, yellow, and cream.

Mature Spread
Covers 1 1/2 to 12 sq. ft. or more.

When, Where, and How to Plant
Lotus and other ornamentals, should cover no more than 1/3 to 1/2 of a 20- by 40-ft. pond; 60 percent to 70 percent of one 10 by 10 ft. A lotus is sold bare root during the few weeks in spring when the rootstock is in tuber form. Plant it at once; when the rootstock puts out runners, the tuber atrophies and planting is impossible. In late summer, the runners form tubers that can be divided the following spring and planted. For a tuber 6 to 18 in. long, provide a pan 16 to 24 in. in diameter and 9 to 10 in. deep. A miniature requires a pan about half this size. Fill the pan with heavy garden soil free of peat, manure, vermiculite, or commercial potting mixes. A lotus tolerates soils ranging between pH 6.0 and 8.0, but optimum is soil and pond water between pH 6.5 and 7.5. Bury the tuber 2 in. deep with the top 1/2 in. above the soil. Push a 10-14-8 water lily fertilizer tablet into the soil, and cover with 1/2 to 3/4 in. of rinsed gravel. Soak the container and place it in the pond.

Growing Tips
A lotus needs six to eight hours of direct sun. Place it on the pond shelf, or on a platform raised to where there will be 2 to 3 in. of water over the growing tip.

Care
Remove yellowing foliage and spent blossoms and fertilize with a water lily pellet twice a month from spring up to a month before the average first frost date for your area. For winter, move the lotus container to a depth beyond the reach of ice. If the pond freezes to the bottom, winter a lotus indoors in a cold, frost-free place and keep the soil from drying out.

Companion Planting and Design
One large lotus takes up as much space as a large water lily, and that is all most home ponds can host.

Our Personal Recommendations
For a small water garden, use the miniature tulip lotus and 'Momo Botan', a double rose dwarf with a golden center; it spreads when growing in a pond, but in tubs and pans stays at 12 in. For a large pond, our favorite is the large, magnificent 'Mrs. Perry D. Slocum'.

Parrot's-Feather
Myriophyllum aquaticum

When, Where, and How to Plant

Parrot's-feather, and other small floating-leaved plants, must be included when you parcel out the surface area of the water garden. Altogether they should cover only $^1/_3$ to $^1/_2$ of a 20- by 40-ft. pond; 60 to 70 percent of one 10 by 10 ft. Parrot's-feather is sold for mid-spring planting, usually in bunches of six cuttings secured by a rubber band. A small water garden likely has space only for one small-leaved floater. Plant it in a 4-in.-deep pan filled with clean sand to within 1 in. of the rim. Rinse the stems, cut the rubber bands, and press the bunch 2 in. into the sand. Cover the sand with rinsed $^1/_2$ to $^3/_4$ in. of gravel and fill the container with water. Set it in the pond a few feet from the lilies on the pond shelf, in full or partial sun, with 3 to 12 in. of water over the crown. Fish love to swim through *Myriophyllum* and to lay eggs there. They're also known to eat it, so provide a protective screen if your water garden includes fish.

Growing Tip

Parrot's-feather has an appetite for naturally occurring pond nutrients, so there is no need to fertilize the plant.

Care

Keep the growth of this rapidly spreading plant pruned back. Just pinch off a stem at any point and pull out and discard the growth beyond. Now and then the delicate, hair-like leaves that cover the stems need to be gently hosed clean. Plant parrot's-feather and other small-leaved floaters with caution: they expand rapidly and easily overwhelm a neglected water garden.

Companion Planting and Design

A nice group for a basin or barrel is the small tropical water lily 'Dauben', with variegated sweet flag for vertical accent, and frills of parrot's-feather cascading over the edge. Among other attractive small-leaved floaters are the tiny water clover, *Marsilea mutica*. For flowers, plant water poppies, *Hydrocleys nymphoides*; floating-heart, *Nymphoides peltata*; and the white or yellow snowflakes, *Nymphoides cristata*, and *N. geminata*.

Our Personal Recommendation

Plant the species.

Parrot's-feather is one of several fast-growing small-leaved floaters planted along with the big water lilies and lotus for visual interest, and to create contrast. It has dainty, floating leaves and tiny flowers, and is grown primarily for its trailing stems that are lovely trained to cascade over a waterfall or the edge of a tub garden. The way it grows is interesting: as the stems rise from their underwater container toward the surface they develop sparse, hair-like leaves. Then, as the stems reach the air, the leaves begin to grow in dense whorls, and trailing silvery blue or lime-green "feathers" stretch out over the water. The foliage opens and closes daily.

Other Name
Diamond Milfoil

Bloom Period and Seasonal Color
Summer; insignificant yellow-green blooms.

Mature Spread
6 in. trailing tips

Water Lily
Nymphaea spp. and hybrids

Water lilies are the pond's stars, its most colorful flowers, and the most important and best loved of the large floating-leaved plants. They come in almost every color including blue and their large, round pads provide the fish with privacy and relief from hot summer sun. There are two types of water lilies, hardy and tropical. The hardy water lilies are perennial here, though they need two to three years to bloom profusely. The tropicals are sure to bloom the first year but must winter indoors. Hardy lilies open only during the day, while the tropical lilies include both day- and night-flowering varieties. The hardy water lilies and the day-blooming tropical lilies open shortly after breakfast and close toward late afternoon. The heavily scented night-blooming tropical lilies open as the stars come out and stay open until late morning.

Bloom Period and Seasonal Color
June to September; all colors and shades.

Mature Spread
Covers 3 to 12 sq. ft.

When, Where, and How to Plant
Water garden plants should cover no more than $1/3$ to $1/2$ of a 20- by 40-ft. pond, and 60 to 70 percent of one 10 by 10 ft. A small water lily covers 90 percent of a tub 2 ft. sq.. Planting time is spring when the water has reached at least 55 degrees Fahrenheit. Lilies usually are sold bare root, ready for planting in the pans, pails, and tubs sold for aquatics. Plant water lilies in heavy garden soil free of peat, manure, vermiculite, or commercial potting mixes. Aquatics tolerate soils ranging between pH 6.0 and 8.0, but optimum is soil and pond water between pH 6.5 and 7.5. Set the water lilies so the growing tips are just above the soil. Push a 10-14-8 fertilizer tablet for aquatics into the soil of each container. Cover the soil with $1/2$ to $3/4$ in. rinsed gravel. Soak the containers and place them in the pond in full sun as soon as the pond is filled; chlorine in tap water is safe for plants. Arrange the containers several inches apart on the pond shelf and on platforms that raise the plants to where they will be covered by the depth of water recommended.

Growing Tips
Containers of newly planted water lilies can be initially placed closer to the water's surface, and then gradually lowered to their recommended depth as they grow, so that their leaves are always afloat.

Care
Remove spent blooms and yellowing foliage. Fertilize the lilies monthly during spring and summer. When the water temperature is over 75 degrees Fahrenheit, increase that to twice monthly. For winter, move containers of tropical lilies to a cold, frost-free storage place and keep the soil from drying out.

Companion Planting and Design
If space allows, grow both day- and night-blooming water lilies for nearly twenty-four hours of flowers, with the added bonus of evening fragrance.

Our Personal Recommendations
Two easy lilies for beginners are the hardy 'Pink Beauty', a shell pink that blooms freely its first year, and 'Dauben', a day-blooming, soft blue-violet tropical. Other favorites are tropical night-blooming 'Wood's White Knight' and day-blooming pink 'General Pershing', 'Pink Pearl', and 'Madame Ganna Walska'.

Yellow Flag

Iris pseudacorus

When, Where, and How to Plant

Water iris transplants easily and grows vigorously in or out of water, as long as there is plenty of moisture around the roots. Growing in moist garden soil, it will bloom consistently. Started in early autumn, water irises bloom the following year; planted in early spring they're shy and, except for the Japanese irises, won't likely flower until the next spring. Plant irises, and other marginals, in sets of three of one type to a container: when you combine various species of marginal plants, one usually overwhelms the others. Irises thrive in full sun at water's edge, or planted in pans with up to 10 in. of water over the rhizomes. Set the rhizomes at a slant, with the bottom 2 in. deep and the growing tip just clearing soil that is heavy, humusy, and slightly acid. Plant three to a 9-in. container and if the pan is to be underwater, cover the soil with rinsed 1/2 to 3/4 in. of gravel. Place hybrids and double-flowered varieties in full sun with only 4 in. of water over the crowns.

Growing Tip

Cut back flowers that have gone by.

Care

In October press a fertilizer pellet into the soil. Before frost, clear away damaged or rotting foliage and move the container to the bottom of the pond. Every three to five years divide yellow flag in mid- to late summer or early fall.

Companion Planting and Design

The most appealing marginal plantings combine narrow-leaved irises with broad-leaved verticals such as *Colocasia*. Cattails and ornamental grasses are a lovely addition to the mix, as are water cannas and dainty umbrella plant, *Cyperus alternifolius*, and arrow-shaped water arum, *Peltandra virginica*. To extend the iris season, add the small Louisiana irises, the regal Siberians, the exquisite Japanese iris, and our native blue flag.

Our Personal Recommendation

The beautiful double-flowered yellow flag variety called 'Flora Plena' is about 2 ft. tall.

These irises, like other upright, narrow-leaved bog plants, move with the wind, adding motion to the design of the water garden. They are winter hardy here, and the most colorful of the narrow-leaved marginal plants. The first iris to flower, the yellow flag, blooms in mid-spring. The vivid yellow blossoms have brown or violet veins and the beautiful sword-like foliage remains handsome all season. This plant is larger than the garden iris and other water-loving irises, such as our native blue flag and the Louisiana irises. It forms attractive clumps of 1- to 2-in.-wide leaves that are bright green. Hybrids range in flower color from white to dark yellow and they are a little smaller. There are double-flowered forms. A stately European species, yellow flag has naturalized beside ponds and quiet streams all over temperate North America.

Other Name

Water Iris

Bloom Period and Seasonal Color

June and July; yellow, and colorful hybrids.

Mature Height × Spread

3 to 4 ft. × 3 to 4 ft.

More About Fertilizers and Plant Nutrition

Our all-purpose recipe for fertilizing, followed by an explanation of why and when we use which product:

Flower and Shrub Garden

For each 100 square feet of new garden space add:

	Sun Garden	Shade Garden
Plant-Tone®	5-10 lbs.	0
Holly-Tone®	0	4-7 lbs.
Rock Phosphate	5-10 lbs.	0
Super Phosphate	0	3-5 lbs.
Greensand	5-10 lbs.	5-10 lbs.
Gypsum (for clay soils)	5-10 lbs.	5-10 lbs.
Osmocote® (8 month)	2 lbs.	2 lbs.

Till all these amendments plus organic matter into the soil, rake smooth, and your bed is ready to be planted.

Know What's in Your Fertilizer

In our experience, plant health depends on more than just the three essential nutrients, nitrogen, phosphorous, and potash provided in an all-purpose chemical fertilizer. The Viette family has been growing plants for over eighty years using natural, organic, blended fertilizers made up of at least ten to fourteen ingredients. These are earth-friendly products that include the three essential nutrients, and in addition, have beneficial effects on the environment and the soil.

Adding natural organics to the soil has a positive effect on soil microorganisms, the micro-fauna and micro-flora of the soil, and beneficial earthworms. The soil structure and aeration is improved. Natural organics don't dissolve quickly and do not easily run off into rivers and lakes. Their breakdown is dependent on three factors—soil moisture, temperature, and microbial activity. The nutrient microbial release is a slow, gradual process that makes nutrients available exactly when the plants need them and over an extended period of time. The result is overall plant health, and plants with luxuriant and robust foliage and superb flowers.

In the past, we mixed our own blends of organic fertilizers in the nursery garage. Today the marketplace offers packaged fertilizers that are blends of natural organics. Bulb-Tone®, Holly-Tone®, Plant-Tone®, and Rose-Tone® are the most complete on the market at this writing. Here's what they contain:

Bulb-Tone® 4-10-6

Ingredients: bone meal, crab meal, dehydrated manure, animal tankage, cocoa meal, dried blood, sunflower meal, greensand, rock phosphate, ammonium sulfate, single super phosphate

Application Amounts: New Bed—10 lbs. per 100 sq. ft.; Established Bed—5 lbs. per 100 sq. ft.

Holly-Tone® 4-6-4

Ingredients: dehydrated manure, animal tankage, crab meal, cocoa meal, cottonseed meal, dried blood, sunflower meal, kelp, greensand, rock phosphate, sulfate of potash, ammonium sulfate, single super phosphate (1 pound = 2²/3 cups)

Application Amounts: New Bed—10 lbs. per 100 sq. ft., 100 lbs. per 1000 sq. ft.; Established Bed— 5 lbs. per 100 sq. ft., 50 lbs. per 1000 sq. ft.

Plant-Tone® 5-3-3

Ingredients: dehydrated manure, animal tankage, crab meal, cocoa meal, bone meal, dried blood, sunflower meal, kelp, greensand, rock phosphate, sulfate of potash

Application Amounts: New Bed—10 lbs. per 100 sq. ft., 100 lbs. per 1000 sq. ft.; Established Bed—5 lbs. per 100 sq. ft., 50 lbs. per 1000 sq. ft.

Rose-Tone® 6-6-4

Ingredients: dehydrated manure, animal tankage, crab meal, cocoa meal, dried blood, cottonseed meal, sunflower meal, kelp, greensand, rock phosphate, sulfate of potash, ammonium sulfate, single super phosphate

Application Amounts: New Plant—4 cups per plant; Established Plant—2 cups per plant

Greensand

Greensand is a mined mineral-rich marine deposit, also known as glauconite. These ancient sea deposits are an all-natural source of potash. It is an iron potassium silicate in which the potassium is the important element in the potash. Thirty-two or more micro ingredients are contained in greensand. There is 0.01% soluble potash in what is a total of 6% total potash K_2O. Greensand is non-burning and helps to loosen heavy clay soil. It also binds sandy soil for a better structure. It increases the water holding capacity of soils and it considered an excellent soil conditioner. Greensand promotes plant vigor, disease resistance, and good color in fruit. Greensand contains nitrogen, phosphorus, potassium, calcium, magnesium, sulfur, chlorine, cobalt, copper, iron, manganese, molybdenum, sodium, and zinc. Greensand also contains silica, iron oxides, magnesia, and lime. Dr. J.C.F. Tedrew, Rutgers University Soil Specialist, mentions that glauconite may have a considerable capacity for gradual release of certain plant food elements, particularly the so-called trace elements (micronutrients). Once greensand is impregnated with micronutrients it will later release them at a very slow rate.

Gypsum

Gypsum is a hydrated calcium sulfate. The actual amounts of calcium and sulfur can vary, but 22% calcium and 17% sulfur occur in some formulations. Gypsum replaces sodium in alkaline soils with calcium and improves the drainage and aeration. Gypsum is an effective ammonia-conserving agent when applied to manured soils or other rapidly decomposing organic matter. The escaping ammonia is changed to ammonium sulfate, which is stable. Gypsum is applied at the rate of 10 lbs. per 100 sq. ft. in heavy clay soil and 5 lbs. per 100 sq. ft. in moderately clay soil. Gypsum improves the structure of the heavier soils rather than the sandy soils.

Osmocote®, Scotts and Scotts-Sierra All-Purpose Fertilizers

All-purpose chemical fertilizers contain balanced proportions of the three essential plant nutrients—nitrogen (N), phosphorus (P), and potassium (K). The numbers on the packaging, 5-10-5 and 10-10-10 for example, refer to the proportions of each element present. When you apply a granular all-purpose chemical fertilizer to the soil, the nutrients last a short time—five or six weeks. To keep the plants nourished using only chemical fertilizers, you must repeat the applications. Because they dissolve easily in water, these elements can contribute to the pollution of nearby streams and rivers, and eventually harm bigger bodies of water like the Chesapeake Bay. Somewhat similar are the soluble chemical fertilizers you mix with water and apply with a hose-end sprayer or a watering can. We use these fertilizers when a plant shows symptoms of nutrient deficiency, as a quick pick-up, or as a starter fertilizer. But for a general liquid fertilization there are organic counterparts of the chemical fertilizers: for example, fish emulsion and liquid seaweed, manure teas made by steeping dehydrated manure, and the compost teas that are becoming popular today.

Scientists have packaged the chemical fertilizers so they act like tiny little time pills, releasing their nutrients over a specified period. Examples are Osmocote® controlled release fertilizers, which come in 3-4 month, 8-9 month, and 12-14 month formulations. A similar product is Scotts controlled-release Agriform™ fertilizer tablets, which can last up to two years.

More About Pruning Trees and Shrubs

Pruning is part of regular garden maintenance, not just a solution to things gone wrong. The thing to keep in mind when you prune is that it stimulates growth, which dictates what you should prune, and when.

What to Prune

To keep trees and shrubs looking their best and growing well, regularly remove weak, crowded stems; branches that will eventually cross each other; suckers, which are shoots growing at the base of a tree or shrub; and water sprouts, which are vigorous upright shoots that develop along a branch, usually where it has been pruned. Pruning is sometimes needed to open up the canopy of a tree or a shrub to let in air and sun. Pruning also causes denser growth, and can be used to encourage height and to control size. For the most appealing results, when you prune, follow the lines of the plant's natural growth habit.

Thinning Before

When to Prune

Our plant pages suggest a best time for pruning each plant. The rule is that trees and shrubs that bloom on this year's growth—hydrangeas for example, rose-of-Sharon, chaste tree, butterfly bush—are pruned early in the year, before growth begins. The growth that pruning encourages provides more places for flowers. Plants that bloom on wood from the previous year—ornamental fruit trees and most spring flowering trees and shrubs such as azaleas—are pruned as soon as possible after they bloom. Shade and evergreen trees typically are pruned every three or four years.

Flowering and evergreen shrubs may need maintenance pruning every season. Young vigorous plants will need more pruning than mature plants. Winter and early spring pruning stimulates plants to produce more unwanted suckers than late spring or summer pruning. So if it's a plant's nature to sucker heavily, as with lilacs and crabapples, summer is a better time to prune. On the other hand, pruning in late summer or early fall can cause growth that won't have time to harden off before winter.

Thinning After

Pruning Large Trees

When a large limb is involved, pruning is best undertaken in spring just before growth begins, or after maximum leaf expansion in June. Pruned then, the tree will likely roll calluses over the external wound, and, internally, it will protect itself by walling off the damaged tissue. Painting a wound has fallen out of favor but the *Cornell Cooperative Extension Illustrated Guide to Pruning* says "certain materials such as orange shellac may provide a temporary barrier to certain pathogens until a tree's natural barrier zones form." The alcohol in shellac is a disinfectant.

Evergreen trees are usually allowed to develop naturally, but deciduous trees may need pruning to grow up to be all they can be. After planting a balled-and-burlapped, or a container-grown, deciduous tree, remove any weak and injured branches, and those that will eventually rub across each other. For bare-root trees, some experts recommend thinning out a quarter of the branches so the canopy will be in better balance with the reduced root system. The year after planting, pruning to shape a deciduous tree begins, and that continues over the next three to five years. The first step is to identify the strongest terminal leader, unless the tree is naturally multi-stemmed: the leader will become the trunk. Then prune all but the main limbs—the "scaffold branches"—that will define the structure of the tree. Choose as scaffolding those branches whose crotch is at a wide angle to the trunk. The height of the lowest scaffold branches depends on the activities planned under the tree. You can leave them in place for the first few years to protect the bark from sunscald and to provide more leaves to nourish the root system. The scaffold branches at each level should be a fairly equal distance from each other: spaced evenly all around the

trunk, they make for better balance. For each next level of scaffold branches, choose limbs developing between or offset from, not directly over, the branches of the level below. In the following years, watch the growth of the tree and trim back any side branches growing taller than the leader.

Limb Removal

Pruning and Rejuvenating Shrubs

At planting time prune out weak and injured branches, and any crossing each other. To keep the shrub airy, then and later, you may need to remove a few branches from the base and to head back others. "Heading back" means cutting an unwanted branchlet back to where there is an outward facing branchlet or bud on the main stem. Shearing shrubs, unless they are growing as a hedge, is discouraged because it stimulates dense growth at the tips of the branches and distorts the natural shape of the plant.

You can use pruning to rejuvenate older shrubs grown leggy or out of scale with their place in the garden. There are three ways to rejuvenate deciduous shrubs, all initiated before growth begins in early spring. The most drastic way is to cut the whole plant back to within 6 to 10 inches of the ground: by July it will be a mass of upright canes. Remove half or more of these, and head the others back to outward facing buds at half or less of the height you want the shrub to be. A slightly less drastic way is to cut half, or more, of the older branches, including any that cross, and all suckers, back to the ground: at midsummer, remove all new canes and head back branching that develops on the canes you kept. The least drastic method is to remove a third to a quarter of the older branches over three, or even four years, each year removing unwanted suckers and heading back crowded branching. You can rejuvenate broadleaved evergreen shrubs that have grown out of scale—rhododendrons, mountain laurels, boxwoods for example—by cutting them back to within 2 to 4 feet of the ground in late winter or early spring before growth begins. Leave branch ends at various heights so re-growth will appear natural. Re-growth will take two to four years.

Rejuvenation

Gardening with Wildlife, Welcome and Otherwise

Birds:

Birds adopt gardens that provide food, water, and shelter. To attract birds, plant trees and shrubs that have berries and small fruits. Let stand the seedheads of ornamental grasses and various flowers for fall and early winter. Provide a water basin/bird bath near a shrub, preferably a dense evergreen, where birds can check for predators before flying in. Plant, or keep, tall trees for perching and nesting: pines and hemlocks provide nesting materials as well. Finally, if you have space, allow milkweed and other wild plants useful to birds to develop in a bramble away from house traffic.

To deter birds: Our feathered friends are beautiful, lovable, inspiring, and useful in that they eat insects, some good and some bad. They also eat your berries and your flower and grass seeds. A mesh cover is almost the only way to protect berries. Remember when planting for birds that they drop seeds everywhere. Bears are eager for birdseed: if there are bears in your area, stocking a bird feeder may not be a good idea.

Hummingbirds:

Hummingbirds rely on sight, not scent, to locate their food. They are attracted by tubular, brightly colored flowers, and prefer single-petaled varieties to doubles. Like butterflies, hummingbirds require a continuous supply of nectar.

Bears, bees, and wasps love nectar, too: think twice before putting out sugared water.

Butterflies:

Ideal for a butterfly garden is the sun-warmed side of a south-facing fence, a wall, or a windbreak. Because this lovely thing is cold-blooded, it can fly only when warmed by the sun and in air that is 55 to 60 degrees Fahrenheit. On sunless days and at night butterflies roost in deeply fissured bark, or a butterfly hotel: a wooden box with perches and an entrance big enough for a butterfly with folded wings to slide through, a slot about 1/4 inch wide by about $3^1/_2$ inches high. For basking, butterflies also need tall verticals that hold warmth—statuary, stones, standing logs. And a puddling place—a patch of damp sand or drying mud where male butterflies can gather and take up moisture and dissolved salts, which we believe are helpful for mating. The food for adult butterflies is the nectar in flowers. They are drawn to brightly colored flowers—purple, yellow, orange, and red. The caterpillars of most species need a specific host plant: *Peterson Field Guide to Eastern Butterflies* can tell you which. Learn to recognize the caterpillars of butterflies, and even many moths, so that you won't be tempted to eliminate them from the garden when you see them eating your plants.

Deer:

To attract Bambi and company, plant fruit trees. They relish apples and pears. They also adore hostas, daylilies, rhododendrons, and other large, succulent leaves, and roses, raspberries, impatiens—anything that doesn't have itsy bitsy leaves or flowers. Provide a salt lick and water in a secluded spot, and for winter put out bales of hay.

To deter these oversize white-tailed rats: Every commercial deterrent we have tried so far has succeeded only until the deer decided it wasn't a sign of danger. Wrapping evergreens with burlap in late fall and winter works: for summer, use chicken wire—at a distance you won't see it. Or plant in small, fully enclosed spaces. To protect a large property, try high tensile fencing 9 to 10 feet high, or double fences 4 to 5 feet apart. If you can't fence, you may be able to discourage them this way: at places where they enter your garden, hang tubes of crushed garlic, or predator urine, chunks of Irish Spring soap, or human hair damp with strongly scented lotions such as Avon's Skin So Soft. Hang them at the height of the deer's nose, a different scent at each entry point. Replace these scents with new different ones every four to six weeks of the gardening season.

Rabbits, Woodchucks, and Other Rodents:

To attract these sweet critters, develop a wilderness bramble with fallen logs far enough from the beaten path to let them feel safe. Provide a source of water. Time and nature will do the rest.

Chicken wire fencing that starts 24 inches underground keeps out most rodents: for woodchucks, make it 4 to 6 feet tall as well and leave it loose and floppy, not stiff enough to climb. Keeping raccoons out too requires enclosing your garden overhead as well.

Good Plants for Birds

Annuals, Perennials, and Grasses:

Ammophila breviligulata, American Beach Grass

Echinacea purpurea 'Magnus', Purple Coneflower

Echinops ritro, Globe Thistle

Helianthus annuus, Sunflower

Panicum virgatum, Switch Grass

Rudbeckia fulgida var. *sullivantii* 'Goldsturm', Black-Eyed Susan

Trees, Shrubs, and Vines:

Abies concolor, White Fir

Acer saccharum, Sugar Maple

Amelanchier arborea, Serviceberry

Arctostaphylos uva-ursi, Bearberry

Buxus spp., Boxwood

Cedrus libani ssp. *atlantica* 'Glauca', Blue Atlas Cedar

Cercis canadensis, Eastern Redbud

Chamaecyparis obtusa 'Nana Gracilis', Dwarf Hinoki Falsecypress

Chionanthus virginicus, White Fringe Tree

Cornus florida, Flowering Dogwood

Cotinus spp., Smoke Tree

Cotoneaster spp., Cotoneaster

Crataegus viridus, Hawthorn

× *Cupressocyparis leylandii*, Leyland Cypress

Euonymus alatus 'Compactus', Dwarf Burning Bush

Fagus grandifolia, American Beech

Juniperus spp., Juniper

Liquidambar styraciflua, Sweet Gum

Liriodendron tulipifera, Tuliptree

Lonicera × *heckrottii*, Goldflame Honeysuckle

Malus spp. and hybrids, Flowering Crabapple

Nyssa sylvatica, Sour Gum

Oxydendrum arboreum, Sourwood

Parthenocissus quinquefolia, Virginia Creeper

Picea pungens 'Glauca', Colorado Blue Spruce

Pinus strobus, Eastern White Pine

Prunus spp., Flowering Cherry

Pseudotsuga menziesii, Douglas Fir

Pyracantha coccinea, Firethorn

Pyrus calleryana, Callery Pear
Quercus spp., Oak
Rosa spp. and hybrids, Rose
Sciadopitys verticillata, Umbrella Pine
Spiraea spp., Spirea

Stewartia pseudocamellia, Japanese Stewartia
Taxus × media, Yew
Thuja occidentalis, Arborvitae
Tsuga canadensis, Canadian Hemlock

Good Plants for Hummingbirds

Annuals, Perennials, and Bulbs

Ageratum houstonianum, Ageratum
Ajuga spp., Bugleweed
Alcea ficifolia, Hollyhock
Allium spp., Flowering Onion
Antirrhinum majus, Snapdragon
Aquilegia spp., Columbine
Asclepias tuberosa, Butterfly Weed
Begonia grandis, Hardy Begonia
Chelone spp., Turtlehead
Crocosmia spp., Crocosmia
Dahlia spp. and hybrids, Dahlia
Delphinium spp., Larkspur
Dianthus spp., Pinks
Digitalis spp., Foxglove
Heuchera spp. and hybrids, Coral Bells
Hibiscus moscheutos, Marsh Rose Mallow
Hosta spp. and hybrids, Hosta
Impatiens walleriana, Impatiens
Kniphofia spp., Red Hot Poker

Lavandula angustifolia, Lavender
Lilium spp., Lily
Lobelia cardinalis, Cardinal Flower
Lobularia maritima, Sweet Alyssum
Mentha spicata, Mint
Monarda didyma, Bee Balm
Nepeta faassenii, Catmint
Pelargonium spp. and hybrids, Geranium
Penstemon digitalis, Beardtongue
Petunia × hybrida, Petunia
Phlox paniculata, Phlox
Rosmarinus officinalis, Rosemary
Rudbeckia spp., Black-Eyed Susan
Salvia spp., Salvia and Sage
Scabiosa spp., Pincushion Flower
Tropaeolum majus, Nasturtium
Verbena spp., Verbena
Zinnia elegans, Zinnia

Trees, Shrubs, and Vines:

Buddleja davidii, Butterfly Bush
Campsis radicans, Trumpet Vine
Caryopteris × clandonensis, Blue Spirea
Chaenomeles speciosa, Flowering Quince
Daphne × burkwoodii 'Carol Mackie', Daphne
Hibiscus syriacus, Rose-of-Sharon

Lonicera × heckrottii, Goldflame Honeysuckle
Sophora japonica, Japanese Pagoda Tree
Stewartia pseudocamellia, Japanese Stewartia
Syringa vulgaris, Lilac
Wisteria floribunda, Japanese Wisteria

Good Plants for Butterflies

(Including plants for butterfly larvae, or caterpillars)

Achillea millefolium, Yarrow

Agastache spp., Anise Hyssop

Alcea spp., Hollyhock

Allium spp., Ornamental Onion

Alyssum saxatile, Alyssum

Aquilegia spp., Columbine

Aristolochia spp., Dutchman's Pipe

Arabis spp., Rockcress

Armeria maritima, Sea Thrift

Asclepias tuberosa, Butterfly Weed

Asimina triloba, Paw Paw

Aster spp., Aster

Astilbe spp., Astilbe

Boltonia asteroides, Boltonia

Buddleja davidii, Butterfly Bush

Caryopteris × clandonensis, Blue Spirea

Centaurea spp., Bachelor's Buttons

Centranthus ruber, Jupiter's Beard

Ceratostigma plumbaginoides, Leadwort

Chelone spp., Turtlehead

Coreopsis spp., Tickseed

Crocosmia spp., Crocosmia

Delphinium spp., Larkspur

Dendranthema spp., Chrysanthemum, Daisy

Dianthus spp., Pinks

Echinacea purpurea, Purple Coneflower

Echinops ritro, Globe Thistle

Eryngium spp., Sea Holly

Eupatorium spp., Perennial Ageratum,
    Joe Pye Weed, White Snake Root

Filipendula rubra, Meadowsweet

Foeniculum vulgare, Fennel

Gaillardia spp., Indian Blanket

Helenium autumnale, Sneezeweed

Helianthus spp., Sunflower

Heliopsis helianthoides, Heliopsis

Hemerocallis spp., Daylily

Iberis spp., Candytuft

Iris pseudacorus, Yellow Flag

Kniphofia uvaria, Red Hot Poker

Lavandula angustifolia, Lavender

Liatris spicata, Blazing-Star

Lilium spp., Lily

Lindera benzoin, Spicebush

Lobelia spp., Cardinal Flower, Blue Lobelia

Monarda didyma, Bee Balm

Nepeta faassenii, Catmint

Origanum spp., Oregano

Passiflora spp., Passion Vine

Petroselinum crispum, Parsley

Petunia × hybrida, Petunia

Phlox spp., Phlox

Physostegia virginiana, Obedient Plant

Primula spp., Primrose

Rosmarinus officinalis, Rosemary

Rudbeckia spp., Black-Eyed Susan

Ruta graveolens, Rue

Salvia spp., Salvia, Sage

Scabiosa spp., Pincushion Flower

Sedum spp., Stonecrop

Skimmia japonica, Skimmia

Solidago spp., Goldenrod

Spiraea japonica, Spirea

Stokesia laevis, Stokes' Aster

Vernonia noveboracensis, Ironweed

Verbena spp., Verbena

Veronica spp., Speedwell

Zinnia elegans, Zinnia

Mid-Atlantic Public Gardens

Delaware

Hagley Museum's E. I. Du Pont
    Restored Garden
Del. 141
Wilmington, DE 19803
(302) 658-2400

Mount Cuba Center for the Study of
    Piedmont Flora
Barley Hill Road
Greenville, DE 19807
(302) 239-4244

Nemours Gardens
Rockland Road
Wilmington, DE 19803
(302) 651-6912

District of Columbia

Bishop's Garden
Washington National Cathedral
Massachusetts & Wisconsin Avenues, NW
Washington, D.C. 20016
(202) 537-2937

Dumbarton Oaks
1703 32nd Street
Washington, D.C. 20007
(202) 339-6401

Hillwood Museum & Gardens
4155 Linnean Avenue, NW
Washington, D.C. 20008

United States Botanic Garden and Conservatory
1st Street & Maryland Avenue, SW
Washington, D.C. 20024
(202) 225-8333

United States National Arboretum
3501 New York Avenue, NE
Washington, D.C. 20002
(202) 245-2726

Maryland

Brookside Gardens
1500 Glenallan Avenue
Wheaton, MD 20920
(301) 949-8230

Clyburn Wild Flower Preserve &
    Garden Center
4915 Greenspring Avenue
Baltimore, MD 21209

Ladew Topiary Gardens
3535 Jarretsville Pike
Monkton, MD 21111
(410) 557-9570

McCrillis Gardens
6910 Greentree Road
Bethesda, MD 20817
(301) 365-5728

William Pica Garden
186 Prince George Street
Annapolis, MD 21401
(410) 263-5553

Virginia

Ashcroft Hall
4305 Sulgrave Road
Richmond, VA 23221
(804) 353-4241

Colonial Williamsburg
Colonial Parkway
Williamsburg, VA 23187
(757) 229-1000

Gunston Hall
Va. 242
Lorton, VA 22079
(703) 550-9220

Kenmore
Fredericksburg, VA

Lewis Ginter Botanical Garden
1800 Lakeside Avenue
Richmond, VA 23228-4700
(804) 262-9887

Maymont
1700 Hampton Street
Richmond, VA 23220
(804) 358-7166

Monticello
Thomas Jefferson Foundation
P.O. Va. 53
Charlottesville, VA 22902
(804) 984-9822

Montpelier Gardens
James Madison's Home
Orange County
Montpelier Station, VA

Mount Vernon Estate & Gardens
South End of George Washington Memorial
    Parkway
Mount Vernon, VA 22121
(703) 780-2000

Norfolk Botanical Garden
Airport Road (off Azalea Garden Road)
Norfolk, VA 23518
(804) 441-5830

Oatlands Plantation
200850 Oatlands Plantation Lane (US 15)
Leesburg, VA 20175
(703) 777-3174

River Farm
American Horticultural Society
7931 East Boulevard Drive
Alexandria, VA 22308
(703) 768-5700

Virginia House
4301 Sulgrave Road
Richmond, VA 23221
(804) 353-4251

Woodrow Wilson Birthplace
Staunton, VA 24401

Sources

Mid-Atlantic Nurseries with a Good Selection of Plants

Behnke Nurseries
11300 Baltimore Avenue
Beltsville, MD 20705
Tel: (301) 937-1100

Homestead Gardens
Route 214
743 West Central Avenue
Davidsonville, MD 21035
Tel: (800) 300-5631

Merrifield Garden Center
12100 Lee Highway
Fairfax, VA 22030
Tel: (703) 968-9600

Merrifield Garden Center
8132 Lee Highway
Merrifield, VA 22116
Tel: (703) 560-6222

Mail Order Catalogs for Perennials, Daylilies, Peonies, Irises, Hostas, Grasses

André Viette Farm & Nursery
994 Long Meadow Road
P. O. Box 1109
Fishersville, VA 22939
Tel: (800) 575-5538
www.inthegardenradio.com

Bluestone Perennials
7211 Middle Ridge Road
Madison, OH 44057
Tel: (800) 852-5243

Borbeleta Gardens
15974 Canby Avenue
Faribault, MN 55021
Tel: (507) 334-2807

Caprice Farm Nursery
10944 Mill Greek Road SE
Aumsville, OR 97325
Tel: (503) 749-1397

Fragrant Path, The
P.O. Box 328
Fort Calhoun, NE 68023

Kuk's Forest Nursery
10174 Barr Road
Brecksville, OH 44141-3302
Tel: (216) 546-2675

Kurt Bluemel Inc.
22740 Greene Lane
Baldwin, MD 21013
Tel: (800) 248-7584

Mellinger's Inc.
2310 W South Range Road
North Lima, OH 44452-9731
Tel: (800) 321-7444

Milaeger's Gardens
4838 Douglas Avenue
Racine, WI 53402-2498
Tel: (800) 669-1229

Plant Delights Nursery Inc.
9241 Sauls Road
Raleigh, NC 27603
Tel: (919) 772-4794

Song Sparrow Perennial Farm
13101 East Rye Road
Alalon, WI 53505
Tel: (800) 553-3715

Prairie Nursery
(Wild Flowers)
P.O. Box 306
Westfield, WI 53964
Tel: (800) 476-9453

White Flower Farm
P.O. Box 50
Litchfield, CT 06759-0050
Tel: (800) 503-9624

Mail Order Seed Catalogues for Flowers, Annuals, Perennials, Wildflowers, Vegetables, Herbs, Rare Seeds, and Heirloom Seeds

Carolina Seeds
P.O. Box 2658
Boone, NC 28607
Tel: (800) 825-5477

Park Seed
1 Parkton Avenue
Greenwood, SC 29647
Tel: (800) 845-3369

Ferry-Morse Seeds
(Seeds, Plants, and Bulbs)
P. O. Box 1620
Fulton, KY 42041-0488

Pinetree Garden Seeds
P.O. Box 300
New Gloucester, ME 04260
Tel: (207) 926-3400

Gurney's Seed & Nursery Co
110 Capital Street
Yankton, SD 57079
Tel: (605) 665-1930

R. H. Shumway Seedsman
P.O. Box 1
Graniteville, SC 29829
Tel: (803) 663-9771

Moon Mountain Wildflowers
P.O. Box 34
Morro Bay, CA 93443
Tel: (805) 772-2473

Seeds of Change
(Heirloom Seeds)
P.O. Box 15700
Santa Fe, NM 87506
Tel: (888) 762-7333

Nichols Garden Nursery
1190 N. Pacific Highway
Albany, OR 97321
Tel: (541) 928-9280

Seeds of Distinction
P.O. Box 86
Toronto, Canada M9C 4V2
Tel: (416) 255-3060

Select Seeds
180 Stickney Hill Road
Union, CT 06076
Tel: (860) 684-9310

Shepherd's Garden Seeds
30 Irene Street
Torrington, CT 06790
Tel: (800) 482-3638

Stokes Seeds Inc.
P.O. Box 548
Buffalo, NY 14240
Tel: (800) 263-7233

Thompson & Morgan Inc.
P.O. Box 1308
Jackson, NJ 08527
Tel: (800) 274-7333

W. Atlee Burpee & Co.
300 Park Avenue
Warminster, PA 18991
Tel: (800) 888-1447

Wildseed Farms
P.O. Box 3000
Fredericksburg, TX 78624
Tel: (800) 848-0078

Mail Order Catalogs for Tender Perennials, Annuals, Tropicals, House Plants, Bromeliads, Bougainvilleas, Cactus, Orchids, Pineapples, Begonias, Gesneriads, and African Violets

Banana Tree, Inc.
715 Northampton Street
Easton, PA 18042
Tel: (610) 253-9589

Davidson-Wilson
    Greenhouse, Inc.
RR2, Box 168
Crawfordsville, IN 47933
Tel: (317) 364-0556

Glasshouse Works
Church Street
Stewart, OH 45778
Tel: (614) 662-2142

Going Bananas
24401 SW 197 Avenue
Homestead, FL 33031
Tel: (305) 247-0397

Good Scents
RR2, P O Box 168
Crawfordsville, IN 47933
Tel: (765) 364-0556

Kartuz Greenhouse
P.O. Box 790
Vista, CA 92085
Tel: (760) 941-3613

Lauray of Salisbury
493 Undermountain Road, RT 41
Salisbury, CT 06068
Tel: (860) 435-2263

Logee's Greenhouse, Ltd.
141 North Street
Danielson, CT 06239
Tel: (860) 774-8038

Lyndon Lyon Greenhouse, Inc.
P.O. Box 249
Dolgeville, NY 13329
Tel: (315) 429-8291

Stokes Tropicals
P.O. Box 9868
New Iberia, LA 70562
Tel: (800) 624-9706

Sunshine State Tropicals
6329 Alaska Avenue
New Port Richey, FL 34653
Tel: (813) 841-9618

Mail Order Catalogs for Roses

Antique Rose Emporium, The
9300 Lueckemeyer Road
Brenham, TX 77833
Tel: (800) 441-0002

Chamblee's Rose Nursery
10926 US Highway 69 North
Tyler, TX 75706-8742
Tel: (800) 256-7673

David Austin Roses Limited
15059 Highway 64 West
Tyler, TX 75704
Tel: (800) 328-8893

Edmund's Roses
6235 SW Kahle Road
Wilsonville, OR 97070-9727
Tel: (888) 481-7673

Hardy Roses for the North
Box 2048
Grand Forks, BC Canada VOH 1HO
Tel: 604 442-8442

Heirloom Old Garden Roses
24062 NE Riverside Drive
St. Paul, OR 97137
Tel: (503) 538-1576

High Country Roses
P.O. Box 148
Jensen, UT 84035-0148
Tel: (800) 552-2082

Historical Roses
1657 W Jackson Street
Painesville, OH 44077
Tel: (216) 357-7270

Jackson & Perkins Co.
1 Rose Lane
Medford, OR 97501-0702
Tel: (800) 292-4769

Lowe's Own-Root Roses
6 Sheffield Road
Nashua, NH 03062
Tel: (603) 888-2214

Meilland Star Roses
P.O. Box 249
Cutler, CA 93615
Tel: (800) 457-1859

Nor'East Miniature Roses, Inc.
P.O. Box 307
Rowley, MA 01969-0607
Tel: (800) 426-6485

Mail Order Catalogs for Trees, Shrubs, and Evergreens

Arborvillage Farm Nursery
15604 County Road CC
Holt, MO 64048
Tel: (516) 643-9347

Arrowhead Nursery
5030 Watia Road
Bryson City, NC 28713
Tel: (440) 466-2881

Camellia Forest Nursery
125 Carolina Forest Road
Chapel Hill, NC 27516
Tel: (919) 968-0504

Collector's Nursery
16804 NE 102nd Avenue
Battle Ground, WA 98604
Tel: (706) 356-8947

Fairweather Gardens
P.O. Box 330
Greenwich, NJ 08323
Tel: (800) 548-0111

Forest Farm
990 Tetherow Road
Williams, OR 97544
Tel: (503) 543-7474

Foxborough Nursery Inc.
3611 Miller Road
Street, MD 21154
Tel: (360) 574-3832

Girard Nurseries
P.O. Box 428
Geneva, OH 44041
Tel: (919) 967-5529

Greer Gardens
1280 Goodpasture Island Road
Eugene, OR 97401
Tel: (609) 451-6261

Porterhowse Farms
41370 SE Thomas Road
Sandy, OR 97055
Tel: (409) 826-6363

Roslyn Nursery
211 Burrs Lane
Dix Hills, NY 11746
Tel: (541) 846-7269

Wayside Gardens
1 Garden Lane
Hodges, SC 29695
Tel: (800) 845-1124

Mail Order Catalogs for Water Plants, Ponds, and Pools

Gilberg Farms
2172 Highway O
Robertsville, MO 63072
Tel: (636) 451-2530

Lilypons Water Gardens
6800 Lilypons Road
Buckeystown, MD 21717
Tel: (800) 999-5459

Springdale Water Gardens
P.O. Box 546
Greenville, VA   24440-0546
Tel: (800) 420-5459

Glossary

Acid soil: soil whose pH is less than 7.0. The pH in which the widest range of flowers thrive is somewhat acid, in the pH 5.5 to 6.5 range. Except for areas where limestone is prevalent, most garden soil in America is in this range. This pH is also suited to most plants described as acid loving.

Alkaline soil: soil whose pH is greater than 7.0. It lacks acidity, often because it has limestone in it. Mid-Atlantic soils vary greatly, ranging from acid to neutral to basic (alkaline).

All-purpose fertilizer: is available in three forms: powdered, liquid, or granular. It contains balanced proportions of the three important nutrients—nitrogen (N), phosphorus (P), and potassium (K). It is suitable for most plants.

Annual: a plant that lives its entire life in one season. It germinates, produces flowers, sets seed, and dies the same year.

Balled and burlapped: a tree or shrub grown in the field and dug, whose soil- and rootball is wrapped with protective burlap and tied with twine.

Bare root: describes plants without any soil around their roots, often packaged by mail order suppliers. The rule of thumb is to soak the roots six to twelve hours before planting.

Bedding plant: usually annuals that are massed (planted in large groups) in a bed for maximum show.

Beneficial insect: insects and their larvae that prey on pest organisms and their eggs. Some that are well known include the ladybug and praying mantis.

Botanical name: plant names given in Latin accurately identifying the genus, species, subspecies, variety, and form. Here's an example: *Picea abies* forma *pendula* is the 1) genus, 2) species, and 3) form (*pendula*, meaning "pendulous" or "weeping") that is the botanical name for weeping Norway spruce. *Picea abies* 'Nidiformis' is the a) genus, 2) species, and 3) variety. When the varietal name is between single quotation marks, it's what is called a "cultivar"—a cultivated variety, or a variety that has been cultivated and given a name of its own.

Bract: a modified leaf structure resembling a petal that appears close behind the flower or head of flowers. In some flowers, that of flowering dogwoods for example, the bract may be more colorful than the flowers themselves.

Bud union: a thickened area above the crown on the main stem of a woody plant. This is the point at which a desirable plant has been grafted, or budded, onto the rootstock of a plant that is strong but less ornamental.

Canopy: the overhead branching area of a tree, including its foliage.

Cold hardiness: the ability of a plant to survive the winter cold in a particular area or zone.

Common name: there is no such thing as an accurate "common name" for a plant. Names commonly used for plants are rarely common the world over, or even in a single country, or state. Because they can vary from region to region, they are not as much help in locating plants as the scientific botanical names. Botanical names find their way into common gardener language. Examples are: impatiens, begonia, petunia, salvia, zinnia, aster, astilbe, phlox, iris. In time, you will find yourself remembering many of the botanical names of the plants that interest you most. Many are British "antiques" which continue to be used for their charm—for example, love-in-a-mist, fleabane, and lady's mantle.

Compost: organic matter, such as leaves, weeds, grass clippings, and seaweed, that has undergone progressive decomposition until it is reduced to a soft, fluffy texture. Soil that has been amended with compost holds air and water better and also has improved drainage.

Corm: an energy-storing structure, similar to a bulb, but actually a specialized stem, found at the base of a plant, such as crocosmia and crocus.

Crown: the base of a plant where the roots meet the stems.

Cultivar: the word stands for "cultivated variety." Cultivars are varieties named by gardeners and gardening professionals. They are developed, or selected, variations of species and hybrids.

Deadhead: the process of removing faded flower heads from plants in order to improve their appearance, stop unwanted seed production, and, most often, to encourage more flowering.

Deciduous: refers to trees and shrubs that loose their leaves in fall, a sign that the plant is going into dormancy for the period of weather ahead.

Division: the splitting apart of perennial plants in order to create several smaller plants. Division is a way to control the size of a plant, multiply your holdings, and renovate crowded plants losing vitality.

Dormancy: the period, usually winter, when plants temporarily cease active growth and rest. Heat and drought can throw plants into summer dormancy. Certain plants, for example oriental poppies, spring-blooming wildflowers, and certain bulbs, have their natural dormancy period in summer.

Established: the point at which a new planting begins to show new growth and is well rooted in the soil, indicating the plants have recovered from transplant shock.

Evergreen: plants that do not lose all their foliage annually with the onset of winter.

Exfoliating: peeling away in thin layers, as with bark.

Fertility/fertile: refers to the soil's content of the nutrients needed for sturdy plant growth. Nutrient availability is affected by pH levels.

Floret: a tiny flower, usually one of many forming a cluster, comprising a single flower head.

Foliar: refers to the practice of making applications to just the plant's foliage of dissolved fertilizer and some insecticides. Leaf tissue absorbs liquid quickly.

Germinate/germination: refers to the sprouting of a seed, the plant's first stage of development.

Graft/union: point on the stem of a woody plant where a stem (scion) from another plant (usually one that is more ornamental) has been inserted into understock so that they will join together.

Habit: the growth pattern and mature form a plant assumes when it is allowed to grow naturally, for example, upright, spreading, rounded, mounded, columnar, twiggy.

Hardscape: the permanent, structural, non-plant part of a landscape, such as walls, arbors, and walkways.

Herbaceous: plants with soft stems, such as annuals and perennials, as opposed to the woody stem tissue of trees and shrubs.

Humus: almost completely decomposed organic materials such as leaves, plant matter, and manures.

Hybrid: a plant that is the product of deliberate or natural cross-pollination between two or more plants of the same species or genus.

Leader: the main stem of a tree.

Loam: a mix of sand and clay. When humus is added, loam is the best soil for gardening.

Low water demand: describes plants that tolerate dry soil for varying periods of time.

Microclimate: pockets that are warmer or cooler than the listed climatic zone. Hilly spots, valleys, nearness to reflective surfaces or windbreaks, proximity to large bodies of water can all contribute to altering the surrounding temperature.

Mulch: a layer of material (natural or man-made) used to cover soil to protect it from water or wind erosion, and to help maintain the soil temperature and moisture. Mulches also discourage weeds.

Naturalize: a plant that adapts and spreads in a landscape habitat. Some plants we think of as "native" are imports that have "naturalized," for example, *Phlox drummondii*, the annual phlox, self-sows and has naturalized in sand in the Outer Banks of North Carolina.

Nectar: the sweet fluid produced by glands on flowers that attract pollinators such as bees, butterflies, and hummingbirds.

Organic fertilizer: a fertilizer that is derived from anything that was living, such as bone meal, fish emulsion, manure, plants.

Organic material/organic matter: any substance that is derived from plants.

Peat moss: acid organic matter from peat sedges (United States) or sphagnum mosses (Canada) often mixed into soil to raise its organic content and sometimes as a mild acidifier.

Perennial: a flowering plant that lives for more than one season; the foliage often dies back with frost, but their roots survive the winter and generate new growth in the spring.

Perennialize: sometimes confused with "naturalize." The two words are not synonymous. Tulips many perennialize, that is come back for four years or more, but they don't become wild plants. "Naturalize" applies to a garden plant that becomes a wildflower of a region that is not necessarily its native habitat. It could be a native plant or an exotic plant.

pH: pH stands for potential of hydrogen. A measurement of the relative acidity (low pH) or alkalinity (high pH) of soil or water. Based on a scale of 1 to 14, pH 7.0 being neutral.

Pinch: to remove tender stems and/or leaves by pressing them between thumb and forefinger. The purpose is usually to deadhead, or to encourage branching and compactness. Hand shearing achieves the same purpose on plants whose blooms are too small to pinch out one at a time, pinks for example.

Planting season: refers to the best time to set out certain plants. The most vigorous growth occurs in spring. Early spring is the preferred planting time in cold zones, particularly for woody plants and for species that react poorly to transplanting. Early fall, after summer's heat has gone by and before cold comes, is an excellent time for planting in the Mid-Atlantic, provided the climate allows the roots two months or so to tie into the soil before cold shuts the plants down. Traditional planting seasons are spring and fall: availability of plants in containers/pots has added a new and valuable season to plant, the summer.

Pollen: the yellow, powdery grains in the center of a flower which are the plant's male sex cells. Pollen is transferred by wind and insects, and to a lesser extent by animals, to the female plants, whence fertilization occurs.

Raceme: describes a flower stalk where the blossoms are an arrangement of single-stalked florets along a tall stem; similar to a spike.

Rhizome: an energy-storing structure, actually a specialized stem, similar to a bulb, sometimes planted horizontally near the soil surface (iris), or beneath the soil surface (trillium). The roots emerge from the bottom and leaves and flowers grow from the upper portion of the rhizome.

Rootbound/potbound: the condition of a plant that has been confined in a container too long. Without space for expansion, the roots wrap around the rootball or mat at the bottom of the container.

Root division/rooted divisions: sections of the crown of a plant, usually of a perennial, that has been divided. This is often the source of containerized perennial plants. A root division will perform exactly like the parent plant.

Rooted cuttings: cuttings taken from foliage growth perennials, usually, or from woody plants, that have been handled so as to grow roots. Rooted cuttings will perform exactly like the parent plant.

Seedling: plantlets started from seed. Flats and containers of annuals are usually seedlings. Seedlings of perennials and especially of hybrids, may perform exactly as the parent did, but can't be counted on to do so. Which is why perennial growers of quality plants sell root divisions or rooted cuttings rather than seedlings.

Self-sow: some plants mature seeds, sow them freely, and the offspring appear as volunteers the following season.

Semi-evergreen: tending to be evergreen in a mild climate but deciduous in a colder climate.

Shearing: the pruning technique where plant stems and branches are cut uniformly with long-bladed pruning shears or hedge trimmers. Shearing is also a fast and easy way to deadhead plants with many tiny blooms, pinks for example.

Slow-release fertilizer: fertilizer that does not dissolve in water and therefore releases its nutrients gradually. It is often granular and can be either organic or synthetic.

Soil amendment: anything added to change the composition of the soil. Most often the product is compost, which results in the end product humus.

Starter solution: all-purpose fertilizer dissolved in water, used to wet roots of plants before placing them in their planting holes.

Succulent growth: the production of (often unwanted) soft, fleshy leaves or stems. Can be a result of over-fertilization.

Suckers: shoots developing at the base of a tree or shrub which can be useful, or not, depending on the plant. Removing lilac suckers keeps the plant strong and attractive.

Summer dormancy: in excessive heat some plants, including roses, slow or stop productivity. Fertilizing or pruning a partially dormant plant will stimulate it into growth.

Tuber: similar to a bulb, a tuber is a specialized stem, branch, or root structure used for food storage. It generates roots on the lower surface while the upper portion puts up stems, leaves, and flowers. Dahlia and caladium are examples.

Variegated: foliage that is streaked, edged, or blotched with various colors—often green leaves with yellow, cream, or white markings.

Variety: the only accurate names for plants are the scientific botanical names and these are given in Latin—genus, species, subspecies, variety, and form. In botany, "variety" is reserved for a variant of a species that occurs in the wild or natural habitat. The "cultivated variety," or "cultivar," is a variety that has been introduced into the nursery trade and named.

Water sprouts: vigorous upright shoots that develop along a branch, usually where it has been pruned.

Wings: the tissue that forms edges along the twigs of some woody plants such as winged euonymus; or the flat, dried extension on some seeds, such as maple, that catch the wind and enable the seeds to fly away to land and grow in another place.

Winter mulch: a heaped-up cover of pine boughs, hay, or similar material placed over perennials, roses, and other plants to protect them during winter.

Photography Credits

Thomas Eltzroth: pages 27, 30, 31, 32, 33, 34, 36, 37, 38, 39, 40, 41, 44, 47, 52, 58, 59, 60, 61, 62, 63, 64, 65, 67, 68, 69, 70, 71, 72, 73, 74, 75, 76, 78, 80, 82, 84, 88, 89, 93, 94, 95, 96, 97, 99, 100, 101, 102, 103, 104, 105, 108, 109, 111, 112, 120, 126, 129, 132, 133, 138, 140, 141, 144, 148, 149, 150, 151, 152, 153, 154, 155, 158, 160, 163, 164, 170, 173, 175, 177, 181, 182, 199, 200, 204, 207, 210, 213, 216, 220, 221, 232, 233, 235, 238

Liz Ball and Rick Ray: pages 24, 26, 45, 51, 54, 56, 57, 77, 79, 85, 86, 92, 98, 122, 124, 127, 139, 165, 174, 178, 179, 180, 186, 188, 190, 194, 196, 197, 198, 201, 203, 206, 208, 209, 211, 212, 214, 217, 223, 228, 230, 234, 236, 237

Jerry Pavia: pages 23, 28, 29, 35, 53, 66, 81, 83, 87, 90, 110, 113, 115, 121, 123, 130, 137, 142, 143, 145, 156, 157, 159, 162, 168, 169, 171, 183, 184, 185, 187, 189, 191, 192, 202, 205, 218, 229, 231, 239

André Viette: pages 10, 12, 15, 16, 18, 22, 25, 46, 50, 55, 106, 107, 116, 117, 119, 125, 128, 131, 134, 135, 136, 146, 147, 167, 193, 222, 224, 225, 226, 227, back cover photos

Lorenzo Gunn: pages 176, 219

Pamela Harper: pages 161, 215

Charles Mann: pages 43, 91

William Adams: page 114

Tim Boland and Laura Coit: page 166

Karen Bussolini: page 42

Ralph Snodsmith: page 172

Trademarked Product Credits

The following products, either trademarked or registered, appear in this book.

Bitrex® (Macfarlan Smith Ltd.)

Bulb-Tone®, Holly-Tone®, Plant-Tone®, and Rose-Tone® (Espoma Company)

First Choice® Sluggo Snail and Slug Bait (Western Farm Service, Inc.)

Nature's Green-ReLeaf™ (Green Relief Biotech, Inc.)

Osmocote® and Agriform™ (Scotts-Sierra Horticultural Products Company)

PermaTill® and VoleBloc™ (Carolina Stalite Company)

Princeton Sentry® Ginkgo (Princeton Nurseries)

Roundup® (Monsanto Company)

Soil Moist™ (JRM Chemical, Inc.)

Stained Glassworks™ Coleus (The Flower Fields)

Supertunia™ Petunias (Proven Winners)

Surfinia® and Million Bells® Petunias (Jackson & Perkins Wholesale, Inc.)

Wave® and Tidal Wave® Petunias; Super Elfin® Impatiens (Pan American Seed Company)

Bibliography

Aden, Paul. *The Hosta Book: 2nd Edition.* Timber Press, 1992.

American Horticultural Society A-Z Encyclopedia of Garden Plants: First American Edition, The. Christopher Brickell and Judith D. Zuk, eds. DK Publishing, 1997.

André Viette Gardening Guide. Viette Staff.

Annuals, A Gardener's Guide (Plants and Gardens: Brooklyn Botanic Garden Record). Brooklyn Botanic Garden, 1993.

Annuals: 1001 Gardening Questions Answered. Editors of Garden Way Publishing, Storey Books, 1989.

Armitage, Allan M. *Herbaceous Perennial Plants: 2nd Edition.* Stipes Publishing Co., 1997.

Armitage, Allan M., Asha Kays, Chris Johnson. *Armitage's Manuel of Annuals, Biennials, and Half-Hardy Perennials.* Timber Press, 2001.

A-Z Horticulture: Annuals for the Connoisseur.

Bales, Susan Fruitig. *The Burpee American Gardening Series: Annuals, Reissue Edition.* Hungry Minds, Inc., 1993.

Ball, Liz. *Pennsylvania Gardener's Guide.* Cool Springs Press, 2002.

Barash, Cathy Wilkinson. *Edible Flowers: From Garden to Palate.* Fulcrum Publishing, 1993.

Bar-Zvi, David, Kathy Sammis, Chani Yammer, Albert Squillance. *American Garden Guides: Tropical Gardening, Fairchild Tropical Garden, Miami, Florida.* Pantheon Books, 1996.

Bath, Trevor and Joy Jones. *The Gardener's Guide to Growing Hardy Geraniums.* Timber Press, 1994.

Bloom, Adrian. *Conifers for Your Garden.* John Markham & Associates, 1987.

Boland, Tim, Laura Coit, Marty Hair. *Michigan Gardener's Guide: Revised Edition.* Cool Springs Press, 2001.

Bost, Toby. *North Carolina Gardener's Guide: Revised Edition.* Cool Springs Press, 2001.

Botanica: The Illustrated A-Z of Over 10,000 Garden Plants. Welcome Rain, 1999.

Bradley, Fern and Barbara Ellis. *Rodale's All-New Encyclopedia of Organic Gardening.* Rodale Press, 1992.

Bremness, Lesley. *Dorling Kindersley Handbooks: Herbs.* DK Publishing, Inc., 2000.

Bridwell, Ferrell M. *Landscape Plants, Their Identification, Culture and Use: 2nd Edition.* Delmar Learning, 2002.

Brown, Deni. *The Herb Society of America Encyclopedia of Herbs and Their Uses.* DK Publishing, 2001.

Brown, George E. *The Pruning of Trees, Shrubs and Conifers.* Timber Press, 1995.

Bruce, James and Lloyd Snyder. *Field Guide to Ferns and Other Pteridophytes of Georgia.* University of Georgia Press, 1986.

Bush-Brown, Louise, James Bush-Brown, Howard S. Erwin, and Brooklyn Botanic Garden. *America's Garden Book: Revised Edition.* MacMillan, 1996.

Chase, A. R., Margery L. Daughtrey, Gary W. Simone. *Diseases of Annuals and Perennials: A Ball Guide, Identification and Control.* Ball Publishing, 2001.

Clarkson, Rosetta E. *Herbs: Their Culture and Uses.* MacMillan Publishing Co., 1949.

Clausen, Ruth Rogers and Nicolas Ekstrom. *Perennials for American Gardens.* Random House, 1989.

Cooke, Ian. *The Plant Finders Guide to Tender Perennials.* David & Charles Publishers, 2001.

Coombes, Allen J. *Dictionary of Plant Names.* Timber Press, 1985.

Courtright, Gordon. *Tropicals.* Timber Press, 1995.

Darke, Rick. *Ornamental Grasses for Your Garden.* Little Brown and Co., 1994.

Daughtrey, Margery L. and Morey Semel. "Herbaceous Perennials: Diseases and Insect Pests (Information Bulletin No. 207)." Cornell University, December 1987.

Davis, Brian. *The Gardener's Illustrated Encyclopedia of Trees and Shrubs.* Rodale Press, 1987.

Den Ouden, P. and B. K. Boom. *Manuel of Cultivated Conifers.* Martinus Nijhoff, 1982.

Dirr, Michael A. *Manuel of Woody Landscape Plants: 5th Edition.* Stipes Publishing Co., 1998.

DiSabato-Aust, Tracy. *The Well-Tended Perennial Garden.* Timber Press, 1998.

Egolf, Donald R. and Anne O. Andrick. *A Check List of Pyracantha Cultivars: U.S. National Arboretum Contribution Number 8.* U.S. Government Printing Office, 1995.

Elias, Thomas S. *Field Guide to North American Trees: Revised Edition.* Outdoor Life, 1991.

Els, David, Jack Ruttle, Barbara Radcliffe Rogers. *The National Gardening Association Dictionary of Horticulture.* Viking Press, 1994.

Encyclopedia of Organic Gardening, The. Rodale Press, 2000.

Everett, Thomas H. *The New York Botanical Garden Illustrated Encyclopedia of Horticulture.* Garland Publishing, 1980.

Foster, Gordon. *Ferns to Know and Grow: 3rd Edition.* Timber Press, 1993.

Fox, Helen Morgenthau. *Gardening with Herbs for Flavor and Fragrance.* Dover Publications, 1997.

Galle, Fred C. *Azaleas.* International Specialized Book Service, 1986.

Galle, Fred C. *Hollies: The Genus Ilex.* Timber Press, 1997.

Good Housekeeping Illustrated Encyclopedia of Gardening, The. William Morrow Hearst & Company, 1972.

Grey-Wilson, Christopher. *Poppies: A Guide to the Poppy Family in the Wild and in Cultivation.* Timber Press, 2001.

Grey-Wilson, Christopher and Victoria Matthews. *Gardening with Climbers.* Timber Press, 1997.

Griffiths, Mark. *Index of Common Garden Plants: The New Royal Horticultural Society Dictionary.* MacMillan Press, 1994.

Grissell, Eric. *Thyme on My Hands: Reprint Edition.* Timber Press, 1995.

Halfacre, R. Gordon and Anne R. Shawcroft. *Landscape Plants of the Southeast: 5th Edition.* Sparks Press, 1989.

Halpin, Anne. *Morning Glories and Moonflowers: A Guide to Climbing, Trailing & Cascading Plants.* Simon & Schuster, 1996.

Harper, Pamela J. *Designing with Perennials.* Lark Books, 2001.

Hériteau, Jacqueline. *Glorious Gardens.* Stewart Tabori & Chang, 1998.

Hériteau, Jacqueline. *The National Arboretum Book of Outstanding Garden Plants.* Simon and Schuster, 1990.

Hériteau, Jacqueline. *Virginia Gardener's Guide.* Cool Springs Press, 1997.

Hériteau, Jacqueline and Charles Thomas. *Water Gardens: How to Design, Install, Plant and Maintain a Home Water Garden.* Houghton Mifflin Co., 1996.

Hériteau, Jacqueline and André Viette. *The American Horticultural Society Flower Finder.* Simon and Schuster, 1992.

Horticulture: Volume 10. Garland Pub., 1980.

Hortus Third: A Concise Dictionary of Plants Cultivated in the U.S. and Canada. Staff of L. H. Bailey Hortorium, Cornell University. John Wiley & Sons, 1976.

Hoshizaki, Barbara. *Fern Growers Manual.* Random House, 1975.

Hudak, Joseph. *Gardening with Perennials Month by Month: 2nd Edition.* Timber Press, 1993.

Hutson, June, Brian Ward, Ruth Rogers Clausen. *The American Garden Guides: Missouri Botanical Garden, Annual Gardening.* Pantheon Books, 1995.

Hyam, Roger and Richard Pankhurst. *Plants and Their Names: A Concise Dictionary.* Oxford University Press, 1995.

Irwin, Howard S. *America's Garden Book.* Brooklyn Botanic Garden, John Wiley & Sons, 1996.

Iverson, Richard R. *The Exotic Garden: Designing with Tropical Plants in Almost Any Climate.* Taunton Press, 1999.

King, Michael and Piet Oudolf. *Gardening with Grasses.* Timber Press, 1998.

Leach, David G. *Rhododendrons of the World.* Scribner, 1961.

Loewer, Peter. *Growing and Decorating with Grasses.* Walker & Co., 1977.

Lowe, Judy. *Tennessee Gardener's Guide: 3rd Edition.* Cool Springs Press, 2001.

Marston, Ted. *Hearst Garden Guides: Annuals.* Hearst Books, 1993.

Martin, Tovah, Diane Whealy, David Cavagnaro. *Heirloom Flowers: Vintage Flowers for Modern Gardens.* Fireside, 1999.

Massey, A. B. *Virginia Ferns & Fern Allies.*

Mazeo, Peter F. *Ferns and Fern Allies of Shenandoah National Park.*

McEwen, Currier. *Japanese Iris.* University Press of New England, 1990.

McEwen, Currier. *Siberian Iris.* Timber Press, 1996.

McVicar, Jekka. *Jekka's Culinary Herbs: A Guide to Growing and Using Herbs for the Kitchen.* William Morrow and Co., 1997.

Meyer, Mary Hockenberry. *Ornamental Grasses: Decorative Plants for Home and Garden.* Scribner.

Moskowitz, Mark, Thomas Reinhardt, Martina Reinhardt. *Ornamental Grass Gardening: Design Ideas, Functions & Effects.* Mark Moskowitz, 1994.

Ottesen, Carol. *Ornamental Grasses: 2nd Edition.* McGraw-Hill, 1995.

Poor, Janet M. and Nancy Brewster. *Plants That Merit Attention: Volume 1, Trees.* Timber Press, 1984.

Rice, Graham. *Discovering Annuals.* Timber Press, 1999.

Rice, Graham and Elizabeth Strangman. *The Gardener's Guide to Growing Hellebores.* Timber Press, 1993.

Rogers, Allan. *Peonies.* Timber Press, 1995.

Rohde, Eleanor Sinclair. *A Garden of Herbs.*

Rose, Jeanne and Michael S. Moore. *Herbs And Things, A Compendium of Practical and Exotic Lore: 19th Edition.* Last Gasp of San Francisco, 2001.

Schacht, Wilhelm, Alfred Fessler, Leo Jellito. *Hardy Herbaceous Perennials.* Timber Press, 1990.

Schmid, W. George. *The Genus Hosta.* Timber Press, 1992.

Shaver, Jesse M. *Ferns of the Eastern Central States with Special Reference to Tennessee.* Dover Publications, 1970.

Snodsmith, Ralph. *The Tri-State Gardener's Guide.* Cool Springs Press, 2001.

Southern Living Garden Guide: Annuals. Lois Trigg Chaplin, ed. Oxmoor House, 1996.

Successful Gardening: A-Z of Annuals, Biennials & Bulbs. Reader's Digest, 1997.

Thomas, Graham Stuart. *Perennial Garden Plants, or, the Modern Florilegium: 3rd Edition.* Saga Press, 1990.

Trehane, Piers. *Index Hortensis: Volume 1, Perennials.* Timber Press, 1990.

Tripp, Kim and J. C. Raulston. *The Year in Trees: Superb Woody Plants for Four-Season Gardens.* Timber Press, 2001.

Van der Laar, Fortgens, Hoffman and Jong. *Naam lijist Van Vaste Planten.*

Van Gelderen, D. M. and J. R. P. van Hoey Smith. *Conifers: The Illustrated Encyclopedia.* Timber Press, 1996.

Viette, André and Stephen Still. *The Time Life Complete Gardener: Perennials.* Time Life.

Winterrowd, Wayne. *Annuals for Connoisseurs.* Hungry Minds, Inc., 1996.

Wyman, Donald. *Easy Care Ground Covers.*

Wyman, Donald. *Shrubs and Vines for American Gardens: Revised Edition.* Hungry Minds, 1996.

Wyman, Donald. *Wyman's Gardening Encyclopedia: 2nd Edition.* Simon and Schuster, 1987.

Yeo, Peter F. *Hardy Geraniums: 2nd Edition.* Timber Press, 2002.

Plant Index

Featured plant selections are indicated in **boldface**.

abelia, 173
  glossy, 173
Abelia × grandiflora, 173
Abies concolor, 72
Abies nordmanniana, 72
Acer japonicum, 209
Acer palmatum, 209
Acer rubrum, 214
Acer saccharum, 214
Acer spp. and cultivars, 214
Achillea filipendulina, 147
Achillea millefolium, 147
Achillea spp. and hybrids, 147
Achnatherum brachytricha, 107
Acidanthera bicolor, 49
aconite, winter, 48
Adam's needle, 119
Adiantum pedatum, 77
Aesculus × carnea 'Briotii', 216
Aesculus hippocastanum, 216
Aesculus pavia, 216
African marigold, 36
ageratum, 26, 41
  blue, 33
  hardy, 26, 119
Ageratum houstonianum, 26
ajuga, 80, 199, 209, 210,
    226, 230
Ajuga genevensis, 80
Ajuga reptans, 80
Alaska false cypress, 67
alder, witch, 168
Algerian ivy, 84
Allegheny
  foamflower, 85
  pachysandra, 88
Allium aflatunense, 55
Allium albopilosum, 55
Allium christophii, 55
Allium giganteum, 49, 55
Allium karataviense, 55
Allium moly, 55
Allium schoenoprasum, 97
Allium schubertii, 55
Allium sphaerocephalum, 55
Allium spp. and cultivars, 55
Allium tuberosum, 55, 97
Alopecurus pratensis, 113
althea, shrub, 133, 186
alumroot, 127
alyssum, 58
  sweet, 26, 27, 30, 33, 44
amaranth
  feathered, 28
  globe, 25
Amaranthus tricolor, 31
American
  arborvitae, 62
  beech, 196

holly, 208
hornbeam, 195
sweet gum, 220
vervain, 30
wall fern, 77
yellowwood, 195
anacharis, 234
andromeda, 169
  Japanese, 175
  mountain, 175
anemone, 78
  Japanese, 114, 131, 137
  poppy, 49
Anemone blanda, 48
anemone clematis, 227
Anemone coronaria, 49
Anemone hupehensis, 131
Anemone × hybrida, 131
Anethum graveolens, 98
Antirrhinum majus, 41
apple, Asiatic, 204
Aquilegia canadensis, 125
Aquilegia flabellata, 125
Aquilegia spp. and
    hybrids, 125
Aquilegia vulgaris, 125
arborvitae, 62
  American, 62
  eastern, 62
  giant, 62
  Oriental, 62
  western, 62
Arctostaphylos uva-ursi, 79
artemisia, 26, 34, 41, 109
  silver king, 119
Artemisia abrotanum, 104, 119
Artemisia absinthium, 104
Artemisia dracunculus, 104
Artemisia ludoviciana var.
  albula, 119
arum, water, 239
Aruncus dioicus, 119
Asarum europeum, 77
Asclepias tuberosa, 35, 119
Asiatic
  apple, 204
  lily, 58
aster, 53, 111, 112, 115, 128,
    135, 137
  Stokes', 119
astilbe, 87, 120, 129
  Chinese, 120
Astilbe × arendsii, 120
Astilbe chinensis, 120
Astilbe simplicifolia, 120
Athyrium filix-femina, 87
Athyrium nipponicum
  'Pictum', 87
aucuba, Japanese, 176

Aucuba japonica, 176
autumn clematis, sweet, 227
avena grass, 109
Avena sempervirens, 109
azalea, 88, 166, 168, 169, 175,
    180, 182, 212
  deciduous, 166, 169
  evergreen, 63, 169
  flame, 166
  Korean, 166
  Kurume, 169
  pinkshell, 166
  royal, 166
  sweet, 166
  Yodogawa, 169
Aztec marigold, 36
baby's breath, 53
bachelor's-button, 25
Balcon geranium, 33
balloon flower, 121
bamboo, heavenly, 181
banana, ornamental, 49
baptisia, 123
Baptisia australis, 123
Baptisia pendula, 123
barberry, purple Japanese, 184
barren strawberry, 77
barrenwort, 78
  bi-color, 78
basil, 31, 96
  holy, 96
  opal, 96
  purple, 53
  purple leaf, 96
  sweet, 96
bearberry, 79, 182
  cotoneaster, 164
bearded iris, 49
beautyberry, 183
  bodinier, 183
  purple, 183
beautybush, 159
bedding begonia, 27
bee balm, 134
beech
  American, 196
  European, 196
  purple, 196
  tricolor, 196
beech fern, 77
begonia, 81
  bedding, 27
  Evans, 27
  fibrous-rooted, 27
  wax, 26, 27, 37
Begonia evansiana, 27
Begonia grandis, 27
Begonia Semperflorens-
    Cultorum Hybrids, 27

bellflower, 119
  Chinese, 121
Ben Franklin tree, 205
Berberis thunbergii, 184
bergamot, 134
bergenia, 113
Betula albo-sinensis, 197
Betula maximowicziana, 197
Betula nigra, 197
Betula pendula, 197
Betula platyphylla var.
  japonica, 197
Betula spp. and cultivars, 197
Betula utilis var.
  jacquemontii, 197
bi-color barrenwort, 78
bigleaf hydrangea, 174
birch, 197
  Chinese paper, 197
  Himalayan, 197
  Japanese white, 197
  monarch, 197
  river, 197
  weeping, 197
bishop's hat, 78
black-eyed Susan, 111, 112,
    115, 126, 139
black
  gum, 217
  princess taro, 235
  tupelo, 217
blazing star, 119
Blechnum spicant, 77
bleeding heart, 85, 87, 122
blood grass, Japanese, 113
bloody cranesbill, 77
blue
  ageratum, 33
  atlas cedar, 63
  beech ironwood, 195
  false indigo, 123
  fescue, 108
  flag, 239
  lily-turf, 92
  oat grass, 109
  pincushion flower, 143
  sage, 40
  salvia, 31, 39
  sheep's fescue, 53, 108
  spirea, 160
  wild indigo, 123
bluebeard, 160
  common, 160
bluebell
  English, 57
  Spanish, 57
blue-mist shrub, 160
bluewings, 25
bodinier beautyberry, 183

boltonia, 111, 115, 141, 142
border forsythia, 172
botanical tulip, 59
bourbon rose, 152
box, 161
    English, 161
    Korean little-leaf, 161
boxwood, 161
    English, 161
    Korean little leaf, 161
    little-leaf, 161
Brassica oleracea, 25
bridal wreath spirea, 187
broom
    prostrate, 159
    Scotch, 159
    Warminster, 159
browallia, 25
Browallia speciosa, 25
brunnera, 119
Brunnera macrophylla, 119
buckeye, red, 216
Buddleja, 35, 162
Buddleja alternifolia, 162
Buddleja davidii, 162
Buddleja davidii var.
    nanhoensis, 162
bugleweed, 80
    carpet, 80
bullbay magnolia, 219
Burford's Chinese holly, 208
burning bush, dwarf, 167
bush
    butterfly, 35, 162
    dwarf burning, 167
    dwarf butterfly, 162
    sweet pepper, 188
bush
    cinquefoil, 159
    violet, 25
busy Lizzie, 34
butter daisy, 25
butterfly
    bush, 35, 162
    weed, 35, 119
Buxus microphylla, 161
Buxus microphylla var.
    koreana, 161
Buxus microphylla var.
    japonica, 161
Buxus sempervirens, 161
cabbage, ornamental, 25, 36
Cabomba caroliniana, 234
caladium, 34, 54
    fancy-leaved, 54
Caladium bicolor, 54
Calamagrostis × *acutiflora*
    'Karl Foerster', 111
Calamagrostis brachytricha, 107
California privet, 159
callery pear, 198
Callicarpa americana, 183
Callicarpa bodinieri, 183
Callicarpa dichotoma, 183
Callicarpa japonica, 183
Calonyction aculeatum, 225
camellia, 163, 212
    fragrant tea oil, 163

    Japanese, 163
    sasanqua, 163
Camellia japonica and
    hybrids, 163
Camellia oleifera, 163
Camellia sasanqua, 163
campanula, 121
Campanula carpatica, 119
Campanula persicifolia, 119
Campanula poscharskyana, 119
Campsis radicans, 231
Campsis × *tagliabuana,* 231
Canadian hemlock, 64
candytuft, 59, 119
canker brake, 81
canna, 49
    dwarf, 49
    water, 239
Canna × *generalis* cultivars, 49
Canna hybrids, 49
Carex buchananii, 107
Carex morrowii, 107
carnation, 138
    miniature, 138
Carol Mackie daphne, 165
Carolina
    hemlock, 64
    jessamine, 226
    silverbell, 195
carpet
    bugleweed, 80
    rose, 152
Carpinus betulus, 195
Carpinus caroliniana, 195
Caryopteris × *clandonensis,* 160
Caryopteris incana, 160
Catawba rhododendron, 185
Catharanthus roseus, 39
catmint, 95, 119, 150
cattail, 239
Caucasian fir, 72
cedar
    blue atlas, 63
    deodar, 63
    eastern red, 68
cedar of Lebanon, 63
Cedrus deodara, 63
Cedrus libani, 63
Cedrus libani ssp. *atlantica*
    'Glauca', 63
Cedrus libani var. *stenocoma,* 63
celery, wild, 234
celosia, 28
Celosia argentea var. *cristata,* 28
Centaurea cyanus, 25
Cerastium tomentosum, 77
Ceratostigma plumbaginoides, 89
Ceratostigma willmottianum, 89
Cercidiphyllum japonicum, 213
Cercis canadensis, 202
Cercis chinensis, 202
Cercis texensis, 202
Chaenomeles speciosa, 171
Chamaecyparis lawsoniana, 61
Chamaecyparis nootkatensis, 67
Chamaecyparis obtusa, 67
Chamaecyparis pisifera, 67
Chasmanthium latifolium, 114

chaste tree, 195
checkerberry, 77
cheddar pink, 138
cherry
    flowering, 203
    Higan, 203
    Sargent, 203
    Yoshino, 203
    weeping, 203
chestnut
    European horse, 216
    red horse, 216
China rose, 155
Chinese
    astilbe, 120
    bellflower, 121
    chives, 97
    dogwood, 201
    flametree, 207
    flowering quince, 171
    fringe tree, 222
    holly, Burford's, 208
    juniper, 68, 82
    paper birch, 197
    parsley, 101
    pennisetum, 112
    plumbago, 89
    redbud, 202
    scholar-tree, 210
    silver grass, 110
    stewartia, 212
    witch-hazel, 191
Chionanthus retusus, 222
Chionanthus virginicus, 222
Chionodoxa luciliae, 48
chives, 97
    Chinese, 97
    garlic, 55
Christmas fern, 81
chrysanthemum, 124, 135
Chrysanthemum
    maximum, 124
Chrysanthemum
    nipponicum, 124
Chrysanthemum
    parthenium, 95
Chrysogonum virginianum, 77
cilantro, 101
cinnamon fern, 77
cinquefoil, bush, 159
Cladastris kentukea, 195
Cladastris lutea, 195
clematis, 85, 227
    anemone, 227
    sweet autumn, 227
Clematis
    maximowicziana, 227
Clematis montana var.
    rubens, 227
Clematis paniculata, 227
Clematis spp., cultivars, and
    hybrids, 227
Clematis terniflora, 227
Cleome hassleriana, 42
Clethra alnifolia, 188
climbing
    hydrangea, 228
    rose, 150, 154

clover, water, 237
cockscomb, 28
coffee tree, Kentucky, 195
colchicum, 49
Colchicum autumnale, 49, 51
coleus, 29, 34, 86
colocasia, 239
Colocasia affinis var.
    jenningsii, 235
Colocasia esculenta, 235
Colorado
    blue spruce, 65
    fir, 72
columbine, 81, 91, 125, 146
    fan, 125
    wild, 125
common
    bluebeard, 160
    garden verbena, 30
    lilac, 178
    quince, 171
    rose mallow, 133
    smoke tree, 200
compact pampas grass, 107
concolor fir, 72
coneflower, 126, 129
    purple, 139
Consolida ambigua, 25
Convallaria majalis, 49, 91
coral
    bells, 127
    honeysuckle, 229
coreopsis, 142, 145
Coreopsis spp. and cultivars, 119
coriander, fresh, 101
Coriandrum sativum, 101
cornflower, 25
corn poppy, 25
Cornus controversa, 201
Cornus florida, 201
Cornus kousa, 201
Cornus kousa var. *chinensis,* 201
Cornus mas, 201
Cornus × *rutgeriensis,* 201
Cornus spp., cultivars, and
    hybrids, 201
Cortaderia selloana, 107
Corylopsis species, 191
cosmos, 31
Cosmos bipinnatus, 31
Cosmos sulphureus, 31, 35
Cotinus coggygria, 200
Cotinus obovatus, 200
cotoneaster, 164
    bearberry, 164
    cranberry, 164
    creeping, 164
    rockspray, 164
Cotoneaster adpressus, 164
Cotoneaster apiculatus, 164
Cotoneaster dammeri, 164
Cotoneaster divaricatus, 164
Cotoneaster horizontalis, 164
crab
    flowering, 204
    Japanese, 204
    Sargent, 204
    tea, 204

crabapple
  flowering, 204
  Japanese, 204
  Sargent, 204
  tea, 204
cranberry cotoneaster, 164
cranesbill, bloody, 77
crape myrtle, **199**
Crataegus laevigata, 195
Crataegus phaenopyrum, 195
Crataegus viridis, 195
creeping
  cotoneaster, 164
  jenny, golden, 86
  juniper, 68, **82**
  lily-turf, 92
  phlox, 59, 85, 137
  thyme, 105
  zinnia, 45
crocosmia, 49, **50**, 128
Crocosmia spp. and
  hybrids, 49, 50
crocus, 49, **51**, 59
  early, 48
  fall, 49
  late, 49
  saffron, 49, 51
Crocus kotschyanus, 49, 51
Crocus sativus, 49, 51
Crocus speciosus, 49, 51
Crocus spp., 51
Crocus vernus, 48, 51
Crocus zonatus, 49, 51
× *Cupressocyparis leylandii*, 70
curly parsley, 101
cushion mum, 34, 137
cyclamen
  hardy, 49
  miniature, 48
Cyclamen coum, 48
Cyclamen hederifolium, 49
Cydonia oblonga, 171
Cymbopogon syriacus, 95
Cyperus alternifolius, 239
cypress
  Alaska false, 67
  dwarf false, 67
  dwarf hinoki, 67
  golden, 67
  golden threadleaf
    sawara, 67
  Japanese, 67
  Lawson's false, 61
  Leyland, 70
  Nootka false, 67
Cytisus decumbens, 159
Cytisus × *praecox*, 159
Cytisus scorparius, 159
daffodil, 37, 49, **52**, 56,
  82, 115
  miniature, 48
  Peruvian, 49
  Tenby, 49
  winter, 49
dagger fern, 81
dahlia, 31, 49, **53**, 135
Dahlia × *hybrida*, 53
Dahlia hybrids, 49

daisy, 124
  butter, 25
  Nippon, 124
  shasta, 31, 124
dancing ladies, 54
daphne
  'Carol Mackie', **165**
  February, 165
  lilac, 165
Daphne × *burkwoodii*
  'Carol Mackie', 165
Daphne genkwa, 165
Daphne mezereum, 165
dasheen, 235
dawn redwood, 61
daylily, **128**
dead nettle, **83**
  spotted, 83
deciduous azalea, **166**, 169
deer fern, 77
delphinium, 123
Delphinium ajacis, 25
Dendranthema pacificum, 124
Dendranthema spp. and
  hybrids, 124
deodar cedar, 63
deutzia, 179
diamond milfoil, 237
dianthus, 30
Dianthus gratianopolitanus, 138
Dianthus spp. and hybrids, 138
Dicentra eximia, 122
Dicentra formosa, 122
Dicentra spectabilis, 122
Dicentra spp. and
  cultivars, 122
Digitalis spp. and hybrids, 119
dill, **98**
dill weed, 98
dogwood, **201**
  Chinese, 201
  giant, 201
Dolichos lablab, 225
doublefile viburnum, 189
Douglas fir, **66**
  green, 66
  Rocky Mountain, 66
drumsticks, 55
Dryopteris erythrosora, 77
dusty miller, 30, 33
Dutch hyacinth, 57
dwarf
  beardless iris, 48
  burning bush, **167**
  butterfly bush, 162
  canna, 49
  false cypress, 67
  fothergilla, **168**
  Hinoki cypress, **67**
  Japanese garden juniper, 82
  sagittaria, 234
  winged spindle tree, 167
early crocus, 48
eastern
  arborvitae, 62
  hemlock, 64
  redbud, **202**
  red cedar, 68

white pine, 69
Echinacea purpurea
  'Magnus', 139
Echinops ritro
  'Taplow Blue', 129
edging lobelia, **32**, 37
Egeria densa, 234
elodea, 234
endymion, 57
English
  bluebell, 57
  box, 161
  hawthorn, 195
  holly, 208
  ivy, **84**
  lavender, 99
  rose, 151
  yew, 73
epimedium, 131
  red alpine, 78
Epimedium colchicum, 78
Epimedium grandiflorum, 78
Epimedium pinnatum, 78
Epimedium × *rubrum*, 78
Epimedium spp. and
  hybrids, 78
Epimedium × *versicolor*
  'Sulphureum', 78
Eranthis hyemalis, 48
Erianthus ravennae, 107
eulalia, 110
euonymus
  European, 167
  wintercreeper, 167
Euonymus alatus, 167
  'Compactus', 167
Euonymus europaeus, 167
Euonymus fortunei, 167
Eupatorium
  coelestinum, 26, 119
Euphorbia dulcis, 119
Euphorbia epithymoides, 119
Euphorbia griffithii, 119
European
  beech, 196
  euonymus, 167
  ginger, 77
  hornbeam, 195
  horse chestnut, 216
Evans begonia, 27
evergreen azalea, 63,
  166, **169**
Fagus grandifolia, 196
Fagus sylvatica, 196
fairy rose, 155
fall
  crocus, 49
  phlox, 137
false cypress
  Alaska, 67
  Lawson's, 61
  Nootka, 67
  dwarf, 67
false indigo
  blue, 123
  plains, 123
fan columbine, 125
fancy-leaved caladium, **54**

feather
  hyacinth, 56
  reed grass, **111**
  Korean, 107
feathered amaranth, 28
February daphne, 165
fennel, 95, 98
fern
  American wall, 77
  beech, 77
  Christmas, 81
  cinnamon, 77
  dagger, 81
  deer, 77
  holly, 81
  Japanese painted, 87
  Japanese shield, 77
  lady, 87
  maidenhair, 77
  marsh, 77
  Massachusetts, 77
  New York, 77
  ostrich, 77
  painted, 87
  royal, 77
  shield, 81
fern-leaved yarrow, 147
fescue
  blue, 108
  blue sheep's, 108
Festuca glauca, 108
Festuca ovina var. *glauca*, 108
feverfew, 95
fibrous-rooted begonia, 27
fir
  Caucasian, 72
  Colorado, 72
  concolor, 72
  Douglas, 66
  green Douglas, 66
  Nordmann, 72
  Rocky Mountain
    Douglas, 66
  silver, 72
  white, 72
firethorn, **170**
  scarlet, 170
flag
  blue, 239
  yellow, 239
flame azalea, 166
flametree, Chinese, 207
flat-leafed parsley, 101
floating-heart, 237
floribunda rose, 151, 154
florist's verbena, 30
flossflower, 26
flowering
  cherry, **203**
  crab, 204
  crabapple, **204**
  onion, 49, **55**
  pear, 198
  quince, **171**
  tobacco, 25
foamflower, **85**
  Allegheny, 85
Foeniculum, 98

Foeniculum vulgare, 95
forget-me-not, 37
forsythia, 166, 167, **172**, 179
   border, 172
Forsythia × intermedia
   'Spectabilis', 172
fothergilla, dwarf, 168
Fothergilla gardenii, 168
Fothergilla major, 168
fountain grass, 112
   Oriental, 112
four o'clock, 25
foxglove, 119
foxtail, golden-leaved
   meadow, 113
foxtail lily, 115
fragrant
   snowbell, 211
   tea oil camellia, 163
franklinia, 212
Franklinia alatamaha, 205
Franklin tree, 205
French
   lavender, 99
   lilac, 178
   marigold, 36
   tarragon, 104
   thyme, 105
fresh coriander, 101
fringe tree
   Chinese, 222
   white, 222
fritillaria, 49
Fritillaria imperialis, 49
full moon Japanese
   maple, 209
funkia, 130
Galanthus nivalis, 48
Galium odoratum, 77, 95
Galtonia hybrids, 49
Galtonia spp., 49
garden
   heliotrope, 25
   mum, 124
   rose, 151
Gardening with Wildlife,
   Welcome or
   Otherwise, 244
garlic chives, 55, 97
garlic
   golden, 55
   Oriental, 55
   round-headed, 55
Gaultheria procumbens, 77
gayfeather, 119
Gelsemium sempervirens, 226
geranium, 33, 101, 119
   Alpine ivy-leaved, 33
   Balcon, 33
   ivy-leaved, 33
   Martha Washington, 33
   scent-leaved, 33
   zonal, 33
Geranium sanguineum, 77
Geranium spp. and
   cultivars, 119
gerbera, 25
Gerbera jamesonii, 25

giant
   arborvitae, 62
   onion, 55
   silver grass, 110
ginger, European, 77
ginkgo, 206
Ginkgo biloba, 206
gladiolus, 49
Gleditsia triacanthus var.
   inermis, 195
globe
   amaranth, 25
   thistle, 129
glory-of-the-snow, 48
glossy abelia, 173
goatsbeard, 119
golden
   creeping jenny, 86
   cypress, 67
   garlic, 55
   moneywort, 86
   privet, 159
   rain tree, 207
   star, 77
   threadleaf sawara
      cypress, 67
golden-leaved meadow
   foxtail, 113
goldenrod, 119
goldflame honeysuckle, 229
Gomphrena globosa, 25
granny's bonnet, 125
grape
   holly, Oregon, 182
   hyacinth, 48, **56**
grass
   avena, 109
   blue oat, 109
   Chinese silver, 110
   compact pampas, 107
   feather reed, 111
   fountain, 112
   giant silver, 110
   Japanese blood, 113
   Korean feather reed, 107
   lemon, 95
   maiden, 110
   mondo, 92, 210, 230
   Oriental fountain, 112
   plume, 107
   ravenna, 107
   swamp foxtail, 112
   switch, 115
   Washington, 234
   zebra, 110
green Douglas fir, 66
ground cover
   juniper, 82
   rose, 152
gum
   American sweet, 220
   black, 217
   sour, 217
   sweet, 220
Gymnocladus dioicus, 195
Halesia monticola, 195
Halesia tetraptera, 195
Hamamelis × intermedia, 191

Hamamelis japonica, 191
Hamamelis mollis, 191
hardy
   ageratum, 119
   cyclamen, 49
   mum, 124
hawthorn
   English, 195
   Washington, 195
   winter king, 195
hazel, winter, 191
heart, bleeding, 85, 87, 122
heartsease, 37
heavenly bamboo, 181
Hedera canariensis, 84
Hedera helix, 84
hedge rose, 153
Helianthus, 128
Helianthus annuus, 43
Helictotrichon sempervirens, 109
heliopsis, 119
Heliopsis, 128
Heliopsis helianthoides
   cultivars, 119
heliotrope, garden, 25
Heliotropium arborescens, 25
hellebore, 78, 85, 90, 182
   stinking, 90
Helleborus atrorubens, 90
Helleborus foetidus, 90
Helleborus orientalis, 90
Hemerocallis citrina, 128
Hemerocallis spp. and
   hybrids, 128
hemlock
   Canadian, 64
   Carolina, 64
   eastern, 64
Heuchera micrantha, 127
Heuchera spp. and hybrids, 127
Heuchera villosa, 127
Hibiscus moscheutos, 133
Hibiscus rosa-sinensis, 133
Hibiscus syriacus, 133, 186
Higan cherry, 203
Himalayan birch, 197
holly, 208
   American, 208
   Burford's Chinese, 208
   English, 208
   Japanese, 208
   longstalk, 208
   Meserve, 208
   Oregon grape, 182
holly fern, 81
holy basil, 96
honeylocust
   thornless, 195
honeysuckle, 229
   coral, 229
   goldflame, 229
hornbeam
   American, 195
   European, 195
horse chestnut
   European, 216
   red, 216
hortensia hydrangea, 174

hosta, 29, 34, 78, 90, 122,
   130, 131, 146, 210, 230
Hosta fortunei, 130
Hosta plantaginea, 130
Hosta spp. and hybrids, 130
hyacinth, 49, **57**
   Dutch, 57
   feather, 56
   grape, 48, 56
   Oriental, 57
   summer, 49
   water, 234
   wild, 49
   wood, 49, 199, 210
hyacinth bean, 225
Hyacinthoides, 57
Hyacinthoides hispanica, 49, 57
Hyacinthoides non-scripta, 57
Hyacinthus hybrids, 49
Hyacinthus orientalis, 57
hybrid tea rose, 151, **154**
hydrangea, 174
   bigleaf, 174
   climbing, 228
   hortensia, 174
   lacecap, 174
   mophead, 174
   oakleaf, 174
Hydrangea anomala var.
   petiolaris, 228
Hydrangea arborescens
   'Annabelle', 174
Hydrangea macrophylla, 174
Hydrangea quercifolia, 174
Hydrocleys nymphoides, 237
Hymenocallis narcissiflora, 49
Iberis, 59
Iberis sempervirens hybrids, 119
Ilex aquifolium, 208
Ilex × attenuata, 208
Ilex cornuta, 208
Ilex crenata, 208
Ilex glabra, 208
Ilex × meserveae, 208
Ilex opaca, 208
Ilex pedunculosa, 208
Ilex spp. and hybrids, 208
Ilex verticillata, 208
impatiens, 29, **34**, 37, 54
   New Guinea, 34, 40
Impatiens hawkeri, 34
Impatiens walleriana, 34
Imperata cylindrica
   'Red Baron', 113
inkberry, 208
intermediate yew, 73
Ipheion uniflorum, 49
Ipomea alba, 225
Ipomea tricolor, 225
iris
   bearded, 49
   dwarf beardless, 48
   Japanese, 87, 129, 239
   Louisiana, 239
   Siberian, 129, 145, 239
   water, 239
Iris hybrids, 49
Iris pseudacorus, 239

Iris reticulata, 48
Iris sibirica, 145
ironwood, blue beech, 195
Ismene calathina, 49
Italian
    oregano, 95
    parsley, 101
Itea virginica, 159
ivy, 84, 226, 230
    Algerian, 84
    English, 84
ivy-leaved geranium, 33
Japanese
    andromeda, 175
    anemone, 114, **131**, 137
    aucuba, 176
    black pine, 69
    blood grass, 113
    camellia, 163
    crabapple, 204
    cypress, 67
    holly, 208
    iris, 87, 129, 239
    kerria, 177
    maple, 209
        full moon, 209
    pachysandra, 88
    pagoda tree, 210
    painted fern, 87
    pieris, 175
    rose, 153
    shield fern, 77
    snowbell, 211
    spirea, 187
    spurge, 88
    stewartia, 159, **212**
    tree lilac, 178
    umbrella pine, 71
    white birch, 197
    wisteria, 230
    witch-hazel, 191
    yew, 73
    zelkova, 223
jessamine, Carolina, 226
Joe Pye weed, 115
Johnny-jump-up, 37
jonquil, 52
Joseph's-coat, 31
juniper, 68
    Chinese, 68, 82
    creeping, 68, 82
    dwarf Japanese garden, 82
    ground cover, 82
    shore, 82
    temple, 68
Juniperus chinensis, 68
Juniperus chinensis var.
    sargentii, 82
Juniperus conferta, 82
Juniperus horizontalis, 68, 82
Juniperus procumbens, 82
Juniperus rigida, 68
Juniperus sabina, 68
Juniperus scopulorum, 68
Juniperus spp. cultivars, and
    hybrids, 68
Juniperus virginiana, 68
kale, ornamental, 25, 36

Kalmia latifolia, 180
Katsura tree, 213
Kentucky coffee tree, 195
kerria, Japanese, 177
Kerria japonica
    'Pleniflora', 177
King Solomon's seal, 146
kinnikinick, 79
Kniphofia spp. and
    hybrids, 140
Koelreuteria bipinnata, 207
Koelreuteria paniculata, 207
Kolkwitzia amabilis, 159
Korean
    azalea, 166
    feather reed grass, 107
    little-leaf box, 161
    pine, 69
    rhododendron, 166
    stewartia, 159, 212
Koreanspice viburnum, 189
Kurume azalea, 169
Lablab purpureus, 225
lacebark pine, 69
lacecap hydrangea, 174
ladies-delight, 37
lady fern, 87
lady's-slipper, 81, 91
Lagerstroemia indica and
    hybrids, 199
lamb's
    ears, 132
    tail, 132
    tongue, 132
lamium, 83, 89
Lamium maculatum, 83
landscape rose, 152
lantana, 35
    trailing, 35
    weeping, 35
Lantana camara, 35
Lantana montevidensis, 35
large-flowered bush rose, 154
larkspur, 25
late crocus, 49
laurel, 180
    mountain, 166, 169, 180
Lavandula angustifolia, 99
Lavandula angustifolia ssp.
    angustifolia, 99
Lavandula intermedia ×
    'Provence', 99
Lavandula stoechas, 99
lavender, 53, **99**, 108, 150, 154
    English, 99
    French, 99
    Spanish, 99
    true, 99
Lawson's false cypress, 61
leadwort, 89
leatherleaf mahonia, 182
leather leaf sedge, 107
leek, lily, 55
lemon grass, 95
Lenten rose, 90
lettuce, water, 234
Leucanthemum ×
    superbum, 124

Leyland cypress, 70
Liatris spicata, 119
Ligustrum ovalifolium, 159
Ligustrum 'Vicary', 159
Ligustrum vulgare, 159
lilac, 178
    common, 178
    daphne, 165
    French, 178
    Japanese tree, 178
    Meyer, 178
    Persian, 178
    Southern summer, 199
    summer, 162
Lilium, 49
Lilium candidum, 58
Lilium spp. and hybrids, 58
lily, 49, **58**
    Asiatic, 58
    foxtail, 115
    Martagon, 58
    Oriental, 58
    plantain, 130
    spider, 49
    toad, 114
    trumpet, 58
    water, 238
lily leek, 55
lily-of-the-field, 49
lily-of-the-valley, 49, 81,
    91, 146
    tree, 218
lily-turf, 92
    blue, 92
    creeping, 92
Lindera benzoin, 159
Liquidambar styraciflua, 220
Liriodendron tulipifera, 221
liriope, 53, 92, 210, 230
Liriope muscari, 92
Liriope spicata, 92
little-leaf boxwood, 161
    Korean, 161
lobelia, 114
    edging, 32, 37
Lobelia cardinalis, 32
Lobelia erinus, 32
Lobelia siphilitica, 32
Lobularia maritima, 44
longstalk holly, 208
Lonicera × *brownii*, 229
Lonicera × *heckrottii*, 229
Lonicera sempervirens, 229
lotus, 236
    sacred, 236
Louisiana iris, 239
lungwort, 119
Lycoris spp., 49
Lysimachia nummularia
    'Aurea', 86
Madagascar periwinkle, 39
magnolia
    bullbay, 219
    saucer, 219
    Southern, 219
    star, 219
Magnolia grandiflora, 219
Magnolia × *soulangiana*, 219

Magnolia stellata, 219
mahonia, leatherleaf, 182
Mahonia aquifolium, 182
Mahonia bealei, 182
maiden grass, 110
maidenhair
    fern, 77
    tree, 206
Malus floribunda, 204
Malus hupehensis, 204
Malus spectabilis, 204
Malus spp. and cultivars, 204
maple, 214
    full moon Japanese, 209
    Japanese, 209
    red, 63, 214
    sugar, 214
    swamp, 214
marigold, 36, 58, 59
    African, 36
    Aztec, 36
    French, 36
marsh
    fern, 77
    rose mallow, 133
Marsilea mutica, 237
Martagon lily, 58
Martha Washington
    geranium, 33
Massachusetts fern, 77
Matteuccia struthiopteris, 77
meadow foxtail,
    golden-leaved, 113
meadow rue, 119
Meidiland rose, 152
Melampodium paludosum, 25
Mentha arvensis, 100
Mentha spicata, 100
Mentha suaveolens, 100
Meserve holly, 208
Metasequoia glyptostroboides, 61
Meyer lilac, 178
milfoil, 147
    diamond, 237
miniature
    carnation, 138
    cyclamen, 48
    daffodil, 48
    rose, 154, **155**
mint, 31, 53, **100**
    pineapple, 100
Mirabilis jalapa, 25
Miscanthus floridulus, 110
Miscanthus sinensis and
    cultivars, 110
mist flower, 119
mock orange, 179
monarch birch, 197
monarda, 134
Monarda didyma, 134
mondo grass, 92, 210, 230
moneywort, golden, 86
moonvine, 225
mophead hydrangea, 174
More About Fertilizers and
    Plant Nutrition, 240
More About Pruning Shrubs
    and Trees, 242

morning glory, 225
moss rose, 25
mountain
    andromeda, 175
    laurel, 166, 169, **180**
    pink, 77
mum, 36, 124, 128
    cushion, 34, 137
    garden, 124
    hardy, 124
Musa velutina, 49
Muscari armeniacum, 56
Muscari azureum, 56
Muscari botryoides, 56
Muscari comosum, 56
Muscari macrocarpum, 56
Muscari spp., 48, 56
Myriophyllum, 234
Myriophyllum aquaticum, 237
myrtle, 89, 93
    crape, 199
nandina, 181
Nandina domestica, 181
Narcissus, 48, 49, 90
Narcissus asturiensis, 49
Narcissus jonquilla, 52
Narcissus spp. and hybrids, 52
nasturtium, 25
Nelumbo spp. and hybrids, 236
nepeta, 109
Nepeta faassenii, 119
Nepeta mussinii, 95
nettle
    dead, 83
    painted, 29
    spotted dead, 83
New Guinea impatiens, 34, 40
New York fern, 77
Nicotiana alata, 25
Nicotiana sylvestris, 25
Nipponanthemum
    nipponicum, 124
Nippon daisy, 124
Nootka false cypress, 67
Nordmann fir, 72
northern
    red oak, 215
    sea oats, 114
Norway spruce, 65
Nymphaea spp. and
    hybrids, 238
Nymphoides cristata, 237
Nymphoides geminata, 237
Nymphoides peltata, 237
Nyssa aquatica, 217
Nyssa sylvatica, 217
oak, 215
    northern red, 215
    scarlet, 215
    shumard, 215
    Southern scarlet, 215
    white, 215
    willow, 215
oakleaf hydrangea, 174
oat grass, blue, 109
oats
    river, 114
    wild, 114

Ocimum basilicum, 96
Ocimum sanctum, 96
old-fashioned weigela, 190
old garden rose, 153
onion
    flowering, 49, 55
    giant, 55
    ornamental, 55
opal basil, 96
Ophiopogon japonicus, 92
orange, mock, 179
orchid, peacock, 49
oregano, Italian, 95
Oregon grape holly, 182
Oriental
    arborvitae, 62
    fountain grass, 112
    garlic, 55
    hyacinth, 57
    lily, 58
    poppy, 135
    spruce, 65
Origanum vulgare, 95
ornamental
    banana, 49
    cabbage, 25, 36
    kale, 25, 36
    onion, 55
    pepper, 44
Ornithogalum nutans, 49
Osmunda cinnamomea, 77
Osmunda regalis, 77
ostrich fern, 77
Oswego tea, 134
Oxalis adenophylla, 49
Oxydendrum arboreum, 218
pachysandra, 88, 91, 93
    Allegheny, 88
    Japanese, 88
Pachysandra procumbens, 88
Pachysandra terminalis, 88
Paeonia hybrids, 136
pagoda tree, Japanese, 210
painted
    fern, 87
    nettle, 29
pampas grass, compact, 107
Panicum virgatum
    'Heavy Metal', 115
pansy, 37, 59
Papaver orientalis, 135
Papaver rhoeas, 25
paper birch, Chinese, 197
paperwhites, 52
parrot's-feather, 237
parsley, 101
    Chinese, 101
    curly, 101
    flat-leafed, 101
    Italian, 101
Passiflora caerulea, 35
passion flower, 35
Paxhysandra procumbens, 88
peacock orchid, 49
pear
    callery, 198
    flowering, 198
Pelargonium × *hortorum*, 33

Pelargonium spp. and
    hybrids, 33
Peltandra virginica, 239
Pennisetum alopecuroides, 112
pennisetum, Chinese, 112
Pennisetum orientale, 112
pentas, 35
peony, 129, 136
pepper, ornamental, 44
perennial
    phlox, 137
    salvia, 142
periwinkle, 93, 199, 210,
    226, 230
    Madagascar, 39
    rose, 39
Perovskia atriplicifolia, 141
Persian lilac, 178
Peruvian daffodil, 49
Petroselinum crispum, 101
petunia, 30, 33, **38,** 58
Petunia axillaris, 38
Petunia × *hybrida*, 38
Petunia integrifolia, 38
Philadelphus coronarius, 179
Philadelphus × *lemoinei*, 179
Philadelphus × *virginalis*, 179
phlox, 137
    creeping, 59, 85, 137
    fall, 137
    perennial, 137
    summer, 137
Phlox divaricata, 137
Phlox paniculata, 137
Phlox stolonifera, 137
Phlox subulata, 59, 77, 137
Picea abies, 65
Picea abies forma *pendula*, 65
Picea omorika, 65
Picea orientalis, 65
Picea pungens, 66
Pieris floribunda, 175
pieris, Japanese, 175
Pieris japonica, 175
pillar rose, 150
pincushion flower, blue, 143
pine
    eastern white, 69
    Japanese
        black, 69
        umbrella, 71
    Korean, 69
    lacebark, 69
    mugo, 69
    umbrella, 71
pineapple mint, 100
pink
    cheddar, 138
    mountain, 77
pink
    spirea, 187
    vinca, 39
pinks, 138
pinkshell azalea, 166
Pinus bungeana, 69
Pinus koraiensis, 69
Pinus strobus, 69
Pinus thunbergii, 69

plains false indigo, 123
plantain lily, 130
Platycodon grandiflorus
    'Mariesii', 121
plumbago, 89, 93
    Chinese, 89
Plumbago larpentae, 89
plume grass, 107
Polianthes tuberosa, 49
Polianthes tuberosa hybrids, 49
polyantha rose, 151, 154
Polygonatum biflorum, 146
Polygonatum commutatum, 146
Polygonatum humile, 146
Polygonatum multiflorum, 146
Polygonatum odoratum, 146
Polygonatum spp. and
    cultivars, 146
Polypodium virginianum, 77
Polystichum acrostichoides, 81
Polystichum braunii, 81
poplar, tulip, 221
poppy, 112, 128
    corn, 25
    Oriental, 135
    water, 237
poppy anemone, 49
Portulaca grandiflora, 25
Potentilla fruticosa, 159
primrose, 81, 91, 146
privet, 159
    California, 159
    golden, 159
prostrate broom, 159
Prunus sargentii, 203
Prunus spp. and hybrids, 203
Prunus subhirtella, 203
Prunus × *yedoensis*, 203
Pseudotsuga menziesii, 66
Pseudotsuga menziesii var.
    glauca, 66
Pulmonaria saccharata, 90
Pulmonaria spp. and
    hybrids, 119
purple
    basil, 53
    beautyberry, 183
    beech, 196
    coneflower, 35, **139**
    Japanese barberry, 184
    leaf basil, 96
Pushkinia scilloides, 48
Pyracantha coccinea, 170
Pyrus calleryana, 198
Quercus alba, 215
Quercus coccinea, 215
Quercus phellos, 215
Quercus rubra, 215
Quercus shumardii, 215
Quercus spp., 215
quince, 171
    Chinese flowering, 171
    common, 171
    flowering, 171
rain lily, 49
ravenna grass, 107
red
    Alpine epimedium, 78

buckeye, 216
horse chestnut, 216
hot poker plant, 140
maple, 63, 214
oak, northern, 215
redbud
Chinese, 202
eastern, 202
redwood, dawn, 61
rhododendron, 88, 90, 166,
168, 169, 175, 180,
182, **185**
Catawba, 185
Korean, 166
rosebay, 185
Rhododendron arborescens, 166
*Rhododendron
calendulaceum*, 166
*Rhododendron
catawbiense*, 185
Rhododendron cultivars and
hybrids, 169
Rhododendron kaempferi, 169
Rhododendron keiski, 185
Rhododendron ×
kosteranum, 166
Rhododendron maximum, 185
*Rhododendron
mucronulatum*, 166
Rhododendron obtusum, 169
*Rhododendron
schlippenbachii*, 166
Rhododendron spp. and
hybrids, 185
Rhododendron vaseyi, 166
*Rhododendron
yakusimanum*, 185
Rhododendron yedoense, 169
river
birch, 197
oats, 114
rockspray cotoneaster, 164
rock polypody, 77
Rocky Mountain Douglas
fir, 66
Rosa hybrids, 154
Rosa rugosa, 153
Rosa spp. and hybrids, 150,
151, 152, 153, 155
Rosa virginiana, 152
rose
bourbon, 152
carpet, 152
China, 155
climbing, 150, 154
English, 151
fairy, 155
floribunda, 151, 154
garden,151
ground cover, 152
hedge, 153
hybrid tea, 151, 154
Japanese, 153
landscape, 152
large-flowered bush, 154
Lenten, 90
Meidiland, 152
miniature, 154, 155

moss, 25
old garden, 153
pillar, 150
polyantha, 151, 154
rugosa, 153
shrub, 153
Virginia, 152
rose mallow
common, 133
marsh, 133
swamp, 133
rose-of-Sharon, 133, **186**
rose
periwinkle, 39
vinca, 39
rosebay rhododendron, 185
rosemary, 102
Rosmarinus officinalis, 102
round-headed garlic, 55
royal
azalea, 166
fern, 77
Rudbeckia, 128
Rudbeckia fulgida var.
sullivantii
'Goldsturm', 126
Rudbeckia speciosa, 126
rue, 95
meadow, 119
rugosa rose, 153
Russian
sage, 108, **141**, 144
tarragon, 104
Ruta graveolens, 95
sacred lotus, 236
saffron crocus, 49, 51
sage, 40, **103**
blue, 40
Russian, 108, 141, 144
scarlet, 40
yellow, 35
sagittaria, dwarf, 234
Sagittaria subulata, 234
salvia, 40, 53, 108, 142
blue, 31, 39
'May Night', 142
perennial, 142
scarlet, 39
Salvia coccinea, 40
Salvia farinacea, 40
Salvia nemorosa, 142
Salvia officinalis, 103
Salvia splendens, 40, 142
Salvia × *sylvestris*, 142
Sanvitalia procumbens, 45
Saponaria officinalis, 77
Sargent
cherry, 203
crabapple, 204
sasanqua camellia, 163
Satureja spp., 95
saucer magnolia, 219
savory
summer, 95
winter, 95
saw leaf zelkova, 223
scabiosa, 143
Scabiosa caucasica, 143

Scabiosa columbaria
'Butterfly Blue', 143
scarlet
firethorn, 170
oak, 215
oak, Southern, 215
sage, 40
salvia, 39
scent-leaved geranium, 33
scholar-tree, Chinese, 210
Sciadopitys verticillata, 71
scilla, 59
Scilla campanulata, 49
Scilla non-scripta, 57
Scilla tubergeniana, 48
Scotch broom, 159
sea oats, northern, 114
sedge, leather leaf, 107
sedum, 77, 111, 112, 115,
132, **144**, 145
Sedum spp. and hybrids, 144
Sedum spurium, 77, 144
Serbian spruce, 65
shasta daisy, 31, 124
shield fern, 81
shore juniper, 82
shrub
althea, 133, 186
rose, 153
shrub, blue-mist, 160
shumard oak, 215
Siberian iris, 129, **145**, 239
silver
bells, 49
fir, 72
grass
Chinese, 110
grass
giant, 110
king artemisia, 119
silverbell, Carolina, 195
skimmia, 90
smoke tree, common, 200
snapdragon, 26, 31, **41**, 59
snaps, 41
snowbell
fragrant, 211
Japanese, 211
snowdrops, 48, 59
snowflake
white, 237
yellow, 237
snow-in-summer, 77
soapwort, 77
*Solenostemon
scutellarioides*, 29
Solidago spp. and hybrids, 119
Solomon's seal, 81, 91,
122, **146**
King, 146
Sophora japonica, 210
sorrel tree, 218
sorrel, wood, 49
sour gum, 217
sourwood, 218
Southern
magnolia, 219
scarlet oak, 215

summer lilac, 199
southernwood, 104, 119
Spanish
bluebell, 57
lavender, 99
spearmint, 100
species tulip, 48, 59, 115
speedwell, 119
spicebush, 159
spider
flower, 42
lily, 49
spindle tree
dwarf winged, 167
winged, 167
Spiraea japonica, 187
Spiraea nipponica, 187
Spiraea prunifolia, 187
Spiraea × *vanhouttei*, 187
spirea, 179, **187**
blue, 160
bridal wreath, 187
Japanese, 187
pink, 187
spotted dead nettle, 83
spruce
Colorado blue, 65
Norway, 65
Oriental, 65
Serbian, 65
spurge, 119
Japanese, 88
squill, 48
striped, 48
stachys, 109, 113
Stachys byzantina, 132
starflower, 49
star magnolia, 219
star-of-Persia, 55
statice, 53
stepmother's flower, 37
Sternbergia lutea, 49
stewartia
Chinese, 212
Japanese, 159, 212
Korean, 159, 212
Stewartia koreana, 159, 212
*Stewartia
pseudocamellia*, 159, 212
Stewartia sinensis, 212
stinking hellebore, 90
Stokes' aster, 119
Stokesia laevis cultivars, 119
stonecrop, 144
strawberry, barren, 77
striped squill, 48
Styrax japonicum, 211
Styrax obassia, 211
sugar maple, 214
sultana, 34
sumac, Venetian, 200
summer
hyacinth, 49
lilac, 162
Southern, 199
phlox, 137
savory, 95
thyme, 105

summersweet, 188
sunflower, 43
swamp
    foxtail grass, 112
    maple, 214
    rose mallow, 133
sweet
    alyssum, 26, 27, 30,
        33, **44**
    autumn clematis, 227
    azalea, 166
    basil, 96
    gum, 220
        American, 220
    pepper bush, 188
        William, 138
    woodruff, 77, 95
sweetspire, Virginia, 159
switch grass, 115
Syringa meyeri, 178
Syringa × persica, 178
Syringa reticulata, 178
Syringa vulgaris and
    hybrids, 178
Tagetes erecta, 36
Tagetes patula, 36
Tagetes spp. and hybrids, 36
taro, 235
    black princess, 235
tarragon, 104
    French, 104
    Russian, 104
Taxus baccata, 73
Taxus cuspidata, 73
Taxus × media, 73
tea
    crab, 204
    crabapple, 204
tea, Oswego, 134
temple juniper, 68
Tenby daffodil, 49
Thalictrum aquilegifolium, 119
Thalictrum flavum ssp.
    glaucum, 119
Thalictrum
    rochebrunnianum, 119
Thelypteris hexagonoptera, 77
Thelypteris noveboracensis, 77
Thelypteris palustris forma
    pufferae, 77
Thelypteris simulata, 77
thistle, globe, 129
thornless honeylocust, 195
Thuja occidentalis, 62
Thuja orientalis, 62
Thuja plicata, 62
thyme, 105
    creeping, 105
    French, 105
    summer, 105

Thymus × citriodorus, 105
Thymus herba-barona, 105
Thymus serpyllum, 105
Thymus serpyllum ssp.
    serpyllum, 105
Thymus spp. and
    hybrids, 105
Thymus vulgaris, 105
Tiarella cordifolia, 85
Tiarella wherryi, 85
tickseed, 119
toad lily, 114
tobacco, flowering, 25
Torenia fournieri, 25
trailing lantana, 35
tree lilac, Japanese, 178
tricolor beech, 196
trillium, 81, 91, 146
Tropaeolum majus, 25
true lavender, 99
trumpet
    lily, 58
    vine, 231
Tsuga canadensis, 64
Tsuga caroliniana, 64
tuberose, 49
tulip, 37, 49, **59**
    botanicaL, 59
    species, 48, 59, 115
tulip poplar, 221
Tulipa, 49
Tulipa saxatilis, 48
Tulipa spp. and hybrids, 59
Tulipa tarda, 48
Tulipa turkistanica, 48
tuliptree, 221
tupelo
    black, 217
    water, 217
umbrella
    pine, 71
    plant, 239
Uniola latifolia, 114
Vallisneria americana, 234
varnish tree, 207
Venetian sumac, 200
verbena
    common garden, 30
    florist's, 30
Verbena bonariensis, 30
Verbena canadensis, 30
Verbena × hybrida, 30
Verbena tenuisecta, 30
Veronica spp. and
    hybrids, 119
vervain, 30
    American, 30
viburnum, 189
    doublefile, 189
    Koreanspice, 189

Viburnum × burkwoodii, 189
Viburnum ×
    carlcephalum, 189
Viburnum carlesii, 189
Viburnum × juddii, 189
Viburnum plicatum, 189
Viburnum spp. and
    hybrids, 189
vinca, 30, 33, 209
    pink, 39
    rose, 39
Vinca major, 39, 93
Vinca minor, 39, 93
viola, 37
Viola odorata, 93
Viola × wittrockiana, 37
violet, bush, 25
Virginia
    rose, 152
    sweetspire, 159
Vitex agnus-castus, 195
Vitex negundo, 195
Waldsteinia fragarioides, 77
Warminster broom, 159
Washington
    grass, 234
    hawthorn, 195
water
    arum, 239
    canna, 239
    clover, 237
    hyacinth, 234
    iris, 239
    lettuce, 234
    lily, 238
    poppy, 237
    tupelo, 217
wax begonia, 26, 27, 37
weed
    butterfly, 35, 119
    Joe Pye, 115
weeping
    birch, 197
    lantana, 35
weigela, 179, **190**
    old-fashioned, 190
Weigela florida
    'Variegata', 190
western arborvitae, 62
white
    birch, Japanese, 197
    fir, 72
    fringe tree, 222
    oak, 215
    snowflake, 237
wig tree, 200
wild
    blue indigo, 123
    celery, 234
    columbine, 125

hyacinth, 49
oats, 114
willow oak, 215
windflower, 48, 131
winged spindle tree, 167
    dwarf, 167
winter
    aconite, 48
    daffodil, 49
    hazel, 191
    king hawthorn, 195
    savory, 95
wintercreeper euonymus, 167
wintergreen, 77
wishbone plant, 25
wisteria, Japanese, 230
Wisteria floribunda, 230
witch alder, 168
witch-hazel, 191
    Chinese, 191
    Japanese, 191
wood
    hyacinth, 49, 199, 210
    sorrel, 49
woodruff, sweet, 77, 95
woolly betony, 132
wormwood, 104
Yakushima
    rhododendron, 185
yarrow, 142, **147**
    fern-leaved, 147
yellow
    flag, 239
    sage, 35
    snowflake, 237
yellowwood, 195
    American, 195
yew, 73
    English, 73
    intermediate, 73
    Japanese, 73
Yodogawa azalea, 169
Yoshino cherry, 203
yucca, 129
Yucca filamentosa, 119
zebra grass, 110
zelkova, 223
    Japanese, 223
    saw leaf, 223
Zelkova serrata, 223
Zephyranthes, 49
Zephyranthes spp., 49
zinnia, 45, 59
    creeping, 45
Zinnia angustifolia, 45
Zinnia elegans and
    hybrids, 45
zonal geranium, 33